Douglas County
Colorado

Prehistory to 2020

Tim Weber and Larry Schlupp, Editors

Historic Douglas County, Inc.

Cover by: Penny Dawson

Editors: Tim Weber and Larry Schlupp

Published by:
Historic Douglas County, Inc., Box 2032
Castle Rock, Colorado 80104

Printed by Amazon Publishing

First Edition
Printed in the United States of America

Acknowledgments

This book was a group effort. Twenty-four local historians used their expertise to provide chapters. Most writers were connected to one or more of DC's local history associations, and many have already written extensively about DC history. Their participation is greatly appreciated.

The editors and authors owe a debt of gratitude to the Archives and Local History department of the Philip S. Miller Library in Castle Rock. Its resources were essential in our combined efforts. Several local history archivists contributed chapters, as well as helped other writers find materials to help them write theirs.

Many authors interviewed community people who had special experience or knowledge of events or subjects in the book. Their names can be found in the footnotes.

The Historical Douglas County, Inc board worked hard to have each of the six book-calendars ready for distribution at the annual Douglas County Fair. Larry and Tim want to thank Jim Weglarz, HDC president. He not only wrote a chapter but lent support during the entire process, making sure that we met our deadlines and got the help we needed. Mary O' Pry, with the assistance of Douglas County Library archivists, helped authors locate appropriate historical photographs for their chapters. She also rendered a valuable service by proofreading the entire document before we sent it to the publisher. For most of the project, Ed Hooks provided continuing support and technical advice. HDC's website (www.historicdouglascounty.org) contains additional information about DC history and is a good source for many other areas of research.

The project benefitted from the assistance of Douglas County historical societies, museums, and historical venues. They have played an important role in keeping different aspects of DC's story alive.

- Castle Rock Historical Society and Museum
- DOTTS Club
- Highlands Ranch Historical Society
- Indian Park Schoolhouse Association
- Larkspur Historical Society
- Parker Area Historical Society
- Roxborough Area Historical Society
- Sedalia Museum and Gardens
- Franktown Museum

- Cherokee Ranch and Castle
- Highlands Ranch Mansion
- Devil's Head Tower and Trailhead

Finally, this multi-year project could not have been completed without the support of several sponsors. They provided needed funds to produce the annual calendars. The present book would have been impossible without their help.

- Castle Rock Bank
- Plum Creek Hollow Farm
- Flying Horse Catering
- RBC Wealth Management, David R. Rhode
- Rockyard American Grill and Brewing Company
- Jaris Realty
- Tri-Lakes Printing
- Douglas County Fair and Rodeo
- Burning Tree Dental and Creekside Family Dental
- Engel & Volkers
- Steps Real Estate
- Edward Jones
- Hometrackr

One final expression of gratitude: Larry Schlupp and Linda Weber deserve special kudos for mastering enormous challenges in preparing the book manuscript for submission to the publisher. We quickly discovered that formatting our text to its specifications took special analytical skills and the ability to maneuver a number of technical complexities, especially in the creation of the table of contents and the index. While Tim stood by in bewildered paralysis, Larry and Linda persisted until they discovered and then applied the almost indecipherable commands to make the text conform to expectations. Without their amazing tenacity and endurance, this book would have never seen the light of day.

Contributors

Edwin Bathke is co-author of *The West in Postage Stamps* and editor of the Denver Westerners *1972 Brand Book*. Ed is active in the Denver, Colorado Springs, and Boulder Westerners and the Ghost Town Club of Colorado. An avid Colorado history buff, he lives in Roxborough Park and has been a resident of Colorado since 1960.

Steve Boand worked as a geohydrologist for more than thirty years. He served for three years as Colorado's State Disaster Recovery Manager after the floods of 2013. He also served as a Douglas County Commissioner and Mayor and Councilman in the Town of Castle Rock.

Shaun Boyd was an archivist with the Douglas County Libraries from 1998-2018. She is currently the Curator of Archives at History Colorado. She is also the Past President of the Society of Rocky Mountain Archivists and a past secretary of the Academy of Certified Archivists. She has taught graduate-level seminars of Introduction to Archives, Arrangement and Description, and Genealogy for Emporia State University and the University of Denver.

Peggy Cummings is President of Literary Research Company, LLC, is a published co-author of *Images of America: Douglas County* and author of chapters in *The Silver Anniversary of Castle Pines Golf Club* and *Horses and Their Women*. Peggy and her husband Wendell have lived in Sedalia since 1988 and own and operate Paynter's Paint Ranch.

Sergeant Attila Denes has been with the Douglas County Sheriff's Office since 1988. He became the agency's historian in 1989 and has written extensively about its history ever since. He has served in every division of the DCSO and oversaw the Special Victims Unit before he retired.

Joan Gandy earned a master's degree in journalism and mass communication from the University of North Carolina, Chapel Hill. She has worked as a reporter, copy editor, and page designer for newspapers such as the *Denver Post*, *The Douglas County News-Press*, and *The Alexander City Outlook*. Since 2017, she has been an archives technician at the Douglas County Library Archives and Local History.

Blake Graham served as an Archivist at Douglas County Libraries and has an academic and professional background in historical research methodologies. After moving to Colorado in 2010, Blake has aided and advised research publications across the Rocky Mountain region. Exploring the culture and community of Douglas County has been a truly rewarding and invaluable experience for him. He now works for the Denver Water Board.

Jim Hansmann has been Collections Curator at the Castle Rock Museum since 2010. He has history degrees from St. Norbert College and the University of Colorado, Denver. He is co-author of *Images of America: Douglas County*, author of *Castle Rock: An Architectural & Historical Walking Tour Paperback*, and past president of the Association of Northern Front Range Museums (ANFRM).

Rebecca Holm is a Colorado native, Air Force Veteran, and Douglas County resident since 2002. She serves on the Roxborough Area Historical Society Board and is Director of Customer Care for Seven Stones Chatfield—Botanical Gardens.

Randall A. Johnson is a former Landscape Architect and has been the Fire Marshal for the Larkspur Fire Protection District for 15 years. He and his wife Susan have resided in Perry Park since 1995 and in Colorado since 1980.

Jamie La Rue is the author of *Douglas County Libraries: 1990-2014*, during which time he was Executive Director of the library. LaRue then served as the Director of the American Library Association's Office for Intellectual Freedom and the Director of the Freedom to Read Foundation. He currently works as a speaker, executive coach, and consultant.

Norma Miller, now retired, was an independent contractor with Douglas County, as a professional archaeologist and curator of the Douglas County Repository. She has served as an advisor to Douglas County Historic Preservation Board. Her participation in several archeological digs led to several published reports. Larry and Norma have lived in the Pinery since 1976, raising two children.

Charlene Nauman has served many years as an officer of the Roxborough Area Historical Society. Char has lived in Douglas County since 1973 when she became a resident of Roxborough Park Community.

Bill Noe is in the fourth of seven generations of Douglas County's pioneering Noe family of the Larkspur area. Retired, Bill has worked as a Douglas County Planning Director, Lockheed Martin project planner, and a quality assurance member for Aero Space Corporation during his long career. Bill is a lifetime member and a webmaster of the Larkspur Historical Society.

Garry O'Hara is a member of History Colorado, Larkspur and Parker Area Historical Societies, and the Smoky Hill Trail Association. Garry also serves as president of the Cherry Creek Valley Historical Society. He is retired from the Air Force and resides in Denver.

Mary O'Pry has been a member of Historic Douglas County, Inc. since 2008 and a member of the Douglas County Historic Preservation Board since 1996. Mary has lived in Douglas County since 1980 and is a resident of Sedalia.

Suzanne Perry served as the dean of the School of Education and Counseling at Regis University for 15 years and holds a doctoral degree from the University of Denver. She serves on the Castle Rock Historical Society Board and resides in Castle Rock, Colorado.

Susan Rocco-McKeel, J.D. is a second-generation Coloradoan. She and her husband Michael have lived in Douglas County for over 25 years. She is co-author of *The Chronicles of Douglas County*, an arbitrator, and a member of The Poetry Society of Colorado.

Larry Schlupp is a longstanding member of Historic Douglas County, Inc., Larkspur Historical Society, and Colorado Preservation, Inc. Larry had a long career in the telecommunications industry in the U.S. and the U.K. Larry and his wife Julia live in Perry Park and have been residents of Colorado since 1993.

Sarah Stevens holds a master's degree in library and information science from the University of Washington. From 2017-2018, she worked as an archives technician in the Archives and Local History department of Douglas County Libraries. Currently, she is an adult services librarian at Douglas County's Parker branch. She resides in Castle Rock with her partner, Matt, and their over-sized orange tabby cat, Fry.

Catherine Traffis is a freelance writer and editor and serves as Vice President of the Parker Area Historical Society. She was formerly a member of Parker's

Historical Preservation Commission, which was tasked with preserving local history and landmarks. Catherine has been happily living in Parker for 16 years.

Tim Weber is on the board of Historic Douglas County, Inc. He has a Ph.D. from the University of Chicago and taught graduate-level history in four different institutions for thirty years in Colorado, Kentucky, Illinois, and Tennessee. He and his wife Linda have lived in Castle Rock since 2005.

Jim Weglarz is a founding member and president of Historic Douglas County, Inc., a member of the Larkspur Historical Society, a Castle Rock Senior Center volunteer, a National Western volunteer, and currently heads Douglas/Elbert Task Force's Senior Food Program. Jim and his wife, Janet, have resided in the Cherry Valley area for 13 years.

Lee Whitely is a member of the Smoky Hill Trail Association and the Oregon-California Trails Association. Lee and his wife, Jan, have written five books on transportation history in the West, including the Cherokee Trail. They are associate producers of the PBS video "Paving the Way."

TABLE OF CONTENTS

INTRODUCTION

Tim Weber and Larry Schlupp

This book grew out of a multi-year project of Historic Douglas County, Inc. (HDC), a non-profit corporation established in Colorado in 2008. Its mission is to expand and enrich public awareness of Douglas County (DC) history through education and communication and through support and coordination among local history organizations and other related groups.

Between 2016 and 2021, HDC published an annual "book-calendar" that traced Douglas County history from prehistoric times to the present:

- 2016 In the Beginning (end of the Ice Age to 1870)
- 2017 The Early Years (1870-1900)
- 2018 Strife and Success (1900-1930)
- 2019 On the Verge of Change (1930-1960)
- 2020 The Big Change (1960-1990)
- 2021 Explosion of Growth (1990- 2020)

The book follows the same content and chronological periodization. It was written at a popular level; but it is based on solid historical research. Its references provide the sources for each chapter's findings, which allow readers to check conclusions and explore other research possibilities.

DC's story began in prehistoric times, whose archeological evidence remains. In recorded time, many "first-comers" made their way to what became Colorado: various Indian tribes; early Spanish, French, and American explorers; mountain men; and those seeking riches in the Colorado Gold Rush of 1859. The coming of the Fifty-niners led to Colorado becoming a U.S. Territory in 1861, with Douglas County as one of its original seventeen counties. The Civil War and the Colorado Indian War followed in the 1860s. DC got new boundaries and a new county seat (Castle Rock) in 1874. Two years later, Colorado became a state; and DC's population numbered only 1,000.

DC towns soon offered a variety of small businesses to serve the needs of DC's residents, who almost all lived on farms, ranches, and dairy farms. The coming of the railroads in the 1870s enabled these residents to "export" their agricultural products and stay connected to the wider world. In the 1880s and 1890s, rhyolite quarries around Castle Rock provided many new jobs for Swedish stonecutters and supplied building products for the Front Range and beyond.

School districts multiplied, each consisting of a single one-room schoolhouse with one teacher. Episcopalians, Catholics, and Methodists built the first churches in DC in the 1880s. From its founding, DC had been a Republican stronghold; but in the late 1880s and early 1890s, the county joined the "agrarian revolt" and voted for Populist Party candidates. A few DC men fought in the Spanish American War of 1898 and returned to find a new world emerging.

DC grew slowly in the early twentieth century, from 3,120 in 1900 to 3,460 in 1930. Most people were born either in Colorado or other parts of the U.S.; but there were many immigrants from Mexico, Germany, Austria, England, Sweden, Canada, and other places. Over 100 people from DC fought in World War I, while people at home supported the war effort in different ways—and suffered from the Spanish Flu pandemic of 1918. Slowly, modern conveniences—electricity, telephones, indoor plumbing, sewer systems, and improved roads—came to DC, though medical care was quite primitive by modern standards. Politics between 1900 and 1930 took pendulum swings from progressive Democrats to conservative Republicans. Unlike other parts of Colorado, DC had little Klu Klux Klan (KKK) activity during the 1920s. For the first time, the recreation industry took root in DC, about the same time as the management of the Pike National Forest improved.

DC was deeply affected by the Great Depression. The Civilian Conservation Corps built a camp just outside the northwest boundary of Castle Rock; and the agricultural community struggled to keep going. The search for adequate water supplies became a constant concern during the 1930s and beyond, which was not helped by the Castlewood Canyon Dam disaster of 1933. World War II affected everyone in DC. Ten DC servicemen died during the war, while civilians conducted scrap drives, bought war bonds, and learned to live with a rationing system for consumer goods.

Politics stabilized during and after the 1930s. DC voted for Franklin Delano Roosevelt (FDR) in 1932 and 1936; but it has not voted for another

Democratic presidential candidate since—with one exception: Lyndon Bains Johnson (LBJ) in 1964. In local elections, however, DC voters often voted for Democratic candidates; and occasionally they supported Democrats for state offices; but in national elections, DC remained staunchly Republican. Because most people in DC liked things the way they were, local politicians found it difficult to provide certain "improvements." In 1925 the state paved US 85, which at that time ran through Castle Rock as Wilcox Street. That was the county seat's only paved road until the late 1950s, when a few blocks around the County Courthouse were also paved.

After 1960, DC began to change. The population grew rapidly; and the economy became less agricultural when ranch and farmland were turned into new housing subdivisions. When DC needed new sales tax support, it built large retail developments—the Outlets Mall in Castle Rock, Park Meadows Mall in Lone Tree—which expanded DC's tax base. Most residents commuted to work outside the county to the Tech Center and other commercial areas; and DC's historic towns decided whether they wanted to grow or stay small. With the coming of Highlands Ranch in the early 1980s, the debate about growth was essentially decided. But development throughout DC was not uniform. After 1990, DC became the fastest growing county in the U.S. Still, while many of DC's existing towns expanded and new towns were established, parts of DC stayed remarkably unchanged.

Some themes recur throughout DC's story: changes brought by population growth; the expansion of its school district; the development of transportation networks—from Indian trails to gravel roads to multi-lane superhighways; the struggle over securing a sufficient water supply; the transformation of its sheriff's department and the establishment of other law enforcement agencies; the growth of town and county governments; and the unpredictable battles with Mother Nature.

At the center of DC's story are its people, an amazing collection of movers and shakers, innovators and standpatters, and hard-working common folks, who loved the county's rural character and its livable lifestyle, even when DC grew and changed. This book celebrates their story.

PART ONE

PREHISTORY TO 1870

Chapter 1

BEFORE THE BEGINNING

Norma Miller

"None of the dead can rise up and answer our questions. But from all that they have left behind, their imperishables or slowly dissolving gear, we may perhaps hear voices 'which are now only able to whisper, when everything else has become silent', to quote Linnaeus." — Bjorn Kurten, *How to Deep Freeze a Mammoth* (1984)

The Ice Age was coming to an end. The glaciers retreated, and the warming land rebounded with new vegetation. The people arrived. Mammoth, ancestral bison, three-toed sloth, saber-toothed tiger, camel, and ancestral horse were prey for the Paleo-Indians whose weapons of choice were the spear and atlatl. As the environment changed, the large mammals became extinct; and over time the small kin-based bands of people, the plant communities, and the animals required new strategies to adapt to the environment. However, new technologies were adopted at different times and in different places, depending on variations in wet and dry decades. It would be another 11,500 years before European explorers (ca. A.D. 1540) arrived to interact with human and animal life.

The people were intimately tied to their environment; and when resources were depleted in one place, they moved on. Animal trails became trails for the bands as they roamed over the landscape, following food and water sources to their favorite places. As they traveled along, they stopped regularly to rest, repair or replace their stone toolkits, and hunt available game. Knowledge of these nomadic locations was passed down from generation to generation and ensured the survival of the group. Mountain valleys became meeting places for nomads in search of resources. Sources of good stone for toolmaking were critical for survival. With the warmer climate, food sources were abundant; and populations grew. Shelters changed from natural caves and rock shelters to shallow pit structures. Interaction with other groups of people brought trade and new technologies. The bow and arrow and pottery were introduced. Smaller game necessitated smaller stone tools, and the differences in these tools left behind inform us of the lifeways of the people.

Archaeologists have developed a timeline for the changes during these thousands of years:

- The Paleo-Indian Stage: 13,000-7500 years before present (YBP),
- Archaic Stage: 7500-1800 YBP, and
- Late Prehistoric Stage: 1800-A.D. 1540.

The Paleo-Indian Stage toolkit contained large lanceolate stone points with a flute (center flake removed at the base) leaving wide grooves for attaching to the spear or atlatl dart. They were made with care and an eye for aesthetics as well as durability and functionality. These distinctive stone tools appear rarely in the western portion of Colorado and the Rocky Mountains, but enough of them have been found to prove that people were there. More sites have been found in other parts of the state: In eastern Colorado at Dent Site, Selby Site, Lindenmeier Site, Hell Gap, Agate Basin, and Olsen-Chubbuck; and in the Rockies at Fourth of July and Caribou Lake. In Douglas County, archeological sites are located at Lamb Spring and Blackfoot Cave. As the large animals disappeared, the Paleo-Indian tools became smaller but retained the familiar flute and fine workmanship.

Projectile Points, Drill, and Scraper

Substantial environmental changes occurred in the Archaic Stage. Although the changes were gradual, large mammals disappeared. In this stage, humans hunted larger animals like deer, elk, and modern bison and small animals like rabbits in larger numbers. A greater variety of plants became an important part of the human diet; and different toolkits were used to accommodate these changes: Grinding stones; smaller stemmed, side and corner notched dart points; scrapers; awls; and perforators provide archeologists with important evidence of Archaic Stage dating. One theory for the disappearance of the fluted points and the emergence of notched points is that notches offered superior hafting (attachment) to the atlatl dart. Populations became larger, the bands stayed longer at the good sites, and basin houses begin to appear. Consequently, more Archaic sites have been found all over Colorado. Within Douglas County, Lamb Spring, Blackfoot Cave, Bayou Gulch, Franktown Cave, and Rueter-Hess have Archaic components.

Through trade and other contacts with eastern and western cultures, important technological inventions changed the Archaic ways of life. The Late Prehistoric Stage saw the introduction of fired clay ceramics and the bow and arrow. On the eastern side of the Rocky Mountains, ceramics were utilitarian with few embellishments. The pots were marked on the exterior with a cord-wrapped paddle and smoothed on the interior with a polishing stone. The cord marks helped to grip the pot when it was hot or wet. The bow and arrow were a much better extension of the atlatl, allowing the hunter more power and the ability to be farther away from prey. Projectile points were small and corner notched. With these changes, the population grew and became more sedentary. Although rock shelters and caves were still used, basin and pit houses were built more often. In Douglas County, evidence of basin houses has been discovered at Rueter-Hess.

Spanish explorers in 1540 brought more changes to the people. For example, the concept of having and riding a horse was new. Now the hunter-gatherers had another element added to their methods of subsistence. Travel was faster, horses were able to transport more possessions. By the 1800s the named tribes we know today—the Utes, Cheyenne, Arapaho, Paiute, Pawnee, Kiowa, and others, were present in the mountains and plains and no longer could be called Prehistoric.

Bibliography of Sources Used for This Chapter:

Benedict, James B. "Getting Away From It All: A Study of Man, Mountains, and the Two-Drought Altithermal," *Southwestern Lore* 45 (1979):1-12.

Cassells, E. Steve. *The Archaeology of Colorado,* rev. ed. (Boulder: Johnson Books, 1997).

Final Environmental Impact Statement: Rueter-Hess Reservoir. Vols. I and II (Omaha: U. S. Army Corps of Engineers, 2003).

Frison, George C. *Prehistoric Hunters of the High Plains,* 2nd ed. (San Diego: Academic Press, 1991).

Gantt, Erik M, et al. *Mitigative Excavations at the Hess (5DA1951), Oeškeso (5DA1957), and 5DA1936 Archaeological Sites at the Rueter-Hess Reservoir, Douglas County, Colorado,* vols. I and II (Ft. Collins: Centennial Archaeology, 2007).

Gilmore, Kevin P., et al. *Colorado Prehistory: A Context for the Platte River Basin* (Salt Lake City: University of Utah Press, 2004).

Vivian, R. Gwinn. *The Chacoan Prehistory of the San Juan Basin* (San Diego: Academic Press, 1990).

Chapter 2

EARLY EXPLORERS

Blake Graham

Spanish explorers were the earliest European group to traverse the Rocky Mountains. In search of gold beyond Mexico in the mythical city of Gran Quivira, Francisco Vasquez de Coronado traveled from the area around Albuquerque, NM, to what became central Kansas in 1540-1541.[1] While earlier historians say otherwise, recent scholarship suggests that Coronado did encounter the Rocky Mountains but did not pass through the southeast corner of what became the Centennial State during his expedition.[2] After Coronado's exploration, Spanish communities were established in Santa Fe and Taos, New Mexico. They became bases for further explorations to the north, especially Colorado, during the early seventeenth century. While earlier contact may have occurred, this timeframe was pivotal for increased interactions and exchanges between other Europeans and Native Americans. In fact, French traders and explorers were also crossing Colorado in their attempts to follow the Arkansas River from Arkansas to its source in Colorado during the middle of the seventeenth century. European explorers hoped to start new settlements while many aboriginal peoples remained dubious about the new cultural encounter and defended their hunting grounds and way of life.

In 1800, Spain agreed to trade much of its frontier land to France, which in turn sold it to the United States as the Louisiana Purchase in 1803. This agreement included land from Louisiana in the South to Montana in the North. President Thomas Jefferson negotiated this transaction and was anxious to explore it. He authorized six expeditions to explore west of the Mississippi basin. "The object of your mission," Jefferson instructed Lewis and Clark, "is to explore the Missouri River & such principal stream of it as by its course . . . may offer the most direct & practicable water communication across this continent for the purposes of commerce."[3] One of these six expeditions included the first U.S. Government-funded exploration and surveying of Colorado.

Zebulon Montgomery Pike, sponsored by Jefferson's commanding general, was tasked with exploring the interior of the Louisiana Purchase in 1806.[4] Pike was assigned to find the sources of the Arkansas and Red Rivers. In November 1806, he led his group of "dam'd [sic] rascals" into the Colorado Rockies.[5] The first summit they encountered was Pike's namesake mountain which, according to his personal journal, had an appearance of "a small blue cloud."[6] Determined to ascend Pike's Peak, the men started the hike but unfortunately were unable to climb to the peak due to harsh winter conditions. Nevertheless, the men continued valiantly into the Rockies until they reached South Park. Soon thereafter, winter conditions and scarce supplies forced them to retrace their steps and trek southward. In February 1807, they were spotted by Spanish scouts after crossing into New Mexico and apprehended for alleged espionage. Pike and his men were hastily escorted to Mexico. In June 1807, they arrived in Chihuahua, Mexico, where they were abruptly pardoned by the Spanish Governor, even though the Mexicans confiscated papers from Pike that allegedly revealed that Pike's second in command was a U.S. spy.[7] Pike was detained for only four months, but other Americans were not so fortunate. A Missouri trader traveling in southwestern Colorado was apprehended by Spanish soldiers, convicted of trespassing, and held prisoner for nine years.[8]

The Jefferson-inspired explorations helped define the characteristics and boundaries of the Louisiana Purchase, but they provided only a partial roadmap of the American West. Major Stephen H. Long, a graduate of Dartmouth College and former mathematics professor at West Point, conducted a "scientific exploration" of the West with instructions to find the source of the Platte, Arkansas, and Red Rivers.[9] Long led his entourage of nineteen men from Nebraska to Colorado in May 1820. In June, after traveling through the Denver area, Long and his men ascended Long's Peak, which they mistakenly believed was Pike's Peak. They continued in a southern direction through the Rockies until they reached New Mexico and eventually headed East with their research and written records. Throughout his journal, Long repeatedly lamented the "incurable barrenness" of the terrain around them. "Our sufferings from thirst, heat, and fatigue were excessive, and were aggravated by the almost unlimited extent of the prospect before us, which promised nothing but a continuation of the same dreary and disgusting scenery."[10] Long's map labeled the region as "the Great American Desert," which greatly influenced those Americans who contemplated migration from the East.[11] Some historians have argued that Long's negative account of the region bought American Indians nearly three more decades of unfettered buffalo hunting.[12]

Lieutenant John C. Fremont is often recognized as the explorer who ignited western expansionism. In 1842, Fremont began the first of five expeditions to survey the major trails crossing the Continental Divide. For the next twelve years, Fremont traveled the Missouri River, Continental Divide, and Great Basin, as well as every trail in between. Fremont employed several mountain men as guides to help navigate the West, including Kit Carson, Old Bill Wilson, and Thomas Fitzpatrick. While the first expeditions were pivotal for mapping the terrain, Fremont's

Kit Carson and John Fremont

fourth expedition represents one of the first attempts to find a suitable railroad route from St. Louis to the Pacific.[13] Regrettably, the mission was aborted when the group encountered extreme winter conditions in San Luis Valley: ten of the thirty-three men died on the journey.[14]

In Fremont's fifth and final expedition in 1854, he competed against surveyor Captain John Gunnison to find an all-weather, transcontinental train route across the Divide by way of Pueblo, Gunnison, and Grand Junction. Fremont won the contest with Gunnison, even though his plans were tabled. For his many successes, Fremont was called "the Pathfinder of the West, by the new Republican Party which made him its first presidential candidate in 1856.[15]

From Spanish explorations north of New Mexico to Fremont's detailed surveys of the Colorado Rockies, the American West was undergoing a significant change in culture and landscape. Historian Phil Carson captured the reality of this change: "[explorers'] cultural arrogance, courage, tactics, and technology had won them a wilderness empire in North America at great cost to the region's native inhabitants."[16]

---

[1] Carl Ubbelohde, Maxine Benson, Duane Smith, *A Colorado History*, 9th ed. (Portland: Westwinds Press, 2006), 10-16.

[2] Phil Carson, *Across the Northern Frontier: Spanish Explorations in Colorado* (Boulder: Johnson, 1998), 8-9.

[3] Gerard W. Gawalt, ed., *Thomas Jefferson and Early Western Explorers*, Manuscript Division, Library of Congress (1803), accessed April 26, 2015, http://"www.;loc.gov/exhibits/lewisandclark/transcript57.html

[4] Matthew L. Harris and Jay H. Buckley, eds., *Zebulon Pike, Thomas Jefferson, and the Opening of the American West* (Norman: University of Oklahoma, 2012), 101.

[5] Daniel Bissell, *Bissell MSS* (St. Louis Mercantile Library,1856), accessed April 26, 2015, http://dl.mospace.unsystem.edu/umsl/slandora/object/umsl%3A40410

[6] Donald DeWitt, *Pike and Pike's Peak: A Brief Life of Zebulon Montgomery Pike and Extracts from His Journal of Exploration* (Colorado Springs: Colorado College, 1906), 13.

[7] Ubbelohde, 19-23; Harris and Buckley, *Zebulon Pike*.

[8] Ubbelohde, 26.

[9] Ibid., 27.

[10] Maxine Benson, ed., *From Pittsburgh to the Rocky Mountains: Major Stephen Long's Expedition, 1819-1820* (Golden, CO: Fulcrum, 1988), 230.

[11] Ibid., 1.

[12] Francis J. Pierson, *Summit of Destiny: Taming the Pike's Peak County, 1858-1918* (Denver: Charlotte Square, 2008), 14.

[13] Ubbelohde, 48.

[14] LeRoy R. Hafen, ed., *Mountain Men and Fur Traders of the Far West: Eighteen Biographical Sketches* (Lincoln: University of Nebraska, 1982),215-219; Ubbelohde, 48.

[15] Larry F. Morris, *The Perilous West: Seven Amazing Explorers the Founding of the Oregon Trail* (Lanham: Rowman & Littlefield, 2013), 193-194.

[16] Carson, *Across the Northern Frontier*, 188.

Chapter 3
THE FIRST IMMIGRANTS

Larry Schlupp

Three American Indian tribes migrated into the Douglas County area and were settled before the large migration of white men from the east: Southern Arapaho, Southern Cheyenne, and Southern Utes. The Utes were a multi-banded, tribal Indian nation of Shoshonean descent that moved from the southwest into Colorado in the early 1500s. Hence, most historians consider the Utes as the only American Indian tribe *"native"* to the state. It was the Mouache band of Utes that migrated into Douglas County, living on the Front Range between Denver and Trinidad to the south. The Caputa band lived east of the Continental Divide, south of the Conejos River, in the San Luis Valley. The Mouache and Caputa bands collectively are known as Southern Utes.[1] The Arapaho and Cheyenne both descended from the large northeastern Algonquian family and migrated into the Colorado Plains in 1820 from Minnesota and the Dakotas. The Arapaho were driven west by the early land-encroaching white men, and the Cheyenne were driven west by the warring Sioux. At the beginning of the nineteenth century, the Arapaho and Cheyenne formed a close, simple alliance without assimilation and continued that relationship during the duration of their time in Colorado. Both tribes moved into the Front Range Mountains *circa* 1835.[2] The Cheyenne settled along the Platte River, which infuriated the Kiowa who considered the area their sacred hunting grounds, even though they did not live there. In 1838, the Kiowa from down on the Arkansas raided a Cheyenne village on the Platte for intruding on their traditional land and massacred forty-eight Cheyenne tribal members.

The Arapaho and Cheyenne were both originally agricultural people, brave but kind and accommodating, and much given to ceremonial observances. Both tribes celebrated the Sun Dance early in their history, a link back to their Algonquian beginnings. Although the Arapahos and Cheyenne intermingled socially, intermarried, shared in religious celebrations, and fought as allies, the two tribes remained separate and the *"Southern"* associated with each of their tribal names primarily was a geographic distinction. One of the few cultural differences between the Arapaho and Cheyenne was that the Arapaho buried their dead in the ground while the Cheyenne placed their dead in trees or on scaffolding.

When they moved into the different environments of the Great Plains and eastern Colorado, the Arapaho and Cheyenne changed their manners and ways of life. While they lived in timbered country, they practiced agriculture, made pottery, and lived in wigwams, which were typical forest-dwelling habitations. After relocating to the prairies, they lost their agricultural and pottery skills. Because bison and antelope were in vast numbers on the plains, they stopped building bark-covered lodges and began living in conical, skin-covered lodges instead, typical teepees. The social work functions of the Arapaho and Cheyenne were similar. Women were responsible for homemaking: making clothing; growing, gathering, and preparing food, and provisioning the family shelter. The men hunted, conducted tribal administration, and managed intertribal and allied relationships that were crucial for security against Kiowa, Sioux, and occasional Comanche war parties.[3]

Tribal leadership differed. The Arapaho were militarily structured, as were most Plains Indians, and had three primary divisions: *Men of the Forked River, Greasy Faces,* and *Bad Pipes.* The Cheyenne were more loosely organized and based on a clan system. As with most Indian tribal structures, both the Arapaho and Cheyenne had multiple chiefs in addition to a principal chief who was usually either a war chief or a significant tribal elder. The multiple chiefs made centralized governance difficult. In defiance of the principal chief, the multiple chiefs often organized splinter or renegade bands to go to war against the Kiowa, Sioux, and Comanche who left their traditional territory to forage along Colorado's Front Range. Such independent activity caused deep divisions within the tribe. These conflicts primarily included providing access to traditional hunting grounds, stealing horses, kidnapping women, or defiling land considered sacred by the tribes. Such hostilities continued until the 1840s when most of the Arapaho and Cheyenne made peace with their enemies in anticipation of a new crisis facing all the tribes: the arrival of a relatively small number of explorers, mountain men, and fur trappers, who brought with them the spread of smallpox. To avoid the contagion, the Colorado tribes took refuge in the mountains in 1837-39; but they were less successful at avoiding other epidemics. In 1849, the tribes were devastated by the spread of cholera.[4]

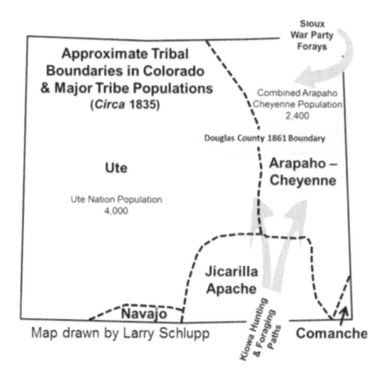

Approximate Tribal Boundaries in Colorado & Major Tribe Populations (*Circa* 1835)

Sioux War Party Forays

Combined Arapaho Cheyenne Population 2,400

Douglas County 1861 Boundary

Ute

Ute Nation Population 4,000

Arapaho – Cheyenne

Jicarilla Apache

Navajo

Map drawn by Larry Schlupp

Kiowa Hunting & Foraging Paths

Comanche

The Utes were always a warlike people. Early on, they acquired horses from the Spanish, which intensified their aggressive character. The Southern Utes were nomadic. They moved in bands through well-known mountain hunting and gathering areas during the spring and summer. The men hunted deer, antelope, buffalo, rabbits, and other small mammals and birds. Women gathered seed grasses, piñon nuts, berries, roots, and greens in woven baskets, and processed and stored meat and plant materials for winter use. Late in the fall, family units would begin to move out of the mountains into sheltered areas for the cold winter. Generally, the family units of the band would live close together which made acquiring fuel for heating and cooking easier. The large family units provided a better line of defense against enemy tribes seeking supplies for the harsh winter weather. Southern Ute families lived in covered hide tepees, enabling relatively easy mobility. The Ute women were well known for their hide tanning, sewing, and bead working ability. Ute men were fierce fighters and warred against the Jicarilla Apache and Navaho, as well as the Arapaho and Cheyenne. The Utes considered the latter two tribes as invaders of their Colorado hunting and wintering areas, as people who had no rights to be in the Colorado Plateau.[5]

The early entrance of the mountain men (*circa* late-1820s) was greeted somewhat amicably by Southern Cheyenne Chief Black Kettle and Southern Arapaho Chief Little Raven who believed in the possibility of coexistence and trading with these mountain men. However, as more whites began arriving, their perspectives began to change. Numerous uprisings in the Great Plains in the late 1840s caused the United States government to negotiate the Fort Laramie Treaty of 1851. The treaty had numerous facets and involved numerous mountain and plains tribes. Chiefs Black Kettle and Little Raven supported the treaty because it recognized permanent lands for the Southern Cheyenne and Southern Arapaho from the North Platte River in the north to the Arkansas River to the south and from the Rockies in the west to the western part of Kansas in the east. After the treaty, Indian life seemed to return to the early days after they had moved from Minnesota and the Dakotas to the Colorado area. The Southern Arapaho and Southern Cheyenne still had to cope with Utes' constant raids on their territory, but for the time being, the Fort Laramie Treaty seemed to establish an agreeable status quo for Colorado's Indian tribes.[6] With the dramatic influx of whites after the discovery of gold in 1859, everything changed.

---

[1] Frederick Hodge, "Ute," *Handbook of American Indians North of Mexico*, Vol. 2 (Washington, D. C.: Government Printing Office, 1910), 874 – 875.

[2] Frederick Hodge, "Arapaho," *Handbook of American Indians North of Mexico*, Vol. 1 (Washington, D.C.: Government Printing Office, 1907), 72-73, 250–257.

[3] "Indians of Colorado, *Family Search*, accessed January 4, 2015, https://familysearch.org.learn/widi/en/Indians-of-Colorado.

[4] Jan Pettit, "Ute Indians of Colorado," *Colorado Spring Pioneer Museum*, accessed January 7, 2015, http://www.cspm.org/learn/regional-history/native-americans/ute-indians-of-colorado.

[5] "Roberts History—Fort Laramie Treaty of 1851," University of Wyoming, accessed December 15, 2014,

http://www.uwyo.edu/robertshistory/fort_laramie_treaty_of_1851.htm; Charles Kappler, "*Arapaho and Cheyenne*," (Articles, Pages 595 -595)." *Oklahoma State University Digital Library* (Washington: Government Printing Office, 1904), 595, accessed December 15, 2014, http://digital.library.okstate.edu/kappler/Vol2/treaties/sio0594.htm#mn11.

[6] Population sizes for Graphic entry designs, accessed December 15, 2014, https://family search.org/learn/wiki/en/Ute_Indians.

Chapter 4
MOUNTAIN MEN

Edwin Bathke

The mountain men were fur trappers and explorers who lived in the Rockies between 1810 and the 1880s. They were usually loners and often social outcasts. To survive and prosper in their environment, they needed to be adventurous and resourceful. Theirs was a precarious life, fraught with dangers from the weather, wild animals, and Indians. The 1830s were the best of times for the mountain men because of the popularity of beaver hats, especially among city folks. But in the 1840s, the fur trade began to decline because the trappers had already depleted the supply of beaver pelts; and silk top hats had suddenly become the fashion rage, reducing the demand for the trappers' "product." As a result of these shifting demands, many mountain men moved onto the eastern plains to hunt for buffalos, since Easterners' tastes demanded "buffalo "robes." Even the independent-minded mountain men were the victim of changing market patterns elsewhere.

In their heyday, the mountain men moved through the Rockies on old Indian footpaths, many of which they improved, and blazed new trails through the wilderness. As a result, they became the pathfinders for western exploration and travel. When fur trapping diminished, many mountain men became guides for exploratory expeditions and wagon trains, as well as scouts for the U.S. Army. Possibly most disturbing to the mountain men was the loss of solitude: the Colorado Gold Rush of 1859 brought thousands of prospectors to the Rockies, many of whom became permanent settlers and homesteaders.

Douglas County played a small role in the evolving story of the mountain men. Neither the Cherry Creek, Plum Creek, or South Platte drainages provided trapping opportunities. But travelers on the way to the Rockies often passed through what became Douglas County on well-established trails used by Indians or the earliest explorers: Trappers Trail, Old Divide Trail, Military Trail, Jimmy Camp Trail, and Cherokee Trail.

Most of the identities of the mountain men are unknown, but a few of them we know well. The first known mountain men to reach the Pikes Peak Region and Douglas County were James Pursley and Baptiste LaLande in 1803-1804. According to the Zebulon Pike's 1806 report, Pursley and his fellow trappers were "driven by Sioux from the plains into the mountains." Pursley reportedly was the first American to discover gold in Colorado along the headwaters of the South Platte River in South Park. When Pike was in Santa Fe a year later, he does not mention Pursley. LaLande came up the South Platte, then went to Santa Fe, where he sold his goods at a fabulous profit. The Ezekiel Williams party (1808), the Philibert Company, and the Choteau-DeMunn party (1815-1817) penetrated the mountains of the Pikes Peak Region, where they suffered much from both the Indians and the Spanish.

Mountain men traveling between Bent's Fort to the south along the Arkansas River, and Forts St. Vrain and Vasquez, to the north, regularly crossed Douglas County. One of these, "Uncle Dick" Wooten, established a regular weekly express between St. Vrain and Bent's Fort about 1842, doing good business in potent rot-gut whiskey known as "Taos Lightning."

In 1831 Thomas "Broken Hand" Fitzpatrick organized a party of trappers in Taos to move into the central Rocky Mountains that included Kit Carson. Fitzpatrick's mule pack train crossed the Arkansas, trail-blazed down East Plum Creek in Douglas County, then went along the South Platte River and later the North Platte River in Wyoming. Fitzpatrick's association with Douglas County would continue in later years when he was appointed the first resident Indian agent for the region of the Upper Platte and Arkansas (by the Fort Laramie Treaty of 1851).

Kit Carson, like Fitzpatrick, continued in the fur trade for over a decade, and became most notable among his peers. Carson and Fitzpatrick were guides for the "Great Pathfinder," John C. Fremont, on his second expedition, which crossed and recrossed Douglas County in 1843. Kit would travel through Colorado considerably in the next twenty-five years. He figured prominently in the Indian unrest in Douglas County in the 1860s. In 1868 as he returned from Washington, D. C., via Denver, he became seriously ill. His party stopped near Wildcat Point near Daniel's Park in Douglas County where he had what is called "his last campfire." He made it as far as Fort Lyons on the Arkansas River, where he died.

James "Jim" Baker was a twenty-year-old when he began trapping for the American Fur Company in 1838. His adventures during the next two decades were typical of a mountain man, including many exploits involving wild animals and Indians. He was a guide for Fremont on his third expedition in 1845. He passed through Douglas County on a journey to Bent's Fort in 1856. He crossed this territory in 1858 when he was a guide on the Marcy expedition. In 1859 Baker settled permanently in Colorado, homesteading on the south side of Clear

JIM BAKER

Jim Baker

Creek, at what is now 53rd and Tennyson streets in Denver. Statements that he was a Colorado Militia member cannot be substantiated. Supposedly he was a guide for Col. Chivington in the Sand Creek fight. His name does not appear on official documents, however, but that is probably because he was a civilian. In 1873 he sold his Denver land and moved to Wyoming, where he resided until he died in 1898.

Among the most prominent of mountain men was James "Jim" Pierson Beckwourth, who entered the fur trade in 1823 with William Ashley and the American Fur Company. In 1859 he worked as a storekeeper in Denver, married in 1860, and worked on a farm a few miles south of Denver. He left Denver in 1861, bought some farmland, ran a saloon, and built a home on the east side of the South Platte River. Although a bit north of Douglas County, he was familiar with this area. In 1862 he became a guide for E. L. Berthoud and the Second Colorado Infantry, and, in November 1864, he served as a guide for Chivington at the Sand Creek Massacre. He was revolted by the atrocities committed there and testified against Chivington at subsequent Congressional investigations. He rebelled against the increasing levels of civilization in Denver, so he returned to trapping on the Green River and working as a scout and guide until he died in 1866.

Little is known of Jimmy Daugherty, who trapped in 1838 and 1839, then made his headquarters in Taos in 1840 and 1841. From there he made trading trips to Arapaho villages on the South Platte, near the present site of Denver. Returning south on the Trappers Trail, through Douglas County, he stopped in El Paso to sell goods. There he was killed in what history now calls Jimmy Camp. Because of Daugherty, many people referred to Trappers Trail as Jimmy Camp Trail.

These notable mountain men serve as good examples of those known as that "reckless breed of men." But they should be considered as businessmen of their era, opening the West, and then as it developed, moving from exploring and trapping, to being guides, and then often settling down. These men left an imprint on Douglas County, and they made valuable contributions to the settlement of the American West.

Bibliography of Sources Used for This Chapter:

Baker, James H and LeRoy L. Hafen, eds. *History of Colorado*, Vol. I. (Denver: Linderman Co., 1927).

Carter, Harvey L. "The Curious Case of the Slandered Scout, the Aggressive Anthropologist, the Delinquent Dean, and the Acquiescent Army," *The Denver Westerners, Brand Book,* Volume 28, edited by Edwin A. Bathke (Boulder, CO: Johnson Publishing Co., 1973).

Carter, Harvey L. *'Dear Old Kit'* (Norman, OK: University of Oklahoma Press, 1968).

Carter, Harvey L. and Thelma S. Guild, *Kit Carson, a Pattern for Heroes* (Lincoln, NE: University of Nebraska Press, 1984).

Conard, Howard Lewis. *"Uncle Dick" Wooten* (Chicago: W. E. Dibble & Co., 1890).

Hafen, LeRoy R. *The Mountain Men and the Fur Trade of the Far West,* 9 volumes (Glendale, CA: Arthur H. Clark Co., 1965-1972).

Marr, Josephine Lowell. *Douglas County: A Historical Journey* (Gunnison, CO: B & B Printers, 1983).

Meyer, Susan. *Our Heritage, People of Douglas County* (Castle Rock, CO: Douglas County Historical Society. n.d.).

Mumey, Nolie. *James Pierson Beckwourth, an Enigmatic Figure of the West, 1856-1866* (Denver: Old West Publishing Co., 1957).

Mumey, Nolie. *The Life of Jim Baker, 1818-1898* (New York: Interland Publishing, 1972).

Smiley, Jerome C. *History of Denver* (Denver: Denver Times, 1901).

Smiley, Jerome C. *Semi-Centennial History of the State of Colorado*, Vol. I (Chicago: Lewis Publishing Co., 1913).

Vestal, Stanley. *Kit Carson* (Boston: Houghton Mifflin Co/ Riverside Press, 1928).

Chapter 5
EARLY TRAILS

Lee Whiteley

Cherry Creek and Plum Creek, with headwaters located in southeastern Douglas County, flow north from the "Arkansas/Platte Divide" to the South Platte River. Providing the essentials of wood, water, and grass, the creeks were natural pathways for north-south travel along the Front Range of the Rocky Mountains. To the west were the Rockies, where only mountain men ventured before the discovery of gold in 1858. To the east was what Stephen Long in 1820 labeled the "Great American Desert."

Trading posts opened east of the Rocky Mountains in the early 1830s: Bent's Old Fort and Pueblo along the Arkansas River, four civilian forts along the South Platte River north of present-day Denver, and Fort Laramie on the North Platte River. The Trappers Trail connected these establishments. Most of the traffic along the trail was the movement of goods by U.S. and Mexican merchants. Rufus Sage accurately described the goods transported along the trail in 1842: "Some twelve or fifteen Mexicans were at this time at the Fort [Fort Lupton]. They constituted a trading party from Taos, escorting a caravan of pack horses and mules, laden with flour, corn, bread, beans, onions, dried pumpkins, salt and pepper, to barter for robes, skins, furs, meats, moccasins, bows and arrows, ammunition, guns, coffee, calico, cloth, tobacco, and old clothes, which were to compose their return freight."[1]

The Trappers Trail followed West Plum Creek, East Plum Creek, and Cherry Creek through Douglas County. The first paths were "pack trails," used not by wheeled vehicles but by horses and mules. Travelers were free to choose the trail desired, depending on water and grass conditions. Stephen H. Long followed West Plum Creek in 1820, while John C. Fremont traveled the East Plum Creek trail in 1843. The Perry Park Road follows closely West Plum Creek while East Plum Creek runs through Castle Rock. The two creeks merge at Sedalia. As trade demands increased in the mid-1830s, wheeled vehicles became a necessity.

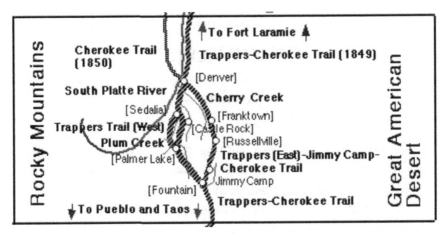

Early Trails Map

The Cherry Creek route proved to be the easiest. As the first wagon road along the Front Range, this trail crossed the southern boundary of the county and descended Russellville Gulch to Cherry Creek, a mile south of present-day Franktown. The trail then descended Cherry Creek to the South Platte River.

Jimmy Camp Trail was an alternate name for the branch of the Trappers Trail along Cherry Creek. It was named for Daugherty, Jimmy, an independent trader, who had a camp on Jimmy Camp Creek, eight miles east of present-day downtown Colorado Springs. With the decline of the fur business, traffic decreased by 1840; but the Jimmy Camp route was still a "trail of many uses." Military expeditions included Lt. Col. Stephen Watts Kearney in 1845 and Captain Randolph Marcy in 1858. Independent travelers Rufus Sage in 1842 and Francis Parkman in 1846, both traveled the trail and wrote of their experiences. A detachment of Mormons, known as the "Mississippi Saints," traveled south from Fort Laramie to Pueblo in 1846. After spending the winter there, they returned north, again along Cherry Creek Road. The Jimmy Camp Trail would see a huge increase in traffic starting in 1849. California-bound gold-seekers, including Cherokee Indians, traveled this east branch of the Trappers Trail.

The Cherokee Trail became the favored name attached to the trail down Cherry Creek. The trail became the primary north-south road between Bent's Old Fort on the Santa Fe Trail "Mountain Branch," and Fort Bridger on the

Oregon-California Trail. Livestock were also driven along the trail, bound for the goldfields of California from Texas, Arkansas, and Oklahoma. Robert M. Peck, a member of the 1857 Col. Edwin Sumner campaign, traveled the Cherokee Trail to present-day Denver. Here he noted: "This part of Kansas Territory was literally a 'howling wilderness,' with

Trader's Cart

little indications of its having been occupied or traversed by white men, except the old wagon-road we have been traveling, with here and there a stump and a few chips by the roadside, as the mark of some California emigrant."[2] This howling wilderness would change a year later.

William "Green" Russell traveled to California via the Cherokee Trail in 1849. He returned in 1858 to present-day Colorado, via the same trail. He discovered small amounts of gold at Russellville, five miles southeast of Franktown. This and other small gold strikes, and major strikes in the spring of 1859, led to the Colorado gold rush. The Cherokee Trail across the Arkansas-Platte Divide became known as the "Southern Route to the Mines."

The use of the Cherokee Trail declined after the Civil War. Shorter, more direct trails linked the developing towns of Denver and Colorado City, now part of Colorado Springs. These new "territorial roads" followed more closely the Trappers Trail along East Plum Creek. All long-distance freighting along the Trappers Trail came to an immediate end with the completion of the Denver and Rio Grande Railroad in 1871.

---

[1] Rufus B. Sage, "Scenes in the Rocky Mountains," *Far West and Rockies Series*, vol. 5, ed. Leroy R. Hafen (Glendale, California: Arthur H. Clark Co., 1956).

[2] R.M. Peck, *Far West and Rockies Series*, vol. 9, ed. Leroy R. Hafen (Glendale, California: Arthur H. Clark Co.), 111.

Chapter 6

THE FIFTY-NINERS

Larry Schlupp

Between 70 and 25 million years ago, a Mineral Belt was formed that cut diagonally across Colorado. It contained veins of gold that had formed within crystalized quartz layers. For many eons, rain and runoff eroded some exposed bedrock in the Mineral Belt, loosening tiny pieces of gold from their original formation that washed down the mountain slopes into the streams of the Front Range.[1]

Native Americans were the first to see gold flecks in Colorado's streams. Although the Indians seldom extracted the shiny gold flecks from the stream bottoms, they told the first white men who entered the area about the gleaming flecks. Eventually, that information made its way to William "Green" Russell. In the summer of 1849, South Carolina-born Russell was mining for gold in northern Georgia. When news of the California gold rush reached him, he and seven friends headed west for the gold fields. After several years of meager results, in 1857 Russell and his friends sold their claims and headed home to Georgia. Once there, Russell's wife, a Cherokee woman named Sukie,[2] learned from other Cherokees about the discovery of gold in streams of the Rocky Mountains.[3] Once in possession of such information, Russell, his brother Oliver, two cousins, and three fellow Georgians headed west to the Rocky Mountains via the Arkansas River, picking up other want-to-be miners along the way. Reaching El Pueblo in May 1858,[4] the Russell party then turned north to the Platte River in their quest for gold. During the first week of July 1858, Russell found trace amounts of placer gold at Dry Creek (close to present-day Englewood) and then moved to the confluence of Cherry Creek and the Platte River, where he found larger amounts of placer gold.[5] After a few weeks, when the gold proved to be in short supply, the miners relocated further north and west. However, news of the discoveries in Dry and Cherry Creeks and the Platte River spread quickly and triggered the Colorado Gold Rush of 1859.

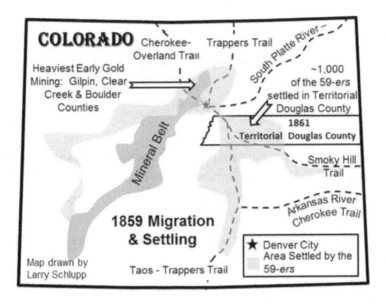

"Pikes Peak or Bust" was the slogan that the Fifty-Niners carried with them across the Great Plains. Most came by wagon trains; but others traveled by mule, on foot carrying a shoulder pack, or pushing a handcart. Colorado-bound wagon trains often had colorful, exciting names like *E. Doty's Lightning Express Train,* while others were simply named after their wagon master, such as *Capt. Willis' Train.* Most wagon trains and coaches included the word *Express* in their names, which was misleading. It took on average six to eight weeks to travel from St. Louis or St. Joseph to Denver City.[6] The Fifty-Niners came in from the north via the Cherokee or Trappers' trails. They came from the south from Taos and El Pueblo;[7] but most followed the trails along the South Platte, Smoky Hill, and Arkansas Rivers. The trip west was dangerous. Travelers reported many unburied bodies or freshly dug graves along the trails. Hundreds of Fifty-Niners died of starvation, lack of water, snake bites, disease, or Indian attacks. Wagon trains in a hurry often did not stop to bury the dead; they pressed on toward the gold fields. In 1859, 100,000 Fifty-Niners came to Colorado. Thousands of them passed through what became Douglas County.

Most Fifty-Niners came to mine for gold, but many of them quickly turned to other pursuits. Many of the migrants settled in Denver and found their fortune selling supplies to the miners and otherwise supporting the enormous influx of people into the area. In significant ways, among the greatest success stories of the Colorado Gold Rush were the shop keepers, grocers, assayers, lawyers, newspaper publishers, and freight-haulers who turned Denver into a thriving base of operations for the gold rush. Long after the rush had subsided, Denver remained a thriving city on which much of Colorado's future would depend.

Many of the Fifty-Niners never made it to the gold fields. Once they arrived in Colorado, they decided to become homesteaders and put down roots along the Front Range and eastern plains. Their efforts shaped Colorado's future as well. It is estimated that about half of the 100,000 Fifty-Niners who came to Colorado eventually abandoned all hope of striking it rich and decided to head for home.[8] Those who stayed behind became the pioneers that made Douglas County and the rest of Colorado home.

The Gold Rush was short-lived in Douglas County. Most historians believe that it was essentially over by 1861 when Congress turned Colorado into a U.S. Territory. While it lasted, gold was mined in Russellville, the gold camp established by "Green" Russell, and a couple of sites along West Plum Creek near what is now Sedalia. After miners gave up on these sites, they moved on to the Boulder-Central City area, where they worked in Clear Creek and nearby Mountain City (now Idaho Springs). Gold was so plentiful there that the region became recognized as the Colorado Mineral Belt.

In 1861, the new Territorial Legislature divided the land into seventeen counties. Douglas County stretched 174 miles from the Platte River to the current Kansas border. It is estimated that of the "permanent population" of about 40-50,000 that remained in Colorado after the end of the gold rush, 1,000 settled in Douglas County. These settlers were a hearty bunch who drove deep cultural pilings into the land and tamed the environment against overwhelming odds. Given the huge geographical size of the County, the population was widely dispersed but tended to stay close to the County's water ways.

One of these "first comers" was Isaac P. Van Wormer who came for gold but did not find any. He decided to settle along Running Creek instead and helped found Elizabeth, which was then in Douglas County. He established a successful ranch there, but during the Indian war of the late 1860s, when a ranch hand and his family were massacred, Van Wormer moved to the western edge of Douglas County where he became a successful horse rancher and served one term as a Douglas County Commissioner.[9] Sarah Coberly, her husband George, and their four children came by wagon train during the summer of 1859 and settled on West Plum Creek at Huntsville, a mile north of present-day Larkspur. Sarah was the first white woman in the County; she became a large landowner and built a hotel or *"halfway house"* at Huntsville along the Denver City-Colorado City territorial road.[10] Daniel Chessman Oakes came to the area in late 1858 and became a Douglas County legend. Oakes was a successful gold miner, a surveyor, the founder of Huntsville, one of the founding fathers of Denver, a lumberman who brought the first steam-powered sawmill to Colorado, a vigilante, a legislator, and an Indian agent.[11] Van Wormer, Coberly, and Oakes were emblematic of the undying spirit, grit, and determination of the founding pioneers in Douglas County, the Fifty-Niners.

Daniel C. Oakes   *Sarah Coberly*

---

[1] Vincent Matthews, Lynn Keller, and Betty Fox, *Messages in Stone, Colorado's Colorful Geology*. Colorado Geological Survey (Denver: Colorado Department of Natural Resources, 2003), 117.

[2] Emma Dill Russell Spencer, *Green Russell and God* (Austin: University of Texas Press, 1966), 39.

[3] E. Bastin, "William Greenbury Russell," accessed December 1, 2014, http://www.ldpierce.com/william_green_russell.html

[4] "History of El Pueblo," accessed January 30, 2015, https://www.historycolorado.org/museums/history-el-pueblo

[5] "The Colorado Gold Rush," accessed May 16, 2006, http://www.westernmininghistory.com/state/colorado; Steven F. Mehls, *The New Empire of the Rockies: A History of Northeast Colorado,* Cultural Resources Series (Denver: Bureau of Land Management, 1983), 33-50.

[6] H. Bromwell, "Precincts and Delegates of 1859," *Fifty-niners' Directory: Colorado Argonauts of 1858-1859,* vol. 1 (Denver: Pikes Peak Region, 1926), 242-243.

[7] "History of El Pueblo," accessed January 30, 2015, http://www.historycolorado.org/museums/history-el-pueblo.

[8] Bromwell, "Precincts and Delegates."

[9] Margee Gabehar, *The Elbert County History* (Raleigh, NC: Curtis Media Corporation, 1926).

[10] Josephine Lowell Marr, *Douglas County: A Historical Journey* (Gunnison, CO: B & B Printers, 1983), 128-29, 180-83, 197-98.

[11] LaVonne Perkins, *D.C. Oakes: Family, Friends & Foe* (Denver: Stony Ridge Press, 2009), 1, 5, 7-9, 12, 14.

Chapter 7

COLORADO TERRITORY

Tim Weber

The Pike's Peak region was part of the Kansas Territory. It included the Front Range and eastern plains in an area stretching roughly between south of Pueblo and just north of Denver. The rest of what became Colorado was part of three other U.S. territories. Utah controlled west of the Continental Divide; Nebraska, the area north of Denver; and New Mexico, a section in the south. After gold was discovered, Kansas governor James W. Denver organized the Pike's Peak region into Arapahoe County; but it lacked a functioning government. As a result, the Fifty-Niners found little law and even less order.

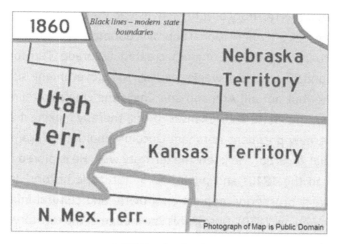

1860 Territories Map

The first settlers developed their own governmental structures. Using models developed elsewhere, people in the new towns utilized "People's courts" to try and execute deserving criminals. Miners established hundreds of "mining districts" where they staked out claims and recorded them in a central office. Elected officers enforced complicated written codes and settled disputes. Agricultural settlers established "claims clubs" with written constitutions and elected officers to record claims and settle disputes between the first comers and later arrivals. Such attempts to establish property rights were technically illegal since the federal government had already given Indians title to the land in the Fort Laramie Treaty of 1851. The Fifty-Niners pressured the government to eliminate the Indian titles so they could legally own the land. Until that happened, they assumed the "law of preemption"—that the earliest people who claimed and settled on lands were given the first chance to acquire them once they were surveyed and made available.[1]

The settlers wanted more government, not less. In November 1858, the inhabitants of the new town of Auraria petitioned Congress to create the Territory of Colona. Congress denied that request in January 1859, along with two others during the winter of 1859. By the spring, a small group of frustrated settlers decided to call a constitutional convention to create the State of Jefferson on their own. But the departure of thousands of disillusioned Fifty-Niners caused them to scale back their plans. In October they organized the Territory of Jefferson instead, but their inability to collect taxes and the lack of Congressional approval doomed their efforts to failure.[2]

On February 28, 1861, Congress created Colorado Territory with its present boundaries. A few weeks earlier, the government succeeded in getting some (but not all) Arapaho and Cheyenne chiefs to relinquish their land between the Platte and Arkansas Rivers, thereby making it available to settlers. The new president Abraham Lincoln appointed William Gilpin the first territorial governor. He knew the territory well. He explored it with John C. Fremont in the 1840s and published a "futuristic history" in which he predicted great prosperity, population growth, and cultural influence (*The Central Gold Region*, 1859). Despite his knowledge of the territory, Gilpin was a disaster as governor. He had enthusiasm and vision, but poor judgment. When Congress refused to fund a territorial militia, Gilpin organized the First Colorado Volunteer Regiment anyway. To pay the troops, he issued drafts that he promised the U.S. Treasury would honor. When the Treasury refused, Gilpin's political days were numbered. Lincoln removed him from office in 1862 and replaced him with his friend John Evans, a successful physician and businessman from Chicago.[3]

Douglas County was one of the original seventeen territorial counties organized in 1861. Its boundaries stretched from the South Platte in the west to the Kansas border in the east. Named after Senator Stephen A. Douglas of Illinois, it included 5,160 square miles and a population of 1000. Most inhabitants lived in the western part of the county, along its waterways: South Platte River, West Plum Creek, East Plum Creek, Cherry Creek, Running Creek, Kiowa Creek, Comanche Creek, Bijou Creek, etc. Most early settlers engaged in agriculture pursuits—farms, cattle ranches, and sawmills. Life was more difficult than originally advertised, thanks to grasshopper invasions, hailstorms, drought, the settlers' lack of experience in such an arid climate, and frequent conflicts with Indians. New territorial roads and the historic Cherokee and Smoky Hill Trails cut through the county and accommodated stagecoach and freight lines, mail routes, and immigrant wagon trains. Five "Mile Houses" marked the final approach to Denver along the Smoky Hill Trail by offering food and lodging. The Twenty-Mile House in the Parker area was famous for its hospitality.[4]

Early county government seemed to depend on the abilities of one man. J. Frank Gardner is considered the "father of Douglas County." Born in NY in 1833, he moved west in phases until he arrived in Colorado as a gold seeker in 1859. Typhoid fever almost killed him. He left the gold fields and began working in the lumber business. In 1860 he took out a squatter's claim at Cherry Creek and Bayou Gulch, near today's Ponderosa High School. The settlement around his ranch became Frankstown (the "s" was dropped in 1877) and was named the county seat in 1861. In 1863 Gardner became county clerk, then

James Frank Gardner

county recorder. The next year he became county treasurer. In 1866 he was appointed county assessor and Justice of the Peace. He served in the territorial legislature (1869-73) and later in the State Senate. He was also a

Douglas County Commissioner (1894-96) and an Indian agent. He conducted county business out of his cabin and in 1863 transferred it to the California Ranch Hotel, a stage stop located at the present intersection of Highways 83 and 86. A fire destroyed the Hotel and all county records in late 1863. The Hotel was rebuilt in 1864, and Gardner purchased it the following year. Frankstown remained the county seat until 1874.[5]

During the 1860s the county grew by only 388 inhabitants, thanks to the Indian War that raged from 1864 to 1869. But the Homestead Act of 1862 laid a foundation for future growth. The law enabled any U.S. citizen or immigrant who planned to become one, who was at least 21 years old and the head of a household, to receive title free and clear to 160 acres of government land after living on it for five years, building a house, making certain improvements, and paying a small registration fee (about $30). The homesteader could receive title much faster by residing on the land for six months and paying $1.25 per acre ($200). But in Colorado's arid climate, 160 acres were not enough to ensure a family's survival.[6] While mountain run-off made irrigation possible in the South Platte and Arkansas River Valleys, most streams in Douglas County were unreliable as irrigation sources.[7] So farmers and cattle raisers had to learn how to conserve water, use dry-land farming techniques, and experiment with new crops. The rugged people of Douglas County made the necessary adjustments and prospered.

By the 1870s, Douglas County was ready to move ahead. The coming of the railroads, the redrawing of the county's boundaries, the building of a new county seat, and the diversification of agriculture turned D.C. into a going concern. But the foundation for success was laid in the turbulent 1860s.

---

[1] Carl Ubbelohde, Maxine Benson, and Duane A. Smith, *A Colorado History*, 9th ed. (Boulder, CO: Pruett, 2006), 89-93.

[2] Carl Abbott, Stephen J. Leonard, and Thomas J. Noel, *Colorado: A History of the Centennial State*, 4th ed. (Boulder, CO: University Press of Colorado, 2005), 56-59.

[3] Elliott West, *Contested Plains: Indians, Goldseekers, and the Rush to Colorado* (Lawrence, KS: University Press of Kansas, 1998), 237-238; Ubbelohde, *Colorado History*, 98-101.

[4] Ann Moore, "History of Douglas County," M.A. Thesis, University of Denver, 1970, 10-27.

[5] Josephine Lowell Marr, *Douglas County: A Historical Journey* (Gunnison, CO: B & B Printers, 1983), 33-45.

[6] Ubbelohde, *Colorado History*, 186-87.

[7] West, *Contested Plains*, 250-54.

Chapter 8
THE CIVIL WAR

Blake Graham

On February 28, 1861, President James Buchanan signed a bill creating the new Territory of Colorado; and Douglas County was recognized as one of the first counties in the Territory. Forty-three days later, on April 12, Confederate forces opened fire on Fort Sumter, near Charleston, South Carolina. This was the first act of aggression that sparked the Civil War. Following the seizure of Fort Sumter by Confederate soldiers, the editor of the *Rocky Mountain News* declared, "For ourselves, we take our stand ON THE SIDE OF THE UNION."[1] While some agreed with this sentiment, others stood in opposition. Nearly one-third of the population in the Colorado territory had an upbringing in the South.[2] Throughout April 1861, merchants in and around Denver proceeded to hang flags over their stores to officially announce their allegiance. The first instance of this occurred on April 22. The *Rocky Mountain News* editor commented that William Graham's City Drug Store "has a fine Union flag flying over his store."[3] Three days later, the Wallingford & Murphy store responded in kind by hoisting a confederate flag over its building. The editor was not impressed: "Aside from the bad taste displayed by the parties who allow such a rag to disgrace their premises, the event is of no importance."[4]

Governor William Gilpin arrived in Denver on May 27, 1861, and intended to dissuade anti-Union attitudes in the Territory and establish a governmental allegiance to the Union.[5] Governor Gilpin immediately mustered volunteers across the territory and raised two regiments within months to build a military-capable Colorado Territory. In October 1861, Confederate soldiers rallied and prepared to move west in hopes of unseating Governor Gilpin, securing the gold mines, and expanding Confederate forces. Gilpin responded immediately by sending troops southbound to New Mexico to stop the offensive strategy. The First Colorado Volunteer Regiment, commanded by Colonel John Slough, led the way from Denver to New Mexico. The opposing forces met at the Battle of Glorieta Pass on March 26, 1862. Major John

Chivington, leading several companies with Colonel Slough's approval, coordinated an attack that crippled the Confederate supply train. Chivington's efforts paved the road to victory for Colorado's volunteer Union soldiers. As a result, Chivington was promoted to full colonel and given command of the regiment, replacing Col. Slough.

The Front Range, particularly in and around Douglas County, remained free of combat engagements between 1861-1865. In fact, many soldiers complained of boredom and unnecessary and repetitive marching. To overcome tedium, they engaged in obsessive gambling and fighting. Romine H. Ostrander, a private in the First Colorado Cavalry, served under Colonel Chivington during the Battle of Glorieta Pass and commented on the behavior of his fellow soldiers traveling through Colorado. On April 13, 1863, a few days after Ostrander camped at California Ranch near Franktown, he noted that a fellow soldier known as Foley had been quarreling with him: "[Foley] has been bragging to the boys that he can whip me; and that he will fight me for fifty dollars; and as I don't think he can, I shall take him up if he challenges me. I do not want the name of a prise [sic] fighter, but the temptation is considerable for fifty dollars."[6] Two years later, in April 1865, Ostrander traveled back through Douglas County and continued to document his and his fellow soldiers' experiences. When his unit stopped for camp near Pretty Women's Ranch in Sedalia, which he mistakenly called "dirty woman's ranch," three new recruits deserted to Taos, New Mexico, in the middle of the night.[7] In a facetious manner, Ostrander did not believe they had any reason to skedaddle: "Oh! The poor private soldiers. How he is fostered and cared for! Furnished with everything the heart could wish, clothing, rations, quarters, and pleanty [sic] of money, what has he to complain of! Who wouldn't be a soldier? . . . "Who wouldn't fight for his country?"[8]

Hubert and Miriam Fonder were introduced near Idaho Springs in 1862. Miriam worked in a boarding house, and Hubert was a laborer at a mining camp. In December 1862, a few months after they married, Hubert volunteered for the army and was assigned to McLain's Light Artillery Battery. Strong-minded Miriam secured a job as a laundress in the same company to be close to her husband. In her autobiography, Miriam notes that many soldiers "had nothing to do but drill only or they volunteered to share guard duty with the others."[9] During their first eight months of military service,

Miriam was pregnant while carrying out her duties in the laundry. The battery relocated from Fort Lyon to Camp Weld in Denver, in July 1863. Shortly after their arrival, Miriam and Hubert's first daughter, Madger, was born. Shortly thereafter, Hubert received orders to join the company's expedition from Denver to Kansas (April 1864). Miriam, like many other wives in Colorado, had little means of subsistence to support herself and her infant after her husband's departure. To survive, she went from mining town to mining town cooking and washing clothes in boarding houses. Providing for

Hubert and Miriam Fonder

herself and her daughter was difficult, so in July 1864, she decided to trek to Kansas and reunite with Hubert until he was discharged in August 1865. Shortly thereafter, they moved back to Colorado and began farming near Pine Grove (near Parker, CO). Miriam's experiences during the Civil War exemplify the widespread illnesses, inadequate earnings, uncertain livelihoods, and harsh winters that many others faced throughout the new Territory during the Civil War.

Though Colorado was far from the carnage and destruction of the Civil War further east, the war's impact on Coloradoans was great. Though most Southern sympathizers left Colorado after the war began, divided loyalties still plagued its population. Miners (what was left of them), laborers, managers, shop keepers, entrepreneurs, homesteaders, and their families were all affected by the war. Like the Fonders, family life throughout the territory was disrupted. Still, while the Civil War in the East, South, and even West along the Mississippi was coming to a close, Colorado experienced another war, the Indian War that extended from the Rockies to beyond its northern and eastern borders. Unlike during the Civil War, Douglas County found itself in the middle of this war and suffered directly from it.

[1] *Rocky Mountain News*, April 22, 1861.

[2] William C. Whitford, *Colorado Volunteers in the Civil War* (Denver: State Historical and Natural History Society of Colorado, 1906), 26.

[3] *Rocky Mountain News*, April 22, 1861.

[4] *Rocky Mountain News*, April 25, 1861.

[5] William H. Wroten, Jr., "Colorado and the Advent of the Civil War: Opinions Expressed in Colorado Newspapers on the Coming Civil War," *Colorado Magazine* 36, no.3 (1959): 186.

[6] Paul A. Malkoski, annotator, *This Soldier's Life: The Diaries of Romine H. Ostrander, 1863 and 1865, in Colorado Territory* (Denver: Colorado Historical Society/History Colorado, 2006), 13.

[7] Ibid., 97.

[8] Ibid., 77.

[9] Kathy Fonder Wait, *My Father's Belgium Fonder Roots and Their American Family Descendants* (South Dakota: K.F. Wait, 1991), 36.

Chapter 9

THE CLASH OF CIVILIZATIONS

Tim Weber

Conflict between whites and Indians was inevitable. Americans believed they were destined to occupy the entire continent ("manifest destiny"), which put them on an unavoidable collision course with Native Americans.[1] The Plains Indians had a nomadic "horse culture" based on migrating buffalo and traditional hunting grounds. The arrival of the Fifty-Niners and later the railroads threatened lands already given to seven tribes in the Treaty of Fort Laramie (1851). By the early 1860s, 30,000 permanent settlers in Colorado outnumbered Plains Indians almost five-to-one.[2] They killed buffalo, cut timber, consumed limited resources, spread disease, claimed title to the land, and demanded protection from the government. To accommodate them, Washington pressured the Arapaho and Cheyenne to abandon most of their lands between the Platte and Arkansas Rivers and move to a small reservation in southeastern Colorado, where the government promised to make them farmers (the Treaty of Fort Wise, 1861). Some chiefs signed the treaty; others refused and decided to fight.[3]

Sporadic violence soon broke out in Kansas, Nebraska, and Colorado. In 1864 Northern Cheyenne, Arapaho, and Lakota Sioux joined Southern Arapaho and Cheyenne, Kiowa, Comanche, and Apache to raid along the South Platte/Denver Road, the Smoky Hill Trail (which cut across Douglas County), and the Santa Fe Trail. They attacked wagon trains, stagecoaches, freight lines, and railroad crews; burned ranches; and stole livestock in order to drive the settlers out. The Colorado Indian War lasted until 1869 in most places, a little longer in others.[4] Up to 700 civilians and over 100 soldiers died, and many women and children were kidnapped.[5] No one knows how many Indians were killed.

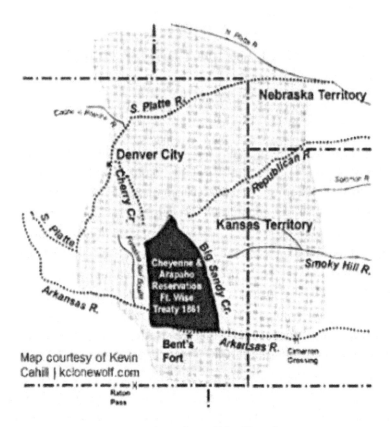

Fort Laramie and Fort Wise Treaties

The Civil War kept the regular army busy back east, so Territorial Governor John Evans organized the 3rd Colorado Volunteer Cavalry under Col. John Chivington, a Methodist minister who advocated the Indians' extermination. In September 1864, at Camp Weld outside Denver, "peace chiefs" from the Southern Cheyenne (Black Kettle and White Antelope) and the Southern Arapahoe (Little Raven) offered peace; but Evans believed full-scale war was imminent. The governor ordered friendly Indians to move to designated forts "for protection" and urged Coloradoans to shoot those Indians who refused to relocate. The army then began raiding non-compliant Indian villages.[6]

Camp Weld Peace Conference

The Sand Creek Massacre made a bad situation much worse. Following Evans' directives, Black Kettle moved his band of Cheyenne to Sand Creek, 40 miles northeast of Fort Lyon on the Arkansas River, where he joined Arapahos who had gathered there under "peace chief" Left Hand. The village contained about 500 people. Early on November 29, 1864, when most warriors were out hunting, Col. Chivington's 700 troopers attacked. They killed and mutilated about 160 Indians, mostly women, children, and old men. White Antelope and eight other chiefs were killed. Left Hand succumbed to his wounds later, but Black Kettle escaped. In Denver, soldiers displayed scalps and other "trophies" and were hailed as heroes, but three subsequent government investigations in 1865 condemned the massacre and blamed Evans and Chivington. Despite much public support, Evans was removed from office; and Chivington resigned before a court martial could punish him. After Sand Creek, Indian attacks multiplied, including the sacking and burning of Julesburg in early 1865.[7]

War parties regularly moved through Douglas County, torching ranches, stealing livestock, and murdering isolated and vulnerable settlers. Probably the best-known incident occurred on June 11, 1864. Nathan Hungate, his wife Ellen, and their two daughters Florence (almost 3 years) and Laura (almost 5 months) were brutally killed on Isaac Van Wormer's ranch near Running

Creek, north of present-day Elizabeth, then in Douglas County. When their mutilated bodies were publicly displayed in Denver, fear and anger escalated and the call for revenge became an important factor leading to the Sand Creek Massacre.[8]

For protection, Douglas County residents constructed stockades: at California Ranch south of Franktown, Fort Washington on Ben Quick's ranch near West Plum Creek, Fort Lincoln in Huntsville near Larkspur, and Spring Valley Fort.[9] At the first sign of trouble, people hurried to the nearest stockade and stayed until the threat passed, though during the day some men left to work their ranches or patrol for Indians. One day Frank Gardner, the founder of Franktown, was working alone at his shingle mill when an Indian war party charged. Nearby lumbermen saved him. In 1864 Charles Engel, Conrad Moschel, and Lorenz Welte left the California Ranch stockade to roundup cattle in Castlewood Canyon, when a dozen Indians attacked. Engel galloped back to the stockade. Welte fell off his horse, hid in the bushes, and later walked back. But Moschel was overtaken and killed. In 1868 Indians killed Jotham Lincoln as he worked alone on his Spring Valley ranch. Later that summer, war parties operated in the Kiowa and Comanche Creek area.[10] On August 25 while Apollinaris Dietemann and a hired hand were in Denver on business, his wife Henrietta, their two children, his sister, and two hired hands saw Indians approaching their ranch. They quickly set out for the settlement of Kiowa. Henrietta (7 months pregnant) and her son John (5) were caught and killed. The others made it safely to Kiowa.[11] Other attacks occurred around Frankstown, Castle Rock, Kiowa Creek, and Bijou Basin.[12]

By the end of 1869, the war in Colorado was mostly over, thanks to the arrival of the U.S. Army and its well-known Civil War generals: Sherman, Sheridan, Hancock, and Custer. In 1867 the army took the offensive against the Indians, which included unprecedented winter attacks. At the Battle of the Washita (western Oklahoma) Custer's 7th Cavalry surprise-attacked another Cheyenne village and killed Black Kettle (1868).[13] The turning point was the Battle of Summit Springs (near Sterling) in 1869, after which Chief Tall Bull's Cheyenne Dog Soldiers, the most feared warriors in Colorado, ceased being a threat.[14] Even during hostilities, new treaties attempted to move non-combatant Indians to reservations in Kansas and Oklahoma. Finally, the Medicine Lodge Treaty of 1867 established a permanent reservation for the Arapaho and Cheyenne in Indian Territory (Oklahoma), far from white settlers. By the early 1870s the Southern Arapaho, Southern Cheyenne, and their allies left Colorado for various reservations; but Lakota Sioux and Northern Cheyenne went north and kept fighting, which culminated in the Battle of Little Big Horn in 1876 and the loss of General Custer's 7th Cavalry.

Only the Utes remained in Colorado. Various bands lived in the Rockies and were the Plains tribes' traditional enemies. After miners and settlers arrived, treaties in the 1860s moved the Utes across the Continental Divide. After a brief Ute uprising in 1879 (the Meeker Massacre and the Battle of Milk Creek), Chief Ouray led most Utes to Utah, though two small reservations were established along the Colorado-New Mexico border and remain the only reservations in Colorado today.

Both sides had peace and militant parties; but neither side was willing or able to accommodate the other, thanks to their competing visions for the land, confusing treaties, broken promises, and unsuitable reservations. Both sides committed similar atrocities against the other. The Indians were not so much defeated as deprived of the necessary resources for survival and overwhelmed by growing numbers of settlers and soldiers. In the West, demographics were destiny.[15]

---

[1] Anders Stephenson, *Manifest Destiny: American Expansion and the Empire of Right* (New York: Hill and Wang, 1996).

[2] Margaret Coel, *Chief Left Hand* (Norman: Oklahoma University Press, 1987), 162.

[3] Ibid., 110-137.

[4] For the most comprehensive study of the war, see Jeff Broome, *Cheyenne War: Indian Raids on the Roads to Denver, 1864-1869* (Sheridan, CO: Aberdeen Books, 2013).

[5] Jeff Broome, "Collateral Damage: Sand Creek and the Fletcher Family Indian Captivity Story," *The Denver Westerners Roundup*, vol. 60 (September-October, 2014).

[6] Coel, *Chief Left Hand*, 237-250.

[7] Stanley W. Hoig, *The Sand Creek Massacre* (Norman, OK: University of Oklahoma Press, 1961); Elliott West, *The Contested Plains: Indians, Goldseekers, and the Rush to Colorado* (Lawrence, KS: University Press of Kansas, 1998), 297-308.

[8] Jeff Broome, "Indian Massacres in Elbert County, Colorado; New Information on the 1864 Hungate and 1868 Dietemann Murders," *The Denver Westerners Roundup*, vol. 60 (January-February, 2004).

[9] Josephine Lowell Marr, *Douglas County: A Historical Journey* (Gunnison: B & B Printers, 1983), 37-38, 48, 182-183, 203.

[10] Broome, *Cheyenne War*, 358, 367-370.

[11] Ibid., 370-374.

[12] Ibid., 377-388.

[13] Stanley W. Hoig, *The Battle of Washita: The Sheridan-Custer Indian Campaign of 1867-1868* (Garden City, NJ: Doubleday, 1976); Evan S. Connell, *Son of the Morning Star* (San Francisco: North Point Press, 1984), 182-197.

[14] Broome, *Cheyenne War*, 450-467; Elliott, *The Contested Plains*, 313-318.

[15] Elliott, *The Contested Plains*, 263.

Chapter 10

EARLY SETTLEMENTS

Larry Schupp

Thomas Jefferson's 1803 purchase provided the land to which immigrants came in unexpected numbers. The people who settled in what would become Douglas County came from the western migration of about 100,000 gold-seeking Fifty-Niners and the surge of Civil War veterans who were looking for a fresh start in the West.[1] When the 1859 Gold Rush busted, most Fifty-Niners left. Most of those who stayed took up farming, using methods learned back home. Thus, these permanent settlers traded the adventure of gold mining for the challenge of farming in a much different environment than they were used to.[2] Their first challenge was to obtain land. Methods varied: Many would-be homesteaders squatted on land whose ownership was undetermined, used military patents, or took advantage of one of the three United States Congressional statutes, the Homestead Act of 1862, the Carey Act, and the Timber Act, which provided land for next-to-nothing to those willing to meet certain requirements.[3]

Between 1858 and 1871, homesteaders formed new settlements, some of which eventually became established towns. The process of town-building was driven by many factors, including cultural similarities of language, nationality, and outlook. Also important in the creation of new settlements were adequate water, building materials, trading opportunities, and the proximity of "transportation," which amounted to dirt trails over which mail, freight, and travel to other settlements occurred.

In 1858, Russellville became Douglas County's first community. The town was named after William Russell from Georgia and began as a gold camp. The "gold rush" there played out quickly, forcing the town to transition to an agricultural-based community. After Russellville, new communities were mainly tied to agriculture or transportation. Most communities began with a single homestead, followed by other homesteads nearby. These early homesteads contained the "basics" needed for survival: a house, privy, and loafing sheds which provided protection and shelter for cattle and other livestock. Cisterns of various kinds stored water; and later on, windmills drew water from wells. Barns and corrals were located away from the house to allow prevailing winds to reduce odors, dust, and flies from livestock. Such steady development enabled settlers to survive the first years after securing their homestead land patent.

When distinct communities formed, they mostly took names based on their geographic surroundings (e.g., Stone Canyon and Pine Grove) or their "founding family" (e.g., Fonder and Williamsville). Stage route stops, post offices, sawmills, and delivery and shipping points often turned into towns that no longer exist, having lost their original purpose after technology transformed farming methods and transportation created new and faster ways of providing goods and services throughout the region. Only six towns formed between 1858 and 1871 in Territorial Douglas County exist today: Elizabeth, Franktown, Kiowa, Larkspur, Louviers, Parker, and Sedalia.

On the eastern plains of early Douglas County, two towns were founded: Elizabeth and Kiowa. The town known today as Kiowa, along the Smoky Hill Trail,[4] was founded as Wendling in 1859. It was named after Henry Wendling, an early settler in the area who ran the Butterfield Overland and Wells Fargo stage station that was established along Kiowa Creek. The name was changed from Wendling to Kiowa in the 1860s.[5] The second plains town, Elizabeth, had its beginning as a Weber Brothers' sawmill camp beside Running Creek in 1855. There was some gold found in the creek, but it was of poor quality and quantity. Even after the gold findings gave out, settlers continued to move into the area. A former Fifty-niner named Isaac Van Wormer was instrumental in establishing Elizabeth in 1858. Shortly after it was founded, the original Weber Brothers sawmill camp site flooded; and the town site was moved to Elizabeth's present location.[6]

Further west, during the the1860s, a few towns were begun that still exist today. Early settler Charles Parkhurst built the California Ranch near what is now the intersection of highways 86 and 83. He sold the ranch property to New Yorker James Frank Gardner who had settled in the area on May 14, 1859.[7] Gardner was an industrious, entrepreneurial character who turned the California Ranch into a hotel that served as a popular stagecoach station on the way to Denver. After Colorado became a U.S. Territory in 1861 and county lines were established, Frankstown became Douglas County's first county seat. Frank Gardner became the County's Clerk and Recorder. He kept all "official" Douglas County documents in a back room at his hotel. In the latter part of the nineteenth century, the "s" in Frankstown was removed.

The Town of Parker began *circa* 1863 at Pine Grove, which was located south of Parker's current location. Parker was eventually named after settler James Samples Parker, who moved to the area from Kiowa. The town developed through a legendary series of multiple sales of property. The first business in the area was a travelers' post office and provisioning store in a one-room cabin that was built and operated by Alfred Butters, who eventually sold out to George Lord. The new owner moved the Pine Grove building and expanded it into the 20 Mile House, a hospitality house for stage travelers on their way to Denver. The 20 Mile House was a magnet drawing other settlers and businesses to the vicinity. George Lord resold the facility to Mr. and Mrs. Nelson Doud who eventually sold it to James Parker. He became the Pine Grove Postmaster in 1870. For some time, then, Parker was known as an important stopping-place on the route to Denver.[8]

Twenty Mile House and Barn

Fifty-Niners John H. Craig, Jack Johnson, and Charles Holmes[9] came to Colorado in May 1859, hoping to get rich mining gold. After their mining attempts were mostly unsuccessful, they settled in the community that became known as Happy Canyon and started raising stock. In 1865, Craig built a corral alongside the new Territorial Road (now Santa Fe Road) which ran near the convergence of East and West Plum Creeks. The corral was circular, and the town near it became known as Round Corral. In 1869, Craig sold the corral to Jonathan House, who renamed it Plum. Later on, a new owner named Henry Clay renamed the town Sedalia, after his hometown in Missouri.[10] The town became an important shipping point for cattle, lumber, and other agricultural products.

Weaver House, Corral and Livery Stable, Sedalia

The town furthest west in Douglas County in the 1858-1871 period had several identities. Jacob Jones came to Colorado in 1858, married, and homesteaded near what became known as Keystone, then Kelley's Station, a stage stop and post office that were noted by cartographers.[11] When the Denver & Rio Grande Railroad (D&RG) was built through the area in 1871, the stage stop became a railroad station called Toluca. In the early 20th century, the station was renamed after its nearby company-town of Louviers.[12]

The last town in the 1858-1871 era was Larkspur, which was named after the purple wildflowers that covered the area. Larkspur, like Sedalia and Louviers, developed after the coming of the D&RG, which reached the future Larkspur town site in September 1871.[13] With the construction of the D&RG

depot there, the importance of Huntsville, located a mile north of the new town declined. It had been a famous stagecoach stop half-way between Denver and Colorado City. It was also Douglas County's first post-office. But with the coming of the train, Huntsville's reason for existence was usurped by Larkspur.

In the first decade after Colorado became a U.S. Territory, its population was small, its towns were few, and its importance to early Colorado was barely recognized. But all that was about to change.

---

[1] Wilbur Fisk Stone. *History of Colorado* (Denver: S. J. Clark Publishing, 1898), 1280.

[2] Alvin T. Steinel, *History of Agriculture in Colorado, 1858 – 1926* (Fort Collins, Colorado: State Agricultural College, 1926), 14-15.

[3] Loretto Dennis Szucs and Sandra Hargreaves Luebking, eds., *The Source: A Guidebook of American Genealogy* (Salt Lake City: Ancestry Incorporated, 1997), 258.

[4] Lee Whiteley, *The Cherokee Trail: Bent's Old Fort to Fort Bridger* (Boulder: Johnson Printing, 1999), 35.

[5] "Kiowa's Story," *Town of Kiowa*, accessed February 18, 2015, http://www.townofkiowa.com/?page_id=295.

[6] "History of Elizabeth, Colorado," *Town of Elizabeth*, accessed February 17, 2015, http://www.townofelizabeth.org/history.html; Margee Gabehart, *The Elbert County* History (Curtis Media Corporation, 1989).

[7] H. Bromwell, *Fifty-Niners' Directory: Colorado Argonauts of 1858-1859*, Vol. 1 (Denver, Pikes Peak Region, 1926), 126.

[8] "A Brief History of Parker, Colorado," *Parker Area Historical Society*, accessed January 18, 2015, http://www.parkerhistory,org.

[9] Frank Hall, *History of the State of Colorado*, Vol. IV (Chicago, Illinois: Blakely Printing Company, 1895), 20; Bromwell, *Fifty-niners' Directory*, 86,185.

[10] Toni Hess, "History of Sedalia," Local History Collection, Douglas County History Research Center; Susan Appleby, *Fading Past: The Story of Douglas County, Colorado* (Palmer Lake, CO: Filter Press, 2001), 163.

[11] Burt Struthers, "So You're Going Ranching!" *Saturday Evening Post*, November 17,1945, 1-5.

[12] Dave Hicks, *Littleton from the Beginning* (Denver: Egan Printing, 1975), 13; Josephine Marr, *Douglas County: A Historical Journey* (Gunnison, CO: B & B Printers, 1983), 104-105.

[13] Appleby, *Fading Past*, 103.

Chapter 11

LAYING THE FOUNDATION

Larry Schlupp and Tim Weber

When Colorado became a U.S. territory in 1861, it lacked almost any kind of infrastructure. During its first decade, Douglas County, like the rest of the territory, struggled to provide the "basics." These included developing a road system to move both people and the supplies necessary for their survival, delivering the mail in a timely and efficient way, establishing a viable system of local government and taxation, and educating its children. By achieving these goals, Douglas County was laying the foundation for its future.

The legislature created a new system of territorial and toll roads to move freight and people through Douglas County. During the 1860s all equipment, supplies, and settlers came from the East over stage, freight, and wagon roads. Territorial roads were created (and often rerouted) over the decade along routes still in use. One followed what is now Santa Fe Road and Interstate 25 to Colorado City; and another went south through Cherry Creek Valley, roughly following the old Cherokee Trail and today's Highway 83 (Parker Road).

The Smoky Hill Trail also became an important highway through Douglas County. During the Gold Rush of 1859, there were two branches of the trail into Denver: the most traveled northern route and a southern "starvation trail" which was shorter but more hazardous. In 1865 the Butterfield Overland Despatch [sic] Company, which ran stagecoaches and freight wagons from Atchison, Kansas, to Denver, surveyed a new southern route that began south of Limon and went through Kiowa, Hill Top, and Parker, where it joined the new territorial road into downtown Denver.

In 1866, the Butterfield route was incorporated as the Lake Station and Douglas County Toll Road. Operators charged $1.00 for a wagon pulled by two animals, 75 cents for a wagon pulled by one, 20 cents for an animal and rider, 10 cents for a loaded pack animal, and 3 cents for each loose stock animal. Such fees added up: each freight wagon train usually had twenty-five wagons, and the trains stretched as far as the eye could see.[1]

Local entrepreneurs also built their own toll roads. In 1866, Frank Gardner, George Engl, J.F. Giles, and others founded the Frankstown and Giles Station Wagon Road Company. Its toll road started at Gardner's California Ranch in Frankstown, passed by George Engl's ranch in Lake Gulch, then went straight south to Giles Ranch in Spring Valley.[2] Most toll roads had a short lifespan, thanks to the arrival of the railroads in Douglas County in the early 1870s.

In the late 1850s and early 1860s, mail service in Douglas County was almost non-existent. Any letters that did arrive in Denver from the East came by individual travelers or regularly scheduled stage or freight lines such as the Leavenworth-Pike Peaks Express or the Butterfield Overland Despatch [sic] Express.[3] As a result, it usually took weeks or months for people in Douglas County to receive any mail, if they received it at all. This situation changed on January 22, 1862, when the first post office in Douglas County opened at Huntsville with Daniel C. Oakes as postmaster.[4] After Huntsville, the number of post offices grew steadily during the 1860s. They were usually established in existing stagecoach and freight line stations. Among the first post offices in Douglas County were in Russellville, which quickly moved to Frankstown under postmaster J. Frank Gardner (1862); Spring Valley at Giles Ranch (1865); and Rock Butte (1869). This eastern mail route was serviced once weekly and then increased to three days a week by the Barnum and Company stage line. In central and western Douglas County four other post offices were established: Bennett Springs (1862), Keystone Ranch at Kellytown (1863), Bear Cañon (1863), and Glen Grove, where Tom Dawson was postmaster (1869). Most of these post offices remained through the decade with mail supplied by stagecoach and freight lines.[5]

The first territorial legislature of 1861 encouraged the development of "common sense" laws to establish simple, effective government infrastructure. Douglas County residents participated in Governor William Gilpin's Vigilante Committee, a rather formidable group of 100 Colorado citizens of good character[6] who dispensed justice in Denver City and the surrounding counties. Among other new governmental structures, Agriculture and Education Committees were established along with much-needed county offices as recorder, treasurer, and assessor, although there were little to no monies available to support them. Colorado's tax situation became even more critical after the Civil War when the U.S. Assessor's Office ordered all states and territories to reassess their tax situation considering the abolition of slavery. Before emancipation, slaves were considered personal property and their value was taxed accordingly. After the War, the taxes from slave owners or others using slave labor were no longer available. As a result, tax revenue in the United States dropped by 75 percent. That meant that the tax system had to be adjusted to make up for lost revenue. According to the *Rocky Mountain News*, Douglas County citizens met together at the Huntsville post office on July 21, 1865, to discuss anticipated adjustments to their property tax assessments.[7] But before the full impact of those changes in property taxes took place, it was decided to raise the needed tax revenue through an income tax.

Benjamin Quick House

Since there were no schools when Colorado Territory was organized, some settlers "homeschooled." Ben Quickof West Plum Creek started a school upstairs in his ranch house and hired a teacher to educate his and the neighbors' children.[8] North of Frankstown, Miriam Fonder taught school in her kitchen until her husband Hubert built a small log schoolhouse nearby.[9]

The Manharts near Sedalia and the Turners in Happy Canyon made similar arrangements.[10]

In 1865, Douglas County began organizing school districts. The first three were Sedalia (Pioneer District), Frankstown, and Spring Valley, which served seventy students. By 1870 the Quick and Fonder schools were official districts, and others followed. Also, in 1870, Frederick Doepke urged County Superintendent of Schools George Lord to divide the Frankstown district to accommodate the German Catholic children around Castlewood Canyon. Lord agreed and appointed Doepke the president of the new Lower Lake Gulch school board.[11]

Each district consisted of a one-room schoolhouse with a single teacher for all grades. The schoolhouses were also used for Sunday school and other community events. Enrollments usually ranged from single digits to twenty students. Each district had a three-person school board and was financed by local taxes, though the Indian War made collecting them difficult. The number of districts increased to twenty-three by 1890 and eventually forty. They were reorganized many times, starting in 1874 when Douglas County boundaries were redrawn.[12]

With these social, economic, and political foundations in place, the people of Douglas County were ready to enter the 1870s, a decade of enormous expansion and development.

---

[1] Josephine Lowell Marr, Douglas County: A Historical Journey (Gunnison, CO: B & B Printers, 1983), 68-73.

[2] Ibid., 48. See also Glenn R. Scott, Historic Trail Map of the Denver 1° x 2° Quadrangle, Central Colorado, Prepared by Denver Public Library, Western History/Genealogy Department (Reston, VA: United States Department of the Interior, U.S.G.S., 1999), 7-22 for a list of all the territorial, toll, and postal roads of this period.

[3] Scott, Historic Trail Map.

[4] LaVonne Perkins, D. C. Oakes: Family, Friends & Foe (Denver: Stony Ridge Press, 2009), 128.

[5] Alice M. Thompson, Walk With Our Pioneers – A Collection (Grand Junction, Colorado: JLM Sales, 2005), 17-18, 167.

[6] Perkins, D.C. Oakes, 111.

[7] "Public Notice," Rocky Mountain News, 30 June 1865.

[8] Marr, Douglas Country, 200-202.

[9] Ibid., 40-41. See also Kathy Fonder Wait, *My Father's Belgian Fonder Roots and their American Descendants* (privately printed, 1991), 42-44.

[10] Susan Meyer, et al, *Our Heritage: People of Douglas County* (Castle RockCO: Douglas Country Historical Society, 1984), 365.

[11] See the correspondence between George Lord and Frederick Doepke. "Superintendent of Schools Papers to F.A. Doepke, 1870-1874," in Douglas County Historical Research Center, Castle Rock, CO.

[12] The Douglas County Historical Research Center has an on-line collection of information on historic school districts: http://douglascountyhistory.org/cdm/singleitem/collection/documents/id/66/rec/9 . Individual districts have their own web pages. See also Marr, *Douglas County*, 35, 40-42, 51, 64, 74, 100, 103, 107.

PART TWO

THE EARLY YEARS, 1870-1900

Chapter 12

TRAILS AND RAILS

Jim Weglarz

Between 1870 and 1900 the people of Douglas County experienced a revolution in transportation. In only a few years, they transitioned from the age of wagon trains and stagecoaches to the age of railroads. The coming of the railroads changed their lives dramatically.

In the early days of settlement, people moved over historic trails created by Indians, trappers, and homesteaders. The best-known and most heavily used trails in Douglas County followed its major waterways—Cherry Creek and Plum Creek. The Cherokee Trail and the Jimmy Camp Trail were often interchangeable names for the trail that followed both West and East Cherry Creek, joined at Russellville, and passed near Franktown and Pine Grove (Parker) until it reached Denver.[1] Wagon trains and freight lines used this trail, as did stagecoach lines like Wells Fargo and Company (1866-1875) and Barlow, Sanderson, and Company (1870-1884).[2] The stagecoaches stopped at Russellville and the "Mile Houses" that were built along the road to Denver: The Twenty Mile House in Pine Grove (Parker), the Seventeen Mile House on the Douglas/Arapahoe County line, the Twelve Mile House at Melvin, and finally the Four Mile House on the border of Glendale and Denver.[3] These stage stops provided the luxury of fresh water, food, and overnight lodging for weary travelers. Such places were no longer needed after the railroads were built.

Another important early trail in Douglas County was Trappers Trail, a name also applied to the Cherokee Trail. It followed both branches of Plum Creek, until they joined at Sedalia, along what is now SR-105 and I-25. It was used mainly by horses and mules since wagons and stagecoaches found the Cherokee Trail much easier going.

During the 1860s, Coloradoans tried to get their territory included in plans to build the transcontinental railroad; but in 1867 the Union Pacific Railroad laid track across southern Wyoming, thereby bypassing Colorado. A group of prominent citizens then organized the Denver Pacific to link Denver and Cheyenne (1870).[4] In the same year, the Kansas Pacific laid track along the Smoky Hill Trail to connect Kansas City and Denver.[5]

In 1871 William Palmer brought the railroad to Douglas County. Palmer was a former Union general, a supervisor of construction for the Kansas Pacific, and a director of the Denver Pacific.[6] He and his partner, former territorial governor A. Cameron Hunt, built the Denver & Rio Grande (D&RG) from Denver to Colorado Springs, which Palmer founded and colonized. The D&RG passed Acequia, Plum (Sedalia), New Memphis, Castle Rock (though the town would not be built until 1874), Douglas, Glade, Huntsville, Larkspur, Greenland, and over the Divide. The initial D&RG rail line was a 3' wide 'narrow gauge,' the first in the U.S.[7] In 1881 it added a third rail to accommodate standard-gauge (4' 8.5" wide) trains. In the 1890s, the D&RG converted all its tracks to standard-gauge.

Colorado Southern Stop at Parker

Another railroad cut across the northeast corner of Douglas County. In 1881 former Governor John Evans organized the Denver & New Orleans Railroad. Its tracks started in Denver, ran by Melvin, Parker, Hilltop, Elizabeth, Elbert, Eastonville, Falcon, and finally Pueblo. By 1888 there was regular service between Denver and New Orleans. This railroad changed names often (Denver, Texas, and Gulf in 1886, Union Pacific, Denver & Gulf in 1890, and Colorado & Southern in 1898) and at times was a collaboration of three or more railroad companies. By 1900 it was losing business to other lines; and by the 1930s, it was no longer operational.[8]

Starting in 1873 the Atchison, Topeka, and Santa Fe (AT&SF) laid track along the old Santa Fe Trail in southern Colorado. In 1881 it began using D&RG's tracks to Denver, which brought it through Douglas County. In 1887, it built its own tracks parallel to D&RG's, which led to head-to-head competition between the two railroads. For example, in 1888 the AT&SF built a depot on the west side of Castle Rock to compete with the D&RG depot on the east side of town. For the first time, there was a real choice in freight and passenger service. Sedalia also enjoyed the convenience and competition of having two depots.[9] Such rivalry continued in Douglas County until both the D&RG and the AT&SF were taken over by other railroads in the late twentieth century.[10]

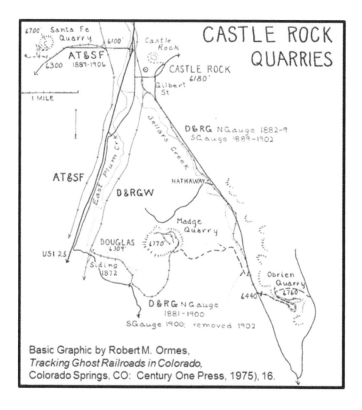

CASTLE ROCK QUARRIES

Basic Graphic by Robert M. Ormes, *Tracking Ghost Railroads in Colorado,* Colorado Springs, CO: Century One Press, 1975), 16.

The coming of the railroads facilitated the economic development of Douglas County. During the 1880s, the rhyolite business flourished because the D&RG built "spurs" from Douglas to the Madge Quarry (now Rhyolite Park) in 1881 and down Sellars Creek in Castle Rock to the O'Brien Quarry in 1882. In 1889 the AT&SF built a spur to the new Santa Fe Quarry west of Castle Rock along Wolfensburger Road. Daily, lines of railroad cars shipped tons of the lava stone to markets in Colorado, Wyoming, Nebraska, and Kansas.[11]

The railroads carried the U.S. Mail; shipped lumber from sawmills around Larkspur, Sedalia, Daniel's Park, and elsewhere; and transported farm and dairy products to Denver and Colorado Springs. The County's burgeoning cattle industry relied on both the D&RG and AT&SF to take beef cattle to market. The residents of Douglas County not only counted on the railroads to ship their products, but they also relished the goods that the trains brought to them from afar. Because of the railroads, people living on isolated farms and ranches had access to both basic and luxury items stocked on the shelves of hardware and dry goods stores throughout Douglas County. Such "imports" connected the people of the County to the rest of the country and even the world and narrowed the gap between how country and city folks lived.[12]

The railroads also carried passengers. According to timetables from the 1870s, the trip from Denver to Colorado Springs on the D&RG took a little over four hours, which meant that travelers could eat breakfast in Denver and lunch in Colorado Springs. The trip from Castle Rock north to Denver or south to Colorado Springs took about two hours, which amounted to a "commute" in the nineteenth century.[13] Before the railroads, no one had ever seen the world go by at 15, 20, or even 30 miles an hour.

In Colorado, over 100 railroads laid track before 1900. While most of them failed, by the turn of the century, trains moved across the eastern plains, along the Front Range, through the high country, and down the western slope. Douglas County's railroads connected people to northern and southern Colorado and beyond, and they provided economic stability and prosperity. But the railroads were also susceptible to economic downturns and were often accused of unscrupulous business practices. Still, the people of Douglas County increasingly depended on the rails.

[1] Alice M. Thompson *Walk With Our Pioneers—A Collection* (Grand Junction, CO: JLM Sales, 2005), 2-5.

[2] Thomas Noel, *Colorado: A Historical Atlas* (Norman: University of Oklahoma, 2015), 167-169.

[3] Thompson *Walk With Our Pioneers*, 86.

[4] Clayton B. Fraser and Jennifer H. Strand, "Railroads in Colorado 1858-1948," *National Register of Historic Places: Multiple Property Documentation Form* (Washington, DC: U.S. Department of Interior, 1997), 6, accessed April 22, 2016, http://www.historycolorado.org/sites/default/files/files/OAH/crforms_edumat/pdf s/625.pdf

[5] Ibid., 10-12.

[6] Carl Ubbelohde, Maxine Benson, and Duane A. Smith, *A Colorado History*, 9th ed. (Boulder: Pruett Publishing, 2006), 117.

[7] Fraser and Strand, "Railroads in Colorado 1858-1948," 15-18; Thompson, *Walk with Our Pioneers*, 89.

[8] Thompson, *Walk With Our Pioneers*, 79, 86-87, 91-92, 121-123.

[9] Josephine Lowell Marr, *Douglas County: A Historical Journey* (Gunnison, CO: B & B Printers, 1983), 122.

[10] Fraser and Strand, "Railroads in Colorado 1858-1948," 18-22; Noel, *Colorado*, 175; Scheuber and Darden Architects, *Colorado Cultural Resource Survey: Architectural Inventory Form*, Resource number 5DA.2039, accessed March 16, 2016, crgov.com/DocumentCenter/View/8953.

[11] Thompson, *Walk With Our Pioneers*, 94-102.

[12] Marr, *Douglas County*, 122-123.

[13] Thompson, *Walk With Our Pioneers*, 67-68.

Chapter 13

NEW BOUNDARIES

Tim Weber

As one of Colorado Territory's 17 original counties (1861), Douglas County stretched from the South Platte River to the Kansas border, with Frankstown as the county seat. In 1874, the legislature reconfigured the county by creating Elbert County in the east and retaining Douglas County's original boundary in the west. The legislature also scheduled an election in late March to determine a new county seat.

New Memphis, Douglas, Sedalia, Glade, and Frankstown campaigned for votes; but Castle Rock had the advantage of being the county's best-known landmark. *The Rocky Mountain News* argued that "Castle Rock is a point. It is somewhere. . . . If the county seat is located at Castle Rock, it will be a permanent location, and a town will grow up there of no ordinary beauty."[1] In short, Castle Rock was an ideal place for a *future* town; but no town yet existed. Of the 597 votes cast, Castle Rock received 315 and second-place Sedalia, 164.[2]

After County Commissioners officially confirmed the new county seat in early April, Castle Rock suddenly came into existence, thanks to Jeremiah Gould, a Civil War veteran from Rhode Island, and one of the area's early settlers. He donated 120 acres for the new town, then he, John Craig, Philip Wilcox, and County Surveyor D.J. McIntyre filed a town site plat with 100 lots, a courthouse square, and streets named Front, Perry, Wilcox, Jerry, and Elbert. At a public auction in June, 77 lots sold for $3,400, which was earmarked for county buildings.

Castle Rock expanded rapidly. In July, Craig and Gould donated more acres east of the original plat that became the town's first residential neighborhood. In 1875 Wilcox donated 80 acres to the north that included Castle Rock itself.[3] Despite such growth, Castle Rock still had a big problem. Though trains from William Palmer's narrow-gauge Denver & Rio Grande Railroad passed by, none stopped because when tracks were laid in 1871, there was no town. The new residents asked Palmer to build a depot and switch, without which Castle Rock could not prosper. At first, Palmer refused, citing the existing stop to the south (Douglas); but he finally relented. In 1875 he constructed a depot just east of the intersection of Perry and 3rd Streets.[4]

Denver and Rio Grande Railroad Depot

Once the depot opened, Perry Street became Castle Rock's first business district. The post office relocated from New Memphis to Castle Rock, as did the Harris Hotel, which was physically moved to Perry Street, near 4th. Several New Memphis and Douglas residents moved to Castle Rock. By 1880, entrepreneurs had opened a variety of businesses: blacksmith, barber, billiard hall, boots and shoemaker, plasterer, building stone, brick maker, carpenter, druggist, physician, cheese factory/creamery, law offices, livery and feed, newspaper, grocery, meat market, dry goods, hardware, two hotels, saloon, undertaker, and cemetery. Three "industries" provided early economic stability. Rhyolite, the popular lava stone taken from four stone quarries nearby, was shipped far and wide. A cheese factory provided a variety of dairy products for Denver and Colorado Springs. County business flourished in the new two-story, wooden Court House at 4th and Wilcox (where B & B Café is now located), built by William Cantril in 1874 for $1,350.[5]

The town's first school was a two-story wooden structure built in 1875. It began as a "common school" (grades 1 through 8), but in the mid-1880s added the county's first high school curriculum. The school burned to the ground in 1896. It was replaced by the imposing Cantril School, made of rhyolite, which still exists on "schoolhouse hill,"[6] east of "downtown."

Other "firsts" followed Castle Rock's incorporation in 1881. When the town was founded, the Territorial Road from Denver to Colorado Springs ran close by; but county roads were few. People from outlying areas had difficulty getting to the new county seat. Over the next two decades, the town and county worked together to build or improve roads from Lake Gulch, Sedalia, West Plum Creek, and points south and east.[7]

Population Growth[8]		
	Castle Rock	Douglas County
1880	88	1,388
1890	315	2,486
1900	304	3,120

In 1882 the town developed its first water system. From an 8-acre reservoir, three miles south of town (later the Lowell Ranch), water flowed by gravity through iron pipes to an open irrigation ditch on the high end of east 2nd Street where it connected to a network of other open ditches that irrigated newly planted trees, gardens, and other vegetation. Residents dug wells for home use. Later, town wells, a pumping station, and pipes provided residents with water free of charge.[8]

In 1881 the Denver & Rio Grande added a third rail to accommodate trains from the standard-gauge Atchison, Topeka, & Santa Fe. In 1887, the Santa Fe laid its own tracks west of town and built a depot the following year. A wooden bridge was built across East Plum Creek from the end of 2nd Street to provide access.[9] In 1881 a flagpole was installed at the top of Castle Rock, and, in 1882, the town held the first Douglas County Fair.[10]

In 1888-1890, a new County Court House was constructed of native rhyolite on Court House Square for $33,000. It had two-and-a-half stories and a 25-foot tower. An iron picket fence surrounded the square to keep livestock off the grass. Soon the block opposite the Court House on Wilcox between 3rd and 4th Streets became the town's most important commercial center.[11]

Douglas County Courthouse

Castle Rock was an enjoyable place to live and visit. The *Castle Rock Journal* kept track of its many social activities. There were dances (sometimes made rowdy by cowboys and stone cutters), picnics, oyster suppers, ice cream or strawberry socials, and potlucks. Young people planned their own dances, hayrides, ice-skating and sledding parties. Men joined the Grand Army of the Republic (GAR), Masons, Odd Fellows, and other fraternal organizations. Women's groups were many and included the Women's Christian Temperance Union, Masonic groups, and the Ladies Aid Society, a charitable organization that sponsored a costumed New Year's Eve Dance and Valentine's Day Dinner. Literary clubs and debating societies provided lectures and other entertainment. Such gatherings met in the large second-floor rooms above many businesses. Churches offered prayer meetings, Bible studies, and young people's groups. But nothing matched the Fourth of July celebration with band concerts, baseball games, speeches, parades, horse races, and a dinner/dance that could last until dawn.

By the turn of the century, only one-tenth of Douglas County's total population (3,120) lived in the county seat (pop. 304). Most people still lived on farms, cattle ranches, and dairy farms. But Castle Rock had become the center of the county's commercial, educational, political, and social life. It provided a full range of goods and services needed by the rural population, thanks to the railroads.

[1] *The Rocky Mountain News*, March 18, 1874, 2.

[2] Josephine Lowell Marr, *Douglas County: A Historical Journey* (Gunnison, CO: B & B, 1983), 141.

[3] Ibid., 142.

[4] Ibid., 148-149; *Rocky Mountain News*, July 12, 1874; *Rocky Mountain News*, July 18, 1874; *Douglas County News*, July 8, 1876.

[5] Marr, *Douglas County*, 149-154.

[6] Ibid., 145-146.

[7] *Douglas County News*, December 22, 1875; *Castle Rock Journal*, May 3, 1882.

[8] *Castle Rock Journal*, April 18, May 3, May 16, July 5, July 12, August 8, October 3,1882; *Castle Rock Journal*, March 28, April 4, July 4,1883.

[9] The history of the depot is summarized by *Colorado Cultural Resource Survey*, Resource number 5DA.2039, accessed on March 16, 2016 at crgov.com/DocumentCenter/View/8953

[10] Marr, *Douglas County*, 161, 168.

[11] Ibid., 164-165; Susan Consola Appleby, *Fading Past: The Story of Douglas County, Colorado* (Palmer Lake, CO: Filter Press, 2001), 10-11, 23-24.

Chapter 14

SCHOOLS AND CHURCHES

Shaun Boyd

Douglas County's school landscape in 1870 was vastly different from today's modern, consolidated school district. In the nineteenth century, a "district" in Douglas County consisted of a single one-room school, managed by its own school board that could hire and fire the teachers. Tax revenues were assessed locally but paid to the County; the curriculum was for the most part recommended by the elected County Superintendent of Schools, and examinations were sometimes open to the public.[1] Each district was governed by a three-person school board; and usually one teacher acted as a daycare provider, school nurse, janitor, and principal. When the student population centers changed, schools were sometimes moved or rebuilt to accommodate shifting needs. In some districts, the schools were a building with a single room. In the bigger districts, there were sometimes two rooms. Occasionally school was held in people's homes, and sometimes there were not enough students in a particular district to hold school at all.

There were 7 locally controlled school districts in the County in 1870.[2] The County had not levied school taxes from 1867-1869 because of "extensive Indian raids."[3] District 1 was the "Pioneer District." It stretched from Sedalia across the northern part of the County to Parker. District 2 was Franktown, and Spring Valley (south of Franktown) was district 3. The other four districts were Platte, Castle Rock, Huntsville, and Bijou Basin.[4] That Castle Rock was mentioned in this early list of schools is interesting, as it predates the creation of the Town of Castle Rock by four years. Probably the district was for the children on ranches near "The Rock" rather than within the current Town boundaries. Most of these original districts were found in the western part of the County. Only one district, "Bijou Basin," covered the area east of Franktown that stretched to the Kansas border. Those widely separated eastern communities were poorly served.[5]

Sedalia School

With the creation of new Douglas County boundaries in 1874 and the founding of Castle Rock to be the county seat, the geographic area covered by County schools decreased; but the number of schools increased. The first list of school districts published in the *Castle Rock Journal* in 1881 shows twenty districts in the County, six of which were collecting special taxes, including Sedalia, Franktown, and Spring Valley.[6] By 1888, there were twenty-six school districts throughout Douglas County; and by 1900 there were eleven more.[7]

Teachers were not always single women, though this was the predominant situation. In an 1888 summary of schools in session, County Superintendent P.H. Hammond reported that eleven of the fifteen teachers were single women; and one was a "Mrs." The remaining three were men, including postmaster, rancher, newspaper editor, and all-around community advocate W.I. Whittier.[8]

In 1896, the largest district in the county was in Castle Rock, with more than 120 students. Castle Rock's first school was built in 1875 at the present-day site of Cantril School and was a two-story wooden structure. That schoolhouse hosted Douglas County's first High School curriculum in the 1880s, but financing was not sustainable, as students outside of the "Castle Rock District" had to pay tuition as well as room and board during the week when classes were in session.[9] This school burned down in November 1896, partially because the fire department did not have a hose long enough to reach the building.[10] The rhyolite Cantril School replaced the original structure and was large enough to accommodate the expanding high school program. Frank Ball and Cole Briscoe sponsored a County High School bill in the Colorado legislature (1900) that eliminated "out of district" tuition and increased financial support for the High School throughout the County.[11]

One of the last one-room school districts established in the County before 1900 was the Dewey School, named for Admiral George Dewey, who defeated the Spanish fleet at Manila Bay in the Spanish-American War. In 1898 Dewey School became District 34 and was located on Crowfoot Valley Road, northeast of Castle Rock.

Churches were also important in early Douglas County. The Methodist, Episcopal, and Catholic Churches all had strong presences before 1900. Religious meetings, particularly in rural areas, were primarily held in the closest one-room school. The ministers traveled on a "circuit" that included Douglas County and beyond.

Colorado history legend Methodist minister John Lewis Dyer, known as the "Snowshoe Itinerant," had the circuit covering "Eastern Douglas County" from 1870-1871. This included Running Creek, Bijou Basin, and those other parts of the future Elbert County and points east, as well as Spring Valley.[12] He was assigned to the Spring Valley and Monument area through 1875. He is buried in the Cedar Hill Cemetery in Castle Rock, where his son Samuel was the first Town Clerk in 1874.

Methodist Episcopal Church, Castle Rock

In Castle Rock, the Methodists secured two lots at the corner of 3rd and Wilcox streets on March 29, 1874, and preached their first sermon a month later in a carpenter shop at 501 Wilcox. The Castle Rock Methodist Episcopal Church was constructed in 1887.[13] A few years later, it moved one block east to 3rd and Perry to accommodate the building of the new First National Bank building (now Masonic Hall).

Saint Philip-in-the-Field Episcopal Church, located by the Bear Canon Cemetery just south of the intersection of today's Highway 105 and Wolfensberger Road, is the oldest standing church in Douglas County. It was originally organized by the "Bear Canon Methodist Church." Its exterior was built in 1872,[14] but the interior had to wait until 1887: a scoundrel posing as a Methodist minister named "Lambert" absconded with $600 he had raised from the community to finish it.[15] In 1888, after hosting several denominations, the church changed its denominational affiliation and was consecrated as the Saint Philip-in-the-Field Episcopal Church.[16]

Today's Scileppi's at the Old Stone Church Restaurant was originally the St. Francis of Assisi Catholic Church in Castle Rock. The building still stands on 3rd street, west of Wilcox, and is made of locally quarried rhyolite. Built in 1888, the church was primarily funded by donations from the uncle of prominent Castle Rock resident William Dillon, as well as contributions from the German Catholic community in the Lake Gulch region southeast of Castle Rock, which included the Ehman family, who were stone masons who helped with the construction.[17]

Before 1900, except for the three churches already mentioned, most religious gatherings met in a variety of places: in homes, schools, or second-floor rooms over hardware stores or other businesses. They formed a network of institutions that contributed to Douglas County's sense of community.

---

[1] Open examinations of students would be completely foreign to our modern culture but were advertised as community events. See *Castle Rock Journal,* May 9, 1888, 4: "The Castle Rock school closes Friday of next week. Examinations will be held Thursday and Friday May 17 and 18. Everybody is invited to attend and note the progress made by the pupils."

[2] Josephine Lowell Marr, *Douglas County: A Historical Journey*, compiled by Joan Marr Keiser (Gunnison, CO: B and B Printers, 1983), 38.

[3] Alice M. Thompson, *Walk With Our Pioneers: A Collection* (Grand Junction, CO: JLM Sales, LLC, 2005), 52.

[4] "Miscellaneous Information on Douglas County Districts," *Our Heritage: People of Douglas County* (Douglas County, CO: Douglas County Historical Society, 1982), 381.

[5] Ibid.

[6] "Commissioners Proceedings," *Castle Rock Journal,* October 12, 1881, 3.

[7] For a list of schools in 1888, see P.H. Hammond, "General School Fund," *Castle Rock Journal,* July 4, 1888.

[8] P.H. Hammond, "Schools," *Castle Rock Journal,* July 4,1888.

[9] Marr, *Douglas County,* 145-146.

[10] Thompson, *Walk With our Pioneers,* 55.

[11] Marr, *Douglas County,* 147.

[12] Ibid, 49.

[13] Ibid, 142.

[14] Ibid, 215.

[15] Ibid.

[16] Ibid, 216.

[17] Ibid, 144.

Chapter 15

DAIRIES, FARMS, AND GRANGES

Bill Noe

In the 1870s Colorado was changing. The Gold Rush was over. About half of the 100,000 Fifty-Niners had returned to their homes back East or moved further West. The rest settled in the mineral belt in the high county or in other parts of Colorado. About 1,000 of the Fifty-Niners stayed in Douglas County. Growth during the 1860s was slow, thanks to the threat of Indian attacks. Even so, the County's residents (1,388 in 1870) were starting to supply larger communities to the north and south with fresh meat, eggs, milk, vegetables, grain, fruit, lumber, building stone, and other products. By the time Colorado became a state in 1876, Douglas County's development as an agricultural community was well underway.

The coming of the railroads made such growth possible. In 1870 the Denver Pacific and the Kansas Pacific had connected Denver to the rest of the country, and in 1871 the Denver & Rio Grande traversed Douglas County to connect Denver and Colorado Springs. Its many stops and train stations provided easy access to growing markets. Later on, two other railroads served the County: the Denver & New Orleans/Colorado & Southern (1881) and the Atchison, Topeka, & Santa Fe (1887).[1]

Most farms in early Douglas County were small, ranging from five to forty acres. Many of them were subsistence farms that barely sustained a family from one year to the next. The County's high altitude posed a huge risk factor for farming. Most of the migrants came from the much lower elevation of the Mississippi River basin where the growing season was about twice as long as Colorado's. Short-season crops were eventually developed for this area, but many farms failed prior to them being available. Livestock needed supplemental feed for seven to eight months of the year, which was almost impossible for a small acreage farm to provide. Most of the tilling of the soil was done by hand or small horse-drawn implements. Even when farmers were able to obtain better implements to increase productivity, many small farmers could not afford them, or the additional draft livestock needed to operate them. Small farmers often had to sell out to larger neighbors. Even the more successful farmers were always looking for a steady income to sustain them between harvests or the annual selling of cattle. Since virtually everyone raised chickens for fresh meat and eggs and kept a cow that provided milk for the family, they sold any surplus beyond the family's needs to a growing market, thereby generating much-needed cash.[2]

Izett Steward Farm and Dairy

By 1900 dairy farming made up the largest part of Douglas County's economy, but it started as a cottage industry on farms with only one or two cows. On a family farm, the size of the dairy herd was limited by how many hands there were to do the milking. A farmer and spouse could milk eight to twelve cows twice a day. When children grew old enough to milk, the family could increase the herd. But because they still had to till, plant, cultivate and harvest their crops, most families found a herd of twenty cows to be optimal.

Milking was only the first step in an involved process. After each pail was full, the milk had to be strained, put into 10-gallon milk cans, and stored in a vat sunk in the ground to be chilled in spring water until it was shipped to a creamery.[3] At first, farmers transported the milk themselves; but soon enterprising types started a pick-up and delivery service to take the milk to the creameries. At the creamery, a milk separator turned whole milk into skim milk and cream, a highly valued commodity whose price was much higher than whole milk. Once separated, the milk could be turned into a variety of dairy products, including butter and cheese that were shipped in ice-cooled train cars to markets in Denver and Colorado Springs. Some farmers chose to ship cans of raw milk to creameries in Denver where the milk was processed, bottled, and delivered to Denver homes. By the 1890s there were eight creameries operating in the County. Between the 1880s and 1900, the annual butter production increased from 97,000 to 750,000 pounds; and the annual production of cheese grew from 22,300 to 300,000 pounds. The number of dairy farms increased during this period. Among them were two standouts: John Welte's Big Dry Creek Cheese Ranch in today's Highlands Ranch and D.R. Williams' cheese factory in Williamsville, north of Spring Valley.[4]

Milk Cans at Larkspur AT&SF Depot

Despite their growing success, farmers became frustrated by the hard work associated with farming, the high cost of transportation, and falling farm prices. They felt like the railroads and the banks were taking advantage of them. In the 1860s they organized to increase their bargaining power and economic clout. In 1867 a national fraternal organization was established called the National Grange of the Order of the Patrons of Husbandry. Popularly known as the Grange, the movement came to Douglas County in the early 1870s and held meetings in schools, churches, and homes. Later some Granges constructed their own buildings where they hosted a variety of educational and social gatherings like dances, dinners, weddings, and even funerals.[5] As membership grew, the Grange became a major voice for agricultural interests. It formed cooperatives for buying and selling, advocated easier access to credit and lower interest rates, and supported the coinage of silver to expand the money supply. The Grange was part of the widespread "agrarian revolt" that transformed national and Colorado state politics in the 1890s (see Ch. 20: Politics in the 1890s). Granges were active for many generations in Douglas County and improved the quality of life for the agricultural community.

In 1900 most people in Douglas County were still living on farms and ranches or in a few small towns, just like most Americans in the nineteenth century. Though urban life was being transformed elsewhere, people here lived like their parents and grandparents before them: they lived on the land, raised crops, tended herds of beef or dairy cattle, sold their products to people who needed them, and developed close relationships with their neighbors. They coped with the unexpected and accepted the risks that came with such a way of life. Douglas County remained overwhelmingly rural until the second half of the twentieth century when agricultural land became neighborhoods for suburban homes, shopping centers, and business parks; and its population grew from 3,120 in 1900 to 314,638 in 2014.[6]

---

[1] Alice M. Thompson, *Walk With Our Pioneers: A Collection* (Grand Junction, CO: JLM, 2005), 66-88.

[2] Susan Meyer, ed., *Our Heritage: People of Douglas County* (Castle Rock, CO: The Historical Society, 1984), 243-244.

[3] Information about the development of dairy farming and the process of milking is from Bill Noe's personal experience growing up on his family's ranch near the Greenland Breeding Farm. See also Josephine Lowell Marr, *Douglas County: A Historical Journey* (Gunnison, CO: B & B Printers, 1983), 40, 43, 57, 78, 134, 197.

[4] Anne Moore, "A History of Douglas County, 1820-1910," M.A. Thesis, University of Denver, 1970, 48-56; Marr, *Douglas County*, 87, 121, 158-59, 189.

[5] Marr, *Douglas County*, 41-42, 48, 100, 119, 170; Thompson, *Walk With Our Pioneers*, 174-175. See also National Grange of the Order of the Patrons of Husbandry, accessed on May 6, 2016, http://www.nationalgrange.org/

[6] U.S. Decennial Census for 1900 and an estimate for 2014.

Chapter 16
RANCHES AND FOUR-FOOTED LIVESTOCK

Larry Schlupp

In 1870, a Douglas County family's non-fowl meat diet primarily consisted of pork, venison, or, once in a great while, buffalo. The only domestic beef to be had was the lanky longhorn, generally "a very tough chew." It was widely avoided because people feared it was infected with Texas fever, a nearly always fatal disease that destroys red blood cells.[1]

Around 1865, William Gilpin Newlin, after whom Newlin Gulch in Parker is named, brought the first *blooded-breed* into Douglas County, Shorthorn beef stock from Minnesota.[2] Newlin's introduction of Shorthorn beef cattle was the seed from which range-ranching in the County started. The defining western provenance of a ranch, as opposed to a farm, is that a ranch's primary purpose is for rearing and grazing livestock.[3]

Newlin's approach to ranching was typical of most ranches that developed in Douglas County in the last third of the nineteenth century. He homesteaded 508 acres in 1862 and ranged an additional unclaimed 1,500 to 2,000 acres adjacent to his ranch. A more extensive example of ranging cattle was the Coberly brothers, William and Joseph, who had a 320-acre homestead in the Dakan area north of Pleasant Park (today's Perry Park). The brothers also ranged cattle in an area east to west from the Front Range to West Plum Creek and south to north from Pleasant Park to Littleton. At roundup time in August, it generally took them between four to six weeks to gather their herd.[4] After Newlin introduced the breed, large Shorthorn beef herds started populating Douglas County. Jacob Schutz, orchard owner, lumberman, and later in life County Commissioner, started raising the breed on his 2,500-acre ranch south of Franktown, circa 1870. Schutz grew his ranch cattle into a large, well-known, high-quality beef herd. Immediately northwest of Greenland, Alvin Daniels started his Greenland Ranch with 8,444 acres and a small herd of Shorthorn stock in the late 1870s. Charles Kountz bought into the Greenland Ranch in the 1880s. Since Kountz was a banker and knew little about cattle, he hired me. J. Noe to manage the enterprise. Noe increased the Greenland Land and Cattle Company to 20,000 acres (1890) and bred, raised, and ranged Shorthorn and the newly introduced Galloway cattle that he brought in from Linwood, Kansas.[5]

Curtis Oakland Ranch

Although the Douglas County population did not grow that dramatically between 1870 and 1900 (from 1,388 to 3,120, according to the official censuses for those years), the demand for beef throughout the country grew exponentially. The Denver & Rio Grande and the Atchison, Topeka & Santa Fe railroads were godsends for getting the beef to market. In the early 1870s, the George Lord Ranch in the Parker area brought the first herd of Herefords (AKA: White Face) into Douglas County. This vigorous, docile, and fast-growing beef animal had great foraging ability and longevity and, from a market perspective, had well-developed and valuable beef cuts.[6] Almost overnight, the Hereford revolutionized the beef market in Douglas County, adding many new ranching operations and hundreds of herds across the County. From the late 1870s through 1900, Douglas County had some 460 ranches raising Hereford cattle with ranch herd sizes from 20 to 10,000-plus head of cattle. Among the pioneering ranch owners were Frank Helmer[7] in the Roxborough area; Henry H. Curtis[8] (Oaklands, Longford Court and Pentilla Ranches), Christian Manhart[9] and Marquis Victor[10] near Sedalia; James Frank Gardner[11] around Franktown; Alvin Daniels[12] and Hiram Bennet[13] (Ben Lomand Ranch) in the Greenland and Divide Country area; Julius Seidensticker[14] and John Hillburger[15] in Lake Gulch and Cherry Valley; George Dakan,[16] George Ratcliffe[17] and John Kinner[18] around Glen Grove; William Rowley (Rowley Ranch) around Parker;[19] and John Wallace Springer (Sunland Ranch) in what is now Highlands Ranch, thanks to his father-in-law Colonel William E. Hughes.[20]

Today's reflection on Douglas County's late nineteenth-century beef cattle ranching appears almost romantic; however, pioneering ranching was anything but romantic! The work was tough, dirty, tiring, and dangerous; and much of ranching's long hours were gruelingly monotonous. With open range foraging (10 to 16 acres were required to feed just one head of stock), fall round-ups and cattle sorting took weeks on end. While cattle rustling and poaching of cattle by Indians had mostly ended by the 1870s, other hazards regularly threatened the herds.

Rancher's Wife, Katherine Shuebert, with Cattle Herd

The 1880s were the toughest years for cattle ranching in Douglas County. In 1883, a blizzard killed a large percentage of ranging cattle; and in 1885, an

April snowstorm had similar results, with some ranchers losing as much as 15 to 20% of their herds. Further out into the plains, some ranchers lost up to 75% of their herds.[21] Wolves killed about 2% of the cattle herds annually, which continued until wolves were totally eradicated in the twentieth century. The biggest impact on cattle ranging was the enactment of the Colorado *"fence out"* law in 1880.[22] This law legalized property fencing to protect crops and farm stock from outside intrusion. In 1885 and 1886, thousands of miles of barbed wire fencing were erected in Douglas County, severely shrinking the availability of range land. Fencing brought another curse for cattle ranchers: the introduction of sheep into Douglas County. Benjamin Hammar of Castle Rock and Axel Preston of Parker owned big sheep herds. Smaller sheep herds were found on other farms in the late 1880s.[23]

By 1890, the competition between grain and dairy farmers, cattle ranchers, and sheepherders escalated almost to the point of a range war. In 1893 a severe drought began that lasted twenty-four years, and the devastating Financial Panic of the same year put one-fifth of the County's cattle ranches out of business. Such disaster brought farmers, cattlemen, and sheepherders together, as they all struggled against the lack of moisture and the failing economy. *"United we stand, divided we fall!*

---

[1] Tamara Miner Haygood, "Texas Fever," *Handbook of Texas Online* (October 2010), 752, accessed February 27, 2016, at http://www.tshaonline.org/handbook/online/articles/awt01.

[2] Wilber Fisk Stone, *History of Colorado*, vol. IV (Chicago, IL: S. J. Clark Publishing Company, 1919), 402.

[3] "Ranch," *American Heritage Dictionary of the English Language,* 5th ed. (Boston: Houghton Mifflin Harcourt Publishing Company, 2011), 708.

[4] Frank Hall, "Portrait and Biographical Record," *History of Colorado,* vol. 3 (Chicago: S. J. Clark Publishing Company, 1919), 455.

[5] Josephine L. Marr, *Douglas County: A Historical Journey* (Gunnison, CO: B&B Printers, 1983), 191.

[6] "Breeds of Livestock—Cattle Breeds," *Oklahoma State University Department of Animal Science* (February, 1995), accessed February 27, 2016, http://www.ansi.okstate.edu/breeds/cattle.

[7] Marr, *Douglas County,* 101.

[8] Ibid., 223-224.

[9] Ibid., 224.

[10] Ibid., 115.

[11] Ibid., 184-185.

[12] Ibid., 190-191.

[13] Ibid., 130-131.

[14] Douglas County Historical Society Book Committee, eds., *Our Heritage, People of Douglas County* (Castle Rock, CO: Douglas County Historical Society, 1981), 255.

[15] Ibid., 245.

[16] Ibid., 72.

[17] Ibid., 236.

[18] Ibid., 140.

[19] Marr, *Douglas County,* 78

[20] Ibid., 212.

[21] Thomas B. McKee et al, *A History of Drought in Colorado* (Fort Collins, CO: Colorado State University Press, 2000), 16.

[22] C.R.S. 35-46 (sections 101-114).

[23] Marr, *Douglas County,* 85.

Chapter 17
MINING, THE NEW GOLD RUSH, AND RHYOLITE

Larry Schlupp

Although Colorado has 774 minerals cataloged today,[1] only four of those minerals addressed the three major human-driven needs of the late nineteenth century: heat, building materials, and acquisition of wealth. Coal was the heat-delivering mineral in early Douglas County. Geologically speaking, coal is an organic sedimentary rock formed over eons from

the accumulation and preservation of plant materials, generally in a swampy environment. That was an accurate ecological description of the massive Denver Basin area some 64 to 65 million years ago.[2] Consequently, the eastern three-fifths of Douglas County is layered with bituminous and lignite coal deposits, much of which is easily accessed either at or close to the earth's surface. Early pioneers generally found coal easily acquired and inexpensive, which made coal the first energy commodity to warm the home, to heat the blacksmith's forge, and to fire the steam engines for early sawmills, farm equipment, and railroads.

The building block from early Douglas County was finely grained rhyolite which is a mixture of quartz, orthoclase feldspar, and plagioclase feldspar. A product of Cretaceous period volcanic formation, rhyolite varies in color, namely pink, bluish gray, and gray.[3] Rhyolite's building qualities were first recognized by Silas W. Madge who owned a ranch two miles south of

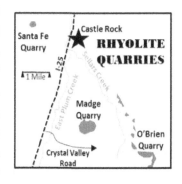

Castle Rock. Madge sent a few of his samples to Denver to be assayed.

Although rhyolite was not found to contain any *precious* minerals, it was lauded as being readily worked, resistant to weather, and extremely strong for its weight. Silas Madge started quarrying the rhyolite on his land in 1872 and became known throughout Colorado as "Father of the Lava Stone Industry."[4] In 1873, the Madge Quarry rail-shipped 600,000 tons of rhyolite that had been hauled 2.6 miles by wagon from the quarry to the Denver & Rio Grande Railroad (D&RG) stop at Douglas.[5]

The largest outcropping of rhyolite was on John Pleasant O'Brien's land along Sellars Creek, southeast of the Madge Quarry. O'Brien purchased the land from General William Palmer and began formal quarrying operations in 1881. The Denver and Rio Grande railroad-built spurs to the Madge and O'Brien Quarries in 1881 and 1882, respectively. As the quarries' outputs grew, so did the small town of Douglas with a rail siding, depot, and boarding houses to accommodate the 100 mostly Swedish quarry workers. Their wages averaged between $2.00 and $2.50 per day. After subtracting $4.50 per week for room and board costs, each worker was left with $7.50 for six days of heavy work.[6]

The height of rhyolite production at the Madge and O'Brien Quarries was in the summer of 1882. Thirty to forty rail cars loaded with rhyolite were shipped daily from the two quarries to Pueblo, Colorado Springs, Denver, Omaha, Cheyenne, and Kansas City. Notable area structures of the period built from rhyolite include the First National Bank (later the Masonic Hall), the D&RG Depot (Castle Rock Museum) in Castle Rock, and the Antlers Hotel at Colorado Springs.

As a result of financial difficulties and several accidents at the quarries in 1883, during 1884-86 there was a decline in business. But it picked up in 1887 when the Santa Fe Quarry along today's Wolfensberger Road opened under the supervision of Gus Nelson from Sedalia. The Atchison, Topeka, and the Santa Fe railroad built a spur to the new quarry, located on the west side of Castle Rock, which made it a profitable enterprise (See Ch. 12 Trails and Rails).[7]

In 1859 there was a dramatic rush of people into what would become Colorado Territory because of the discovery of gold at Russellville in 1858. But the Gold Rush in Douglas County was short-lived. By 1861, gold in the County was but a memory and not a happy memory at that! However, in the mid-to-late 1880s, there was another outbreak of gold fever. Geographically, three areas within the County caused the fever: Newlin Gulch in Parker and the new gold-mining towns of Dakan and West Creek along the Front Range. In the 1890s, the Colorado Gold Producing Company employed 22 men in the Newlin Gulch area, which made it the largest gold mining operation at the time. However,  the low quantity and relatively low quality of the gold, plus the lack of water, led to the demise of gold mining in the Parker area. Today the site of this mining operation lies beneath the water of the Rueter-Hess Dam.[8]

The Dakan area north of Perry Park was another gold repository. Gold was first discovered there by pioneer farmers and ranchers like A. S. Cove, Hiram Dakan, and George Nickson. A limited amount of silver was also found in the area, but gold was more plentiful. The Dakan area grew overnight, with 75 claims. In 1896, prospector William Wanner founded the town of Dakan which grew to 300 tent-housed residents and eight wooden buildings, including a hotel, restaurant, saloon, grocery store, and post office. The gold was assayed as high in quality. Unfortunately, the supply was extremely limited. By the coming of the twentieth century, the Dakan mines closed, and the town disappeared. The Dakan gold mining era was short but colorful, with mines sporting such names as the Invincible Tunnel, Kentucky Belle, and Chicago Girl.[9]

In 1895, Captain George F. Tyler, who ranched adjacent to West Creek in the extreme southwest corner of Douglas County, discovered gold on his ranch. The gold assayed as possessing satisfactory quality and, consequently, several claims were filed in the area. Like Dakan, the surrounding area grew almost overnight. Tyler had a town site surveyed in the middle of his ranch and wanted to name it Tyler, Tyler City, or Bunker Hill.[10] The town, which ultimately became West Creek (incorporated March 16, 1896),[11] grew rapidly, thanks to the prospectors who arrived from all along the Front Range, including Woodland Park, Palmer Lake, South Platte, Jarre Canyon, and Dakan. The gold rush there seemed strong and lasted into the twentieth century but dissipated shortly thereafter.

The only well-known gold deposit still being hunted today in Douglas County is a strongbox containing $60,000 face value of gold double eagles that was robbed from a Colorado-Southern train by an outlaw gang. The strongbox of gold was purportedly buried by the gang at a discreet location, adjacent to a Douglas fir with a knife stuck in it some twelve feet above the ground, someplace near Devil's Head Mountain. So far, the search has been unsuccessful.

[1] James A. Cappa et al, *Messages in Stone: Colorado's Colorful Geology* (Denver, CO: Colorado Geological Survey, 2003), xi.

[2] Ibid., 122-123.

[3] Kirk R. Johnson and Robert G. Reynolds, *Ancient Denvers* (Denver: Denver Museum of Nature & Science, 2006), 20-22.

[4] Mr. and Mrs. James Rose Harvey, "The Quarries of the Castle Rock Area," *The Colorado Magazine* 23, no. 3 (May, 1946): 115.

[5] Ibid., 118.; Alice M. Thompson, *Walk With our Pioneers: A Collection* (Grand Junction, CO JLM Sales, 2005), 96-97.

[6] Ibid.

[7] Ibid.

[8] Ruth L. Miller et al, *Parker, Colorado: An Historical Narrative* (Parker, CO: Parker Area Historical Society, 1996), 44.

[9] Josephine Lowell Marr, *Douglas County: A Historical Journey* (Gunnison, CO: B & B Printers, 1983), 212-213.

[10] Ibid., 248.

[11] A. B. McGaffery, *Biennial Report of the Secretary of State of Colorado, 1895-1896* (Denver: Smith Brooks Printing Co., 1896), 224.

Chapter 18

NEW INDUSTRIES

Larry Schlupp

In her master's thesis on the history of Douglas County, Anne Moore calls the years from 1870 to 1900 "A Period of Steady Growth."[1] As the economy prospered, the residents' livelihoods became more diversified; and new industries and sources of income took hold.

For both agricultural and non-agricultural industries, two factors were responsible for the steady growth of Douglas County in the early 1870s. The most important factor for the economy was the coming of the railroads. Starting with the Denver & Rio Grande (D&RG) in 1871, railroads allowed farmers, cattlemen, and other business owners to market their goods beyond their local areas and to access goods from far away. The D&RG was later joined by the Denver & New Orleans, and the Atchison, Topeka, and Santa Fe railroads. The National Land & Improvement Company was initiated by the D&RG to sell railway land along the railroad's right of way, which greatly stimulated the economy.[2]

The advent of the railroads fostered the other important factor in the steady economic development of Douglas County: the rapid growth of the town of Castle Rock. Recognized for its central location when it was still barely a campsite for travelers, Castle Rock became the county seat in 1874. After it was named county seat, the construction of roads connecting Castle Rock to other parts of Douglas County became its own industry. Castle Rock was incorporated as a town in 1881, but by then it had become the major supply center and shipping point for the County.[3]

Timber cutting and sawmilling remained among the most profitable Douglas County industries in the 1870s and 1880s. The towns of Larkspur, Greenland, and Sedalia became major railroad shipping points for wood products to places all along the Front Range.[4] Early on, the lumber industry concentrated on providing railroad ties, then shifted to cutting lumber for new town construction. The demand for lumber was so high that in 1882 the

Castle Rock Journal reported that Mr. Bowen's lumber mill in Garber Canyon had nine teams of horses and needed more to haul an average of 12,000 feet of lumber per day to his shipping point of Sedalia.[5] The timber industry was so extensive that around the turn of the century many people began voicing concern that timber was quickly being depleted in the County.[6]

The post office, general store, and blacksmith shop were the first businesses to appear in most towns in the County. They were followed by numerous other small businesses and cottage industries. Such new retail establishments served townsfolk and those living in outlying areas. According to Josephine Marr in *Douglas County: A Historical Journey*, "The small town of Parker boosted (sic) the typical pioneer businesses — Henry Goddard's livery stable, John Oswald's lumber store, a blacksmith shop, shoe shop, saloon, drugstore, barbershop, hotels, notary public and mercantile stores, which supplied nearly everything needed by the pioneer—food supplies, clothing, shoes, dry goods, coal, kerosene, farm supplies, grain, and feed—the 'pioneer supermarket'."[7] These businesses were soon augmented by the professional services of physicians, dentists, and lawyers.

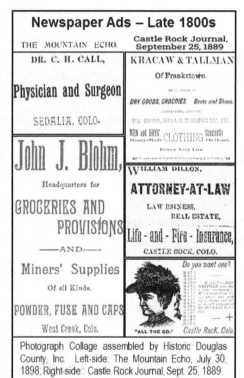

Newspaper Ads – Late 1800s

Photograph Collage assembled by Historic Douglas County, Inc. Left-side: The Mountain Echo, July 30, 1898; Right-side:: Castle Rock Journal, Sept. 25, 1889.

New inventions of farm machinery were available, although in the late 1800s the horse remained the major source of power for farm implements and certain types of transportation. Short-haul horse-drawn conveyances were still in operation, although long-distance freighting and stagecoach operations were put out of business by the railroads. Among the new industries were the icehouses. During the winter, people used horsepower to cut blocks of ice from the county's lakes and creeks. They then packed the ice in sawdust and stacked them in the icehouses. The ice was used in butcher shops, creameries, and refrigerated railroad cars to keep dairy and meat products from spoiling on their way to market.[8] In addition to the increasing number of meat markets, dairy farming became Douglas County's chief industry by 1900.[9] At the same time, farmers grew various money crops: wheat, corn, barley, hay, alfalfa, and a variety of fruits and vegetables.[10] E.R. Parsons established the first commercial orchard in Colorado when he planted 50 acres of fruit trees and berry bushes south of Parker. Soon other growers were shipping fruit products throughout the area, particularly the Lambert Orchard Company and the Perry farm near Sedalia. Denver-area canneries were happy to receive their products. Some fruit growers went out of business because of droughts and early frosts.[11]

The rhyolite quarries around Castle Rock continued to operate throughout the late 1800s, but by 1900 their importance was declining, largely due to the increased use of cement in the building trades.[12] The deposits of clay found in several areas of the County were extracted for making bricks used in building houses and chimneys and making pipes and jewelry cases. Among the most successful brickmakers were Charles and James Woodhouse of Castle Rock. Other operators of fireclay pits were also successful for a time.[13]

In the late 1800s, it became obvious that Douglas County needed more and better forms of irrigation than small wells, ditches, and earthen dams for private use. The irrigation industry provided short-term employment for many Douglas County residents at this time. Among the largest projects was the High Line Canal, completed in 1883 on the border of Arapahoe and Douglas Counties. But the canal provided water for agriculture only in the far northwestern part of the County. Another large project was the Castlewood Canyon Dam, south of Franktown, which was completed in 1890 to control the unpredictable flow of Cherry Creek on its way to Denver. Seen as a milestone in irrigation and flood control, the dam collapsed during a major storm in 1933 and caused a major flood downstream.[14]

In about 1880 Edward Kreutzer moved to the Jarre Canyon area and began manufacturing cigars, which his wife Jane sold in Denver. A few years later he opened a cigar factory in Sedalia. The cigar industry did not last long here, however, mainly because of the problems of supply: tobacco could not be grown in Douglas County or other parts of Colorado and had to be "imported."[15]

Weaver Boarding House, Plum Avenue, Sedalia

Innkeeping grew into a major occupation for more and more people. Two miles south of Castle Rock a boardinghouse was established to accommodate the workers at the Madge rhyolite quarry. Hotels sprang up in Franktown, Sedalia, Parker, and Castle Rock, often advertising themselves as year-round health resorts, especially for people with lung diseases. Hotels sometimes also served as post offices and general stores, and they often provided meals to travelers. But the days of the "hospitality industry," such as at the popular resorts in Perry Park, Roxborough, and Deckers, were still several years away.[16]

---

[1] Anne Moore, "A History of Douglas County, 1820-1910," M.A. Thesis, University of Denver, 1970, 42.

[2] Ibid., 43-45.

[3] Josephine Lowell Marr, *Douglas County: A Historical Journey*, compiled by Joan Marr Keiser (Gunnison, CO: B & B Printers, 1983), 149-152; Susan Consola Appleby, *Fading Past: The Story of Douglas County, Colorado* (Palmer Lake, CO: Filter Press, 2001),104.

[4] Moore, "History of Douglas County," 45; Appleby, *Fading Past*, 104.

[5] *Castle Rock Journal*, June 14, 1882.

[6] Ibid., May 22, 1903.

[7] Marr, *Douglas County*, 78; Ruth L. Miller, *Parker, Colorado: An Historical Narrative* (Parker, CO: Parker Area Historical Society, 2005), 44.

[8] Barbara Belfield Machann, *Sedalia, 1882-1982* (Self-published, 1982), 4.

[9] Moore, "History of Douglas County," 48-56.

[10] *Castle Rock Journal*, September 10, 1890.

[11] Miller, *Parker,* 43; Marr, *Douglas County*, 78.

[12] Moore, "History of Douglas County," 64-69.

[13] Marr, *Douglas County*, 78-79, 160.

[14] Moore, "History of Douglas County," 62-64.

[15] William Reich, *Colorado's Industries of the Past* (Boulder, CO: Johnson, 2008), 121-123.

[16] Susan Meyer, ed., *Our Heritage: People of Douglas County* (Castle Rock, CO: The Historical Society, 1984), 346.

Chapter 19
DOUGLAS COUNTY'S THREE REGIONS

Larry Schlupp

In the last three decades of the nineteenth century, there was an interaction between economic, ethnic, social, and geographical factors in Douglas County. Eventually, three distinct regions took shape based on these elements: *Platte-Plum Creek*, roughly the northwest quadrant of the County that included Littleton in Arapahoe County; *Cherry Creek Valley*, the northeast quarter of the County that reached from Melvin in Arapahoe County, to just south of Castlewood Canyon, and east into Elbert County; and *Divide Country*, the southern half of Douglas County that included Palmer Lake and Monument in El Paso County (minus the Pike National Forest). *Pike* could be identified as a fourth region comprised of the small communities along the Platte River (Westcreek, Deckers, Trumbull, Oxyoke, and Nighthawk). However, the low population density there had little impact on Douglas County's economic and social identity.[1]

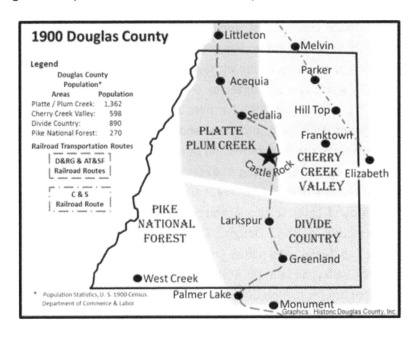

1900 Douglas County

Legend

Douglas County Population*

Areas	Population
Platte / Plum Creek:	1,362
Cherry Creek Valley:	598
Divide Country:	890
Pike National Forest:	270

Railroad Transportation Routes

D&RG & AT&SF Railroad Routes

C & S Railroad Route

Littleton
Melvin
Parker
Acequia
Sedalia
Hill Top
PLATTE PLUM CREEK
Franktown
CHERRY CREEK VALLEY
Castle Rock
Elizabeth
PIKE NATIONAL FOREST
Larkspur
DIVIDE COUNTRY
Greenland
West Creek
Palmer Lake
Monument

* Population Statistics, U. S. 1900 Census Department of Commerce & Labor

Graphics: Historic Douglas County, Inc.

In the beginning, the most important factors that shaped the identity of the County's first communities were economic and ethnic. The first mass migration into Douglas County was during the Gold Rush of 1859. But after prospecting for gold died out, about half of the County's Fifty-Niners returned home; about 40% moved to the mineral belt in the Rockies, and only 10% stayed in Douglas County. A large percentage of them were foreign-born immigrants.[2] These pioneers tended to settle in communities with people who had the same nationality, spoke the same language, and shared the same religious faith. The settlers wrote to friends and family in the "old country" and encouraged them to join them in Douglas County, which gave many early communities in the County a discernible ethnic flavor. For example, among others, the largest ethnic group in the Divide Country consisted of German-speaking Catholics. Most settlers in Cherry Creek Valley region were Methodists from England, Scotland, and Wales. The Platte-Plum Creek region was a melting pot of cultures and nationalities, including English, Scandinavian (most stonecutters in Castle Rock's rhyolite quarries were Swedes), French, German, and Austrian. That meant that the people in the County heard many languages. As a result, being bi-lingual was highly valued. For example, in the Divide Country where there were many German-speaking immigrants, the clergy had to be able to speak both German and English to conduct marriage ceremonies, since intermarriage was common, and the families of the bride and groom needed to be included.[3]

In addition to ethnicity, economic factors defined the three regions. From 1870 to 1900, agriculture accounted for 69% of the County's revenue; mining, 7%; retail, 7%; and lumber, 5%.[4] Farmers and ranchers needed markets for their hay, grains, fruit, dairy products, and beef; and they needed supplies from the outside to run their farms and ranches. Lumbermen and quarrymen needed access to the expanding markets in Denver, Colorado Springs, and beyond.[5] At the beginning of the era, early trails and wagon roads were the way to get around. Later, territorial and county roads connected communities and markets that defined Douglas County's three regions: Frankstown, Parker, Hill Top, Melvin (Arapahoe County), and Elizabeth (Elbert County) in Cherry Creek Valley; Sedalia (AKA: Round Corral and Plum Station), Kassler, Acequia, Littleton (Arapahoe County), and Castle Rock in Platte-Plum Creek; and Larkspur, Greenland, and Palmer Lake and Monument (El Paso County) in the Divide Country. These towns served as markets and supply centers for the regions' residents. With the introduction of the railroads, markets multiplied, which enabled production and sales to increase almost overnight. "The economy and the population of the county seemed to grow with the length and number of trains that served it."[6]

Social at the Case Grange

Also helping to distinguish each region were their social activities. Schools, churches, and Granges were important in establishing local identities. "Socials" were gatherings for fellowship and food, which might include ice cream, strawberries, desserts, oyster suppers, potlucks, etc. There were picnics, dances, town bands, hayrides, literary clubs, lectures, home-craft clubs, fraternal organizations for men and women, professional groups, horse racing, and riding clubs. Such gatherings met in town halls (large rooms over businesses), churches, schools, or even barns. Many towns organized baseball teams (Parker, Larkspur, Littleton, and Plum Creek).[7] In some places, ethnicity remained a strong social factor. In the Lake Gulch area southeast of Castle Rock, the population had come from southern Germany and Austria and consisted of a tight social network of family and friends from the old country. They socialized often, usually at Fred Doepke's Twin Creek Ranch. Likewise, this social group made up most of the founding members of St.

Francis of Assisi Catholic Church in Castle Rock, whose bi-lingual priest understood the customs and practices of his parish. Because the American-born second generation's mother tongue was English, over time such ethnic-centered social gatherings became less important. Throughout the late 19th century, then, social gatherings were the glue that held human relationships together, even during difficult times.

As the twentieth century drew near, the Platte-Plum Creek and Cherry Creek Valley regions gravitated strongly to the Denver area for both market and supplier needs. For obvious reasons, the Divide Country felt a strong economic and social pull toward Colorado Springs. Those ties were so strong that in 1891 people in the Divide Country proposed the formation of a new Divide *County*. However, that proposal never came to fruition.[8]

Each region relied heavily on its railroads and water supply. The three regions were served by the Denver & Rio Grande; Atchison, Topeka & Santa Fe; and the Denver & New Orleans/Colorado & Southern railroads. Each region viewed water as a tightly held, much-conserved resource. Water rights were carefully allocated and protected in the County. Most farmers and ranchers dug shallow wells and reserve ponds for their own use. Surface water was used for ditch irrigation of food crops. The 84-mile long Highline Canal was constructed during 1877-1889 along the border of Arapahoe and Douglas Counties[9] and was a boon to Platte-Plum Creek agriculture, and the Castlewood Dam (1890) and Arapahoe Ditch supported Cherry Creek Valley.[10] For all these reasons, the people of Douglas County naturally identified with one of its three regions.

---

[1] Department of Commerce and Labor Bureau of the Census, *Population by Counties and Minor Civil Divisions: 1890, 1900, and 1910* (Washington, DC: Government Printing Office, 1912), 47

[2] Loretto Dennis Szucs and Sandra Hargreaves Luebking, *The Source: A Guidebook of American Genealogy* (Salt Lake City: Ancestry Publishing, 1997), 258.

[3] Anne Moore, "A History of Douglas County, 1820-1920," M.A. Thesis, University of Denver, 1970, 45.

[4] Robert Gallman, "Gross National Product in the United States, 1834–1909," in *Output, Employment, and Productivity in the United States after 1800*, ed. Dorothy Brady (Cambridge, MA: National Bureau of Economic Research, 1966), 3-90.

[5] Fleta Nockels, "Douglas County Branch History," *AAUW*, accessed April 28, 2016, at https://douglascounty-co.aauw.net/about/history.

[6] Moore, "A History of Douglas County," 43.

[7] Ibid., 85-94.

[8] Josephine Lowell Marr, *Douglas County: A Historical Journey* (Gunnison, CO: B & B Printers, 1983), 191.

[9] Ibid., 99.

[10] Ibid., 66.

Chapter 20

POLITICS IN THE 1890S

Tim Weber

Republicans more or less dominated both Douglas County and Colorado politics in the last quarter of the nineteenth century. In the six presidential elections between 1880 and 1900, the state and the county voted Republican four times. In the eleven gubernatorial elections during the same period, Colorado elected six Republicans and five non-Republicans, while in Douglas County, Republican candidates won nine of the eleven contests. Only in the elections of 1896 and 1900 did both the state and the county vote for non-Republicans in what was a radical departure from politics-as-usual.

Between 1870 and 1900, the United States underwent an unprecedented social, economic, and political change. Almost 12 million immigrants came to America. Urban populations exploded: New York and Philadelphia doubled; Kansas City increased four-fold, Chicago ten-fold, and Denver twenty-seven-fold (4,759 to 133,000). The U.S. became an industrial power controlled by Eastern financial and business elites. Workers organized labor unions whose strikes sometimes turned violent. Two depressions (1873-79 and 1893-97) caused widespread bank and business failures and massive unemployment.[1]

Farmers like those in Douglas County suffered during this period. They complained of exorbitant shipping costs by railroads, high-interest rates by creditors, unfair prices by merchants, and a steady decline in farm prices. Through the Grange movement (the 1860s) and the Farmer Alliances (the 1870s), they formed cooperatives to create more buying and negotiating power.[2] In the 1880s they tried to change the country's monetary system. They believed the single gold standard, adopted in 1873, unfairly disadvantaged farmers and advocated a monetary system based on gold and silver. In 1878 and 1890 the government tried to appease the "Silverites" by purchasing a set amount of silver every month. But the Silverites demanded the coinage of silver and gold at a ratio of 16 to 1 to increase the money supply, expand available credit, and promote inflation so farmers could pay off debts with cheaper money. In 1890 Colorado produced 58% of the silver mined in the U.S., and Coloradoans became fierce supporters of "Free Silver." They formed hundreds of "silver clubs" in support of the cause which became a burning issue in the 1892 general election.[3]

This "agrarian revolt" led to the formation of the People's or Populist Party to protect the farmers' interests. In its defining *Omaha Platform*, it advocated the nationalization of the railroads, telephone, and telegraph industries; a graduated income tax; popular election of senators; the Australian secret ballot; the use of referendums and initiatives; the eight-hour workday for industrial workers; and the "free and unlimited coinage of silver and gold at the present legal ratio of l6 to 1."[4] The Populists nominated James Weaver for president. He came in a distant third to Democrat Grover Cleveland and Republican Benjamin Harrison; but Weaver did receive over a million popular votes, 22 electoral votes, and carried five Western states. Populists also elected 1,500 state legislators, three governors, five senators, and ten congressmen.

In 1892, Colorado went overwhelmingly for the Populist ticket. Weaver beat Harrison by a large margin (57% to 41%). Populists also elected two congressmen, a governor (Davis H. Waite), lieutenant governor, secretary of state, auditor, treasurer, attorney general, and superintendent of public instruction. Despite the election of many Populists to the Colorado House and Senate, Republicans had a narrow majority that kept Governor Waite from carrying out his Populist agenda.[5] Despite Douglas County's agrarian population, it swam against this Populist tide. It voted a straight

Davis Harmon Waite

Republican ticket. The editor of the *Castle Rock Journal* proudly proclaimed, "We want it distinctly understood that Douglas County is the banner Republican county in the state."[6]

Colorado felt the full force of the Panic of 1893, a financial crisis surpassed only by the Great Depression. Within a few months, 377 businesses failed, 435 out of 895 mines closed, 45,000 workers lost their jobs (20% of the workforce), and violent strikes spread. In Douglas County, 20% of the beef cattle ranches failed. When the silver market crashed, Congress stopped all silver purchases. Governor Waite was unable to do much, except support the campaign that secured for Colorado women the right to vote in 1893, 27 years before the 19th Amendment.[7] In 1894, he was replaced by Republican A.W. McIntire.[8]

In the election of 1896, there was a major change in the political landscape. When the Republicans endorsed the gold standard and nominated William McKinley, a group supporting Free Silver left the party. The Democrats nominated William Jennings Bryan, who was for Free Silver and against big business, the railroads, and the banks. The Populists decided to "fuse" with the Democrats and endorsed Bryan who lost badly to McKinley in the general election. But in Colorado, Bryan won a resounding victory (85% to 14%). He even won in Douglas County (1049 votes to 192), along with the entire slate of fusion candidates supported by an alliance of Silver Republicans, Democrats, and Populists.[9]

The 1900 election was a rematch between McKinley and Bryan. The return of prosperity and victory in the Spanish-American War brought McKinley an easy victory. Once again Colorado went for Bryan (55% to 42%). In Douglas County, the fusion alliance lost ground; but Bryan still eked out a narrow victory, as did the fusion candidates for Congress and the Colorado legislature. In the other state races, the Republicans won. The fight for Free Silver was over.[10]

Throughout this tumultuous period, there were some political success stories. J. Frank Gardner, "the father of Douglas County" and an unflinching Republican, held almost every County office: county clerk, county recorder, county treasurer, county assessor, and Justice of the Peace. He served in the territorial legislature (1869-73), the Colorado Senate (1876-78), and the Colorado House (1896-98) when he ran on the Fusion ticket. When he sought re-election in 1898 as a Republican, he lost badly.[11]

Elias M. Ammons was another huge political success. Born in North Carolina in 1860, his family came to Colorado in 1871. After graduating from Denver High School at age 20, he became a newspaperman and then started the Oxyoke cattle ranch in western Douglas County. In 1890 he became clerk of the District Court in Castle Rock. He was elected as a Republican to the Colorado House in 1890 and 1892, serving as Speaker of the House from 1892-94. When the Republicans endorsed the gold standard, he left the party and was elected to the Colorado Senate twice: in 1898 on the Fusion ticket and in 1902 as a Democrat. After campaigning unsuccessfully for Lieutenant Governor in 1904 and 1906, he was elected Governor in 1912 as a Democrat.

Elias M. Ammons

He was a progressive reformer but is best known for calling out the National Guard to confront striking coal miners in southern Colorado. The result was the "Ludlow Massacre" (1914) in which 19 people were killed, including 11 children. As a result, his popularity plummeted; and he served only one term, after which he became a prominent business and civic leader.[12]

Douglas County fully participated in the raucous state and national politics of the 1890s, during which it sometimes abandoned its Republican roots. Since its population was small (3,120 in 1900) its political process was hands-on, in-your-face, and intensely personal.

---

[1] Gary Nash et al., *The American People: Creating a Nation and a Society*, Concise 7th ed., vol. 2, (Boston: Prentice Hall, 2011), 489-645.

[2] James I. Stewart, "The Economics of American Farm Unrest, 1865-1900," *EH.net*, accessed on March 26, 2016, https://eh.net/encyclopedia/the-economics-of-american-farm-unrest-1865-1900/

[3] For a good explanation of the "free Silver movement," see Carl Ubbelobde, Maxine Benson, and Duane A. Smith, *A Colorado History*, 9th ed. (Boulder, CO: Pruett, 2006), 206-225.

[4] "The Omaha Platform: Launching the Populist Party," *History Matters*, accessed on March 26, 2016, http://historymatters.gmu.edu/d/5361

[5] G. Michael McCarthy, "The People's Party in Colorado: A Profile in Populist Leadership," in *Agricultural History*, vol. 4, no. 2 (April, 1973): 146-155.

[6] *Castle Rock Journal*, November 16, 1894, 1.

[7] Carl Abbott, Stephen J. Leonard, and Thomas J. Noel, *Colorado: A History of the Centennial State*, 4th ed. (Boulder, CO: University Press of Colorado, 2005), 177-190.

[8] Ubbelobde, Benson, and Smith, *A Colorado History*, 216-223.

[9] Ibid., 222-225; *Castle Rock Journal*, November 13, 1896, 4

[10] *Castle Rock Journal*, November 16, 1900, 5.

[11] Ibid., November 13, 1896, 4; ibid, November 18, 1898, 3; Alice M. Thompson, *Walk With Our Pioneers: A Collection* (Grand Junction, CO: JLM, 2005), 7.

[12] *Castle Rock Journal*, November 12, 1890, 1; ibid., November, 16, 1892, 1; ibid., November 18, 1898, 2; ibid., November 14, 1902, 5; ibid., November 15, 1912; Ubbelobde, Benson, and Smith, *A Colorado History*, 247-249; Abbot, Leonard, and Noel, *Colorado*, 147-153; Wilbur Fisk Stone, ed., *History of Colorado*, vol. 2 (Chicago: S.J. Clarke Publishing Co., 1918), 32-38, accessed March 29, 2016, http://files.usgwarchives.net/co/denver/bios/ammonsem.txt

Chapter 21

MOVERS AND SHAKERS

Mary O'Pry

Douglas County in the late nineteenth century had many forward-looking entrepreneurs. The West attracted such people, and Douglas County's list of movers and shakers was long. These pacesetters found new ways of doing things, set standards for others to follow, and left an indelible mark. Among them were a big-dreaming dairyman, a fruit grower with an innovative irrigation system, and a well-educated and cultured attorney with an international reputation.

David Rice Williams was born in 1837 in Worcester County, Massachusetts. At age 20, he set out for the California gold fields by sailing from New York to Panama, crossing the Isthmus, and taking another ship to San Francisco. He spent the next eight years in California, Oregon, Washington, and Idaho before returning to Massachusetts, where he spent the next seven years in the furniture business. In 1867 he married Elvira Pond with whom he had five children. In 1871 he left his family behind for a train trip to California. After

David Rice Williams

narrowly escaping the Chicago Fire, he arrived in Denver and decided to stay. He called for his family and started a boot and shoe store on Larimer Street with merchandise his wife brought from New England shoe factories. In 1873 he sold the store and homesteaded on Antelope Creek in Douglas County. In 1881 he moved to a new spread on West Cherry Creek, north of Spring Valley. In time the ranch grew to 1,180 acres. There he farmed, raised livestock, and went into the dairy business.

He dreamed big. In his creamery, he processed milk from his 85 dairy cows and the 10,000 gallons he purchased each day from his neighbors. In 1890 he hired an experienced cheesemaker from New York to run a new cheese factory that included a steam boiler to heat six 5,000-gallon vats. The 30-day cheese-making process turned out about 1,100 pounds of cheese per day. To serve his vendors and customers, he added a blacksmith shop, grocery, general merchandise store, and eventually a post office, which turned his ranch into "Williamsville," one of the Divide Country's most popular commercial centers.

He served three terms as a Douglas County Commissioner and was active in Democratic politics. In 1905 he decided to shut down his cheese-making business and sold off his cows and equipment. All the people who had depended on him felt the loss. While it lasted, his was the largest and most advanced dairy operation in the County. He died in 1912.[1]

William Thompson Lambert was born in 1850, near Portland, Maine. His family moved to Colorado in 1861 because of William's health. They settled on Indian Creek, near Wildcat Mountain outside Sedalia. William worked with his father as a bricklayer during his teens, after which he went to the University of Kansas to study civil engineering. He married Rachel Parman in 1874, and together they had four children. In 1875 his father bought 160 acres near Sedalia from Rachel's uncle, Greenlief Lowell. Eventually, William used this land to start his life's work.

During the 1880s and early 1890s, William served three terms as Douglas County Surveyor and one term as County Assessor. Then in 1894, he started the family-owned Lambert Orchard Company. Lambert's original 160 acres grew to 2,000. He cleared the land and purchased the inventories of tree nurseries in western Iowa. By 1896 he had planted twenty-eight thousand apple, plum, and cherry trees. The saplings in his nursery numbered in the tens of thousands. By 1898 his orchard was fully operational.

What made the Lambert Orchard unique was its advanced irrigation system. After studying such systems in California, Lambert designed one for his Colorado orchard. He dug a well 900 feet deep and installed a windmill to draw the water to the surface, where it went into a reservoir from which buried pipes took it throughout the orchard. Thus, each tree had its own water supply. Lambert patented his irrigation system, and people came to investigate it. Under his "Pure Apple Brand Fruit Products" trademark, he sold apple juice, boiled cider, apple jelly, apple butter, and sweet cider. When a series of early frosts ruined the orchard, the Lamberts became successful ranchers. William Lambert died in 1940 and was remembered for his orchard and a rancher son (William Jr.) who also served as the Speaker of the Colorado House.[2]

William Dillon was born in Brooklyn, NY, in 1850, the son of Irish immigrants who fled to America after his father was convicted of high treason in English courts. In 1857 the Dillons were able to return to Ireland, where William received a classical education which enabled him to read Greek and Latin texts for the rest of his life. He studied law in London, was admitted to the Irish bar in 1874, and practiced law in Dublin. In 1880, he contracted tuberculosis and moved to Colorado for his health. He lived on George Ratcliff's T-Ranch on West Plum Creek. His health was restored after two years, and he returned to Ireland, but

William Dillon

political unrest led him back to Douglas County where he and Ratcliff became business partners. They bought the Crull Ranch, and William married Ratcliff's daughter Elizabeth in 1885. They had ten children, four of whom died in infancy.

In 1888 Dillon moved his family from the ranch to Castle Rock, where he built a house on Cantril Street and opened a law office. He served as County Attorney, represented both the D&RG and AT&SF railroads, and helped farmers win a legal battle over water rights. He was a founder of the Castle Rock Creamery; and he and George Ratcliff opened a meat market, icehouse, stockyard, slaughterhouse, and feed store. He also sold real estate and insurance and helped start St. Francis of Assisi Catholic Church. Like his father-in-law, Dillon was active in Democratic politics. In 1890 he ran for a seat in the Colorado House but lost to Republican Elias Ammons,[3] who eventually was elected Colorado Governor in 1912.

In 1893, Dillon moved his family to Chicago, where he became editor of *The New World*, a Catholic weekly newspaper; joined the prestigious O'Donnell, Dillon, and Toolen law firm; was the founding dean of the Loyola University law school;[4] and hobnobbed with Chicago's social and political elite. In 1916, the Dillons returned to Castle Rock, where they built a three-story house across the street from their first home, and William re-started his law practice. When he died in 1935, many people were surprised when so many condolences arrived from prominent people, including Clarence Darrow, the famous Chicago defense attorney. As it turned out, William Dillon was a famous man, admired from Ireland to Chicago, who had also made a name for himself in Douglas County.[5]

There were other movers and shakers in Douglas County in the late nineteenth century, but these three were standouts who clearly made the County a better place.

---

[1] Susan Meyer, ed., *Our Heritage: People of Douglas County* (Castle Rock, CO: The Historical Society, 1984), 309; Josephine Lowell Marr, *Douglas County: A Historical Journey*, compiled by Joan Marr Keiser (Gunnison, CO: B & B Printers, 1983), 53-57; Anne Moore, "A History of Douglas County, 1820 to 1920," M.A. Thesis, University of Denver, 1970, 49-52; "Williamsville—Cherry," *Larkspur Historical Society*, accessed on May 14, 2016, at http://larkspurhistoricalsociety.org/?page_id=63. See the D.R. Williams Biographical File in the History Research Center, Philip S. Miller Library, Castle Rock, CO.

[2] Meyer, *Our Heritage*, 150-153; Marr, *Douglas County*, 107-109. See the William Thompson Lambert Biographical File in the History Research Center, Philip S. Miller Library, Castle Rock, CO.

[3] *Castle Rock Journal*, November 12, 1890, 1. Dillion lost by 112 votes.

[4] Thomas M. Haney, "The First 100 Years: The Centennial History of Loyola University Chicago School of Law," accessed May 14, 2016, at http://www.luc.edu/media/lucedu/law/students/publications/llj/pdfs/haney_100yrs.pdf

[5] Meyer, *Our Heritage*, 77-79; Marr, *Douglas County*, 99, 144, 158, 160, 163-64, 166-167; "Castle Rock History: William Dillon," *Castle Rock Magazine*, accessed on May 14, 2016, at http://castlerockmagazine.com/experience-castle-rock/ See also the William Dillon Biographical File in the History Research Center in the Philip S. Miller Library, Castle Rock, CO.

Chapter 22

WINDOW TO A NEW WORLD

Larry Schlupp

Most historians view 1890s Colorado as a "period of change."[1] In Douglas County, the number of farms and ranches grew significantly from 1870 to 1900, though by 1890 "most of the good land had been taken up."[2] But on the whole, life in Douglas County remained pretty much the same. Farm life was still characterized by grinding manual labor, day in and day out. There had been some change in small-town life in terms of new amenities and improving living conditions. But overall, as the twentieth century approached, most people expected life to continue as before. Then the United States went to war with Spain; and Americans experienced progressive change and rapid modernization, even in Douglas County.

In the nineteenth century, Spain was an imperial power, with colonies in the Atlantic (Cuba and Puerto Rico) and the Pacific (Guam and the Philippines). In the early 1890s, Spain promised Cuba independence, which prompted the United States to invest $50 million in Cuba and earn twice that amount in annual trade. When Spain reneged on its promise, in 1895 Cuban insurgents started a war for independence, led by Jose Marti. He was killed a few weeks into the fighting, but the rebellion continued in Cuba and spread to Puerto Rico and the Philippines.[3] Spain responded by tightening its grip on its colonies and using brutal tactics to put down the insurrections.

Stories of Spanish atrocities infuriated the American public, egged on by sensational reporting in the press. Popular support for war with Spain grew. Few knew that the American military had been planning for such a possibility since 1894. When the American battleship *USS Maine* blew up in Havana Harbor with the loss of 260 lives on February 15, 1898, most people blamed the Spanish, which quickly led to war. Spain declared war on the U.S. on April 24, and the U.S. declared war on Spain the next day. Five days later Admiral George Dewey's U.S. Asiatic Squadron destroyed or captured the entire Spanish fleet in Manila Bay, the Philippines.[4] U.S. landings followed in the

Philippines, Cuba, and Puerto Rico. The war lasted ten weeks and formally ended with the Treaty of Paris in December 1898, which ceded Puerto Rico, Guam, and the Philippines to the U.S. and made Cuba an American protectorate. The United States was now an imperial power.

Colorado played a minor role in "the splendid little war."[5] President McKinley issued a call for 200,000 troops after Congress' Declaration of War. Colorado's quota was 1,600 troops from the National Guard,[6] but Colorado sent fewer than 1,000. Only nine of them were from Douglas County.[7] The soldiers from Colorado were sent to the Philippines and arrived at Manila Bay on July 26, 1898. In mid-August, the Coloradans fought courageously against Spanish entrenchments; but their time in combat was short. They received orders to leave the Philippines on July 4, 1899.[8]

Upon returning home, the Douglas County troops found life was just as they had left it, except for the people's change of attitude. The war had been fought for a variety of reasons; but when it concluded, America was suddenly a world power, the holder of colonies in the Pacific and Atlantic.[9] Colorado and Douglas County saw a world full of new possibilities. Most of the people back home went about their business with new confidence for the future.[10]

In the last two years of the decade, one could see in Douglas County towns an increased sense of business competitiveness, especially in merchandising and the feed and grain business. New businesses opened, some specializing in unusual commodities like confectioneries (candies) and millinery shops (fancy women's hats).[11] There were also unusual new industries as well: for example, Sedalia's rather exotic cigar factory.[12]

Threshing on the Lorraine Ranch Spring Valley

Agriculture became increasingly mechanized and modernized. Franktown farmer-rancher Frank Graves built the first silo in Douglas County in 1887, and many others followed. Growing mechanization greatly reduced the time it took to bring in a good crop. To produce 100 bushels of wheat from a five-acre field, farmers greatly reduced the time required by using an iron-wheeled riding double-bottomed gang plow (which replaced the single bottom plow) to till their field, a seeder for planting, and a binder, thresher, wagon, and horses for reaping.[13] Needless to say, farm implement dealers did a land-office business, like Lewis Store's McCormick Farm Equipment in Parker and Holcomb & Whitney in Castle Rock. The Panic of 1893 resulted in the loss of many small Douglas County cattle ranches; but after 1895, cattle prices actually increased.[14] The lingering eleven-year drought that started in 1889 initiated dry farming methods,[15] as used by farmers Jacob Shutz, and extensive irrigation, as used by William Lambert Orchard Farm in Sedalia.[16] Despite everything, the agricultural economy in Douglas County grew in the 1890s.

Mechanized Corn Picker on Bihlmeyer Ranch

People living in Douglas County towns also experienced the advent of new technologies. In 1900 Castle Rock got the first telephone exchange in Douglas County.[17] In the same year, residents of Douglas County heard about the arrival of the first automobile in Colorado; and *The Rocky Mountain News* reported that John B. Walker was the first person ever to attempt to climb Pikes Peak in an automobile: he made it to 11,000 feet![18] New technology

119

came to the home as well in the form of the Akron treadle sewing machine ($16.95).[19] In the last five years of the nineteenth century, County and municipal governments began to be concerned about controlling growth. The Town of Castle Rock drew the line at building sidewalks to accommodate a large eastern canning company that wanted to move to Castle Rock. Was it just the cost or the fear that too much change would alter the character of the town? Whatever the reason, the canning company located elsewhere.[20]

A significant cultural change also occurred at the end of the century in the areas of education, journalism, and women's rights. Education began to shift its focus in the curriculum: in addition to the liberal arts, new courses were added in the sciences. Local newspapers followed the lead of mainstream journalism by eliminating fluff pieces on how many cousins attended Aunt Gertrude's 80th birthday party and filed more realistic articles about social change, foreign affairs, and new technologies. On November 7, 1893, Colorado women received the right to vote, second only to Wyoming doing so. Colorado was the first state to elect women legislators in 1894.[21] With the dawn of the twentieth century, Douglas County was poised to throw open the window sash to a new world.

---

[1] Leroy R. Hafen and Ann Hafen, *The Colorado Story: A History of Your State and Mine*, Unit VI (Denver: The Old West Publishing Company, 1953), 308.

[2] Leroy R. Hafen and James H. Baker, eds., *History of Colorado*, vol. 1 (Denver, CO: Linderman Company, Inc., 1927), 528.

[3]"The World of 1898: The Spanish-American War," *Library of Congress, Hispanic Division*, accessed May 5, 2016, http://loc.gov/rr/hispanic/1898/intro.html.

[4] Hafen and Baker, *History of Colorado*, vol. 3, 980.

[5] Secretary of State John Hay quoted in Gary Nash et al, *The American People: Creating a Nation and a Society*, vol. 2 (concise 7th ed.) (Boston: Prentice Hall, 2011), 594.

[6] Ibid., 979.

[7] Ibid., 981.

[8] Ibid., 988.

[9] Ibid., 991.

[10] Anne Moore, "A History of Douglas County, 1820-1920," M.A. Thesis, University of Denver, 1970, 94-95.

[11] William L. Reich, *Colorado Industries of the Past* (Boulder, CO: Johnson Books, 2008), 67-80.

[12] Ibid., 123-143.

[13] "A History of American Agriculture, 1769-1990," accessed May 5, 2016, http://inventors.about.com/library/inventors/blfarm1.htm.

[14] "Farm Report," *Castle Rock Journal*, August 24, 1900, 2.

[15] Ibid., December 21, 1900.

[16] Our Heritage: People of Douglas Country (Castle Rock, CO: Douglas County Historical Society, 1984, 1984), 151-154.

[17] Moore, "History of Douglas County," 95.

[18] Hafen and Baker, *History of Colorado*, 504.

[19] Advertisement, *Castle Rock Journal*, December 28, 1900.

[20] Moore, "History of Douglas County," 100.

[21] Hafen and Hafen, *The Colorado Story*, 308-309.

PART THREE

STRIFE AND SUCCESS, 1900-1930

Chapter 23
GOING MODERN

Joan Gandy

When Douglas County settlers first arrived, the pioneers burned buffalo chips for fuel, cooked on bare ground, and constructed firepots from stones.[1] Over the next eighty years, modern systems steadily replaced antiquated technologies. As the population grew, local governments weighed the costs and benefits of modernization. While the bureaucracy moved slowly, individual homeowners, farmers, and businesses often acted independently to install the latest conveniences. By the 1920s, Douglas County residents possessed electric lights, filtered water, statewide communication, and community septic systems—many of the fixtures of a progressive and up-to-date town.

Hauling Telephone Poles

The Colorado Telephone Company expanded to Douglas County at the turn of the century. In May 1900, cedar poles arrived by train in Castle Rock, and plans for a local exchange developed. "Many is the time when a telephone would save a trip to one of the depots or would enable a housewife to order goods from the stores without having to interrupt her cooking and change her raiment in order to be attired suitably for the street," read an article in the *Castle Rock Journal*.[2] Public telephones at Woltzen's Store and the *Castle Rock Journal* office provided free service to people checking on train schedules and freight shipments. In 1901, some early adopters of in-home phones were cattle rancher George Ratcliff, Colorado Senator Elias M. Ammons, Highlands Ranch mansion resident John W. Springer, Douglas County Sheriff Edward Hoffman, and Douglas County Commissioner John R. Campbell.[3] By the end of 1902, phone lines connected Castle Rock to Colorado communities such as Franktown, Elizabeth, Elbert, Kiowa, Calhan, Eastonville, Fondis, and Peyton, and even cities in Utah, southern Wyoming, New Mexico, Washington State, and Idaho.[4]

After phone lines connected the County to the wider world, community members concentrated on issues of water. In the early twentieth century, water from Plum Creek quenched the thirst of those living nearby. While the stream was sufficient when the population was small, growth adversely affected water quality. Instead of the "purest of water,"[5] residents drank contaminated "swill."[6] For decades, most improvements to the area's water systems were restricted to individual buildings. On June 18, 1909, *The Record Journal* reported the County Commissioners contracted to install a "six horsepower engine and two steel tanks on the courthouse grounds" to provide water for the courthouse lawn and anticipate connecting to a future sewer system.[7]

Castle Rock Water Works Pumping Station

In 1910 Pete Smith purchased a Kewanee Air Pressure water system and bathroom outfit for his new house south of Castle Rock. This "enterprising" rancher believed in having a "modern and up-to-date" water system that could provide both fire protection and water for domestic needs.[8] Not to be outdone, Joseph H. Bassell, who already had gas lights in his home, built an extensive and convenient water system at his Parker farm. "A large windmill furnishes the power to force the water into the big cement reservoir just above the house, from which it is piped to the dwelling and hot water connections made." Additional lines carried water to the barns, garden, and lawn.[9] Finally, in December 1914, J.C. Babcock, owner of the Bay State Dairy Ranch of Greenland, bathed with hot and cold water carried through a gravity water system, making his house a "modern country home."[10]

Still, most of the County's population lacked access to such amenities. In Castle Rock, candidates for the Citizen's Party first proposed the construction of a water system with a filtering plant in the spring of 1913.[11] However, as the *Record Journal* reported, the Castle Rock electorate was equally split on the 1916 bond measure to finance the water system. The tie vote meant the measure would have to wait until the next spring's election, and *The Record Journal*'s staff worked hard to swing the vote to yes.[12] "Don't allow yourself to be influenced by anyone who would rather drink swill if it didn't cost anything than to pay a moderate price for pure water."[13] What turned the tide toward a new water system was a March 1916 report that an examination of the local water revealed sewage contamination.[14] With that piece of information, the electorate passed the bond measure by a 57-17 vote a month later. *The Record Journal* approved the result: "It is the biggest step forward putting Castle Rock in the list of live towns that has ever been made."[15] People living in the country still relied on their own wells.

Within months of the water system bond's approval, discussions began about Castle Rock's next modernization project: a sewer system. Up to this point, most Douglas County residents used vault toilets. Hired "scavengers" cleaned out the underground waste vaults once a year. Despite sanitation concerns, the project failed to gain traction primarily due to anxieties about the county's water supply. Some homeowners opted to construct private septic systems, but most county residents continued to use vaults. More than a decade after the water system was approved, Castle Rock seriously began considering a sewer system plan. The town council approved the sewer system with a 4-2 vote in September 1931.[16] The construction project came with a caveat: all of the labor used in the installation must be provided by Castle Rock citizens, if available.[17] As the Great Depression tightened its grip, sewer construction provided a boost to the local economy as well as a step toward modernization.

In the years between the construction of a water plant and the adoption of a sewer system, electric lights began glowing across the county. The lights first shone in Louviers, a "Modern, Industrial, Growing Village," according to *The Record Journal*.[18] In 1921, the Louviers' school building and ninety private homes glowed with electric lights thanks to the DuPont Powder Plant company, which located its dynamite business in the community.[19] Castle Rock decided against building its own municipal power plant due to costs but was able to connect to the DuPont lines in 1922.[20] Four months after the lines were activated, sixty-one Castle Rock homes were wired. On April 6, 1923, in *The Record Journal,* J. Grant Hesseltine, a Castle Rock electrician, wrote that his family utilized an electric iron, sewing machine, toaster, and vacuum. He encouraged the forty-three homes in town not wired to join the modern world and "lessen labor in the home."[21]

Over eighty years in Douglas County, the electric light bulb replaced the flames from burning buffalo chips. Filtering plants restored water quality to the contaminated water of Plum Creek. Telephone lines enabled the coroner, the doctor, and law enforcement to respond rapidly to deaths, accidents, and crimes in rural areas. Instead of annual cleanings of underground vaults, sewers safely carried off the community's waste. In all, by 1930, Douglas County had entered the modern age.

---

[1] "Douglas County in Legends and Stories," *Record-Journal*, December 16, 1921, 1.

[2] "Local Telephone System." *Castle Rock Journal*, June 22, 1900, 1.

[3] "Additional Local News," *Castle Rock Journal,* May 17, 1901; "Elbert County," *Castle Rock Journal,* November 29, 1901.

[4] "Telephone Extensions," *Castle Rock Journal,* June 13, 1902; "Telephone Extensions," *Castle Rock Journal,* March 4, 1902.

[5] "Castle Rock, Colorado," *Castle Rock Journal*, January 3, 1908; 1.

[6] "Why Not Investigate," *Record-Journal*, February 18, 1916, 1.

[7] "A Big Improvement," *Record-Journal*, June 18, 1909, 1.

[8] "Local Happenings," *Record-Journal*, November 18,1910, 1.

[9] "Improves His Ranch," *Record-Journal*, April 7,1911, 1.

[10] "A Modern Country Home," *Record-Journal*, December 11, 1914, 1.

[11] "Citizens' Party Nominates Candidates," *Record-Journal*, March 4, 1913, 1.

[12] "Election Results in Tie," *Record-Journal*, January 7,1916, 1.

[13] "Why Not Investigate," *Record-Journal*, February 18,1916, 1.

[14] "Castle Rock Water Analyzed," *Record-Journal*, March 17,1916, 1.

[15] "Bonds Voted by Big Majority," *Record-Journal*, April 7, 1916, 1.

[16] "Town Council Votes to Create Sewer District," *Record-Journal*, December 11, 1931, 1.

[17] "Town Council Votes to Create Sewer District," *Record-Journal*, December 11,1931, 1.

[18] "Louviers, Modern, Industrial, Growing Village," *Record-Journal*, December 16, 1921.

[19] "Town Council Votes to Create Sewer District," *Record-Journal*, December 11, 1931, 1.

[20] "Electric Lights Will Soon Twinkle from the Homes of Castle Rock," *Record-Journal*, February 17, 1922, 1.

[21] J. Grant Hesseltine, "Castle Rock's Electric Light System---Detailed Statement Regarding the Plant," *Record-Journal*, April 6,1923, 1.

Chapter 24
WORLD WAR I

Susan Rocco-Mckeel

The U.S. formally entered World War I on April 6, 1917. Known as "The Great War," it was a conflict on a previously unknown scale. Modern weapons such as poison gas, long-range artillery, tanks, and airplanes with bombs augmented trench warfare, resulting in record numbers of death and widespread destruction.[1] Soldiers and military personnel also suffered psychological wounds, "shell shock" or neurasthenia.[2]

Douglas County followed the War's events from the beginning. The local paper often headlined news about the War, including articles from British papers, as did neighboring papers from Denver and Littleton.

Due to inadequate record keeping at the time, some of which were attempted retrospectively, it is difficult to determine the exact number of Douglas County men who served. According to the National Archives, "Not all of the men who registered for the draft actually served in the military, and not all men who served in the military registered for the draft."[3]

Robert Rowley and Soldiers

In 1918, Douglas County's *Honor Roll* of men who had or were serving reported the names of 107 men.[4] The actual number was certainly larger. Omissions included Cam Wilson who had worked at the Louviers Du Pont plant;[5] civil engineer Leslie Gore; German immigrant Fred W. Kugler;[6] Italian immigrant Mike Mingen, a Parker barber; Parker farmer John D. Cecil, Jr.; and William John Hoskin, who was drafted in Douglas County and wounded fighting near Verdun.[7]

Some service experiences have been lost, but at least six County men enlisted in the Rocky Mountain Rangers (cavalry);[8] Frank Alred Cantril of Perry Park participated in the sinking of submarines; Raymond W. Maxwell of Castle Rock fought in the St. Michiel Offensive;[9] and Andrew Garrison was killed on a French battlefield the same day that his brother, John, also "died for his country."[10]

The local newspaper published some of the soldiers' letters home, which were often optimistic but homesick. A letter signed by Dennis Schenk, Walter Lawson, and Arthur R. Law was written from Camp Funston, Kansas, where the barracks were unheated. They praised the YMCA that "furnished our only pleasure and the only place in which we can get warm."[11] They wrote that the YMCA was even more important in France "as they are the means for keeping the boys from wandering the streets and as a consequence finding their way into a house of ill-repute."[12]

Colorado, with its large areas of both agricultural and unplowed land and strong production of livestock and mineral deposits, was situated to help the nation. The War opened new agricultural markets in Europe. Nationally, wheat acreage tripled and opportunities for livestock production were publicized.[13]

According to the Douglas County records, most of the men who enlisted or were drafted listed their previous occupation as "farmer."[14] Such recruits or draftees earned about $32 a month as an Army private or ordinary seaman in the Navy.[15] Though they sent most of their pay back home to their families, their departure from the farm to the battlefield left behind a serious economic deficit. In a County whose population was only 3,192,[16] it was difficult to find substitutes for lost labor and talent. As a result of the war-caused labor shortage on Colorado farms, the state advertised for out-of-state labor to make up the difference.[17]

During the War, women acquired jobs usually reserved for men. First prize essay winner, Ivalu Boegel wrote: "Today in addition to her natural duties as a wife, homemaker, and mother, she is a Red Cross nurse, Red Cross worker, munitions worker, mechanic or soldier of the soil."[18] Women served in the Navy and Marines as nurses; and on the home front, they worked in factories and government offices, all of which not only helped the war effort but contributed to the support for Women's Suffrage.[19] The Women's Service League met to discuss women's roles and as a result, the National League proclaimed it could rely on Douglas County's help when needed.[20]

To finance the War, the federal government relied upon a mix of one-third new taxes and two-thirds borrowing from the populace through the sale of Liberty Bonds. By the end of the War, the Nation had raised $17 billion from Liberty Bonds from twenty million individuals.[21]

Line Up and Sign Up
on June 28th

Enlist as a war saver in the great "army that stays at home"—the second line of defense behind our boys in the first line trenches.
The government has officially set Friday, June 28th, as

National War Savings Day

Be ready to step forward on that day and prove your patriotism. You are summoned on Friday, June 28th, to "sign the pledge"—to agree to invest in a definite amount of War Savings Stamps each month during 1918.

W. S. S. Cost $4.17 in June
Worth $5.00 Jan. 1st, 1923

Be Ready to Go the Limit—Line Up and Sign Up on June 28th

WSS   NATIONAL WAR SAVINGS COMMITTEE

This Space Contributed for the Winning of the War by
The First National Bank of Douglas County

Douglas County was active in the campaign to encourage the purchase of Liberty Bonds, using posters, newspaper ads, and local initiatives.[22] If Douglas County women couldn't nurse or do direct war work, they were urged to buy Liberty Bonds.[23] When Larkspur exceeded its Liberty Bond quota, its people celebrated at a Red Cross dance. Mr. Frink, owner of a large creamery in Larkspur, donated the use of his hall for the dance while Mr. Riggs donated the use of his hall for refreshments.[24]

County residents were creative in their efforts to raise funds. For example, they sponsored a men's knitting contest in Fetherolf's Hall. Men paid a one-dollar entrance fee, which included bringing a six-inch square of knitted wool. The contest consisted of finishing a knitted project with the already-completed knitted square. Women of Castle Rock, Sedalia, Louviers, and Larkspur served as judges. Prizes were awarded for "neatness, gracefulness of handling the needles, speed, and the way you hold your mouth".[25] T. Christensen won, while Dr. Gray got the "booby prize." Harold Strange won the boys' contest.[26]

The people of Douglas County raised funds to help the Red Cross care for wounded soldiers.[27] They planted victory gardens and participated in wheatless Mondays, meatless Tuesdays, and porkless Saturdays, as well as gasless and lightless days. By 1918, U.S. exports of bread products, sugar, and meat had increased threefold.[28] When the armistice began on November 11, 1918, Governor Julius Gunter proclaimed it a state holiday. Douglas County joined in the celebrations. [29] The local paper suggested celebrating with doughnuts since the food board had lifted the ban on powdered sugar.[30]

Herbert Hoover, as head of the U.S. Food Administration, created in 1917 by President Woodrow Wilson's executive order, proclaimed that "No government nor nation can stand if its people are starving. We must do our part if the world be not consumed in a flame of anarchy."[31] Again Colorado and Douglas County did their part, this time in Conservation Week for World Relief to help supply food to European nations until their next harvest. While Hoover stated that there was a surplus of coffee, a sufficient supply of sugar, a sufficient supply of beef, and that wheat, rye, beans, peas, and rice were sufficient "with economy in consumption," he stated that there was a shortage of pork products, dairy products, vegetable oils, and high protein feeds for dairy animals.[32]

As Douglas County people assisted in the War effort and the recovery from its aftermath, they were unaware that more sacrifice would be asked. Although "the war to end all wars" was over, in a little over twenty years, Douglas County would again be participating in a devastating world conflict.

134

[1] Russell Freedman, *The War to End All Wars: World War I* (Boston, New York: Clarion Books, 2010), X.

[2] Jack Batten, *The War to End All Wars* (Canada: Tundra Books, 2009), 92.

[3] National Archives, "Draft Registration Cards," accessed January 18, 2017, www.archives.gov/research/military/ww1.

[4] "Douglas County Honor Roll," *Record-Journal*, May 31, 1918, 4.

[5] "Our Honor Roll," *Du Pont Magazine,* January 1919, 28, accessed February 15, 2017), http://digital.hagley.org/1919_10_01?solr_nav[id]=d907c9393699cd159a49&solr_nav[page]=0&solr_nav[offset]=13#page/30/mode/1up/search/DuPont%2C+wwI+honor+roll.

[6] *World War I War Records 1/5*, Department of History, University of Colorado, accessed January 14, 2014, archived at Douglas County History Research Center.

[7] "War Record," *World War I Archives of Douglas County,* Douglas County History Research Center.

[8.] "Douglas County Boys Enlist," *Record-Journal*, June 22, 1917, 1.

[9] "War Record."

[10] "Andrew Garrison Killed in Action," *Record-Journal*, December 27, 1918, 1.

[11] "More News From the Boys at the Front," *Record-Journal*, November 2, 1917,1.

[12] Ibid.

[13] R. W. Clark, "Livestock Production Farmer's Opportunity," *Record-Journal,* June 22, 1917, 1.

[14] "War Record."

[15] "Pay of Army and Navy on Foreign Service," *Record-Journal*, June 29, 1917, 2.

[16] Richard L. Forstall, *COLORADO: Population of Counties by Decennial Census: 1900 to 1990* (U.S. Bureau of the Census), accessed March 7, 2017, https://www.census.gov/population/cencounts/co190090.txt.

[17] "Demand for Farms Continues," *Record-Journal*, April 13, 1917, 1.

[18] "Woman's Work in the War," *Record-Journal,* May 31, 1918, 4.

[19] Nation Women's History Museum, "Women in World War I," accessed January 28, 2017, https://www.nwhm.org/online-exhibits/progressiveera/worldwarI.html.

[20] "Women's Service League Meeting," *Record-Journal*, April 13, 1917, 1.

[21] Campbell Brown, "Liberty Bonds 04/1917-09/1918," *Federal Reserve,* accessed March 2, 2017, https://www.federalreservehistory.org/Events/DetailView/100.

[22] "Women Must Help Raise War Funds," *Record-Journal*, April 19, 1918, 7.

[23] Ibid.

[24] "Red Cross Dance at Larkspur," *Record-Journal,* May 17, 1918, 1.

[25] "Did You Know?" *Record-Journal* (February 8, 1918): 1.

[26] "Knitting Bee," *Record-Journal,* February 22, 1918, 1.

[27] "Douglas County Does Her Bit," *Record-Journal,* June 29, 1917, 1.

[28] National Archives, "Sow the Seeds of Victory! Posters from the Food Administration During World War I," accessed February 2, 2017, https://www.archives.gov/education/lessons/sow-seeds.

[29] "Centennial State Items," *Record-Journal*, November 15, 1918, 7.

[30] "Celebrate with Doughnuts," *Record-Journal*, November 29, 1918, 1.

[31] "Colorado's Part in World Rebuilding to be Begun Week of Dec. 2," *Record-Journal,* November 29, 1918, 1.

[32] Ibid.

Chapter 25

THE PEOPLE OF DOUGLAS COUNTY

Tim Weber

The decadal U.S. Census reports provide a wealth of information about changing population patterns and the kinds of people who lived in Douglas County. From 1900 to 1930, Colorado's population increased by 92%; and Denver's grew by 115%. In contrast, Douglas County's population grew by only 12%. In short, while other parts of the state grew dramatically, DC maintained a small but stable population that was mostly engaged in agriculture (various kinds of farming and ranching), lumber, and railroads.

After Colorado became a U.S. Territory in 1861, legislators established Douglas County as one of 17 original counties. The territory's population numbered about 50,000; and the County's about 1,000. In the 1870 Census, there were 1,388 County residents. Many of them were foreign-born. Between 1865 and 1920, 28 million immigrants came to the U.S.[1] In this period immigrants settled in Douglas County from Canada, England, Wales, Scotland, Ireland, Austria, Germany, Switzerland, Denmark, Sweden, France, Mexico, and other places.

The Census reports of 1910, 1920, and 1930 provide information on three population groups: Colorado-born, other American-born, and foreign-born.[2] While the number of Colorado-born increased throughout the period, the number of the other American-born increased, then slightly decreased. The number of foreign-born residents steadily declined. In 1910, almost one-in-five Douglas County residents was foreign-born (17%). The five largest immigrant groups were German (98), English (75), Mexican (60), Canadian (55), and Swedish (54). In 1920, the foreign-born population declined to 11%. The top five groups were the same, but their order changed: Mexican (63), English (60), German (57), Swedish (38), and Canadian (32). In 1930, foreign-born residents declined to 9%; and the order of the top five changed again: Mexicans (56), Canadians (53), Germans (38), English (33), and Swedish (27).

Population Groupings	1910 Census[3]	1920 Census[4]	1930 Census
Total DC Population	3185	3522	3469
Colorado-born	1329 (42%)	1559 (44%)	1622 (47%)
Other U.S.-born	1318 (41%)	1589 (45%)	1540 (44%)
Foreign-born	541 (17%)	374 (11%)	307 (9%)

Why did these population patterns change? The answer is obvious: people are born, move around, and die. Few immigrants entered the U.S. after 1920 because of restrictive quotas,[3] and many immigrants who settled here did not stay. For example, only 19 Swedish individuals were on both the 1910 and 1920 lists; and 11 carried over from 1920 to 1930. Only 9 were listed in all three census reports. Among them was John Anderson, who served as county sheriff (1909-12) and judge (1912-32).[4] All three population groups produced Colorado-born children, which accounts for that category's growth.

Like immigrants elsewhere, families with immigrant parents and American-born children underwent a sometimes-difficult assimilation process. At first German, Swedish, or Spanish were spoken at home; and families socialized with others from their ethnic group. Over time, however, their Colorado-born children began pulling away from Old-World ways. They went to Douglas County schools, picked up English quickly, and identified primarily as Americans. Of course, the parents went through a much different assimilation process, which was probably made easier because nearly everyone in Douglas County made their living working the land or supporting those who did. Many immigrants and their descendants married outside their ethnic group. Within a generation or two, they lost the ability to speak their mother tongue. Knowledge of or attachment to the Old Country faded, and most ethnic distinctions disappeared, except for some family recipes or holiday traditions. Full assimilation could take up to three generations.[5]

A few remnants of the original ethnic settlement patterns remained into the twentieth century. In the early years, immigrants preferred living around people who spoke the same language and observed the same customs. Such proximity was a natural outgrowth of "social networking:" Many immigrants followed family or friends who got here first and invited them to come too. The resulting family and ethnic enclaves remained strong by frequent associations. For example, the Germans and Austrians who settled in Lake Gulch often got together for picnics, dances, hayrides, and parties at Fred and Anna Doepke's Twin Creek Ranch.[6] Some of these ethnic concentrations remained well into the early twentieth century. These same German-speaking immigrants and their descendants continued to live in Cherry Creek Valley (Lake Gulch, Parker, Franktown, Case, and Spring Valley). Mexicans had been in Douglas County from the beginning, but by the early 1900s, they congregated mainly in Larkspur and Sedalia where they worked on the railroads. Not all such patterns endured. In the 1890s, many Swedes lived in and around Castle Rock because they had a near monopoly on stonecutting in the quarries there. After the quarries closed, they dispersed throughout the County, as did the English and Canadians.

Frederick and Anna Deopke Family

One immigrant group had a curious story: the Bulgarians. Between 1903 and 1910, 50,000 Bulgarians came to the United States in search of economic opportunity due to Bulgaria's overpopulation and high unemployment. Many of them had no intention of staying in America: they came to find work, earn money, then return home.[7] Most Bulgarian immigrants found work in industrial areas of the East and Midwest, but some went West. According to the 1910 Census, 477 of them lived in Colorado, including 46 Bulgarian men in Douglas County. Most were married (30 of the 46); and their ages ranged from 19 to 50, with the majority in their 20s. All of them worked as laborers at the new DuPont Powder Plant in Louviers and lived on Woodhouse Road, south of town. Bulgarians liked to live together in boarding houses, but none existed in Louviers in 1910. Most likely, then, they lived in tents, adobe huts, or shelters dug into the hillsides until other facilities could be constructed.[8] They played an important role at the powder plant: of the 86 laborers in 1910, 46 were Bulgarians.

By the 1920 Census, not a single Bulgarian lived in Douglas County. Where did they go? Many of them probably returned to Bulgaria. Between 1910 and 1929, more Bulgarians left America than immigrated to it.[9] But records remain for a few of the 46. Four registered for the draft as enemy aliens in 1917-1918 (Bulgaria allied with the Central Powers). They lived in Illinois, Pennsylvania, Missouri, and Michigan. Two showed up in the 1920 Census in Erie, Colorado, and Floyd, Iowa. Two spent the rest of their lives in the U.S. and died in 1946 and 1981.

The Bulgarian story shows that not all immigrants who came to Douglas County stayed. But many did. They and their descendants provided ethnic diversity and contributed to the County's economic development, alongside their Colorado-born and other American-born neighbors. People from all three population groups were essential to Douglas County's future.

---

[1] Winthrop S. Hudson, *Religion in America*, 3rd ed. (New York: Charles Scribner's Sons, 1981), 239; "Mass Immigration and World War I," *U.S. Citizenship and Immigration Services*, accessed March 9, 2017, https://www.uscis.gov/history-and-genealogy/our-history/agency-history/mass-immigration-and-wwi.

[2] All the data found here came from the U.S. Census for 1910, 1920, and 1930, accessed March 3-14, 2017, http://search.ancestry.com/search/group/usfedcen.

[3] "Era of Restriction," *U.S. Citizenship and Immigration Services*, accessed on March 9, 2017, https://www.uscis.gov/history-and-genealogy/our-history/agency-history/mass-immigration-and-wwi.

[4] "Judge Anderson Passed Away Last Sunday," *Record-Journal*, September 3, 1943, 1.

[5] Susan K. Brown and Frank D. Bean, "Assimilation Models, Old and New: Explaining a Long-Term Process," *Migration Policy Institute* (October 1, 2006), accessed on March 16, 2017, http://www.migrationpolicy.org/article/assimilation-models-old-and-new-explaining-long-term-process.

[6] Josephine Lowell Marr, *Douglas County: A Historical Journey* (Gunnison, CO: B & B Printers, 1983), 62-65.

[7] Eleanor Yu, "Bulgarian Americans," *Countries and their Cultures*, accessed on March 9, 2017, http://www.everyculture.com/multi/Bu-Dr/Bulgarian-Americans.html.

[8] Susan Consola Appleby, *Fading Past: The Story of Douglas County, Colorado* (Palmer Lake, CO: Filter Press, 2001), 16.

[9] Yu, "Bulgarian Americans."

Chapter 26
GETTING SICK AND STAYING ALIVE

Peggy Cummings

In 1900, the top ten causes of death in the United States were pneumonia/flu, tuberculosis, gastrointestinal infections, heart disease, stroke, kidney disease, accidents, cancer, senility, and diphtheria.[1] Medical care in Douglas County consisted of a handful of doctors and no medical facilities. Still, the few small-town doctors who served between 1900 and 1930 often made the difference between life and death.

Dr. George Everett Alexander dominated Douglas County medicine during this period. He moved to Castle Rock in 1893 and began his legendary practice. He and his wife Bessie quickly became a well-known part of the community. They were "talented and cultured musicians;"[2] and when he was not making house calls, he was umpiring in local baseball games.[3] In 1899, Dr. Alexander joined Dr. McLennan in part-time practice in Sedalia.[4] At first, he made his house-calls by horse and buggy, then on a bicycle; and finally, in his "Reo," one of the first automobiles in the County.[5]

Dr. George E. Alexander

In 1902, Dr. Alexander moved his family and medical office to the Hammar House, a large, fashionable home built out of rhyolite in 1881 by Benjamin Hammar at 203 Cantril Street in Castle Rock. It became known as "the Doctor's House" because Dr. Alexander's office occupied a room on the first floor.[6] Dr. Alexander treated all types of medical issues: A railroad employee's dislocated shoulder; a nail in the foot of a Larkspur resident; appendicitis attacks; a man knocked unconscious by a team of runaway horses; and countless childbirths. When a diphtheria epidemic hit the County, Dr. Alexander had to act fast. Since diphtheria was highly contagious and caused difficulty breathing, heart failure, and paralysis, he quarantined those infected.[7] In some cases, Dr. Alexander sent patients to Denver by train for hospital treatment. He served as County Coroner from 1923-1928.[8] Dr. Alexander's death in 1947 ended his nearly sixty-year medical career.[9] He was buried in Castle Rock's Cedar Hill Cemetery,[10] alongside many of his former patients.

Other medical personnel served Douglas County. One notable doctor was W.J. Maxwell, an honors graduate of the College of Physicians and Surgeons, Ontario, Canada. He left a successful practice in Toronto and moved to Castle Rock in 1891 to cure his tuberculosis. Despite his disease, Dr. Maxwell saw patients in Castle Rock and Sedalia. Eventually, he moved to Tucson for a drier climate but died there, leaving his wife and two children behind in Castle Rock.[11] Dr. Walter Aaron Palmer moved from Illinois to Castle Rock in 1906. He opened a practice in the City Hotel on Perry Street. He used the south wing of the building for "consultations and operating room and the remainder of the hotel as a residence." Later on, he moved his practice to a new home on Third Street and also ran an off-and-on part-time practice in Sedalia.[12] In 1946 he sold his practice and home to Dr. Charles J. Keller, the physician for the DuPont dynamite plant in Louviers.[13] Clearly, while Dr. Alexander was a constant presence in Douglas County, other doctors served too.

Most people in Douglas County lived a long way from medical care, so they had to take care of themselves. The County's drug stores sold a variety of do-it-yourself remedies. For example, Scott's Drug Store on Third Street in Castle Rock sold an "array of pharmaceutical bottles and paraphernalia [that] conjured up the images of the peddler's wagon with the magic elixirs of life, liniments, Lydia Pinkham's compound, Ayer's Sarsaparilla, salves and ointments which cured a variety of ailments."[14] Lydia Pinkham's "Vegetable Compound was a popular remedy for "female ailments."[15] It consisted of life root, unicorn root, pleurisy root, fenugreek, black cohosh, and 18% alcohol. Enormous sales here and abroad made Lydia Pinkham's company the first successful U.S. business run by a woman. So many women swore by the product that some physicians prescribed it for feminine complaints.[16]

During the worldwide outbreak of Spanish influenza in 1918-1919, an estimated 25% of soldiers in the American Expeditionary Force stationed in the U.S., England, and France were infected. Thousands died of the flu's main complication—pneumonia. In fact, as many soldiers died of the flu as died in combat.[17] The flu also spread throughout the U.S., including Colorado. At the height of the epidemic in the fall of 1918, every issue of the *Record Journal* published the names of those newly infected, along with those who had recovered or succumbed to it.[18] Advertisers claimed that taking quinine kept one from catching the disease, and the newspaper published elaborate instructions for taking care of the sick.[19] Since population density in the County was low, spreading the disease here was less likely than in more congested places like Denver, where reports of the sick numbered in the hundreds. In October 1918, the Colorado Board of Health ordered the cancellation of all public meetings until the epidemic abated. In Douglas County, schools were closed, meetings were postponed, and people in towns began wearing gauze masks to reduce the chance of infection.[20] The crisis passed: by late November/early December, communities in the County reported a dramatic decline in new flu cases.[21]

In 1928 an outbreak of rabies hit Parker and decimated its dog population. Three residents, E.P. Haskins, Homer Sandrige, and Elsie Halley were bitten by the Halleys' dog. After it tested positive for rabies, the three were transported to Denver to receive the standard treatment for rabies: a series of injections in the abdomen. Subsequently, many other dogs in Parker tested positive for rabies too and were destroyed. Fortunately, the three infected people survived.[22] In fact, Elsie lived another 73 years.

Following World War, I, the role that nurses played in Public Health dramatically increased. Mary Cole Briscoe pioneered public health nursing in Douglas County. She was born and educated in Castle Rock. After one year at what became C.S.U., she finished nurses training at Mercy Hospital School of

Nursing in Denver. Briscoe was an outstanding student and was admitted to the first national Public Health Program at the Universities of Minnesota and Washington. In 1937 she was appointed the first Douglas County Nurse by the Colorado State Board of Health.[23] She organized the Douglas County Nursing Council, whose Executive Committee was led by Dr. Alexander. Nurse Briscoe focused on public health issues and delivered talks in schools and to community groups and gave immunizations. In 1939, she married Henry A. Enderud,[24] a widower with a daughter, Bonnie. Mary practiced nursing for the rest of her life. She died in 1958.[25]

Mary Briscoe

By contemporary standards, medical practices in the early twentieth century were primitive. Today the people of Douglas County have access to hundreds of doctors, local emergency services, the latest medical technology, and four major hospitals. But back then, people did the best they could with what they had.

---

[1] Jesus Diaz, "Fascinating comparison of the top 10 causes of death in 1900 and 2010," SPLOID, http://sploid.gizmodo.com/fascinating-comparison-of-the-top-10-causes-of-death-in-1657638574

[2] "Funeral Services Held Friday for Dr. Alexander," *Record-Journal*, November 14, 1947, 1.

[3] *Castle Rock Journal,* September 30, 1904, 4.

[4] Ibid., June 2, 1899, 3.

[5] "Two New Autos in Town," *Record-Journal,* March 24, 1911, 1.

[6] Susan Consola Appleby, *Fading Past: The Story of Douglas County, Colorado* (Palmer Lake, CO: Filter Press, 2001), 26.

[7] "The Country Doctor," *Alexander Display Notation* (Castle Rock, CO: Castle Rock Museum).

[8] "List of Douglas County Coroners, 1879-1968" (Castle Rock, CO: Douglas County History Research Center, n.d.).

[9] "Dr. George E. Alexander," *Alexander Display Notation* (Castle Rock, CO: Castle Rock Museum).

[10] "Funeral Services Held Friday for Dr. Alexander."

[11] "Informational Poster: Additional Castle Rock Doctors," Douglas County History Research Center Display.

[12] "Announcement," *Record-Journal*, December 20, 1918, 8.

[13] Ibid.

[14] Josephine Lowell Marr, *Douglas County: A Historical Journey* (Gunnison, CO: B&B Printers, 1983), 174.

[15] Sammy R. Dana, *Lydia Pinkham: The Face that Launched A Thousand Ads* (Lanham, Maryland: Rowman & Littlefield, 2015), 1, 9.

[16] Belle Waring, "Commodification Meets Black Cohosh: NLM Seminar Focuses on 19th Century Patent Medicine," *NIH Record*, LVIII no.7 (April 7, 2006), https://nihrecord.nih.gov/newsletters/2006/04_07_2006/story04.htm.

[17] "Respiratory Infections in the U.S. Military: Recent Experience and Control," *Clinical Microbiology Reviews,* 28 no. 3 (July 28, 2015): 743-800, https://www.ncbi.nlm.nih.gov/pmc/articles/PMC4475643/

[18] Sample coverage: *Record-Journal*, October 11, 1918; November 8, 1918, 8; and November 15, 1918, 1.

[19] *Record-Journal*, March 21, 1919, 6; ibid., October 25, 1918, 7.

[20] "Meetings Prohibited," *Record-Journal*, October 18, 1918, 3.

[21] Ibid., December 20, 1918, 8.

[22] "Mad Dogs Cause Much Excitement in Parker Section," *Record-Journal,* January 6, 1928, 1.

[23] "Miss Mary Briscoe Will Take Position as County Nurse," *Record-Journal*, September 10, 1937, 1.

[24] *Record-Journal*, January 13, 1939, 1.

[25] "Obituary," *Douglas County News*, October 9, 1958, 3.

Chapter 27
MOTHER NATURE TAKES AIM

Larry Schlupp

In the first three decades of the 20th century, there were on average 332 farms and ranches in Douglas County.[1] Their grain, dairy, and meat products accounted for 65 percent of the County's annual revenue.[2] Agriculture made Douglas County's economy hum, but at times Mother Nature brought drought, hail, cinch bugs, and fungal rust. The farmers' tenacity and ingenuity helped blunt the impacts of Nature's fury.

The most potent weapons in Mother Nature's arsenal were drought and hail. Douglas County experienced severe droughts from 1889 to 1905 and 1920 and 1921. Many farmers resorted to dry farming techniques, which included deep plowing to conserve subsoil moisture, a large amount of cultivation, summer land fallowing, well and reservoir-supplied water irrigation, and planting drought-resistant crops such as alfalfa and Kaffir corn.[3] Because most of these methods required significant capital investments, many farmers—especially those with smaller acreage—were unable to cover such expenses. To stem small farm loss, the Congress of 1909 and 1910 passed the Enlarged Homestead Act, "giving each settler 320 acres of free land on which to build a dry-farming empire."[4] Inventive men developed unique water systems to nurture their crops: William Lambert of Lambert Orchard Company built a well-fed underground irrigation system;[5] and many ranchers such as Henry Curtis, John Lowell, John Schneider, Jacob Schutz, and James Killin built small reservoirs (farm ponds) to trap water from springs on their properties and fashioned delivery ditches to gardens and fields.

Most of these efforts were rather limited: only 76 springs, approximately 115 reservoirs, and 150 ditches were registered in Douglas County during this period.[6] Larger reservoirs serving a broader area were built by developers and Denver Water in order to create thriving agricultural areas. In the northern part of the County, the 71-mile-long High Line Canal delivered water from the

Platte River's Cheesman Reservoir. Completed in 1905, it replaced the O. J. Hill Reservoir at Westcreek.[7] In 1890 a developer built the Castlewood Canyon Reservoir in the Lake Gulch area. It served central Douglas County via the Arapahoe Ditch that flowed north into the Clark Reservoir on the County Line north of John Schweiger's ranch.[8]

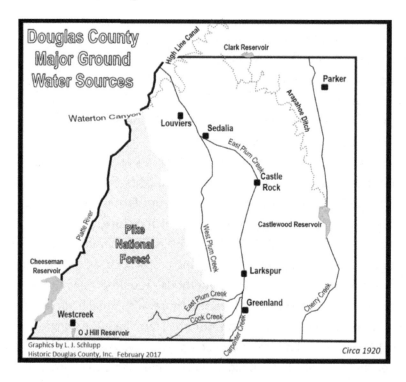

Douglas County
Major Ground
Water Sources

High Line Canal
Clark Reservoir
Parker
Arapahoe Ditch
Waterton Canyon
Louviers
Sedalia
East Plum Creek
Castle Rock
Platte River
Pike National Forest
West Plum Creek
Castlewood Reservoir
Cheeseman Reservoir
Larkspur
East Plum Creek
Cook Creek
Greenland
Cherry Creek
Westcreek
O J Hill Reservoir
Carpenter Creek
Graphics by L. J. Schlupp
Historic Douglas County, Inc. February 2017
Circa 1920

When moisture broke the relentless drought in the last half of the era, most of it came in the form of hail. Some storms brought hail stones that measured 1 to 2 inches in diameter that pummeled and destroyed crops and killed small livestock. From 1915 to 1927, major hailstorms occurred along the watersheds of both forks of Plum Creek and Cherry Creek. Sedalia, Hill Top, Cherry, Spring Valley, and the Lake Gulch areas got hammered. Especially hard-hit were farms and ranches owned by the Blunts and Kings near Sedalia; the Seidenstickers of Lake Gulch; and William Rhine of Cherry Creek Valley. In some cases, the hail measured three feet deep; but most farmers measured these storms not by the depth of hail left behind, but by the large and unrecoverable crop losses.[9]

Starting at the turn of the century, insurance companies such as Farmers' Mutual Hail of Kansas City offered crop protection policies. County farmers who had experienced hail were quick to buy policies, but they often were not paid after crop losses because many insurance companies were massively undercapitalized.[10] It was not until the latter part of the era that reliable insurance policies became available. The First National Bank of Douglas County was a leader in providing such insurance.[11] Many farmers shifted from grains to forage crops because even if damaged by hail, they could be salvaged as silage and stored in silos as feed for livestock. Frank Graves of Franktown built the first silo in Douglas County in 1897, but many others were built in the County between 1918 and 1930.[12]

Spring Valley Silo Filling

Cinch and potato bugs impacted potatoes and orchards, and rust ruined grain and row crops. Generally, such blight had little long-term impact on farm income because farmers quickly switched to crops resistant to insects and fungus, since insecticides and fungicides were not widely used. Other natural menaces included cloudbursts, cyclones, lightning, and blizzards They had less impact on crop production than drought and hail, but people and structures were at a much higher risk. From 1900 to 1930, on average one to two people were killed annually by lightning, along with more numerous ranging livestock.[13] Tornadic cyclones occurred frequently in southern Douglas County in the middle of the decade, hitting Greenland and destroying railroad structural material. Other cyclones demolished the Larkspur School, the Nanichant Inn at Perry Park, and the Sedalia firehouse.[14]

Nature's arsenal also included blizzards, many of which were dangerous to the people of Douglas County. The most notable was the 1913 blizzard that trapped Cherry School students in the schoolhouse for two days![15] As people of the land, farmers and ranchers of Douglas County realized that their livelihood often depended on forces beyond their control.

---

[1] United States Department of Agriculture, *"Census of Agriculture Historical Archive,"* Table 4: Farms, Land in Farms, Land Use, United States: 1850 to 1969, accessed January 22, 2017, http://agcensus.mannlib.cornell.edu/AgCensus/getVolumeTwoPart.do?volnum=2&year=1969&part_id=331&number=2&title=Farms:%20Number,%20Use%20of%20Land,%20Size%20of%20Farm.

[2] United States Census Bureau, *Reports and Statistics, 1900 – 1930 Overviews,"* accessed December 21, 2016, https://www.census.gov/history/www/through_the_decades/overview.

[3] "Dry Farm Factors – Two Plants Resist Drought," *Record-Journal*, August 24,1900.

[4] David J. Wishart, editor, "Dryland Farming," *Encyclopedia of the Great Plains*, accessed January 27, 2017, http://plainshumanities.unl.edu/encyclopedia/doc/egp.ag.027.

[5] Josephine Lowell Marr, *Douglas County: A Historical Journey* (Gunnison, CO: B&B Printers, 1983), 108-109.

[6] "Colorado-Water, Douglas County," accessed January 1, 2017, http://www.colorado-water.com/douglas-county.

[7] "Denver Water," accessed December 20, 2016, http://www.denverwater.org/AboutUs/History/SouthPlatteCollection.

[8] Marr, *Douglas County*, 66.

[9] "Drouth Broken," *Record-Journal*, July 11, 1913; "Hail Brings Destruction," ibid, August 6, 1915; "Rain and Hail Storm," ibid, August 15, 1919; "Hail Storm Causes Heavy Crop Loss," ibid, August 20, 1926; "Hail Damages Crops in Spring Valley," ibid, August 5, 1927.

[10] "Hail Insurance Failure," *Castle Rock Journal*, January 24, 1902.

[11] "Every Property Owner," *Record-Journal*, May 12,1922.

[12] "Pencil Points," *Castle Rock Journal*, May 25,1887.

[13] "An Experience with Lightning," *Record-Journal*, July 24, 1914; "Parker," *Castle Rock Journal*, May 24, 1902.

[14] "Perry Park," *Castle Rock Journal*, August 14, 1903; "Cloudburst at Larkspur," *Record-Journal*, July 26, 1912; "Cyclone at Larkspur," ibid; August 9, 1912; "Rain, Hail and Cyclone Visit Douglas County," ibid, August 8,1913; "Sedalia Items," ibid, December 10, 1926.

[15] "Cherry School," Douglas County History Research Center, accessed February 2, 2017, http://douglascountyhistory.org/cdm/search/searchterm/1913%20Blizzard/order/nosort.

Chapter 28
TAKING IT EASY

Joan Gandy

From the beginning, people recognized the natural beauty of Douglas County. Both residents and visitors praised its fresh air, clean water, mountain views, and unsurpassed summer weather. But the first steps in developing parts of the County for recreation did not occur until the late nineteenth century.

Nanichant Inn, Perry Park

In 1888 several Denver entrepreneurs recognized Perry Park's potential as a vacation destination. They purchased land, constructed a 20-room hotel and several vacation homes,[1] and began advertising Perry Park as "one of the most beautiful summer resorts in Colorado."[2] In July 1891, the Nanichant Inn opened for business. According to the advertisement in the *Castle Rock Journal*, the hotel was under the management of Miss Hammand.[3] She already had experience in the hospitality business, having worked in a hotel and managed a cooking school. Potential patrons were lured with the following low-key come-on: "Persons visiting this beautiful resort may be assured of satisfactory treatment by stopping at this hotel."[4]

The Inn garnered praise for its "natural attractions," "pure and sparkling water," "romantic resting place," and freedom from the "annoyances of businesses."[5] The Inn's promoters were not afraid to take on the competition—the nearby Garden of the Gods. While the Colorado Springs attraction was much better known, Perry Park had obvious advantages: "That place is entirely arid and therefore uninhabitable, while Perry Park . . . is amply provided with water, is easily accessible, and is a most enjoyable place of resort."[6] Guests could enjoy golf, horseback riding, home-cooked meals, scenic views, and beds "ready to induce healthful refreshing sleep."[7] The Nanichant Inn became a leisure destination in the fall as well as the summer. Over the Thanksgiving holiday in 1902, the Inn hosted a turkey shoot with 100 "big fat turkeys" from Nebraska. Mr. Underwood, the Inn's new manager, promised a 1-year-old horse to the person who shot the most birds. During Thanksgiving dinner, when the victims of the turkey shoot were consumed, guests could also dance to the music supplied by six members of the Schroeder orchestra.[8] Despite its popularity, the Nanichant Inn burned to the ground in the 1920s.

Even before the turn of the 20th century, resorts were being developed in the area around the South Platte River. Western Douglas County was peppered with small resorts that catered to fishermen, hikers, rock climbers, and those drawn to the mineral springs that peppered the area nearby. For example, Deane's Hotel operated as a European-style health spa thanks to its mineral spring. Eventually, Cecil Deane added a general store, bakery, and post office, and offered the usual fishing, hiking, and rock climbing.[9] A little later (1897), Stephen Decker turned his property at the junction of Trout Creek and the South Platte River into a health resort he named Daffodil. Long before he changed the resort's name to Decker's Mineral Springs and Resort, Decker was bottling and distributing water from his Lithia mineral springs whose curative powers were attested to by several Denver physicians.[10] For those less inclined to "take the waters," Decker also advertised the typical mountain activities like fishing, site-seeing, and the "healthful influence of sleeping amid the odor of the pines."[11] Decker's marketing and the variety of activities available turned his resort into a huge success. "It is amazing how

156

popular Decker's mineral springs have become in a single season. The ten or twelve cottages . . . are all occupied nearly all the time and applications for rates and information come in by the dozen in every mail. Last Sunday 91 meals were served at the resort."[12] Deckers and the other resorts in the area were easily accessible to recreation-hungry Denver residents. The Colorado & Southern railroad scheduled a regular "fish train" that transported people the twenty miles from Denver to its South Platte Station. There, vacationers took stagecoaches (later motor coaches) the remaining 10 to 15 miles to Deckers and the other resorts.[13] This was the early twentieth century's version of taking I-70 to the mountains on the weekends.

As the new century wore on, the desire for leisure in Douglas County grew. In 1915 Joe Buckman opened Woodbine Lodge in Jarre Canyon, west of Sedalia. It included a restaurant and resort cabins and offered fishing, hiking, dancing, and good eating. Fraternal organizations liked to meet there,[14] and business owners sometimes treated their employees to weekend getaways.[15] The Lodge scheduled various events to attract visitors: on July 4, 1921, the Lodge hosted bronco busting, steer riding, and picnicking.[16] During Prohibition, the Lodge added to its leisure-time offerings—booze, gambling, and prostitution.[17] For some time, evidently, DC law enforcement, which was severely understaffed, had to look the other way.

As a result of its changing emphasis, Woodbine began attracting unsavory characters during the 1920s. Two of the most controversial were Dean O'Banion and Louis "Diamond Jack" Alterie, Chicago gangsters and rivals of Johnny Torrio and Al Capone. When Diamond Jack won half-interest in the Round-Up Ranch in Jarre Canyon, he turned it into a cowboy/rancher wanna-be venue.

Diamond Jack

When in Colorado, he dressed in Western clothes, wore a big Stetson, drove around in a fancy car, and wore two .45 automatics on his hip. He turned his ranch into a playground for the mob. He arranged rodeos for his Chicago friends and took them deer hunting with Thompson submachine guns.[18] His boss O'Banion was assassinated in Chicago in 1924,[19] and Diamond Jack was involved in a shoot-out in Glenwood Springs. To avoid arrest, Diamond Jack agreed to stay out of Colorado for five years.[20] He returned to Chicago, where he was assassinated in 1935. In the 1930s, Woodbine reclaimed its family orientation. It became famous for its chicken dinners, which were served by respectable teen-aged girls from some of Douglas County's best families.[21] In the 1950s Woodbine was purchased by Baptists who turned it into a church camp; and in 2002, it became the Woodbine Ecology Center.[22]

Douglas County resorts, lodges, and mineral springs enabled residents and tourists to enjoy the natural wonders of the area. Some people came looking for rejuvenation. Others wanted to hunt or fish. More folks just wanted to have a good time as the country entered more difficult years. Douglas County businesspeople harnessed the area's beauty to fill all those needs.

---

[1] *Castle Rock Journal*, June 22, 1888, 1.

[2] "Improvements at Perry Park," ibid.

[3] *Castle Rock Journal*, July 1, 1891, 1.

[4] Ibid., 4.

[5] "Perry Park: A Beautiful Summer Resort Located Amid Many Picturesque Natural Attractions," ibid., December 21, 1900, 8.

[6] Ibid.

[7] "Lovely Perry Park," ibid., July 6, 1990, 1.

[8] "Perry Park," ibid., November 14, 1902, 8.

[9] Josephine Lowell Marr, *Douglas County: A Historical Journey* (Gunnison, CO: B&B Printers, 1983), 238.

[10] "New Summer Resort," *Castle Rock Journal*, November 26, 1897, 2.

[11] Ibid.

[12] "Mountain Echoes," *The Mountain Echo*, August 6, 1898, 1.

[13] Susan Consola Appleby, *Fading Past: The Story of Douglas County, Colorado* (Palmer Lake, CO: Filter Press, 2001), 37.

[14] "Shriners will Picnic at Woodbine Park," *Record-Journal*, September 19, 1920, 1; ibid., August 7, 1925, 8.

[15] Ibid.; ibid., September 19, 1920, 1.

[16] Ibid., July 1, 1921, 8.

[17] "The Evolving History of Woodbine," *Woodbine Ecology Center*, accessed April 7, 2017, https://woodbinecenter.org/evolving-history-woodbine, "Hottest Gambling Spot This Side of Reno Running Wide Open in Jarre Canon," *Rocky Mountain News*, August 10, 1936, 1-2.

[18] "Rodeo at Woodbine," *Record-Journal*, October 31, 1924, 1; "The Evolving History of Woodbine."

[19] "Chicago Gagster Shot; Known Here," *Record-Journal*, November 24, 1924, 1.

[20] The Castle Rock Writers, *A Photographic Journey: Douglas Country, Colorado* (Castle Rock, CO: The Douglas County Libraries Foundation, 2005), 167, 169; *Record Journal*, January 9, 1925; ibid., January 16, 1925; "The Story of Diamond Jack Alterie," *The Hotel Denver*, accessed April 7, 2017, www.thehoteldenver.com/the-story-of-diamond-jack-alterie/

[21] Castle Rock Writers, *Photographic Journey*, 169.

[22] "The Evolving History of Woodbine."

Chapter 29
GOOD POLITICS AND BAD

Tim Weber

After 1900 American politics entered the Progressive Era that expanded the role and size of government. Reform-minded Presidents Teddy Roosevelt and Woodrow Wilson dismantled business monopolies, regulated industries to ensure safety and fair treatment, and passed new laws to help working people, give women the vote, and introduce Prohibition. After World War I, however, Americans rejected reforming Progressivism for Republican conservatism.

How did Douglas County fit into this changing political scene? In the nineteenth century, the County was overwhelmingly agricultural and Republican. But starting in the 1890s it showed openness to political change. As part of the "agrarian revolt," both Colorado and the County voted for populist Democrat William Jennings Bryan in 1896 and 1900. In the second election, Bryan took 57% of the state vote but squeaked by in the County by only 8 votes.[1] In 1904 the political winds shifted again: Republican Theodore Roosevelt carried both the state and

Woodrow Wilson

County by a large margin.[2] In 1908 William Jennings Bryan won the state for the third time but lost badly in the County to Republican William Howard Taft. In the same County election, Republicans won 11 of 14 state and County offices.[3]

There was a Democratic tidal wave in 1912. Progressive Democrat Woodrow Wilson won big in both Colorado and the County, where

Democrats won races for the U.S. Senate, House of Representatives, all state contests, and 5 of 10 County positions.[4] In 1916 Wilson again carried both the state and the County, where Republicans won only 7 of 16 state and County contests.[5] But America changed dramatically by 1920. After the trauma of World War I, which took 675,000 American lives, rancorous political division over the League of Nations, and the new pressures that came with America's becoming a world power, most people abandoned the Progressive agenda and longed for simpler times. Consequently, the Republican Warren G. Harding won a landslide victory in 1920. Harding got 59% of the vote in Colorado and a big plurality in Douglas County. In addition, of the other 23 national, state, and local races on the County ballot, Republicans won 18.[6] The people had voted for "normalcy." What they got were the Roaring Twenties.

Republicans maintained power throughout the 1920s. Calvin Coolidge won a resounding victory in 1924 (57% of the Colorado vote; and almost a 4 to 1 margin in Douglas County);[7] and in 1928, Herbert Hoover won 65% of the state vote and a large majority of County votes.[8] In both elections, Republicans came close to sweeping the other state and local races. But Republican rule was not without controversy.

Herbert Hoover

Contributing to Republican power during the mid-1920s was the resurgence of the Ku Klux Klan.[9] First organized in the South after the Civil War to terrorize former slaves, the Klan was mostly defunct by 1900. After 1915, however, it experienced a comeback. Instead of spouting racist rancor, the "new Klan" promoted "100% Americanism," which it defined as a commitment to traditional Protestant values (that "old time religion"), opposition to the teaching of evolution in the schools, an emphasis on law and order to eliminate crime and corruption, and protection of the rights of native-born Americans if they were White and not Catholics or Jews. They portrayed themselves as law-abiding and God-fearing reformers. Such emphases struck a responsive chord in many places in the Midwest and West; and Klan membership grew: 5,000 in 1915, 85,000 in 1921, and over 3 million in 1925. Their goal was to make America safe for White native-born Protestants, and their strategy was to win elections. They were not averse to using violence if it served their purposes.

The Klan began organizing in Colorado in 1921 under the leadership of Grand Dragon Dr. John Galen Locke. In 1923, it supported the election of Ben Stapleton as Denver mayor, who then appointed many Klansmen to city posts, including chief of police. By then there were 17,000 dues-paying Klansmen in Denver who launched boycotts against Catholic and Jewish businesses. Klansmen then tried to infiltrate both political parties but succeeded only with the Republicans. Klan candidates swept the Republican primaries in 1924, then ran a full slate of Klansmen in the general election. They elected most of them: two U.S. Senators, a governor, lieutenant governor, secretary of state, attorney general, auditor, and justice of the state Supreme Court. Klan-dominated Republicans controlled both houses of the Colorado legislature.[10] While Douglas County voted for 8 of the 10 Klan candidates, it also elected 8 Democrats and 4 non-Klan Republicans to County offices.[11]

Klan power was short-lived. The newly elected Klansmen were political novices and easily outmaneuvered by their opponents. Governor Clarence Morley's pro-Klan legislative agenda flopped. He served only one term (1925-27), as did most of his fellow Klansmen. The Klan had been strong in Pueblo, Canon City, Walsenburg, and Trinidad; but it never gained a foothold in El Paso and Douglas Counties. Despite Klan victories in 1924, there was no record of Klan meetings, parades, cross-burnings, or intimidation in those counties. Douglas County lacked the conditions necessary for Klan success: its population was small, there was little crime, and its immigrants and Catholics were well-integrated into the community and not seen as a threat. After the 1924 election, Douglas County Democrats complained about a Klan mailing that went out two days before the vote; but County Republicans claimed that the mailing was a fraudulent attempt to discredit legitimate candidates.[12] The only public Klan event in Douglas County was a well-attended meeting in the County Court House on February 25, 1925—six months *after* the election. The *Record Journal* published two articles on the gathering, one descriptive and neutral, the other quite critical. Its author (William Dillon) accused the speaker of not telling the whole truth.[13] According to both accounts, the speaker defended Klan principles and methods, sometimes with humor; and the crowd was mostly appreciative since many Klansmen had been imported from Denver. This meeting had no discernible result. The Klan had already proved that it was inept at governing, and the Klan was unraveling after its Grand Dragon was forced to resign following a kidnapping by the Denver Klan. If there were any Klansmen in Douglas County, they operated underground and kept themselves out of the papers.

By the 1928 election, the Klan had virtually disappeared. Republican Herbert Hoover won 65% of the Colorado vote and had a 500-vote edge in the County. Of the other national and state candidates, County voters selected 8 Republicans and 1 Independent. To County offices, voters favored 6 Republicans, 5 Democrats, and 1 Independent. There was only one Klan hold-over from 1924, State Treasurer William MacGinnis, for whom County residents voted enthusiastically.[14]

For the most part, then, Douglas County followed national political trends in the early 20th century. But the optimism surrounding Herbert Hoover's election in 1928 was quickly quashed by the Stock Market Crash of 1929 and the Great Depression.

---

[1] "Official Election Results," *Castle Rock Journal*, November 16, 1900, 5.

[2] Ibid., November 11, 1904, 1; ibid., November 18, 1904, 1, 2, 7.

[3] *Record-Journal*, November 13, 1908, 4.

[4] Ibid., November 15, 1912, 4.

[5] Ibid., November 17, 1916, 4.

[6] Ibid., November 19, 1920, 10.

[7] Ibid., November 21, 1924, 2.

[8] Ibid., November 16, 1928, 8.

[9] The summary that follows relies heavily on Robert Alan Goldberg, *Hooded Empire: The Ku Klux Klan in Colorado* (Urbana, IL: University of Illinois Press, 1981).

[10] Carl Abbott, Stephen J. Leonard, and Thomas J. Noel, *Colorado: A History of the Centennial State*, 4th ed. (Boulder: University Press of Colorado, 2005), 271-278. See also James H. Davis, "Colorado Under the Klan," *Colorado Magazine*, 42, no. 2 (September, 1965): 95-108, accessed March 30, 2017,

http://www.historycolorado.org/sites/default/files/files/Researchers/ColoradoMagazine_v42n2_Spring1965.pdf.

[11] *Record-Journal*, November 21, 1924, 2.

[12] Cole Briscoe, "Democratic Editorial," ibid., November 7, 1924, 3; Walter A. Palmer, "Republican Editorial," ibid.

[13] "Speaks to a Large Audience," *Record-Journal*, February 27, 1925, 1; William Dillon, "The Ku Klux Klan Meeting," ibid.

[14] Ibid., November 16, 1928, 8.

Chapter 30

FOREST MANAGEMENT

Randal R. Johnson

As the nineteenth century faded into the twentieth, Douglas County was facing a natural resource crisis. In large part, the degradation of the forested federal lands in Douglas County was due to several Congressional Acts[1] and the fraud, theft, and corruption by some unscrupulous persons that followed.[2] Also contributing to the environmental destruction was the lack of law and policy enforcement by the Department of the Interior's General Land Office (GLO) which was charged with the management of the Public Domain.[3]

As a timber conservation measure, the Plum Creek Timber Land Reserve was established by a Presidential proclamation on June 23, 1892. It was the eighth Timber Reserve established in the U.S. and the third established in Colorado.[4] The Reserve was 278.87 square miles in size and was located wholly within the boundaries of Douglas County within the Rampart Range.[5] By 1900, of all the Federal Timber Land Reserves in the U.S., the three in Colorado—the Plum Creek, Pikes Peak, and South Platte Reserves—had received the most damage by fire and timber cutters.[6] The destruction was so extensive that only several thousand acres of merchantable timber remained in each Reserve.[7]

On August 8, 1898, Colonel W. T. S. May, a lawyer in Denver, was appointed Forestry Superintendent for the Timber Land Reserves in Colorado. On that same day, he appointed William Richard Kreutzer as the first United States Forest Ranger in the nation and assigned him to the Plum Creek Timber Preserve. Known as Billy, he was an ambitious young man with great integrity. The son of Edward and Jane Kreutzer, he was born and raised on the family homestead near Indian Creek, west of Jarre Canyon in Douglas County, and was working on the H. H. Metcalf Ranch at the time of his appointment. At the time of Kreutzer's selection, Colonel May told him, "Right now, I want you to go back to the Plum Creek Reserve, ride as far and as fast as the Almighty will let you and put out those forest fires. That will be the first duty of you rangers. Other things will follow, but, to me, there is nothing so important."[8] For over two and a half years, Billy worked on the Plum Creek Reserve fighting fires, stopping the illegal cutting of timber, and preventing grazing trespass. He was a "Nemesis on the heels of wrongdoers,"[9] bringing the rule of law to the Reserve. Billy was the beginning of the end of resource destruction in the Plum Creek Timber Land Reserve.[10]

On July 1, 1905, the U.S. Forest Service was established, replacing the Bureau of Forestry within the Department of Agriculture.[11] The early years of the U.S. Forest Service were focused on practical field forestry: fighting wildfires, timber and grazing trespass, game poaching, and

William R. Kreutzer

mapping.[12] This practical approach, along with more personnel in the field, made a difference in the lawless degradation of timber resources and overgrazing that had occurred when the Timber Land Reserves were under GLO management.[13]

Fire Tower on Devil's Head

The Pikes Peak Timber Land Reserve became the Pike National Forest on July 01, 1908.[14] Fighting wildfires continued to be a priority in the new National Forests.[15] To preserve the forest's resources, wildfires were no longer allowed to burn themselves out. Rangers were instructed to detect them early and mount a quick response. Consequently, Forest Ranger Billy Kreutzer started climbing to high elevations to look for smoke from forest fires. One of the high points he used was the Devil's Head formation, which in time became the most well-known fire lookout station in the Pike N.F. in Douglas County.[16] The first lookout station on Devil's Head was a small log cabin with a telephone, constructed in 1912. A mechanical instrument called a "fire finder" was bolted to the highest boulder next to the lookout station. It was used to determine the direction and distance of a fire from the lookout's position. A shelter cabin was built about two hundred feet below the lookout cabin. Big trees were used to construct the stairs leading up the rocks to the lookout cabin. In 1919, a ten-by-ten-foot wood and glass observatory replaced the cabin and exists to this day.[17] Helen Dowe was one of the first female fire lookouts in the Forest Service and was assigned to the Devil's Head Lookout from 1919 through 1921.[18]

Conservation practices increased in the Pike N.F. as forest science and research advanced in the U.S. and universities added forestry programs. Reforestation of the Pike N.F. for watershed protection and wood production began in earnest in 1906 with tree seedling planting. Several tree nurseries were established to grow seedlings and camps were set up for tree planters until 1917. Monitoring livestock grazing practices and enforcing grazing regulations also improved during this time.[19]

The coming of World War I placed a great strain on forest management within the Pike N.F. The personnel went off to serve in the war; and even though staffing was down, more timber harvests and heavier grazing were needed to support the war effort. Forestry research and the seedling nurseries were temporarily shut down. Grazing damage increased during this period, and reforestation efforts were halted. Despite those cutbacks, tourist traffic in the forest increased during the war and added to the drain on resources.[20]

During the 1920s, the concept of multiple-use management and the development of new forest products within the Pike N.F. were the order of the day. New management policies were developed for timber, grazing, mining, wildlife, and recreation. Conservation of wood, range, game, water, scenery, and wilderness was implemented. A successful experiment in the Pike N.F. was the selling of Christmas trees that started in 1920 and continues to the present. It encouraged private growers to develop better cutting practices and improve young Douglas-fir stands in the Forest, which brought them additional income.[21] By 1930, the Pike National Forest was largely recovered from the land abuses of the past and on its way to a more successful future.

---

[1] Anthony Godfrey, *From Prairies to Peaks: A History of the Rocky Mountain Region of the U.S. Forest Service, 1905-2012* (Washington, DC: USDA), 33.

[2] Gerald W. Williams, *The USDA Forest Service: The First Century,* revised ed. (Washington, DC: USDA Forest Service Office of Communication, 2005), 24.

[3] Len Shoemaker, "Saga of a Forest Ranger," *Pike and San Isabel National Forests, Cimarron and Comanche National Grasslands: Culture and History* (Boulder, CO: University of Colorado Press, 1958), accessed December 27, 2016, https:/www.fs.usda.gov/Internet/FSE_DOCUMENTS/stelprd38256000.doc.

[4] Lands and Realty Management Staff, *Establishment and Modification of National Forest Boundaries and National Grasslands, a Chronological Record 1891-2012* (Washington, DC: United States Department of Agriculture, Forest Service, 2012), 1.

[5] U.S. Surveyor General's Office, "Plum Creek Forest Reserve Map," *Pike and San Isabel National Forests, Cimarron and Comanche National Grasslands: Culture and History* (Boulder, CO: University of Colorado Press, 1958), accessed January 3, 2017, https://www.fs.usda.gov/Internet/FSE_DOCUMENTS/stelprdb5446242.tif.

[6] Charles D. Walcott, "Twentieth Annual Report of the United States Geological Survey, 1898-1899, Part V—Forest Reserves Annual Report 20," *USGS Publications,* accessed December 27, 2016, http://pubs.usgs.gov/ar/20-5/report.pdf., 4.

[7] Godfrey, *From Prairies to Peaks,* 39.

[8] Shoemaker, *"Saga of a Forest Ranger."*

[9] Ibid.

[10] Ibid.

[11] Williams, *The USDA Forest Service,* 17.

[12] Ibid., 18.

[13] Ibid., 19.

[14] Lands and Realty Management Staff, *Establishment and Modification of National Forest Boundaries and National Grasslands, a Chronological Record,* 1891-2012, 17.

[15] Godfrey, *From Prairies to Peaks,* 123.

[16] Shoemaker, "Saga of a Forest Ranger."

[17] Ingwal S. Horgen, "History of Pike National Forest *Pike and San Isabel National Forests, Cimarron and Comanche National Grasslands: Culture & History*, 68, accessed December 27, 2016, https://www.fs.usda.gov/Internet/FSE_DOCUMENTS/stelprdb5446198.pdf.

[18] Godfrey. *From Prairies to Peaks*, 104.

[19] Ibid., 127.

[20] Ibid., 141-142.

[21] Ibid., 152-155.

Chapter 31

THE MORPHING ECONOMY

Shaun Boyd

The period between 1900 and 1930 was a time of great economic and social change in the United States, and some of those changes affected the local communities in Douglas County as well. The County's total investment in agriculture in 1900 was around $1 million. By 1925, the value of farm operations had risen to $7.3 million; but the number of farms had declined from 457 in 1900 to 438 in 1930.[1]

Agriculture was the main industry in Douglas County for about 100 years, from its beginnings in the 1860s, through the 1960s. The Homestead Act of 1862 greatly accelerated the number of farmers in Colorado. By the early twentieth century, Douglas County's homesteads were mostly claimed. The Pike National Forest was established in 1905 from the unclaimed land on the west side of the county. The last homestead in Douglas County was awarded in 1940 to Vera Burton for an area just north of Dawson Butte, between Castle Rock and Larkspur. In fact, after 1930 there were only five homesteads issued throughout the County, in comparison to the 1,000 issued before 1930, signaling the end of the homestead era in the region. About 20% of the homesteads in Douglas County were filed after 1900.[2]

Throughout the early twentieth century, new technologies such as the invention of the tractor increased the yields of the average farm or ranch. The widespread adoption of trucks over wagons made transportation to shipping points along the railroads much cheaper. Douglas County's railroads were fully converted to standard gauge track in 1902. The rail lines in the County were critical for moving farm products, manufactured or quarried goods, and people. Between 1900 and 1930, at least 11 passenger trains per day left Castle Rock for Colorado Springs or Denver.[3] The chaos in Europe caused by World War I positively affected Western U.S. farm prices, as American products were shipped to hungry, war-torn Europeans. The federal government also set prices for wheat and other commodities that were grown in Douglas County at the time, and those prices were relatively high.[4] In fact, Douglas County's agricultural economy appeared to boom throughout the late 1910s and 1920s. The maturing banking system helped farmers during this boom period by giving out loans; but many farmers borrowed too much, which led to losses during the post-war downturn.

Even long-term changes in the weather affected the types of products that could be grown in the area. When settlers first arrived in Douglas County, the area was experiencing an unusually wet period. Scientists now believe that this type of situation is cyclical in the west, but the amount of moisture in the early twentieth century had a positive impact on people more than ever before. As can be expected, the wet period was followed by a dry one: the severe drought that produced the Dust Bowl of the 1930s.[5] In Douglas County, silos were built on farms for the first time in the 1910s; but silo construction ended in the early 1920s. They were no longer needed because, in the drier environment, farmers shifted to ranching.

Socially and politically, the Grange movement was a significant force in Douglas County. Local Granges met frequently for dances and other events, but they also advocated for political issues important to farmers at state and national levels. A pair of local Granges organized races, exhibits, and a rodeo at the Douglas County fairgrounds in September 1915, which were the first events to be scheduled at the venue since 1894.[6] The Douglas County Fair became a permanent fixture in 1918 when the County purchased the fairgrounds and planning was taken over by a County-appointed Fair Board.[7]

Between 1900 and 1930, the larger U.S. economy shifted from primarily an agriculture-based economy to a more service-based economy. In 1900, about 40% of U.S. workers were involved in agriculture. By 1930, the number had dropped to 25%. Service and manufacturing were on the rise throughout this period, from 35% and 25% in 1900 to about 50% and 30% in 1930.[8] A sign of the changing economic environment in Douglas County occurred with the closure of the rhyolite quarries in Castle Rock. This major local industry began in the 1870s and for the most part, ended by 1906.[9] At their height in the 1880s and early 1890s, the quarries had employed more than 150 people. According to the U.S. Census of 1900, only 45 people in Douglas County were employed in manufacturing. In 1904 the Silicated Brick Factory in the Roxborough area was established, which employed 27 men, a significant percentage of the manufacturing jobs in the County. In 1913 the company failed but was reorganized as the Silica Brick and Clay Company. It ceased operations in 1916. Three years later, the plant and its associated land were returned to the Helmer Family, which had originally sold the land to the company.[10]

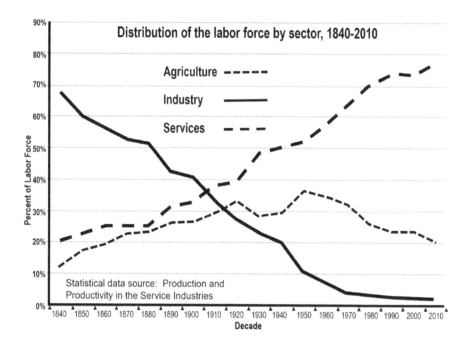

The largest expansion in manufacturing during this period was the rise of the E. I. du Pont de Nemours and Company factory at Louviers, Colorado. This plant manufactured dynamite for use in mines and infrastructure projects throughout the western United States. Louviers was laid out as a "company town" for employees, and homes were built starting in 1908.[11] Housing was based on one's position at the factory, so as one moved up in rank, the family moved to a larger house. Louviers was one of the largest employers in the county. In 1920, they had around 152 employees, drawing from both the town of Louviers and from nearby ranches. Those figures increased dramatically over the years.

Silica Brickyard and Bricks

The Carlson and Frink Creamery and the Littleton Creamery were among the first dairy companies to take advantage of the County's changing road infrastructure. Clarence Frink incorporated his Larkspur creamery in 1902 but quickly built additional creameries in El Paso and Elbert Counties, which together processed 800 pounds of milk a day.[12] When Clarence died in 1945, his company outlived him for at least another 20 years, becoming one of the main dairy distributors in Colorado.

Between 1900 and 1930, Douglas County's economy changed, but not to the same extent as other parts of the U.S. economy. Though there were increases in manufacturing and the service economy, the County remained overwhelmingly agricultural.

---

[1] Minnesota Population Center, *National Historical Geographic Information System: Version 11.0* [Database] (Minneapolis: University of Minnesota. 2016), accessed March 22, 2017, http://doi.org/10.18128/D050.V11.0.

[2] Bureau of Land Management, *Official Federal Land Records Site* (United States Department of the Interior, Bureau of Land Management), accessed March 22, 2017, https://glorecords.blm.gov/.

[3] "The D. & R. G. Timecard" and "The A. T. & S. F. Timecard," *Record-Journal,* March 4, 1910, 8.

[4] "Crops and Food Prices," *Record-Journal,* August 17, 1917, 1.

[5] Robert Kunzig, "Drying of the West," *National Geographic,* February 2008, accessed March 22, 2017, http://ngm.nationalgeographic.com/print/2008/02/drying-west/kunzig-text.

[6] "Grange Frontier Day Almost Here," *Record-Journal,* September 24, 1915, 1.

[7] "County Fair Board Organizes," ibid., July 12, 1918, 1.

[8] Robert E. Gallman and Thomas J. Weiss, "The Service Industries in the Nineteenth Century," *Production and Productivity in the Service Industries,* ed. Victor R. Fuchs (New York: Columbia University Press, 1969), 287-352, accessed March 22, 2017, https://www.minnpost.com/macro-micro-minnesota/2012/02/history-lessons-understanding-decline-manufacturing

[9] Mr. and Mrs. James Rose Harvey, "The Quarries of the Castle Rock Area," *Record- Journal,* January 7, 1949, 4.

[10] Susan Trumble, *Douglas County Register of Landmark Properties Nomination Form for the Silicated Brick Company also known as Silica Brick and Clay Company, #M106-017* (Castle Rock, CO: Douglas County, May 7, 2006), in Records of Douglas County Community Development Department, Douglas County History Research Center, accessed March 23, 2017, http://www.douglas.co.us/about-us/historic-preservation/county-landmarks/silicated-brick-company/

[11] "Louviers, Colorado: A Model for a Company Town" (Castle Rock, CO: Douglas County Repository, 2014), accessed March 23, 2017, http://www.douglas.co.us/museum/vex16/index.htm.

[12] "Larkspur Creamery" (Larkspur, CO: Larkspur Historical Society, 2009), accessed March 23, 2017, http://larkspurhistoricalsociety.org/locations/larkspur/creamery.html.

Chapter 32

LASTING LANDMARKS

Suzanne Perry

Many buildings constructed in or already built by the early twentieth century no longer exist. But a few remain important landmarks in the history of Douglas County. Among our "lasting landmarks" are the Cantril School in Castle Rock, the Charlford/Cherokee Castle in Sedalia, and the Village Club in Louviers.

The Cantril School has existed on "schoolhouse hill" in Castle Rock since 1897. It replaced a two-story wooden structure that served as the town's first schoolhouse after 1875. Cantril School, which was named after William Cantrilone of Castle Rock's early leaders,[1] was constructed of locally quarried rhyolite. It was two stories, included six classrooms, and had an imposing bell tower. Every weekday morning, its bell summoned students to school. Like its predecessor, Cantril School functioned as a "common school" with grades 1 to 8. In 1885, it added a high school curriculum. Because it was Douglas County's only high school, about half of its students came from outside Castle Rock. For practical reasons, most of them had to board with local families during the week. Because they did not live in the Castle Rock school district, they were charged $1/month for tuition. The high school occupied the entire second floor of Cantril School, with grades 1-8 on the ground floor.[2]

Castle Rock Public School - Cantril School circa 1905

Castle Rock's 350 residents found it difficult to finance a full high school curriculum. Starting in the late 1890s, a bill was introduced in the state legislature by Cole Briscoe, Douglas County's state representative, to create a County High School that all 34 County districts within the County supported, which would eliminate tuition charges for those who did not live in Castle Rock. The plan made sense to legislators and educators across the state, and the new law passed in 1900. The Douglas County High School graduated its first class of students in 1902.

The DCHS quickly outgrew its allotted space in Cantril School. In 1907 a new brick high school was built on Wilcox Street, but it burnt down in 1910. It was immediately replaced with a large rhyolite structure with all the amenities required for a first-class high school program. Cantril School continued to serve students in grades 1-8. Because it sat on a hill east of downtown, it was visible from most places in Castle Rock. In 1984, Cantril School, which was then called Castle Rock Elementary School, was officially listed on the National Register of Historic Places.[3]

Boston-born Charles A. Johnson and his wife Alice Gifford Phillips moved to Colorado in 1891. Charles was a successful real estate investor who wanted to build a summer home in Douglas County on the old Flower homestead near Sedalia, between Highway 85 and Daniels Park Road.[4] He hired his friend and noted architect Burnham Hoyt of Denver. His design eventually exceeded the Johnsons' original desire for a simple "thatched roof cottage" that they could use for weekend getaways. After numerous changes, their "cottage" became a 10,000 sq. ft. mansion modeled after a fifteenth-century Scottish castle. Hoyt promised authenticity, so he hired stonemasons from Cornwall in southwest England to build the castle according to Old World specifications, using the local rhyolite. As one might expect, the house included luxurious touches: it had 24 rooms, including 8 bedrooms, "leaded and bottle-glassed windows, four towers, gargoyles, turrets, battlements, a walled courtyard, and several chimneys."[5] Its great room measured 25x40 feet. From nearly every window, there were spectacular views of the Front Range. Construction took two years (1924-1926), during which the Johnsons toured Europe acquiring art and furniture for their new home. When they moved in, they named the castle after their two sons Charlie and Gifford—Charlford Castle.[6]

East Elevation of Charlford during Construction

The Johnson family maintained the Castle until 1954 when they sold it to "Tweet" Kimball from Tennessee. She changed the name to Cherokee Castle and Ranch and developed a cattle breeding operation that specialized in Santa Gertrudis, a breed that had never been raised in a cold climate. In the 1990s, after Cherokee Ranch had been put on the National Register of Historic Places, she sold it to Douglas County with the provision that the Ranch remain an open space and the Castle remain a museum open for various public events.[7] The Charlford/Cherokee Castle was the only rival to John Springer's Mansion in Highlands Ranch as the most imposing property in Douglas County.

The third "lasting landmark" is the Louviers Village Club. In 1907 the Du Pont Company of Delaware started construction on a powder plant for the manufacture of dynamite and nitroglycerin. Surrounding the plant Du Pont built a company town for its workers and named it Louviers, located a few miles north of Sedalia. Workers lived in company-built and –maintained homes, for which they paid from $8 to $24 a month, depending on their place in the company pecking order; sent their children to the company-built school; attended the company-built church; shopped in the company-owned store; and played in the company-owned park. In short, Du Pont took care of its own. It also supplied free electricity and maintained the lawns and roads.

Louviers Village Clubhouse 1917

The center of social activity in Louviers was the two-story, brick Village Club, whose grand opening was in October 1917.[8] The company deducted a fifty cents membership fee from everyone's monthly paycheck. The Club provided a billiard table, card room, grocery store, post office, two-lane bowling alley (the oldest in the state), a library, and a "women's talk room" upstairs. Monthly dances and free weekly movie nights were held in the large community room. The people of Louviers—and their guests from elsewhere—were well entertained. No other community in Douglas County had a facility like the Village Club.

During the 1918 Spanish influenza epidemic, the Village Club was transformed into a temporary hospital for flu victims. Starting in the 1960s Du Pont leased the Club to the town, under its Village Club Board; and in 1975 Du Pont donated the Club to Douglas County. Since then, the Club has housed a branch of the Douglas County Library, a gym, a reception hall, and a kitchen. On September 20, 1995, the Louviers Village Club was placed on the National Register of Historic Places.[9] For over a hundred years, the Village Club has served as the heart of the Louviers community.[10]

---

[1] Susan Consola Appleby, *Fading Past: The Story of Douglas County, Colorado* (Palmer Lake, CO: Filter Press, 2001), 20.

[2] Josephine Lowell Marr, *Douglas County: A Historical Journey* (Gunnison, CO: B & B Printers, 1983), 145-148.

[3] "Castle Rock Elementary School," National and State Register of Historic Places: Douglas County, *History Colorado*, accessed April 6, 2017, http://www.historycolorado.org/oahp/douglas-county.

[4] Marr, *Douglas County*, 110-111; "Wonder House on Promontory Near Sedalia Realizes Daydream of Denver Business Man," *Rocky Mountain News*, August 29, 1926.

[5] Appleby, *Fading Past*, 170-171.

[6] The Castle Rock Writers, *A Photographic Journey, Douglas County, Colorado* (Castle Rock, CO: The Douglas County Libraries Foundation, 2005), 64-65.

[7] Appleby, *Fading Past*, 171.

[8] "Louviers Club to Have Opening," *Record-Journal*, October 12, 1917, 1.

[9] Appleby, *Fading Past*, 122.

[10] Elizabeth Hernandez, "Louviers Village Club remains heart of community for more than 100 years," *Denver Post*, January 15, 2015, accessed April 7, 2017, http://www.denverpost.com/2015/01/13/louviers-village-club-remains-heart-of-community-for-more-than-100-years/

Chapter 33
NOTABLE PEOPLE

Shaun Boyd and Tim Weber

In the early twentieth century, people contributed to the Douglas County community in different ways: through politics, generous donations, and the simple act of operating a telephone switchboard.

Elias Ammons was the first Colorado governor from Douglas County. He was born in 1860 in North Carolina and came to Colorado with his family in 1871. As a young teen, he worked a variety of jobs before starting school as a 14-year-old fourth grader. He graduated from Denver (now) East High School six years later. After five years as a reporter and editor at the *Denver Times*, he partnered with his editor Thomas Dawson to start the Oxyoke Ranch in western Douglas County.[1] As managing partner, Ammons made the ranch a huge success and became a founder of the Colorado Cattle and Horse Growers' Association and the National Western Stock Show.[2]

Elias Ammons

In 1889 he married Elizabeth Fleming, with whom he had five children. The next year he started his political career. He became Clerk of the District Court in Castle Rock then served the County as a Republican in the Colorado House from 1891 to 1894, his last two years as Speaker.[3] Later he was elected as a Democrat to the State Senate (1899-1902).[4] After two unsuccessful runs for Lieutenant Governor (1904, 1906), he was elected Governor in 1912.[5] He served one term (1913-1915) during which he championed school and tax reform, new road construction, new banking and insurance laws, a state park system, support for agriculture, an eight-hour work day, minimum salaries for teachers, and the like. He was an energetic and productive reformer.

Ammons' involvement in the Ludlow Massacre (1914) ruined his political career.[6] Coal miners in southern Colorado went on strike, then constructed a tent-city in defiance of the mine owners. When the strike dragged on and grew violent, Ammons ordered in the Colorado National Guard; and President Wilson sent in Federal troops. In the ensuing conflict, 19 people died, including 11 children. When his term was up, he had no choice but to return to private life. Ammons got involved in many civic causes including the Denver and Douglas County School Boards and became president of the Farmers Insurance Company. He died in 1925, twelve years before his son Teller also became Colorado governor (1937-1939).[7]

Florence Martin was born on Christmas Day, 1867 in Sydney, Australia to a politically connected and wealthy family.[8] Florence attended the University of Sydney where she studied physics and became a re-search assistant, which was rare for a woman of the time.[9] In around 1904, she became fast friends with William C. Daniels, one of the young owners of the Daniels & Fisher Department Store in Denver, and his fiancé Cecily Banner, who arrived in Australia before Daniels left for a year-long scientific expedition to New Guinea. Cecily needed a place to stay in his absence while he went to New Guinea on a year-

Daniels and Fisher Tower

long scientific expedition.[10] In his absence, Cecily stayed in Florence's large home. After William returned, he and Cecily were married in 1907.[11] The three friends then left together on a world tour that lasted until 1914, which included a buying expedition to bring exotic products to the Denver store.

William and Cecily both died of the Spanish influenza epidemic of 1918 and left their estate to Florence.[12] "Miss Martin" thus became part owner of the department store and moved to Colorado to take care of her new business responsibilities. She bought a beautiful ranch in northern Douglas County in 1920, built a "summer home," and became involved in civic and arts organizations, including the Denver Civic Theater and the Denver Art Museum.[13] Her ranch employed many people, and the Round Top School was built there to accommodate the children of her employees.[14] She was uncommonly brave. While at home alone, Miss Martin was the victim of a home invasion, which she repelled by talking to the criminals while her chauffeur drove down to Sedalia to call the sheriff.[15] Between 1920 and 1937, Miss Martin donated her ranch to the Denver Mountain Parks system, the only one in Douglas County. Today it is known as Daniels Park, named for the friends who changed her life.[16] She died in 1956. All that remains of the store, which once covered a city block on 16th Street in Denver, is the Daniels & Fisher Tower, modeled after the campanile at St. Mark's in Venice.[17]

Helen Josephine "Josie" Doepke was born June 3, 1878, in the Lake Gulch region of southeast Castle Rock, the oldest child of a German Catholic immigrant family. Her early years were spent among German-speaking immigrants and their American-born children. She lived almost all her life on or near the Twin Creek Ranch or in Castle Rock.[18] Josie attended the Lake Gulch School, which was built at the urging of her father, Fred Doepke, and

Helen "Josie" Doepke

the wooden Castle Rock School, from which she graduated (8th grade) just before it burned down in 1896.[19]

187

Miss Doepke's life seemed typical for a young woman in Douglas County at the turn of the twentieth century: attending parties with other young people, visiting neighbors with her mother and friends, participating in community organizations, and helping out on the ranch.[20] Josie never married. After her parents died, she continued to live on the ranch and acted as senior advisor to her three younger brothers in its development.

She found her own path by acting as secretary of the local school board that her father had once served as President, participating as an election judge, and remaining active in St. Francis of Assisi Catholic Church and the Cherry Homemakers Club. It appears that Josie left the ranch briefly to try out her own homestead with one of her brothers in Weld County around 1911, but she was back in Douglas County by the end of 1912.[21] Josie's father was one of the early adopters of the telephone from the Elbert exchange in 1904. Josie and her mother shared duties as operators at the switchboard set up in their ranch house. When her mother Anna died in 1929, Josie continued as the sole operator into the1950s. In that way, she provided a valuable service that kept her neighbors well connected: for years every telephone call made in the local exchange came through her switchboard, for which she kept detailed records.[22] She passed away in 1956 at the age of 77.

All kinds of people made a difference in Douglas County: A newspaperman-turned cattleman who served the County in the state legislature and became governor; an Australian immigrant who used her fortune in various causes and gave the people of DC and Denver the gift of Daniels Park; and the daughter of immigrants who connected with everyone in her community by becoming a telephone operator, well-known by her neighbors and fellow townspeople.

---

[1] Elias Ammons, "A Tribute to Thomas F. Dawson," *The Colorado Magazine*, vol. 1, no. 1 (November 1923).

[2] Wilbur Fish Stone, ed., "Hon. Elias Milton Ammons," *History of Colorado*, vol. 2 (Chicago: S.J. Clarke Publishing, 1918), 32, 34-38, accessed March 15, 2017, http://files.usgwarchives.net/co/denver/bios/ammonsem.txt

[3] *Castle Rock Journal*, November 12, 1890, 1.

[4] Ibid., November 16, 1892, 1; ibid., November 18, 1898, 2; Ibid., November 14, 1902, 5.

[5] Ibid., November 15, 1912.

[6] Carl Abbott, Stephen J. Leonard, Thomas J. Noel, *Colorado: A History of the Centennial State*, 4th ed. (Boulder: University Press of Colorado, 2005), 147-153.

[7] "Succumbs After Long Illness," *Record-Journal*, May 22, 1925, 1, 4.

[8] G.J. McCarthy, "Biographical Entry for Martin, Florence (1867-1957)," *Encyclopedia of Australian Science,* 20 Oct 1993, accessed March 31, 2017, http://www.eoas.info/biogs/P001282b.htm

[9] Ibid.

[10] "Denver Explorer," *Silver Cliff Rustler*, January 4, 1905, 3.

[11] R.W. Home, "Martin, Florence (1867-1957)," *Australian Dictionary of Biography* (National Centre of Biography, Australian National University), accessed April 1, 2017, http://adb.anu.edu.au/biography/martin-florence-7504/text13085.

[12] "Cecily Banner Daniels," *Creede Candle*, November 2, 1918, 4; "Denver Woman Buys Summer Home Site in Douglas County, *"Record-Journal,* January 16, 1920, 1.

[13] "Denver Woman Buys Summer Home Site in Douglas County, *"Record-Journal,* January 16, 1920, 1.

[14] Sarah Gleason, *I'd Do It Again: Teaching in Colorado for Over Half a Century* (Colorado Springs: Century One Press, 1982); "She Defied Bandit Trio," *Carbondale Chronicle* (Leadville, CO), April 24, 1922.

[15] Ibid.

[16] "Daniels Park," *Denver Mountain Parks,* accessed March 31, 2017, https://denvermountainparks.wordpress.com/daniels-park-history/

[17] Deb Stanley, "Secrets of Colorado: Go Inside the Daniels and Fisher Clocktower on the 16th Street Mall in Denver," accessed March 31, 2017, http://www.thedenverchannel.com/news/front-range/denver/secrets-of-colorado-go-inside-the-daniels-and-fisher-clocktower-on-the-16th-street-mall-in-denver.

[18] "Obituary," *Douglas County News*, March 22, 1956, 8.

[19] "Graduation Exercises," *Castle Rock Journal*, April 22, 1896, 4.

[20] "Lake Gulch," ibid., April 24, 1903, 1.

[21] "Miss Josie Doepke," *Record-Journal*, July 14, 1911, 5. Note: no Doepkes appear on the Homestead records at the General Land Office outside of Douglas County. This was likely a reference to her purchasing a ranch that had once been a homestead.

[22] "Helen Josephine Doepke, *Lake Gulch-Twin Creek Area Phone Records, 1905-1950*, Douglas County History Research Center (Castle Rock, CO, 2010), 1992.001.0012, accessed April 12, 2017, http://douglascountyhistory.org/cdm/compoundobject/collection/collguides/id/23/rec/4.

PART FOUR

ON THE VERGE OF CHANGE, 1930-1960

Chapter 34

THE GREAT DEPRESSION AND THE CIVILIAN CONSERVATION CORPS

Susan Rocco-McKeel

After the stock market crash of 1929, severe unemployment and natural disasters plagued Douglas County throughout the 1930s. The Dust Bowl ravaged Colorado's eastern plains by blowing topsoil miles away. The Great Depression exacerbated the struggle of ranchers and farmers who were reeling from the deflated prices and debt accrued during a period of over-production in World War I. These conditions brought declining prices for produce and land, the decrease of available credit, the calling in of loans, and foreclosures on property.[1] For many, hardship and sacrifice became the new reality after the prosperity of the 1920s. Extreme measures were needed to relieve the toll on people and their livelihoods. Experimental legislation and programs initiated by local, state, and federal governments left a notable legacy.

Livestock prices fell further during the Depression. In the 1930s, Douglas County was mostly ranchland[2] with incomes based on crops, dairy, and livestock.[3] In Colorado, hogs sold for $12.10 in 1929 and $3.10 in 1933. Potatoes once selling at $1.40 a bushel dropped to 24¢ in 1932.[4] Colorado State University (CSU) developed drought-resistant varieties of wheat, corn, and other crops.[5] Bill Noe of Larkspur, a grandson of Eagle Mountain Ranch owner Isaac Noe, recalls stories of ranch foreclosures and that CSU experimentation at Eastonville near Larkspur determined that winter wheat could grow in an area once dominated by turnips and potatoes. CSU also assisted the farmers in growing grains because horses did better on them than on plain grass.[6]

Douglas County banks suffered as well. Sixty-six of Colorado's 237 banks failed during the Depression.[7] In 1932, the Castle Rock State Bank closed its doors due to market conditions.[8] Eventually, the federal government declared a "bank holiday" to determine which institutions had enough capital to survive and created the Federal Deposit Insurance Corporation (FDIC) to insure the deposits of those that did.[9]

Elected in 1932, President Franklin D. Roosevelt (FDR) launched the New Deal, a succession of experimental programs and legislation aimed at relieving those suffering from poverty and unemployment. These programs addressed a wide range of issues including banking, child labor, unemployment, conservation, and agriculture.[10] For example, the Agricultural Adjustment Act of 1933 paid farmers to decrease the production of crops and animals.[11]

The Works Progress Administration (WPA) hired men from Douglas County relief rolls to build new bridges in response to flooding.[12] The WPA also employed women to work on various sewing projects, thus providing badly needed income for impoverished families.[13] WPA workers also installed curb and gutters on Wilcox Street in Castle Rock.[14] In 1936 WPA workers designed and constructed Castle Rock's iconic Star which the town's Volunteer Fire Department installed. George P. Stewart sold the prominent rock and surrounding land to the town for a token amount. Laurie Marr Wasmund's mom, Willa (Scott) Marr, and Willard Monk (8th graders) sang at the first Castle Rock Starlighting Service."[15] Every year at Thanksgiving the Star was lit for the holiday season. The WPA was terminated after the start of World War II when close to full employment was achieved.

Christmas Star over Castle Rock 1940

193

Colorado ranked tenth out of forty-eight states in per capita expenditures from New Deal agencies. To receive such government grants, states were required to make their own contributions. In order to comply, Colorado passed sales and income tax legislation.[16] In 1933, it also appropriated funds to buy cattle to feed those in need[17] and earmarked a 2% sales tax for public relief.[18] Colorado amended its Constitution in 1936 to provide pensions for elderly citizens in need, using money from taxes on the sale of liquor and liquor license fees.[19] The same year the State voted its first individual and corporate income tax with the initial proceeds going to public education.[20]

Despite the Depression, County people enjoyed themselves by playing cards, engaging in turkey shoots, and organizing box socials. Louise Beeman Hier and Florence Campbell Beeman recalled "canned music" from a record player brought to the Grange Hall on Saturday nights for dances that charged a fifty-cent entrance fee.[21] Local activities were plentiful: In April 1938, there was a track meet for County schools,[22] a County music festival,[23] a dance at Franktown sponsored by the American Legion,[24] and a Mother-Daughter Tea put on by the Hilltop Social Club.[25]

The County's population did not grow during the Depression,[26] but the people of Douglas County worked to update their schools. County taxpayers voted for bond issues that matched federal dollars to improve the Douglas County High School building. It was the County's only high school at the time.[27] Its graduating classes numbered between 20 and 33 students during the 1930s.[28]

With 54% of the nation's young men between the ages of 17-25 out of work or under-employed, in 1933 FDR created the Civilian Conservation Corps (CCC) to put young, inexperienced, and unemployed men to work.[29] Unlike the WPA which worked with local governments to hire local people for local projects, the CCC was an operation of the federal government, under the direction of the U.S. Army.[30] The young men in the program received food, clothing, and housing, plus $30 a month, most of which the men were required to send home to their families.[31] Ninety percent of the men took classes offered on a variety of subjects. In nine years, the CCC taught 40,000 illiterate men to read.[32]

In 1934, a CCC camp was established in McMurdo Gulch, northeast of Castle Rock. The camp had five barracks, a recreation hall, a mess hall, a headquarters building, a latrine, and a washroom.[33] It accommodated about 130 young men. In the beginning, most of them were from Colorado, including 11 from nearby Castle Rock. But over time, the camp's population changed. Initially, the men worked on flood control projects around Franktown, especially those caused by the 1935 flood there.[34] Later on, the emphasis shifted from erosion control to fire fighting[35] and soil conservation.[36] CCC workers dug diversion ditches, built earth-filled dams to help farmers retain water, fought grasshopper plagues, and the like.[37]

Civilian Conservation Corp SCS-7-C 1938

By 1939, farmers were working with the CCC on soil conservation. They built terraces on 196 acres, adopted flexible crop systems on 1,561 acres, and used contour tillage methods. Ranchers cut contour furrows on 19,075 acres, constructed 63 stock water ponds, developed springs, distributed grazing more effectively, and planted 2,000 black locust trees for gully control.[38]

The CCC camp became an important part of the Douglas County community. The CCC boys sponsored dances at the camp, fielded basketball and baseball teams to play against the locals, and were appreciated by County residents.[39] But by 1941, enlistments and appropriations were way down. On July 1, 1941, the Castle Rock CCC camp was closed, along with 263 other camps around the country. By then young men were enlisting in the Army, Navy, and Marines in anticipation of the coming war. In 1943, a public auction sold off what remained of the camp.[40]

Out of the economic difficulties, Douglas County gained a legacy of a reshaped landscape. While federal programs helped the country recover from the Great Depression, the nation did not fully rebound until WW II, when many people from Douglas County joined the Armed Forces and others raised cattle and grew crops to feed them.

---

[1] Alvin T. Steinal, *History of Agriculture in Colorado: A Chronological Record of Progress in the Development of General Farming, Livestock Production and Agricultural Education and Investigations of the Western Border of the Great Plains and in the Mountains of Colorado 1858-1926* (Ft. Collins: State Board of Agriculture, 1926), 498.

[2] Thomas J. Noel and Debra B. Faulkner, *Colorado: An Illustrated History of the Highest State* (Sun Valley, CA: American Historical Press, 2006), 110.

[3] Bill Noe, Interview by Susan Rocco-McKeel and Alice Aldridge-Dennis, Larkspur, February 6, 2014.

[4] Carl Ubbelohde, Maxine Benson and Duane Smith, *A Colorado History*, 8th ed. (Boulder: Pruett Publishing, 2001), 298-299.

[5] Noel, *Colorado: The Highest State*, 234.

[6] Noe, Interview.

[7] Noel, *Colorado: The Highest State*, 231.

[8] "Directors Close Castle Rock State Bank," *Record-Journal*, November 4, 1932, 1.

[9] Noel, *Colorado: The Highest State*, 231.

[10] PBS, "American Experience, The New Deal," accessed February 13, 2014, www.pbs.org/wgbh/americanexperience.org.

[11] Richard N. Ellis and Duane A. Smith, *Colorado: A History in Photographs* (Niwot: University Press of Colorado, 1991), 121.

[12] "WPA Workers Finish Bridge Projects; Total Cost, $38,065.46," *Record-Journal*, May 8, 1936,1.

[13] "WPA Sewing Project Ladies Honor Mrs. Prescott," *Record-Journal*, May 8, 1936, 1.

[14] "Castle Rock Streets Are Being Improved by W.P.A. Workers," *Record-Journal*, June 12, 1936, 1.

[15] Laurie Marr Wasmund, Interview with Alice Aldridge-Dennis, Castle Rock, March 19, 2014.

[16] Ellis and Smith, *Colorado: A History in Photographs*, 122.

[17] Ubbelohde, *A Colorado History*, 301.

[18] Leroy Hafen and Ann Hafen, *The Colorado Story: A History of Your State and Mine* (Denver: The Old West Publishing Co., 1953), 333.

[19] Ubbbelohde, *A Colorado History*, 301.

[20] Ibid., 315.

[21] Louise Beeman Hier and Florence Campbell Beeman, Oral History Interview (Douglas County History Research Center, 2001), accessed March 20, 2018, douglascountyhistory.org.

[22] "Douglas County Schools Will Hold Track Meet Today," *Record-Journal*, April 22, 1938, 1.

[23] "County School Music Festival Will Be Held Next Friday," *Record-Journal*, April 22, 1938, 1.

[24] "American Legion Will Give Dance at Franktown," *Record-Journal*, April 22, 1938, 1.

[25] "Hill Top Social Club Met at Home of Mrs. Nancy Walden," *Record-Journal*, April 22, 1938, 1.

[26] "Colorado Schools Decrease While Pupils on Increase," *Record-Journal*, May 25, 1923, 4.

[27] "Taxpayers Vote Bond Issue for High School Improvement," *Record-Journal*, May 8, 1936.

[28] "Douglas County High School Graduation by Year 1899-1964," Douglas County History Resource Center, accessed March 3, 2014, www.douglascountyhistory.org.

[29] Douglas County Television, *Landmarks,* 2nd ed., DVD (2001-2009), www.TheNetworkDC.us.

[30] *Civilian Conservation Corps Legacy*, accessed December 10, 2013, www.ccclegacy.org; see also *Record-Journal*, September 28, 1934, 1.

[31] Ibid.

[32] Ibid.

[33] L.A. Greyre and C.N. Alleger (supervised by the Commanding Officer of the Littleton District), *History of the Conservation Corps in Colorado: That the Work of Young America May Be Recorded* (Denver: Press of the Western Newspaper Union, no date), 2.

[34] "CCC Brief History."

[35] "Fire-Fighting Cooperation," *Record-Journal*, July 21, 1939, 1.

[36] K. J. Kelmick, "Work of CCC Boys in Elimination of Soil Erosion," *Record-Journal*, December 7, 1934.

[37] *Landmarks*, 2nd ed., DVD.

[38] "Many Ranchers are Cooperating with CCC Camp," *Record-Journal*, January 13, 1939, 1.

[39] *Record-Journal*, July 5, 1940, 1.

[40] "Looks Like We'll Lose Our CCC Camp," *Record-Journal*, June 27, 1941, 1; *Record-Journal*, June 4, 1943, 1, 5.

Chapter 35

THE POLITICAL PENDULUM

Tim Weber

What were politics in Douglas County like in the 1930s, 1940s, and 1950s? While the people of Douglas County did follow national trends, they never departed for long from their basic Republican orientation. When they voted at the state and local level, however, party affiliation seemed to be less important. In short, voters in DC often crossed party lines to support people they knew and liked.

In the seven presidential elections during this period, the people of DC voted Republican five times and Democratic two times. In the four national elections won by Franklin D. Roosevelt, he took DC and Colorado in 1932 and 1936. But in 1940 and 1944, the Republican candidates beat him decisively in Douglas County: Wendell Wilke won by 24% and Thomas Dewey by 32%. In the same years, the two Republicans also won state-wide, but by a narrower margin. In Harry Truman's surprise national victory over Thomas Dewey in 1948, the voters of DC gave Dewey a 12% edge, though Colorado gave him only a 5% victory. In the 1950s, DC and Colorado voters gave Dwight Eisenhower landslide wins over Adlai Stevenson. In 1952 Ike had a 38% advantage in the County; and in 1956, he had a 36% margin.

Douglas County Votes in Presidential Elections. 1932-1956					
Year	**Republicans**		**Democrats**		
1932	43%	Hoover (836)	55%	Roosevelt	(1061)
1936	46%	Landon (895)	54%	Roosevelt	(1046)
1940	62%	Wilke (1298)	38%	Roosevelt	(801)
1944	66%	Dewey (1214)	34%	Roosevelt	(638)
1948	56%	Dewey (979)	44%	Truman	(767)
1952	**69%**	**Eisenhower (1427)**	31%	Stevenson	(637)
1956	**68%**	**Eisenhower (1508)**	32%	Stevenson	(697)
County Winners: Republicans=5 Democrats=2					
Research and chart by Tim Weber		**Bold=National Winners**			

At the state and county levels, results were often quite different. In the first Roosevelt landslide of 1932, DC voters elected eight Democrats and seven Republicans to County offices. For state-wide offices, they voted for nine Republicans and six Democrats.[1] But in FDR's second landslide in 1936, Democrats came close to sweeping both County and State-wide races. At the County level, Democrats won eighteen of twenty-two contests. For national and state offices, Democrats took twelve of fourteen races. It was nearly a complete blowout.[2]

Franklin Delano Roosevelt

One of the winners in the 1936 landslide was Teller Ammons, the Democratic candidate for governor. He was a 1912 graduate of DCHS and the son of former governor Elias Ammons (1913-1915). Despite these local connections, in DC he beat his Republican opponent by only 55 votes.[3]

Two years later, in the mid-term election of 1938, the political pendulum started swinging in the other direction. Ammons ran for re-election in 1938, but he lost to Republican Ralph L. Carr by 301 votes in DC and 50,000 votes state-wide. DC voted for ten Republicans and four Democrats for national and state offices, but for County offices, they elected ten Democrats and five Republicans.[4]

By 1940, DC Republicans were clearly in charge. Republican Presidential candidate Wendell Wilke defeated FDR in DC with 61.6% of the vote and in Colorado with 51%, but FDR won the national election by 10%. Colorado's two Democratic but anti-Roosevelt U.S. Senators, Alva Adams and Edwin Johnson, supported Wilke in the election.[5] Both County and Colorado results supported the re-election of Governor Ralph Carr. In the DC election, Republicans won nine of the national and state races; and the Democrats won three. At the County level, the Democrats edged passed Republicans nine to eight.[6]

In the DC mid-term election of 1942, DC Republicans won all sixteen of the national and state-wide races. But in the County contests, they split evenly with the Democrats, each side winning seven offices. One of the most interesting stories in this election was the U.S. Senate race between Governor Ralph Carr and the incumbent Democrat Senator Edwin Johnson. Carr defeated Johnson in DC by 161 votes but lost in the state-wide election by fewer than 4,000 votes.[7] Carr remained in the governor's office until 1943, but his 1942 campaign turned out to be his last. Before he entered politics, Carr was a highly respected lawyer who became U.S. Attorney for Colorado. In his first days as governor, he saved Colorado from imminent bankruptcy and then consistently opposed New Deal bureaucracy. He was financially conservative and socially progressive. When FDR issued Executive Order 9066 in February 1942 to send people of Japanese descent to internment camps, Carr was one of the few American politicians to defend them on humanitarian and constitutional grounds. When an internment camp was built in Amache, near Granada in southeastern Colorado, he did what he could to support the people living there. Such actions were very controversial and probably contributed to his loss in 1942 mid-term.[8] Nevertheless, the people of DC gave him a narrow victory in his last election.

In FDR's run for a fourth term in 1944, he received 53% of the votes in the general election. In DC he made his poorest showing. The Republican Thomas Dewey beat him 66% to 34%. Republicans won all thirteen national and state-wide offices and eight of eleven County contests.[9] The three winning Democrats were often the "exception to the rule" of Republican dominance: Charles Prescott, County Clerk and Recorder (1937-1971);[10] Robert T. Jones, County Treasurer (1933-1947);[11] and C. Douglas Andrews, County Coroner (1941-1970).[12] Andrews had an advantage over other candidates: he was a successful funeral director in Castle Rock and owned a florist shop. Sooner or later, he got to know nearly everyone in the County. No matter how the political winds were blowing, these three Democrats got elected over and over. The Republican with the greatest electoral longevity was John Hammond, who served as Sheriff from 1947 to 1970.[13]

In 1948 Democrat Harry Truman upset Thomas Dewey by 5% in both the national and Colorado elections. But in DC, Dewey beat Truman 56% to 44%. Republicans also won twelve of fourteen national and state races and six of ten County contests.[14] Republican power was firmly established in the County, but its dominance was about to become even greater.

The Republicans dominated national and DC politics in the 1950s. In 1952 Republican Dwight D. Eisenhower (Ike) defeated Adlai Stevenson 55% to 44% in the general election, but in Colorado, Ike won 60% to 39%. In DC, Ike crushed Stevenson 69% to 31%. Republicans took all fifteen national and state-wide races; but at the County level, voters elected five Republicans and five Democrats.[15] In 1956 Ike defeated Stevenson 47% to 42% in the general election and 59% to 40% in Colorado. In the County, Ike beat Stevenson 68% to 32%; and Republicans

Dwight David Eisenhower

swept ten of twelve national and state races. At the County level, the voters split: seven Republicans and five Democrats.[16] In the 1958 mid-term, Republicans won ten of thirteen state contests and six of nine County offices.[17]

Political patterns were set early and continued for decades. During the early years of the Depression, voters in Douglas County broke with tradition and strongly supported FDR's efforts to pull the country out of a financial crisis. But after two terms of FDR and the Democrats, DC reverted to its historic Republican ways. In the next five presidential races, its voters supported Republican candidates, often by huge margins. They also overwhelmingly chose Republican candidates for state offices. But voters were remarkably even-handed when it came to County elections. Though Republican sentiments were strong there too, Democratic candidates were often elected and re-elected for many terms. At the local level, then, DC voters knew the candidates well and preferred the person over the party.

[1] "Democrats and Republicans Divide County Offices," *Record-Journal*, November 11, 1932, 1; "Official Returns," *The Record Journal*, November 18, 1932, 1.

[2] "Final Election Returns for Douglas County," *Record-Journal*, November 13, 1936, 1.

[3] Ibid.

[4] "Republican Make Gains in the Election on Tuesday, *Record-Journal*, November 11, 1938, 1, 4; "The Douglas County Vote," *Record-Journal*, November 11, 1938, 1.

[5] Carl Ubbelohde, Maxine Benson, and Duane Smith, *A Colorado History*, 9th ed. (Boulder: Pruett, 2006), 302.

[6] "Democrats Win in Nation, Colorado Goes Republican," *Record-Journal*, November 8, 1940, 1.

[7] "Republicans Win Big Victories in Election, Tuesday," *Record-Journal*, November 6, 1942, 1.

[8] "Ralph Carr," *Colorado Encyclopedia*, accessed on April 11, 2018, https://coloradoencyclopedia.org/article/ralph-carr.

[9] "Large Vote Registered in General Election," *Record-Journal*, November 10, 1944, 1.

[10] *Record-Journal*, November 13, 1936, 1; ibid., "Charles Prescott to Retire: Flowers to Come First Now," *Douglas County News*, July 2, 1970, 13.

[11] "Democrats and GOP Divide County Offices, *Record-Journal*, November 11, 1932, 1; "GOP Capture Most Offices in General Election," *Record-Journal*, November 8, 1946, 1.

[12] "C. Douglas Andrews Takes Office As County Coroner," *Record-Journal*, January 24, 1941, 1; his last election was in 1968: *Record-Journal*, November 7, 1968, 2.

[13] "GOP Capture Most Offices." *Douglas County News*, November 5, 1970, 8.

[14] "List of Nominations," *The Record-Journal*, October 22, 1948, 2; "General Election Returns in County," *Record-Journal*, November 5, 1948, 1.

[15] "Douglas Co. Voters Favor Republican Dwight Eisenhower by 956 to 378," *Douglas County News*, November 6, 1952, 1, 4. State of Colorado, *Abstract of Votes Cast . . . the General Election Held on the Fourth Day of November, A.D. 1952*, 1C.

[16] "Douglas County Gives Big Majority to Republicans on State, National Level," *Douglas County News*, November 8, 1956, 1.

[17] "Warren Christensen is New County Commissioner," *Douglas County News*, November 6, 1958, 1.

Chapter 36
LOOKING FOR WATER

Steve Boand

Water is key to life in the arid west. But far too often there is far too little or too much. Between 1930 and 1960, Douglas County saw drought, floods, and the beginning of population growth. During this period, the County population increased by 38% from approximately 3,500 to nearly 5,000 residents.[1] The Town of Castle Rock saw its population increase by more than 140% to 1,152 people.[2] People needed water, and Castle Rock improved the Town's water facilities in the 1920s to meet the demands of a growing community.

Water in Douglas County is the story of floods and drought. It is the same across most of Colorado where there is infrequently an average year. The "average" is made up of extremes at both ends of the water spectrum. Average precipitation years occur between 2% and 6% of the time.[3] With those reference points in mind, precipitation across the County ranges from slightly over 18 inches per year in the foothills and Palmer Divide downward to slightly more than thirteen inches northeast of Parker.[4]

The 1930s were very dry. Colorado experienced a decade of drought, and it was the "most widespread" and "long-lasting drought in Colorado recorded history."[5] The drought was severe between 1930 and 1932.[6] Rains returned in the summers of 1933 and 1938; but severe drought occurred in 1934, 1937, and 1939.[7] From 1930-1932 and again in 1937 and 1939, precipitation in north central Douglas County at the Kassler weather station was just over 12 inches annually.[8]

The 1890s and 1900s brought great strides in reservoir construction in Colorado. During this period, more than four hundred new reservoirs of various sizes were built.[9] A plan to water a large proposed agricultural development project began with the construction of Castlewood Canyon in 1889.[10] Waters of the upper reaches of Cherry Creek were captured in this new reservoir which had a capacity of approximately 5,300 acre-feet.[11]

Castlewood Dam before the Flood.
Note the water leaking from the dam in the center and to the right.

The water stored in Castlewood Reservoir was meant to irrigate 15,000 acres. It was delivered by a large ditch, the Arapahoe Canal, which flowed for some 85 miles to the irrigated farmlands.[12] Remnants of the canal system are still visible in the County. The Castlewood Reservoir and irrigation system operated for just over forty years. Ownership of the water system changed hands several times with the actual irrigated area dwindling to 2,500 acres by the early 1930s.[13]

The Castlewood dam was not without controversy. Inspections soon after its construction raised questions as to the safety and integrity of the dam.[14] A series of leaks and washouts supported assertions that the dam was a hazard to those living along Cherry Creek, including the residents of Denver. In response to those calling for the reservoir to be drained, the dam's engineer wrote: "The Castlewood dam will never, in the life of any person now living, or in generations to come, break to an extent that will do any great damage to itself or others from the volume of water impounded, and never in all time to the city of Denver."[15]

During the 1930s drought, a deluge hit the Cherry Valley area above the reservoir. By the morning of August 3, 1933, the surging streamflow caused a massive breach in the Castlewood Dam. The advancing flood wave reached eight feet in height as it entered Denver.[16] Telephone exchange operators near Cherry Creek's path into Denver saved the day by sending warnings of the on-rush.[17] Only two lives were lost.[18] Property damage exceeded a million dollars.[19] As is so typical in Colorado, floods can ravage communities during drought.

The wall of water from the Castlewood Dam collapse as it moved down Cherry Creek through Denver

A month later, the County suffered another flood. In September 1933, heavy rains fell on the divide separating Cherry Creek and Plum Creek.[20] Severe flooding damaged the area around Franktown and Parker. The years from 1941 to 1949 were generally wetter than normal, causing eight major floods on Cherry Creek by 1945.[21] Drought returned to the County in the early 1950s.[22] Only 10.68 inches of moisture fell at Kassler in 1956.[23] Nevertheless, Cherry Creek Reservoir was completed in 1950 to protect Denver from future flood catastrophes.

The first electric well pump in the County was installed near Sedalia in 1922.[24] Pumped wells emerged as the water supply of choice in Colorado due to drought, floods, the widespread availability of electricity, and the efficiency of a pumped water supply.[25] Changes in the Town of Castle Rock's water supply system over the decades reflect this change.

The Town's original water system was constructed in the early 1880s and consisted of the ditches taking water from East Plum Creek to feed three small reservoirs in Town.[26] By 1895, the Town had improved its water supply facilities to include a system bringing water from approximately two and a half miles south of Town via wooden stave pipeline into an enlarged reservoir system. By the 1920s, Castle Rock's primary source was groundwater pumped by windmill from shallow wooden cribs one foot below the channel of Sellars Creek. The system pumped five gallons per minute into the Town's reservoirs.[27]

A new Town water supply was initiated in the early 1940s with the construction of a large diameter well in the alluvium of Sellars Creek on the north side of Douglas County Fairgrounds.[28] This first well was dug to a depth of 57 feet for $4,561.65.[29] Use of the well began in April 1942, and the well was used for 33 years until it was replaced in 1975.[30] A second alluvial well was drilled at the Fairgrounds and put into use in September 1950.[31] This well produced 200 gallons per minute and was 92 feet deep.[32]

In March 1954, the Town completed its first deep well (1,608 feet) into the Dawson and Denver aquifers.[33] The availability of electrical power meant that water users across Douglas County gained access to the deep groundwater reserves of the Denver basin aquifers. By 1990, the number of wells in the Town's water supply portfolio had increased to 34.[34] More than 70% of these wells were deep wells.[35]

Sedalia found another way to set up its first water and sewer system. From the beginning, Sedalia residents had individual wells and septic systems. In 1958 the AT&SF railroad donated to the town its 154,000-gallon water tank, well, and pipe system that had previously been used by the town's fire department. After laying some additional pipes throughout town, Sedalia had its first Water and Sanitation District.[36]

Douglas County was now truly on the verge of change with access to vast supplies of deep groundwater to serve the rapid population growth of coming decades. There was an inherent problem with this new system: water from the deep aquifers of the Denver basin is a non-renewable water source. Studies in more recent decades found that "pumping from the Denver Basin bedrock aquifers is not indefinitely sustainable and that renewable water supplies will be needed for the future."

---

[1] Colorado Department of Local Affairs, *Historical Census Data—Counties and Municipalities,* accessed April 1, 2018, https://demography.dola.colorado.gov/population/data/profile-county/.
[2] Ibid.

[3] Thomas Mckee, et al, "Water in the Balance," *A History of Drought in Colorado: Lessons Learned and What Lies Ahead*, no. 9, 2nd ed. (Fort Collins: Colorado Climate Center and Colorado Water Resources Research Institute, 2000), 8.

[4] Wallace R. Hansen, John Chronic, and John Matelock, *Climatology of the Front Range Urban Corridor and Vicinity, Colorado,* United States Geological Survey Professional Paper 1019 (Washington: United States Government Printing Office, 1978), 39.

[5] Ibid., 15.

[6] *Access Colorado Data.* Colorado Climate Center (Fort Collins: Colorado State University, n.d.), accessed April 1, 2018, http://climate.colostate.edu/data_access.html.

[7] Ibid.

[8] Ibid.

[9] *Colorado's Water Plan* (Denver: Colorado Water Conservation Board, 2015), 4-16.

[10] Sharon Randall,Tracy Dixon, and Patty Horan,*The Night the Dam Gave Way: A Diary of Personal Accounts* (Franktown: Castlewood Canyon State Park, Colorado Division of Parks and Outdoor Recreation, 1997), 10-11.

[11] Ibid., 10.

[12] *The Denver Suburban Homes and Water Co. vs. A.E. Gray et. al.* 280 No. 20 (District Court, County of Douglas, State of Colorado, September 25, 1910).

[13] Randall, *The Night the Dam Gave Way,* 13-14.

[14] Ibid., 11-12.

[15] A.M. Wells, "The Castlewood Dam Controversy," *The Denver Times,* May 2, 1900.

[16] Robert Follansbee and Leon R. Sawyer, *Floods in Colorado,* Water Supply Paper 997, United State Department of the Interior, Geological Survey (Washington: United States Government Printing Office,1948), 67.

[17] Randall, *The Night the Dam Gave Way,*19.

[18] Ibid., 10.

[19] A.N. Thompson, *Report on the Cherry Creek Project—Colorado* (Washington: Bureau of Reclamation, United State Department of the Interior, 1938), D.

[20] Follansbee, *Floods in Colorado,* 28.

[21] Hansen, *Climatology of the Front Range Urban Corridor and Vicinity,* 43.

[22] Mckee, *History of Drought in Colorado,* 15.

[23] *Access Colorado Data.*

[24] "Colorado's Well Permit Search," *Ground Water Administration and Well Permitting* (Colorado Division of Water Resources, Department of Natural Resources. n.d), accessed March 25, 2018, http://www.dwr.state.co.us/WellPermitSearch/default.aspx

[25] Susan M. Ryan, "Colorado's Answer to the Tributary Well Question: Maximum Utilization of Surface and Ground Water Through Conjunctive Use," *31st Annual Water Law Conference* (Las Vegas: American Bar Association Section of Environment, Energy, and Resources, 2013), 2-3.

[26] *Revised Findings and Ruling of the Referee and Decree of the Water Court Concerning the Application for Water Rights of The Town of Castle Rock in Douglas County,* 79CW281 (District Court, Water Division 1, Colorado, February 25,1983).

[27] *In the Matter of Priorities of Water Rights in Water District Number Eight and Water Division Number Four of the State of Colorado—Decree in Behalf of the Town of Castle Rock,* 998 (District Court, County of Douglas, State of Colorado, May 10,1926).

[28] E.C. Peterson, *Registration of No. 2 Well.* Form F (Rev.) (Castle Rock: State of Colorado Division of Water Resources Office of the State Engineer, Ground Water Section, 1960).

[29] R.W. Chandler & Sons, "Cost of New Water System, Town of Castle Rock, Colorado" (Littleton, April 18, 1942).

[30] Ibid.

[31] E.C. Peterson, "Interview by Metropolitan Water Study, Basic Data Summary," *Town of Castle Rock Water Facilities Worksheet,* October 6, 1964.

[32] Ibid.

[33] E.C. Peterson, *Registration of No. 1 of Well.* Form F (Rev.) (Castle Rock: State of Colorado Division of Water Resources Office of the State Engineer, Ground Water Section, 1960).

[34] Billie Owens, interview by Steven Boand, *Town of Castle Rock Active Well Drilling Dates Summary* (January 5, 1995).

[35] Ibid.

[36] "Sedalia Folks Will Vote on Water and Sewage District," *Douglas County News,* March 14, 1957, 1; "Sedalia Receives Santa Fe Railroad Water Systems," *Douglas County News,* December 18, 1958, 1; Susan Consola Appleby, *Fading Past: The Story of Douglas County, Colorado* (Palmer Lake, CO: Filter Press, 2001), 167.

Chapter 37

GOING TO WAR

Susan Rocco-Mckeel and Tim Weber

The U.S. entered World War II after the Japanese bombed Pearl Harbor on December 7, 1941. It was the largest war in history with millions killed.[1] Precise statistics are sometimes unavailable because the various branches of the service compiled and stored statistics differently. As a result, their statistics do not always agree.

People from Douglas County were killed during the war. Its population was small (3,498 in 1940);[2] and during the 1930s, the military-age population of Douglas County was relatively small. For example, during this period, the Douglas County High School (DCHS) averaged fewer than thirty graduates a year,[3] more than half of whom were females. Of course, not all military-age males went to high school. According to official sources, of the 2,688 Coloradoans who died of all causes in WW II, ten were from DC: Seven from the Army and Army Air Corps, and three from the Navy.[4]

Army 1st Lieutenant Tony Perez of Larkspur was a 1934 graduate of DCHS. He joined the Army before Pearl Harbor and became a photography instructor at Lowry Field. After receiving his commission, in 1945 he became the Photography Officer for a heavy bomber squadron in India, where he was killed in action. He left behind his wife Sicilia and a 17-month-old son.[5]

2nd Lieutenant Fred Angell also was a DCHS graduate. He became a navigator on a B-17 bomber. In 1943, his plane was hit by German artillery. Though gravely injured, he put out fires and saved the plane. He died of his wounds and was awarded the Silver Star posthumously. He left behind Helen, his wife of three months.[6] Jack Cain of Larkspur was killed in 1945 crossing the Danube River in Germany. Also killed were Leonard Martinez of Sedalia, Alton Wyatt of Jarre Creek, and Harold New, an engineer from the local CCC camp. Jack Higgins of Parker was killed in the Philippines.[7]

Navy Lieutenant (j.g.) Bernard Curtis was born on Oaklands Ranch, Sedalia, in 1918. After graduation from DCHS, he attended Mesa College and the

University of Colorado. He enlisted in the Navy in 1940 and was at Pearl Harbor on December 7. He piloted a float plane off the cruiser USS San Francisco. In May 1942, he married Mary Van Lopik, the daughter of a leading merchant and mayor of Castle Rock. Six months after the wedding, he was killed off Guadalcanal.[8]

Jack Nipko of Castle Rock was a youth leader at the Community Methodist Church and an award-winning musician (piano, cornet, and voice). A 1941 DCHS graduate, he joined the Navy and served on the battleship, *USS Colorado*. He was wounded off Saipan in July 1944 and was killed in a kamikaze attack in Lingayen Gulf in the Philippines in January 1945.[9] Edward Lee Arment of Louviers served on the destroyer *USS Evans* and was killed in a kamikaze attack off Okinawa on May 11, 1945.[10]

Those who fought and survived had stories to tell. Of the twelve Parker men who served, three were the Motsenbocker brothers. Everett served with the Army in Germany; Jesse was in the Pacific with the Navy; and John flew with the Air Corps in North Africa, Sicily, and Italy.[11] William Anderson of Larkspur led a platoon onto Omaha Beach during D-Day and later helped liberate Nazi concentration camps.[12] Ken Malick of Parker fought on Okinawa.[13] Darrell Bell from Larkspur served in the China-Burma-India theater.[14]

USS Colorado BB45 off Tinian, July 24, 1944

Benjamin Esquibel was a cowboy near Sedalia who ended up guarding German POWs in Normandy and fighting across northern France.[15] Marine 1st

Lieutenant Edward Seidensticker, Jr. fought on Iwo Jima and was part of the occupation forces in Japan.[16] Vera Foy Briscoe served in the Women's Reserve of the Marine Corps as a Technical Sergeant.[17] Arlie Gordon was with the Navy in the Marianas, the Philippines, Iwo Jima, and Okinawa. Simon Ehmann, Jr fought in Normandy and Germany and received the Bronze Star. John Higby was a Tech 5 in Northern France and the Ardennes. Geneva Hier Thomson was a Lieutenant in the Naval Reserve (WAVES) stateside.[18] Staff Sergeant Alan Omans fought in the Battle of the Bulge.[19] Fred Quintana of Franktown served in the Pacific with the Navy.[20]

The people of Douglas County were affected by the war in many ways. A complicated rationing system controlled the consumption of consumer goods. War Rationing Books containing coupons were issued for processed foods, meats, fats, oils, sugar, coffee, shoes, gasoline, tires, and the like.[21] The sugar ration provided less than one pound of sugar per person every two weeks. People who lost their Ration Book had to wait two months before receiving a new one.[22] Gasoline was strictly rationed according to how one's auto was used.[23] Everyone had to "make do."

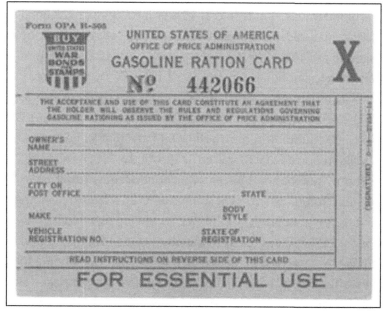

Gasoline Ration Card

Food rationing forced people to be self-reliant. Since most canned fruit and vegetables went to the military, the government urged civilians to plant "victory gardens" to provide fresh produce for their families. That request was easy to follow in DC, but people in some places needed help. In Louviers, where the company-owned houses sat on small lots, additional garden plots were allocated.[24]

Civilians also conducted scrap drives "to salvage every available scrap of metal, paper, old rags, and rubber."[25] Such recycled materials were essential in the manufacturing of war materiel. October 12, 1942—Columbus Day—was designated "Scrap Collection Day" in DC.[26] Since schools and businesses were closed for what was then a national holiday, everyone was able to participate. Collection depots in Castle Rock, Parker, Sedalia, Hill Top, Larkspur, Spring Valley, Lower Plum Creek, and Golddale amassed 131 tons of scrap material, including a 3,000-pound safe from the second floor of the County Courthouse.[27] "Summer Paper Week" was scheduled for July 29 to August 5, 1944, with drop-off sites at Castle Rock, Louviers, Parker, Sedalia, Larkspur, and Franktown.[28]

Tax increases could not pay for the war, so the government sponsored eight War Bond Drives. Bonds sold at 75% of face value (a $25 bond sold for $18.75) that matured in ten years (a 2.9% rate of return). People were encouraged to use 10% of each paycheck to buy Bonds. Over time, 85 million Americans purchased bonds worth $185.7 billion.[29] DC did its part. In each bond drive, counties were assigned dollar quotas; and DC always surpassed theirs. In the Second War Bond Drive in April 1943,[30] DC raised $61,648, well over its $37,900 quota.[31] In the Third Drive later that same year, Chairman Philip S. Miller reported that DC raised $119,448, 144% of its quota.[32] Children participated by purchasing ten-cent war bond stamps to fill their *Defense Stamp Albums*. It took 187 10-cent stamps to fill an album and another nickel to obtain a $25 War Bond.[33]

The people of Douglas County were committed to winning the war. Many sons and daughters served in the military. All but ten came home to resume their lives after the war. For many, it had been the greatest—and most terrifying—adventure of their lives. But everyone in the County experienced the war in one way or another. Unlike any other time in DC's history, the war years meant "all hands on deck."

[1] John Graham Smith and Thomas Hughes, "World War II," in the *Encyclopedia Britannica*, 1-2, accessed March 12, 2018, www.britannica.com/event/World-War-II.

[2] Douglas County Research Center, "Table 4 Population of Counties by Minor Civil Divisions," in *Douglas County Colorado Demographics*, 56.

[3] "Douglas County High School Graduation by Year 1899-1964," Douglas County History Resource Center, accessed March 3, 2014, www.douglascountyhistory.org.

[4] Compare V.F.W. Post 4664 and Castle Rock/Community Business Men, *Service Record WWII, Castle Rock and Community* (Marceline, MO: Walsworth Bros., 1948), 1-43, that lists sixteen dead, with the Adjutant General, World War II Honor List of Dead and Missing, State of Colorado (Washington DC: War Department, 1946) which lists ten, which are the official results.

[5] "Lt. Anthony Perez Reported Killed in Line of Duty," *Record-Journal*, May 18, 1945, 1.

[6] "Silver Star Awarded Posthumously to Lt. Angell," *Record-Journal*, December 3, 1943, 1.

[7] "WW II Army and Army Air Force Casualties," *Military Records, National Archives*, accessed March 29, 2018, https://archives.gov/research/military/ww2/army-casualties.

[8] "Lt. Bernard Curtis Reported Killed in Line of Duty," *Record-Journal*, November 27, 1942, 1 and "Memorial Service for Lt. Bernard J. Curtis," *Record Journal*, January 1, 1943, 1.

[9] *Service Record WWII, Castle Rock and Community*, 1-43.

[10] Ibid.

[11] Ibid., "12 Served, 2 died," *Supplement to Douglas County News-Press*, June 15, 1984, 13B. Here Raymond Woodbury is reported as a fatality, but his name does not appear in official records.

[12] Jim Staats, "Larkspur Resident was World War II veteran and Social Activist," *Marin Independent Journal* (2008), accessed March 20, 2018, www.marinij.com.

[13] Chris Michiewicz, "Parker vet remembers bloody battle of Okinawa," *Douglas County News-Press*, April 7, 2005, in Military Veterans Notebook assembled by the Douglas County History Research Center.

[14] *Service Record WW II*.

[15] Benjamin Esquibel, Veterans History Project Oral History Interview (Douglas County History Research Center, 2010), accessed February 25, 2018, douglascountyhistory.org.

[16] *Service Record World War II*.

[17] Ibid.; *Record-Journal*, November 17, 1944, 1.

[18] *Service Record World War II*.

[19] *Record-Journal*, November 2, 1945, 1; *Record-Journal*, February 22, 1946, 5.

[20] *Service Record WW II*.

[21] *Record-Journal*, November 17, 1944, 1.

[22] "A Few Items Regarding the Sugar Ration Books," *Record-Journal*, May 29, 1942, 5.

[23] "'A' Applications Should Be Filed Immediately," *Record-Journal*, September 8, 1944, 1.

[24] "Victory Gardens at Louviers Exceptionally Fine," *Record-Journal*, April 17, 1942.

[25] "U.S. Requests Citizens' Aid In Scrap Hunt," *Record-Journal*, April 17, 1942, 2.

[26] "October 12 Will Be Scrap Collection Day in Douglas County," *Record-Journal*, October 2, 1942, 1.

[27] "Lots of Scrap Iron Collected for the Japs Last Monday," *Record-Journal*, October 16, 1942, 1.

[28] "July 29 to August 5 to Be Summer Paper Week," *Record-Journal*, July 28, 1944, 1

[29] "U.S. War Bonds," *United States History*, accessed April 13, 2018, http://www.u-s-history.com/pages/h1682.html

[30]Second War Bond Drive Will Start Next Monday," *Record-Journal*, April 9, 1943, 1.

[31] "Douglas County Makes 162% of Bond Quota," *Record-Journal*, May 7, 1943, 1.

[32] "Douglas County Goes Over the Top in War Bond Drive," *Record-Journal*, October 1, 1943, 1; "Douglas County Makes 144 Per Cent of its War Bond Quota," *Record- Journal*, October 8, 1943, 1.

[33] "War Stamp Sales Over Half Billion Dollars, Album Drive Opens," *Record-Journal*, May 7, 1943, 4.

Chapter 38

MURDER AT THE B & B CAFÉ

Tim Weber

In the 1940s, law enforcement in Douglas County consisted of an elected Sheriff and an appointed Undersheriff. They were responsible for patrolling the entire county in their private vehicles since there were no patrol cars. A few volunteer deputies kept peace at local dances or helped with local disasters. No DC town had its own police force, though Castle Rock had a Town Marshall who patrolled the town after hours and checked for unlocked doors. In other words, the Marshall was a night watchman, not a sworn law officer.

The Town Marshall in Castle Rock (population 580) was Raymond Burr Lewis. He also served as Street and Water Commissioner and the first assistant chief in the volunteer fire department.[1] Ray was well-known and well-liked in the community. He, his wife Ruth, and their four children (ages 18 months to 12 years) lived at the corner of Fourth and Elbert Streets, one block west of Courthouse Square.[2]

About 10 p.m. on Tuesday, February 14, 1946, a 17-year-old fugitive named Manuel Blanco Perez entered the B & B Café, directly across from the County Courthouse. Two days earlier he shot two Denver policemen and had been on the run ever since. He fled on foot to Douglas County and hid outside Castle Rock. By late Tuesday night, Perez was hungry and came to town. B & B Café was still open because at that time it operated around the clock.[3] He ordered two hamburgers to eat there and four more "to-go."[4]

Three café patrons recognized Perez from newspaper photos—Martin "Boots" Nelson, Dale Ridenour, and Dale's brother Perry. Boots and Dale were WW II vets in their early twenties. While Dale kept an eye on Perez, Boots retrieved a handgun from his nearby home, and Perry left to phone Undersheriff Duncan Lowell since Sheriff Robert Campbell was on vacation. He also informed Ray Lewis who was finishing his evening rounds. When Nelson, Ridenour, and Lewis returned to the café at about the same time,

Perez got suspicious and got up to leave. Ridenour bolted the door, and Lewis blocked it. When the unarmed Marshall told Perez to raise his hands because he was under arrest, Perez pulled his gun and shot him through the heart. Lewis died instantly. He was only 44 years old.[5]

L to R - Perry Ridenour, Martin Nelson, and Dale Ridenour
(Murder at the B & B)

Boots Nelson and another patron named Gene Dodge jumped on Perez. Perry Ridenour grabbed a flowerpot, intending to hit Perez with it. In the ensuing mêlée, shots were fired. Boots grazed Perez's ear and finger, and Perez shot Boots in the hand. Two stray bullets hit the ceiling and the back of the bar, where the holes can still be seen. The scuffle ended when Dodge put his hunting knife to Perez's throat.[6]

By the time Undersheriff Lowell arrived and took Perez into custody, an angry crowd on Wilcox Street was debating whether to hang Perez from a tree in Courthouse Square.[7] Lowell dissuaded the crowd and hustled Perez into the Courthouse's basement jail cell. He then arranged to transfer him to the El Paso County jail for safekeeping. In May 1946, Perez was tried and convicted of first-degree murder; but because he was under 18 when he shot

Lewis, he could not be executed and was sentenced to life in prison.[8] Not long after arriving at Canon City, Perez died in a prison knife fight.[9]

Over 700 people, including fifty Denver policemen, attended Ray's funeral on February 19.[10] He was buried in Castle Rock's Cedar Hill Cemetery. A fund started for Ruth and the children by community leaders collected over $6,000, which enabled Ruth to pay off the $2,000 mortgage.[11] In 1953 the Town Council voted to change Main Street in the Craig-Gould neighborhood to Lewis Street in honor of the Town Marshall.[12]

Ruth Lewis and the children stayed in Castle Rock after the funeral. To support the family, she started a telephone answering service, took in laundry from a local motel, and worked as a part-time secretary for the fire department.[13] Ruth never remarried. She died at age 82 and was buried next to Ray. Various family members owned the house until 1991. Currently, it is occupied by Neighbor Networks Helping Seniors Stay Independent.

Despite the Lewis murder, serious crime was extremely rare in those days. Most of DC's population lived on ranches and farms, so nothing like urban crime existed. Guns were everywhere, but gun violence seldom occurred. According to one person who lived through that period in DC, "In those days, people settled disputes with their fists, not with guns."[14]

John Hammond served as the County Sheriff from 1947 to 1970, the longest term in DC history. For a long time, his "uniform" consisted of a badge, cowboy boots, a western shirt, and a cowboy hat. He did not wear a uniform or carry a side-arm until the 1960s. He kept an annual diary to keep track of his mileage, for which the County reimbursed him. Hammond did a lot of driving: some months his reimbursements exceeded his monthly salary. In his *Yearbook for 1947*, he listed calls for car wrecks; "family troubles;" runaway kids; escaped

John Hammond

prisoners and other missing persons; vandalism; home break-ins; livestock loose on the highway; robberies; cattle rustling; drunkenness; taking sick people to the hospital; connecting indigent and transient people to social services; locating stolen merchandise; escorting gypsies through the County; auto thefts; transporting prisoners to different venues; bad checks; confiscating slot machines and other gambling paraphernalia; child neglect; dead or wounded wildlife on the highways; locating plane crashes; drownings; suicides; business disputes; illegal deer hunting; counterfeit money; hit and run accidents; fires; disputes over cattle brands; and serving warrants.[15]

Hammond developed into a first-rate Sheriff, though his only prior experience was serving as a volunteer deputy under Sheriff Buckner (1932-1942). Before that, among other things, he raised cattle, ran a garage in Larkspur, and owned a fleet of trucks that transported milk to Frink's creamery. He developed his investigative skills on the job. He ran a low-key office. The jail in the County Courthouse had no kitchen, so prisoners were marched across the street twice a day to the B & B Café for meals. He also took non-violent prisoners home for Thanksgiving dinner with his family. According to his daughter, the Hammond family moved to Castle Rock after her father became Sheriff; but every year he made sure he visited all the ranchers and farmers in the County to say hello.[16]

DC's population increased by 37% in the 1950s, so law enforcement had to grow too. Paid-part-time deputies were added to the Sheriff's Office; and Castle Rock, whose population increased to 1,152 by 1960, started its own police department. In the beginning, it consisted of Police Chief John Westbrook and his newly purchased patrol car. For financial reasons, the town eliminated Ray Lewis's old Town Marshall position and the overnight telephone answering service provided by his widow Ruth.[17] In time, two other town police forces were established in DC: Parker (1983) and Lone Tree (2004).

---

[1] "Firemen Held 28th Annual Banquet Tuesday Night," *Record-Journal*, February 26, 1943,1.

[2] "Funeral Rites for Ray Lewis Held on Tuesday," *Record-Journal*, February 22, 1946, 1.

[3] B & B Café advertisement, *The Record-Journal*, January 4, 1946, 5.

[4] Ray Humphreys, "Bullet Bargainer: Two Shots Spelled Freedom; The Third Meant Doom," *Timely Detectives*, undated, 44-47, 64-66, Douglas County History Research Center.

[5] "Ray Lewis Killed by Hunted Youth Thursday Night," *Record-Journal*, February 15, 1946, 1.

[6] Humphreys, "Bullet Bargainer."

[7] Jim Duffy, "B & B Killing Occurred 50 Years Ago Today," *Douglas County News-Press*, February 14, 1996.

[8] "Perez Given Life Sentence Friday," *Record-Journal*, May 10, 1946, 1

[9] Virginia Grantier, "B & B Shootout," *Douglas County News*, October 9, 1991; "Ray Lewis Killed by Hunted Youth Thursday Night."

[10] "Funeral Rites for Ray Lewis Held on Tuesday."

[11] Grantier, "B & B Shootout."

[12] "More New Names Suggested for Main," *Douglas County News*, July 23, 1953, 1; "Changing of Street Name from 'Main' to 'Lewis'," *Douglas County News*, October 15, 1953, 1.

[13] "Proceedings for the Town of Castle Rock, September 1960," *Douglas County News*, October 13, 1960, 4.

[14] Interview of Mrs. Bonnie Bell, the daughter of Sheriff John Hammond, on February 23, 2018, in the Philip Miller Library, Castle Rock.

[15] Thanks to Bonnie Bell for making Sheriff Hammond's *Yearbook for 1947* available for examination.

[16] Bonnie Bell Interview.

[17] "C.R. Establishes Town Police Department," *Douglas County News*, December 22, 1960, 1.

Chapter 39
CHANGING LANES

Jim Hansmann

Nothing changed more in Douglas County between 1930 and 1960 than its road system. In the mid-nineteenth century, trails first used by Indians and early explorers carried settlers across eastern Colorado and along the Front Range, making the future DC the "bridge" between northern and southern Colorado. Later, over the same pioneer and territorial roads, farmers and ranchers used horse-drawn wagons to bring DC's agricultural goods and dairy products to train depots for shipment to Denver, Colorado Springs, and beyond. In the early twentieth century, it soon became apparent that the old roads needed to be redesigned and paved for the "automobile age."

US 85 North of Castle Rock circa 1930

After World War I, two north-south routes linked Denver and Colorado Springs through DC. In the west was State Highway 1, which was also known as the "North-South Highway" and finally Highway 85.[1] It entered DC south of Littleton and was popularly known as Santa Fe Drive. It passed by Acequia, Louviers, Gann, and Sedalia; ran through Castle Rock as Wilcox Street; and then continued south by Larkspur and Greenland and over Monument Hill. In the eastern part of the County was Highway 83. It was the premier farm-to-market road that followed the old Cherokee Trail. It entered DC from Arapahoe County and passed through Parker, Franktown, Cherry Valley, and Spring Valley. Both highways were two-lane dirt and gravel roads that were unsuitable for the increasing volume of auto traffic.

During the 1920s the state highway department started paving its major roads. In the mid-1920s, crews paved US 85 from Sedalia through Castle Rock.[2] The highway that continued south to Monument Hill was hazardous in many places, causing many accidents. It became known as the "ribbon of death." Consequently, state engineers decided to make US 83 the preferred north-south route between Denver and Colorado Springs. Crews laid down a two-lane concrete road between Denver and Franktown. To straighten out the road south of Franktown (US 83 originally followed Russellville Road to the east), they built an arched concrete bridge across the 232-foot-wide Castlewood Canyon located a few miles south of Franktown.[3] Just before the bridge was completed in 1949, the state highway commissioner reversed himself and made US 85 the preferred route. Since the finished bridge ended in a cow pasture, locals called it the "Bridge to Nowhere."[4] Paving the rest of US 83 to the south was not finished until the mid-1960s.[5]

In the 1920s, State Highway 86 connected Castle Rock and Franktown, following a trail that had existed since the early days of DC. Like other state highways, it began as graded dirt, then gravel road. It was oiled in the 1930s and given a layer of blacktop in 1953.[6] Highway 86 eventually went beyond Franktown to Elizabeth and Kiowa in Elbert County and Limon in Lincoln County, making it the only connection between the three counties.

By the 1930s there were two other secondary state highways with tie-ins to Sedalia. Highway 67 started at highway 85 then went west up Jarre Canyon and wound its way through the Pike National Forest to Deckers on the South Platte River.[7] From there 67 continued south until it entered Teller County south of Westcreek. Highway 105, also known as Perry Park Road, began at Highway 67 just west of Sedalia and headed south through scenic ranchland and by what became future housing developments (e.g., Christy Ridge, Valley Park, and Perry Park). There were no towns along 105, though the highway passed a few miles west of Castle Rock and Larkspur and was connected by Wolfensberger Road and Perry Park Avenue. The highway finally entered El

Paso County near Palmer Lake.[8] By the mid-1950s, Jarre Canyon was paved; but 105 was not.[9]

US 85 South of Castle Rock circa 1950

After World War II, the number of autos on America's roads increased dramatically. The 1940s and 1950s were the eras of modern freeways. In 1944 construction began on "the Valley Highway," a north-south freeway through Denver. Officially designated US 87 the highway entered Colorado from Wyoming, with plans to be extended through DC, the rest of southern Colorado, and into New Mexico.[10] The Valley Highway was completed in 1958. By then President Eisenhower had signed into law the National Interstate and Defense Highways Act (1956) that created the Interstate Highway System. Under the new law, US 87 eventually became Interstate 25.

US 87 was extended into DC in 1949. By 1952 the stretch between the Arapahoe County line and Castle Rock was finished. It consisted of a two-lane concrete road with four lanes on ascending grades to accommodate both slow and fast vehicles.[11] Just above Castle Rock, the new US 87 merged with US 85, bypassed the town, and continued south past Larkspur and Greenland to El Paso County. Accordingly, Interstate 25 was also designated US 85/US 87. The merchants in Castle Rock were not happy about being bypassed, fearing a significant loss of business. In 1958 a study showed that there had been only a slight decrease in the rate of economic growth, especially in the areas of gasoline and food sales.[12]

There was still a lot of work to be done. When plans for Interstate 25 were announced, much of the proposed route through DC had only two lanes. A map of DC roads in 1955 showed that north of Castle Rock, US 85/US 87 consisted of both two- and four-lanes; but the stretch between Castle Rock and Tomah Road had four lanes. From Tomah Road south to Monument Hill, the road had only two lanes. Thus a "four-laning" project added lanes where needed north of Castle Rock and south of Tomah Road to the El Paso County line. High schooler Bill Noe worked on the Tomah to Monument section in the summer of 1957.[13] In August 1957, the last phase of the four-laning project began—from Castle Rock to Denver.[14] By August 1958, there were four lanes open to traffic between Denver and Pueblo.[15] But this achievement was only the first step in building an Interstate System. By law, it required controlled access, interchanges, overpasses, drainage systems, medians, frontage roads, extensive lighting and signage, and even rest-stops in some places.

In the late 1950s, engineers divided this larger I-25 construction project into three segments, with the following priority: Denver to Castle Rock, Monument to Larkspur, and Larkspur to Castle Rock.[16] In this way, numerous contractors were able to bid on individual parts of the whole. Yet to be determined was the location of future interchanges, overpasses, and other structures. There were many planning meetings, opportunities for citizens to express their preferences, and adjustments to plans along the way. It was one thing to have an Interstate run through Douglas County, but it was another to have easy access to it. What the residents of DC in the late 1950s did not realize was that it would take another decade of non-stop road work to finish I-25.

---

[1] "State Highway Plans for 1924," *Record-Journal*, November 30, 1923, 7.

[2] "Castle Rock Will Pave Wilcox Street," *Record-Journal*, December 19, 1924.

[3] Interview with Lee Whiteley on May 26, 2018.

[4] Bert Hanna, "State Builds Road That Goes Nowhere," *Denver Post,* September 1, 1948; Bert Hanna, "Road to Nowhere Goes Nowhere," *Denver Post,* June 8, 1949.

[5] *Castlewood Canyon State Park: "The Bridge to Nowhere,"* Colorado State Parks.

[6] "Paving of Highway No. 86 Due For Finish in 60 Days," *Douglas County News,* August 13, 1953, 1; "Douglas County Map, 1955."

[7] "Work Commenced on Sedalia—Deckers Road," *Record-Journal,* May 16, 1919.

[8] Castle Rock Chamber of Commerce, *"Free Map & Guide"* (Mt. Vernon, MO: Spring Hill Press, 2013).

[9] "Douglas County Map, 1955," REFMP 4313.D6G4, 1955.D6, Douglas County History Research Center.

[10] "U.S. Highway History of Denver, Colorado," US Ends.com, accessed May 15, 2018, https://www.usends.com/blog/us-highway-history-of-denver-colorado.

[11] Jack Mohler, "New Denver—Castle Rock Highway Opened," *Rocky Mountain News,* August 31, 1952, 10.

[12] "Effects of By-Pass Study Released," *Douglas County News,* October 23, 1958, 19.

[13] Correspondence with Bill Noe, May 24, 2018.

[14] "Denver and Nebraska Contractors Awarded Finish Job on US 87," *Douglas County News,* August 1, 1957, 1; "4-Lane Completion Set for Start Next Monday," *Douglas County News,* August 15, 1957, 1.

[15] "Denver-Pueblo 4-Lane Now Open to Traffic," *Douglas County News,* August 28, 1958, 7.

[16] "Interstate 25 History," *About CDOT,* accessed May 1, 2018, https://www.codot.gov/about/CDOTHistory/50th-anniversary/interstate-25.

Chapter 40

FROM SMALL TOWN TO LITTLE CITY

Joan Gandy

Between 1930 and 1950, Douglas County's population added only 9 people; but Castle Rock added 263. In the 1950s, the County increased 37% (to 4841) and its County Seat 56% (to 1,152). By 1960 almost one-quarter of all DC residents lived in Castle Rock, DC's only incorporated town (1881).[1] During these decades, Castle Rock showed signs of becoming more than a country town. It improved its water supply, added DC's first sewer system, and started paving its streets. None of these changes was easy. Finances were always difficult, and some residents resisted change.

Growth of any kind required a better water supply. In March 1930, the Castle Rock town council contracted with the Platt Rogers Construction Company for a price of $17,942 to extend the water lines further up East Plum Creek to ensure cleaner water for a greater number of property owners.[2] "This improvement of our water system is meeting with the general approval of the citizens, many of whom have made the statement that it will be money well spent if only good, clear water can be secured for the town."[3] In the following decades, there were additional improvements in the water supply. In the 1940s, the town dug new wells near the DC Fair Grounds, and in the 1950s, it dug its first deep well into the Denver and Dawson Aquifers.

The completion of this modest water project in 1930 provided enough water to construct a sewer system to replace the town's septic tanks. "Plans have been drawn and the proposed sewer will take care of every house in town and the lines will be laid sufficiently deep to care for every basement in the district also."[4] While the local newspaper argued in favor of the sewer system, many residents feared the cost. Forty-one percent of property owners in Castle Rock filed protests with the town council, forcing a postponement of plans. The council concluded that 'this is not the psychological time to do the work, because of the depressed times."[5]

Proponents continued to press the argument that costs would be cheaper during the Depression than later, that mandatory connection to the sewer lines would not happen immediately, and that the project would create jobs for local people. "A stipulation in the contract will be to the effect that outside of three skilled men, all labor used in the installation of this system shall be Castle Rock citizens if available, and if not available then Douglas County citizens will be given preference. It is expected that quite a crew of men will be necessary to do this work."[6] These arguments swayed public opinion. The town council voted 4-2 to create a sewer district in September 1931.

The Schwartz Construction Company worked on the sewer system for the rest of 1931.[7] Frozen ground slowed the work, but the jobs generated by the project were greatly appreciated. The project "is furnishing some much-needed labor for many Castle Rock and Douglas County people. Not only this, but these people have to eat, wear clothes, and use fuel and other supplies which are for sale in town. Thus, it is a help to the whole community."[8] Once the sewer system was operational, residents no longer had to hire "scavengers" to clean out their septic vaults once a year.

Shady Drive - Highway 85 through Castle Rock

In the 1930s, 1940s, and most of the 1950s, US 85 ran through Castle Rock as Wilcox Street, so all north-south traffic came through the center of town. In 1925 the State Highway Commission paved an 18 ft.-wide concrete strip down Wilcox,[9] but in 1926 voters turned down a plan to pave the remaining

14 ft. wide strips on each side of the road.[10] Ten years later, WPA workers installed curbs and gutters down Wilcox, around Courthouse Square, and on 3rd Street to the train depot.[11] In 1937, the town finished paving its "main street" to the curbs.[12] For twenty years, Wilcox remained the only paved street in Castle Rock.

In the late 1950s, Ray E. Mohler, publisher of the *Douglas County News,* declared that "Paving makes a town." He argued that paved streets would "get ourselves and those who are sure to be attracted to us out of the mud and dust that, more than anything else, can keep us a small town instead of a little city. . . . Paving for a growing town is not an expense; it is an investment." [13]

Paul Synder

Mayor Paul Snyder, a respected attorney, and the town council accepted the challenge.[14] After a fact-finding survey in February 1957,[15] the council adopted a plan to pave the streets around Courthouse Square, plus a few residential blocks. To gauge public support, the council asked affected property owners to make a "Paving Pledge" to pay $1.50 per running foot in front of their property within thirty days of completion or in installments over twelve months with interest.[16] The pledges trickled in. Mayor Snyder declared, "We want more pledges as we realize that we must have the citizens behind us if we are to try to get the town out of the mud and dust."[17]

After receiving fifty pledges,[18] the council decided to move ahead with paving 3rd Street from Jerry east to Gilbert, Jerry Street from 3rd to 4th, 4th Street from Jerry to Wilcox, Perry Street between 2nd and 5th Streets, and Lewis Street from 3rd Street south to what was then the entrance to the DC Fair Grounds.[19]

Councilmen considered different ways of financing the project, but finally adopted a pay-as-you-go plan in which one-third of the budget came from increased taxes and two-thirds from property owners who were assessed

$1.75 per running foot.[20] The paving was completed in September 1957, with the final seal applied in November.[21]

There was opposition before and after the paving. It took years to pave 4th Street between Wilcox and Perry because property owners refused to make Paving Pledges.[22] Five other citizens pledged but refused to pay. Mayor Snyder sent them final notices with a warning: "Some persons have gotten the idea that the town is powerless to collect for the paving but that is a mistake. We will also charge interest on unpaid items."[23] In February 1958, only $1,000 remained to be collected.[24] The Mayor considered the project a great success.

But Mayor Snyder was also concerned about the high level of opposition. When he called a public meeting in January 1958 to consider paving more streets, only five critics showed up: where were those in favor?[25] The mayor's popularity was waning. Three months later the mayor was voted out of office.[26] Still, the process started by Snyder continued over the next couple of decades. Such slow but steady progress pleased the publisher of the *Douglas County News:* "We like the kind of growth that has been shown. We don't like boomtowns. We don't like 'ghost towns.' Neither extreme indicates good civic health."[27] Progress continued; but it was not easy.

---

[1] Colorado Department of Local Affairs, *Historical Census Data—Counties and Municipalities,* accessed April 1, 2018, https://demography.dola.colorado.gov/population/data/profile-county/.

[2] "Contract is Let for Improvement of Water System," *Record-Journal*, March 21, 1930, 1.

[3] Ibid.

[4] "Councilmen Plan a Sewer System for Castle Rock," *Record-Journal*, June 5, 1931, 1; "Town Council Wants to Put in a Sewer Here," *Record-Journal*, July 10, 1931, 1.

[5] "Town Council Gets Protests on Sewer Plan," *Record-Journal*, August 7, 1931, 1.

[6] "Councilmen Plan a Sewer System for Castle Rock."

[7] "Work on Sewer Goes on Nicely in Spite of Weather," *Record-Journal*, December 4, 1931, 1.

[8] Ibid.

[9] "All for All Colorado," *Record-Journal*, August 21, 1925, 4.

[10] Editorial, *Record-Journal*, April 16, 1926, 4.

[11] "Castle Rock Streets Are Being Improved by WPA Workers," *Record-Journal*, June 12, 1936, 1.

[12] "Asphalt Paving Will Be Laid on Wilcox Street," *Record-Journal*, May 28, 1937, 1.

[13] "Paving Makes a Town," *Douglas County News*, April 21, 1955, 1.

[14] For an account of the entire project, see Paul Snyder, "Town and Citizen Cooperation Results in Paved Streets for Castle Rock, *Colorado Municipalities*, April 1958, 90-91, 96.

[15] "Town Board to Survey Paving Possibilities," *Douglas County News*, February 7, 1957, 1.

[16] "Town Board Offers 'Trial Balloon' on a Paving Program," *Douglas County News*, March 28, 1957, 1.

[17] "Town Board's Paving Plan is Launched Tuesday Night," *Douglas County News*, May 9, 1957, 1.

[18] "Town and Citizen Cooperation," 91.

[19] "Town Board Shaping Final Paving Plans," *Douglas County News*, July 18, 1957, 5.

[20] "Town and Citizens Cooperation," 91.

[21] "Town to Press for Payment of Unpaid Paving Accounts," *Douglas County News*, February 6, 1958, 1.

[22] "Castle Rock Gets a Paving Program," *Douglas County News*, September 12, 1957, 2; "Paving," *Douglas County News*, August 4, 1960, 6.

[23] "Town to Press for Payment."

[24] Ibid.

[25] "Board Talks Paving with Small Group," *Douglas County News*, January 16, 1958, 12; "Town and Citizen Cooperation," 96.

[26] "Rossmeisl Is In as Mayor," *Douglas County News*, April 3, 1958, 1.

[27] "Castle Rock is Showing Healthy, Normal Growth," *Douglas County News*, July 9, 1953, 2. See also "We're on Our Way!" *Douglas County News*, September 5, 1957, 1.

Chapter 41

BIG CHANGES IN AGRICULTURE

Larry Schlupp

During this three-decade era, Douglas County was classified as overwhelmingly rural. Sixty percent of the County's generated revenue came from agriculture; and farms covered 67% of the land, of which 83% was farmer-owned.[1] The Depression and two severe droughts in 1930-1941 and 1951-1960 had a damaging impact on farms. WW II pulled young men from farms for military service so that farm help was almost impossible to find. War-induced price controls and rationing dramatically lowered the profitability of farm commodities and limited the availability of material for the repair and maintenance of farm machinery. These obstacles combined to have a strong effect on Douglas County's farms: it reduced the total number of farms, increased average farm acreage, and changed the types of cash crops produced.

The severe drought of the 1930s was accompanied by incessant winds, causing large soil erosion. In 1935, the Federal Soil Conservation Act was established to provide farmers and ranchers assistance and technical support to prevent the loss of productive land. In Douglas County, the West Plum Creek Soil Erosion District (1940) and the Cherry Creek Soil Conservation District (1943) were instrumental in the widespread adoption of new farming practices. The soil conservancy applications of field contouring, wind protection tree planting, application of erosion-protective pasture grasses such as buffalo and blue grama, and weed control dramatically combated soil erosion by the end of WW II. In 1960, a referendum was held to merge the two erosion districts into one, the Douglas County Soil Conservation District.[2]

Agriculture's revenue came from three primary areas: dairy products, beef cattle, and winter wheat. Dairy and wheat farming were heavily concentrated in the valleys of Cherry and Plum Creeks. Beef ranches were more prevalent in the western region of the County with large pasture lands adjacent to the

Pike National Forest. Dollar-wise in the 1930s, driven by Shorthorn and Holstein milk production, dairy was king.[3]

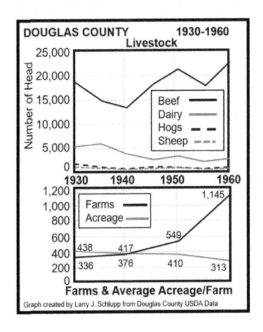

DOUGLAS COUNTY 1930-1960
Livestock

Farms & Average Acreage/Farm

Graph created by Larry J. Schlupp from Douglas County USDA Data

At the turn of the twentieth century, seven creamers-separators and four cheese factories existed in the County. Clarence Frink and C.G. Carlson acquired creameries in Castle Rock, Sedalia, Spring Valley, Kiowa, and Monument;[4] but due to hard times in our period, only Frink's Creamery in Larkspur survived. It processed 80% of the milk produced on mainly southern and western dairy farms.[5] In 1942, a group of dairy farmers from northern and eastern parts of Douglas County formed the Denver Milk Producers consortium that shipped milk from Franktown, Hill Top, and Parker to Denver milk plants.[6] The consortium ultimately merged with Mountain Empire Dairymen's Association (MEDA), including some El Paso County areas. MEDA was headed by Frank Race, whose farm straddled the Arapahoe-Douglas County line.[7]

During the mid-1930s, dairy farmers faced declining milk prices and escalating farm operation expenses due to Federal price controls and regulations that required investments in new dairy equipment and dairy barn remodeling.[8] Dairy farmers had to add hot water and steam production for cleaning barns and milk handling equipment, milk cooling tanks, and filtration systems.[9] Small dairy farmers, even when associated with multi-farm cooperatives, were unable to acquire such improvements and maintain a positive cash flow. Thus, many small dairy farmers went out of business and sold out to larger dairy farms equipped to meet regulations, increase production, and ease manual workloads. New inventions like milking machines, vacuum tank trucks, and new techniques of artificial insemination for dairy cows were adopted during the 1940s and 1950s. Although overall dairy production increased slightly in the era, the number of dairy farmers diminished; and beef ranching increased dramatically in the early years of WW II. As the County cattle industry shifted from dairy to beef, the number of farms decreased;[10] and the average farm acreage increased, which extended beef-supporting pasture lands and hay acreage.[11] These trends continued throughout the 1940s and 1950s.

Greenland Ranch Reserve Champion Feeder Cattle circa the 1950s

The cash value of the beef market surpassed that of the dairy market in the early 1940s. From 1940 to 1960, the annual average number of beef cattle increased by 3.5%. Impacted by severe drought in the first half of the 1950s, the total number of beef cattle in the County experienced a downward dip; but by 1955, the downward trend stopped and the number of cattle steadily rose.[12] From 1930 to1960, three beef breeds dominated the County's beef industry: Shorthorn, Hereford, and Angus.[13] The Shorthorn was an early entry into Douglas County (circa 1865) and dominated the 1930s. Quality Shorthorn breeders such as Joseph Winkler and A. H. Grant were well known both at the National Western Stock Show and in the Douglas County Fair championship arenas.[14] By the 1940s, Hereford cattle outnumbered the Shorthorn breed on most pasture lands in western Douglas County ranches. Names like Louis R. and William E. Higby, John Paulk, Dave, and Jim Curtis, and R. P. Lamont were well known for their championship Hereford stock. In 1933, Edward Serrell introduced Black Angus beef stock to the County; and the breed became the County's strongest breed in the 1950s, raised by ranchers such as Paul Brown and Norman Smith.[15] For his work in the Black Angus cattle industry, Edward Serrell was named "Cattleman of the Year" by the National Cattlemen's Association in 1942. There were other beef breeds in the County, such as the Santa Gertrudis introduced by "Tweet" Kimballin in 1956; but during the era, Shorthorn, Hereford, and Angus accounted for 95% of the County's beef market.

Hogs and sheep were raised but generally for farm use only, as were feed crops like corn, oats, and alfalfa. Turkeys for market entered the County in 1947, and sheep were raised commercially in the late 1950s. However, neither sheep nor turkeys garnered any significant market share.

Innovations in agriculture had a dramatic impact on farm processes and production. In 1930, one farmer could feed 9.8 people; by 1960, one farmer could feed 25.8 people.[16] The use of new inventions like the three-gang plow (1930), rubber-lugged tractor tires (1937), milking machines (1937), commercial fertilizers (the 1940s), and herbicides and pesticides (1948) impacted farms almost overnight. New heavy equipment allowed the digging of farm ponds in the early 1950s. Interestingly, despite the new manual work-easing inventions introduced during the era, horses still played a large part in farm work in Douglas County. It was 1954 before tractors overtook the use of workhorses in the County.[17]

The most significant impact on County farms was the establishment of the Rural Electric Association (REA) in 1936. In 1930 only 13% of the farms had electricity; by 1950 that percentage reached 80%. Innovation upon innovation eased all kinds of manual work in agriculture. In 1930, 60% of Douglas County's workforce worked in agriculture. By 1960, only 30% of the workforce was in agriculture; and farm production had increased sevenfold![18] The period from 1930 to 1960 was truly a revolutionary era for Douglas County agriculture

[1] Douglas County CO, *USDA Data Files 1930-1960*, accessed December 24, 2017, http://places.mooseroots.com/1/310459/Douglas-County-CO(USDA).

[2] Douglas County Conservation District, *"A Brief History of Conservation Districts,"* accessed December 24, 2017, http://www.dcconservation.com/Districtis/Districts%20info.htm.

[3] Ruth L. Miller, "Time Traveler," *Douglas County News-Press*, May 1, 1996.

[4] Josephine Lowell Marr, *Douglas County: A Historical Journey* (Gunnison, Colorado: B & B Printers, 1983), 189.

[5] Charles E. Kirk, "Douglas County Agriculture Diversified," *Douglas County News*, December 17, 1953, 7.

[6] Ibid.

[7] Helen Daley, "Brief History of Dairying," *Douglas County News,* date unknown. *Douglas County Clippings Notebook*, "Dairy." Douglas County History Research Center.

[8] Helen Daley, "Turning Back the Leaves," *Douglas County News-Press*, November 11, 1980.

[9] Ibid.

[10] Sid Scheiner, "Respected Tradition in Elbert, Douglas Counties," *Douglas County News*, June 28, 1973.

[11] United States Department of Agriculture, "Census of Agriculture Historical Archive: Livestock and Poultry on Farms, Number and Value (Census 1920 to 1959)," 9, accessed December 24, 2017, http://agcensus.mannlib.cornell.edu/AgCensus/getVolumeOnePart.do?year=1959&part_id=468&number=41&title=Colorado.

[12] Ibid.

[13] Kirk, "Douglas County Agricultural Agent."

[14] "Douglas County Cattle Win Honors at Denver Stock Show," *Record-Journal,* January 22, 1937, 1.

[15] Charles E. Kirk, "County Agents Notes," *Record-Journal*, January 10, 1947, 1

[16] "History of American Agriculture," *Growing a Nation: The History of American Agriculture*, accessed January 11, 2018, https://www.agclassroom.org/gan/timeline/1930.htm, https://www.agclassroom.org/gan/timeline/1940.htm,

https://www.agclassroom.org/gan/timeline/1950.htm,
https://www.agclassroom.org/gan/timeline/1960.htm.

[17] "Douglas County History," *Graphic MooseRoots*, accessed December 24, 2017, http://places.mooseroots.com/l/310459/Douglas-County-CO.

[18] Ibid.

Chapter 42

DOUGLAS COUNTY'S TWO CASTLES

Joan Gandy

Two Douglas County mansions were transformed in the decades from 1930 to 1960. Guided by Tweet Kimball, Charlford Castle and the 4,000-plus acres surrounding it became the internationally known Cherokee Ranch and Castle, featuring Colorado's first herd of the Santa Gertrudis breed. Just a few miles north, Lawrence Phipps Jr. breathed new life into a floundering but beautiful property by making Highlands Ranch a hub for upper-class events, including the Arapahoe Hunt Club.

For thirty years, Charlford Castle was a beautiful Douglas County home for the Johnson family. The Scottish castle-inspired home was commissioned by Charles Alfred Johnson and was completed in 1926, after two years of construction. Architect Burnham Hoyt borrowed details from existing English and Scottish castles; and Ben Saunders supervised a large force of workers, including thirty imported Cornish stone masons. The Johnsons' home was an enormous "24-room mansion, built of native stone" with "eight bathrooms, swimming pool, [and] immense library."[1] It also had numerous chimneys, turrets, gargoyles, towers, and a walled courtyard. The great hall measured 25 by 50 feet.[2] Its setting was no less spectacular: "The 'Castle' occupies a commanding site, and a wonderful panorama of the mountains is to be seen from this vantage point."[3]

Over the following decades, three generations of Johnsons lived in the castle home until patriarch Charles' health began to fail. A few months before Charles' death in 1954, the Johnson family and neighbor Ray Blunt sold their adjoining properties, including all the Blunt cattle and Charlford, to Merritt Ruddock,[4] who gave the property to his soon-to-be-former-wife Mildred Montague Genevieve "Tweet" Kimball according to a recent CEO of Cherokee Castle and Ranch, "Her first husband bought her this place because he said there wasn't room on the same side of the Mississippi for both of them. So, he stayed east of the Mississippi; and she got this place west of the Mississippi and lived here happily without him."[5]

Cherokee Castle

Shortly after taking ownership, Tweet, who was from Chattanooga, Tennessee, rechristened her property Cherokee Ranch and launched her Santa Gertrudis cattle business. This breed had been developed on the King Ranch in Texas, and the conventional wisdom was that these heat-tolerant cattle would not do well in Colorado's cooler climate. Tweet thought otherwise. In October 1954, she brought to her ranch twenty-eight head of Santa Gertrudis, including two bulls, twenty-two cows and heifers, and four calves.[6] "The unique operations at Cherokee Ranch, near Sedalia, have attracted national attention and are being observed by breeders throughout the west as an innovation in this part of the country."[7]

Under Tweet's guidance, Colorado's first Santa Gertrudis bull was born in 1955.[8] Ranchers from Australia traveled to Douglas County to view Tweet's herd and operation,[9] as did breeders from Colorado, Nebraska, Wyoming, and Kansas to see "Colorado's most famous herd of Santa Gertrudis cattle."[10]

As Tweet's cattle business thrived, the castle continued to serve as a home for her and her two adopted sons, Kirk and Richard, and a venue for Douglas County social events, including her own wedding to Glenn Walker in March

242

1958 in front of the great fireplace in the main drawing room.[11] As Tweet's vision for her Douglas County ranch materialized, she credited her success to her beloved Colorado land. "As an ardent booster of Colorado and all things to do with the Rocky Mountains, it is a pleasure to report on the small success we just had," Tweet wrote in a letter to the editor. "I think the credit goes to the Rocky Mountain country and grass. The buyers all told us that our animals had the best bone."[12]

North of Sedalia another historic ranch and its manor house became Douglas County's other castle. This property had many owners and name changes: Samuel Allen Long (1884-93); Orin Waid (1893-97); John Springer (1897-1913); John Hughes (1913-1918, Sunland Ranch); Waite Phillips (1920-26, Highland Ranch); Frank Kistler (1926-37, Diamond K Ranch); and Lawrence Phipps, Jr. (1937-1976, Highlands Ranch).[13]

In 1930 Kistler completed a major renovation that transformed the exterior to English Tudor and added a new west wing. Thus, the mansion grew to 22,000 square feet with fourteen bedrooms, eleven bathrooms, five fireplaces, a ballroom, and numerous other rooms.[14] While retaining it as a working ranch, Kistler invited the Arapahoe Hunt Club, headquartered at the Denver Country Club, to use Diamond K Ranch; but after Phipps purchased the property from Kistler, he permanently moved the Hunt to Highlands Ranch.[15]

Highlands Ranch Mansion West Extension

243

On most Thursdays and Sundays, fox hunters bedecked in English fox hunting garb gathered at the 23,000-acre property to follow their hounds toward the prey. "A group of 30 to 40 horsemen all rigged up in 'Pink' coats, astride English saddles, [bounded] over the lone prairie at the foot of the Rockies as if it were a meadow in Merry England. The big difference is that the quarry is not a fox but a coyote. . . . Despite their good horsemanship and fancy eastern togs, the hunters manage to kill only three or four of the wily coyotes every year."[16]

"Without Mr. Phipps' keen insistence on having the best of everything for the Hunt, without his knowledge and love of horses and hounds, without his sporting and gentlemanly instincts, and without his staunch devotion to the highest standards of behavior and dress in the hunting field, we would have no Arapahoe Hunt in any sense of the word."[17]

While Easter egg hunts, birthday parties, political events, and picnics all took place in the shadow of the mansion, Phipps' passion for the English fox hunt exposed many riders to the natural beauty of his land. During a ride on March 11, 1948, a small group of riders traversed more than twenty-five miles across at least seven 640-acre sections of the property.[18]

The scenery was spectacular. A rider described one winter fox hunt: "The going was deep and each time we crossed [Bennet's] Gulch we had to stumble through deep drifts, although on the flat the snow had not drifted too badly. The galloping across the north pastures was gorgeous. . . . When we hit the slow uphill rise to Rocky Hill on the anticline to the Rocky Mountains, one of the most dramatic ends of a hunt it has ever been my privilege to see took place. . . . With the sun setting over Devil's Head in the deep twilight, we saw the coyote trotting slowly up a cow path in the white snow. This is the only hunt I can remember at the end of which the horses, hounds, field, staff, and coyote were completely exhausted."[19]

Both properties became protected spaces in the county. Tweet Kimball worked with Douglas County to create a conservation easement through which the Cherokee Ranch and Castle Foundation holds title to the land for use as a wildlife sanctuary and host for various special events. The Highlands Ranch Metro District bought the mansion in 2010, finished new renovations in 2012, and now offers free public tours and rental space for business meetings, receptions, weddings, and holiday parties.[20]

[1] "Charlford and Vel-Ray Properties Sold This Week to Utah Woman," *Douglas County News*, May 13, 1954, 1; "Cherokee Ranch and Castle History," accessed March 23, 2018, http://cherokeeranch.org.

[2] Susan Consola Appleby, *Fading Past: The Story of Douglas County, Colorado* (Palmer Lake: Filter Press, 2001), 171.

[3] "The C.A. Johnsons Now Live in Castle," *Record-Journal*, July 8, 1928, 1.

[4] "Charlford and Vel-Ray Properties Sold This Week to Utah Woman."

[5] "Celebrate Tweet Kimball's 100th birthday at Waterloo at Cherokee Ranch and Castle," *Westworld*, June 10, 2014, accessed March 31, 2018, http://www.westword.com/arts/celebrate-tweet-kimballs-100th-birthday-at-waterloo-at-cherokee-castle-and-ranch-5781127

[6] "Santa Gertrudis Cattle Now at Cherokee Ranch," *Douglas County News*, October 21, 1954, 1.

[7] "Mrs. Ruddoch Adds to Santa Gertrudis Herd on Texas Buying Trip," *Douglas County News*, November 24, 1955, 8.

[8] Ibid.

[9] "Stockmen from Australia Visit Cherokee Ranch Sunday," *Douglas County News*, May 24, 1956, 1.

[10] "Santa Gertrudis Day at Cherokee Ranch," *Douglas County News*, September 19, 1957, 2

[11] "Walker-Kimball Wedding Held at Cherokee Castle," *Douglas County News*, March 20, 1958, 11.

[12] "Colorado Grass the Best Cow Builder," *Douglas County News*, June 16, 1960, 1.

[13] "L.C. Phipps, Jr., Buys 'Diamond K' from Kistler," *Record-Journal,* December 24, 1937, 1.

[14] Appleby, *Fading Past*, 71.

[15] Highlands Ranch Metro District, "Highlands Ranch History," accessed on March 23, 2018, https://highlandsranch.org/community history.

[16] "Life Goes to the Arapahoe Hunt," *Life Magazine*, May 30, 1949, 107-108.

[17] William W. Grant, *A Quarter Century of the Arapahoe Hunt* (Colorado: Privately printed, 1954).

[18] Ibid.

[19] Ibid.

[20] www.highlandsranchmansion.com

Chapter 43

CONSOLIDATING THE SCHOOLS

Shaun Boyd

In 1930, there were thirty-two school districts in Douglas County. In 1960, there was only one. The transformation from these independent school districts to a single Douglas County RE-1 School District in 1958 was part of a wave of school consolidations throughout the state. The School District Reorganization Act of 1949[1] encouraged school districts to consolidate; and local elections greatly reduced the number of school districts state-wide, from 2,105 in 1953 to 937 in 1965.[2]

In Douglas County, each of the thirty-two "one-room school" districts had its own 3-person school board that managed buildings, raised money for school events, and kept records of attendance and grades. Ever since schools were founded in Douglas County in 1861, a Superintendent of Schools was elected by popular vote to oversee all County schools. The Superintendent chose the curriculum, set expectations for teachers, and kept records of all potential students aged 6-17 who had not completed the 8th grade. The first elected Superintendent of Schools on record was George Redman, an early settler in the Spring Valley area of southern Douglas County.

Douglas County High School 1943

The one-room schools included grades 1-8. In the beginning, few students went on to high school. In 1939 there were two high schools in the County. Parker High School met in the Consolidated School building on Mainstreet. Douglas County High School had separate facilities on Wilcox Street in today's Douglas County School District Administration Building.

In 1950, the legislature asked all County Superintendents to form committees to explore school consolidation. In 1951-1952, the consolidation process was already underway in Douglas County. First, the Jarre Creek and Round Top Schools merged with Sedalia in March 1951. In May, four districts in the southeastern part of the County merged into Cherry Valley School, which opened in September 1952. The Rattlesnake School, a joint district with Elbert County, closed in October 1951, when its students were transferred to the school in Parker, which deprived generations of eastern Douglas County children of the fun of saying that they attended Rattlesnake Elementary.

Despite the state's encouragement, on January 10, 1952, DC voters rejected the idea of a County-wide School district by a vote of 864-101. Nevertheless, school consolidation continued because of shifting population patterns and access to new transportation options. New schools were built that year at Gann, Plum Creek (near Chatfield State Park), and Sedalia; and five small schools near the borders of Douglas, Arapahoe, and Elbert Counties began sending their children to Parker. Total school enrollment in January 1952 was 740: 207 in the two high schools and 533 in grades 1-8.[3]

Consolidation remained a live issue both at the local and state levels over the next few years. The state legislature passed another School Reorganization Act in 1957 that required counties to reassess the benefits of forming a single county-wide school district. Meanwhile, school bus drivers, nurses, and other non-teaching personnel were hired in Douglas County.

In April 1958, the Douglas County School Reorganization Committee, consisting of members from each of the smaller districts in the County, presented a plan for approval to both the public and the state. Committee members included Chairman Ed Rodine, Parker; Secretary Robert Metzler (Superintendent—ex officio); Bess Albin, Franktown; Don Brown, Larkspur; Charles Tannin, Cherry Valley; David Stump, Westcreek; Charles Higby, Greenland; George Manhart, Castle Rock; Frank Fenton, Louviers; Mary Wilkinson, Plum Creek; Archie Hier, Sedalia; Helen Arfsten, Spring Valley; and

William Lane, Indian Park. John Paulk, representing the Douglas County High School; Dorothy Woodhouse, Gann; Hank Kimbrough, Deckers; and William Higman, Hilltop were ex-officio members.[4] To be eligible to vote in the County-wide referendum, one had to be over 21, reside in the County for at least 90 days, and be a taxpayer on real or personal property (car taxes did not count).[5]

The new school district plan was adopted in May 1958, by a vote of 714 to 161. Only Cherry Valley voted against the plan, though it had already gone through its own consolidation in 1952.[6] The plan significantly altered the leadership of the district: now there would be a County-wide election to select seven school board members, the same number elected today. The first elected Douglas County RE-1 School Board included several well-known names from the community: Frank Fenton of Louviers; Dr. W. G. Duncan of Sedalia; Dr. H. R. Gannon of Castle Rock; Willis Buboltz of Castle Rock; Darrell Bell of Larkspur; Emery Larreau of Franktown; and Ed Rodine of Parker.[7] Under the new plan, the School Superintendent would no longer be elected by popular vote but appointed by the school board and have more administrative and oversight duties than previously. The last popularly elected Douglas County School Superintendent was Robert Metzler, a native of Castle Rock and by then a nationally recognized school administrator. He was first elected in 1952 and re-elected in 1958, just as the Douglas County RE-1 School District was taking shape.

Dr. Lowell Baumunk 1970 DCHS Huskies

It took a few years to make the new plan fully operational. For the next four years, Metzler helped the new school board get organized. Finally, in 1962 the board reviewed seventy applicants and selected its first Superintendent, Lowell Baumunk, a Kansas native and school administrator from Yuma, Colorado. He got a three-year contract and an annual salary of $9,400.[8] Though there were now two superintendents in the County, Baumunk was clearly in charge. He was the one who met with the school board, carried out its policies, hired new teachers, and guided the district's day-to-day operations. Metzler, on the other hand, did public relations. He met with various PTAs and other civic groups to explain and promote the new system, judged local and state spelling bees, hosted district music festivals, and attended educational conferences at which he often spoke on the growing use of technology in public education, what he called "tele-education."[9] After being elected a third time, Metzler left DC to become the Superintendent of Schools in Clear Creek County.[10] In the 1966 election, the people of Douglas County voted to abolish Metzler's old position.[11]

Consolidation changed County schools. In May 1958, Parker High School had nine graduates; and Douglas County High School had forty-one.[12] One of the first decisions of the new school board was to close Parker High School and move its forty students to Douglas County High School, whose facilities had been updated and expanded for the 1958-1959 school year. There were now eleven elementary schools in the new county-wide district: Sedalia, Franktown, Indian Park, Larkspur, Plum Creek, Louviers, Castle Rock, Cherry Valley, Gann, Parker, and Westcreek, which was the County's smallest school with only ten students.[13] Between 1950 and 1960, the County's population grew by 37% (3507 to 4816). The school enrollment grew to 1204, up from 740 in 1952, a 63% increase. Almost half of these students were in Castle Rock, which enrolled 313 in its elementary school and 285 in the high school.[14]

In time, Douglas County Schools became one of the finest school districts in Colorado. The consolidation of its schools in the 1950s laid a firm foundation for its future greatness.

¹ School Reorganization Act of 1949:
https://www.coloradohistoricnewspapers.org/cgi-
bin/colorado?a=d&d=EVE19490624-01.2.14&srpos=3&e=-------en-20--1--txt-txIN-
%22School+District+Reorganization+Act+of+1949%22-------2-#
²http://coloradopreservation.org/crsurvey/ranching/sites/rch_contexts_educati
on.html.
³ *Douglas County News*, January 10, 1952; ibid., May 22, 1952.
⁴ Ibid., January 10,1952; "School Reorganization Plan is Announced/Ready for
Submission to State Board of Education," ibid., April 10, 1958.
⁵ "1600 Qualified to Ballot One Committee Proposal," ibid., May 1, 1958.
⁶ Ibid., May 8, 1958.
⁷ Ibid., July 3, 1958.
⁸ Ibid., August 14, 1958.
⁹ Ibid., February 18, 1959; ibid., May 14, 1959; ibid., November 26, 1959; ibid.,
February, 1960; ibid., April 13, 1961.
¹⁰ Ibid., October 1, 1964.
¹¹Ibid., November 3, 1966; ibid., November 10, 1966.
¹² Ibid., May 22, 1958.
¹³ "DCHS to Launch School Year Next Tuesday Morning with Expanded
Curriculum," ibid, August 28, 1958; "County Grade Schools to Open Next Tuesday
AM," ibid., May 22, 1958.
¹⁴ "Enrollment in County up 7.5%," ibid., September 22, 1960.

Chapter 44

PHILIP S. MILLER

Jim Hansmann

Philip Simon Miller, Jr. was born in Peoria, Illinois, on October 11, 1895. In 1906 Philip, Sr., known as Butch, moved his wife, Lena, and sons, Adam and Philip, Jr., to Denver. Lena had been diagnosed with tuberculosis and needed a drier climate. Unfortunately, within two years Lena's consumption caught up with her; and she died on November 12, 1908. Butch, whose profession was meat cutting, had opened a meat market in downtown Denver; and he and his two sons stayed busy in that profession.

Philip S. Miller 1915

Butch Miller grew tired of the big city, so in 1917 he and Philip moved to Elizabeth, where he already raised hogs and cattle for his business.[1] Father and son also opened the Miller Meat Market. His older brother, Adam, remained in Denver and soon enlisted in the Army to serve in World War I. He joined the family in Elizabeth after his discharge in 1919. The Millers then opened stores in Kiowa and Castle Rock. During this time Philip met Jessie Ethel Stewart, who preferred the name "Jerry." Married in 1921, she became the love of his life, constant companion, and business partner.

In the 1920s the Millers made some difficult business decisions. The Millers had partners in the Kiowa and Castle Rock stores; and when the Castle Rock partner decided to retire, it created a dilemma for the Miller family. Philip, who was now running the business, determined that the Castle Rock store was the most promising and therefore decided to buy out the partner, which required a bank loan. "I went in to borrow a couple of thousand dollars—and that was a lot of money in those days."[2] The banker turned him down. Miller said he never forgot that snub and decided that if he ever owned a bank, he would look out for small business owners.[3] Without the bank loan, he had to sell the farm and the Millers' interest in the Elizabeth and Kiowa stores and then moved to Castle Rock in 1921.

Castle Rock and Douglas County became home to Philip and Jerry. They moved into the second-floor apartment of the old Douglas County Courthouse on 4th Street. Philip bought out his former business partner and opened his meat market in a corner of the Keystone Hotel, a short half-block walk for him each day. He also built a slaughterhouse on Lake Gulch Road. At the market, Jerry worked side-by-side with her husband. "She ground hamburger, rendered lard, sliced bacon, and unpacked meat."[4]

The business quickly outgrew its location and moved across the street to 320 Wilcox Street, which today is the south dining room of the B & B Café. Phil also changed its name from Miller's Meat Market to Castle Rock Meat Market. Miller sold the market in 1928 and opened a fuel and feed store just a block away, in a former livery stable at 413 Wilcox Street. As usual, Jerry was right there with him as office manager in this new endeavor. The business looked promising, but then disaster struck: the Stock Market Crash of October 29, 1929.

Douglas County and the Millers were hit hard by the Great Depression. By 1932, Miller's business was in dire straits which forced him to lay off everyone except his wife who just happened to be working for free. He had to shovel the coal himself but still earned only a dollar a ton. "I'd have to go up and load a truckload of coal off the railroad car. I'd load it on my truck and then shovel it off to all my customers."[5] He was going broke and decided it was time to go back to what he knew best.

In July 1933, Miller was again running the meat market at 320 Wilcox Street.[6] He managed to keep the fuel and feed store for two more years, then sold it to a former employee, Ben Saunders. Meanwhile, the Depression forced the closure of Castle Rock State Bank (1932) and First National Bank (1933). Area businessmen were concerned about the loss of the banks and were determined to do something about it.

This crisis was Philip Miller's opportunity to go into the banking business. Several businessmen came to him with the idea of organizing a local bank.

Under his guidance, they determined that a State Bank would be preferable because it was much more expensive to obtain a charter for a National Bank. Still, raising the required $25,000 was not easy; but Miller's determination paid off.

Under Miller's leadership, The Bank of Douglas County was established. "He was forty-four years old, and this time there was no turning back!"[7] To support the new venture, in 1938-1939, Miller sold the meat market and all his cattle to Fred White; and several DC ranchers, farmers, and businesspeople contributed to the new enterprise. There were twenty-seven shareholders.[8] On August 28, 1939, the bank opened across from the Keystone Hotel in Castle Rock with Louis R. Higby, Sr. of Greenland as President and Philip S. Miller, Jr., as Vice President and Chief Operating Officer.[9] Two years later, Philip sold the slaughterhouse to Fred White. The butcher was now a banker.

The 1940s were years of change for the Millers. Though there were difficult times, the bank prospered. Within two months of opening, the bank had $30,000 in deposits. Six months later, that figure had more than doubled.[10] During the war years, the bank grew slowly but steadily; and Miller found ways to serve the community. In 1943, he chaired the Third War Bond Drive in the County and collected 144% of the assigned quota.[11] In the same year, he bought an insurance agency, renamed it the P.S. Miller Insurance Agency, and moved it into the bank.[12] Phil and Jenny also purchased the Cole Briscoe Ranch south of the DC Fair Grounds, where they built a beautiful ranch house and raised prize-winning Shorthorn cattle.[13] Finally, he gave his wife ten shares of stock in the bank, thus allowing her to sit on the Board of Directors, a position she held for the next forty years.[14]

In 1950, Miller began buying out the other major stockholders, thus becoming "majority stockholder, owner and President of The Bank of Douglas County."[15] In practical terms, that meant that Phil did nearly everything. While he handled bank loans and wore a coat and tie during the week, on weekends he and Jerry were the janitors. They "put on grubby clothes [to] dust and mop the floors, wash the windows, clean the bathrooms, and clean out the coal furnace!"[16] He knew his customers and was committed to the growth of both his hometown and the County. Throughout his banking career, Miller looked out for local businesspeople, ranchers, and farmers. He did not hesitate to extend or refinance a small dairy loan. He could be counted on to help "a newcomer to the community."[17] At first, most loans were agricultural but as Castle Rock and the County grew, The Bank of Douglas County lent its generous support to the changing community.

In the following decades, the Millers became DC's biggest benefactors. Over two decades he and Jerry donated $700,000 to the Douglas County Library[18] and supported several other local causes, including 4-H and the DC Fair. Jerry died in 1987, but Phil retained his position as Bank President until 1993.[19] He died in 1995 at the age of 99. The Millers had no children, so they left behind a Perpetual Charitable Trust of over $30 million. Every year its earned income is distributed to nine beneficiaries including Castle Rock, Douglas County, high school

Philip Simon Miller

scholarships, and the Douglas County Library.[20] As a result, his trust has helped to finance major projects throughout the County, including the Miller Activities Complex and the adjoining 270-acre Philip S. Miller Park in Castle Rock. According to Jamie LaRue, the former Director of DC Libraries, "Miller's keen business instincts and attendant success allowed him to raise the quality of life for children and adults in the county for which he felt great loyalty."[21]

---

[1] Debbie Buboltz-Bodle, *Philip Simon Miller Butcher, Banker and Benefactor: His Life and Legacy in Douglas County, Colorado* (Phoenix: Phoenix Publishing Group, 1998), 27.

[2] Dianna Gordon, "Philip S. Miller—Quiet hero in fast-paced world," *Douglas County News-Press,* August 12, 1980, 2.

[3] Buboltz-Bodle, *Philip Simon Miller,* 49.

[4] Dianna Gordon, "Jerry Miller takes pride in husband's accomplishments," *Douglas County News-Press,* August 12, 1980, 7.

[5] "Salute to Miller," *Douglas County News-Press,* August 30, 1979, 2.

[6] Buboltz-Bodle, *Philip Simon Miller,* 63.

[7] Ibid., 118.
[8] Ibid., 119 for a complete list of these stockholders.
[9] Ibid., 119-120.
[10] Ibid., 124.
[11] "Douglas County Makes 144% of its War Bond Quota," *Record-Journal*, October 8, 1943, 1.
[12] Buboltz-Bodle, *Philip Simon Miller*, 151-157.
[13] Ibid., 139-149.
[14] Ibid, 126.
[15] Ibid.
[16] Ibid, 125.
[17] Ibid, 161-162.
[18] Ibid, 207-234.
[19] *Douglas County News-Press*, January 12, 1984.
[20] Buboltz-Bodle, *Philip Simon Miller*, 257.
[21] Jamie LaRue, "20 Who Made a Difference: Philip S. Miller," *Douglas County News- Press*, January 21, 1995, 16B.

PART FIVE

The Big Change, 1960-1990

Chapter 45
TRAINS, TRUCKS, AND AUTOMOBILES

Tim Weber

In the 1910s it took about five and a half hours to drive the 75 miles between Denver and Colorado Springs on US 85, a rutted gravel road with steep grades and sharp turns that locals called "the ribbon of death." By 1915, 250 cars were making the perilous trip every day.[1]

Even after US 85 was paved in the late 1920s,[2] most travelers took the train. By the late 1880s, two railroads connected Denver and Colorado Springs through DC: the Denver & Rio Grande and the Atchison, Topeka & the Santa Fe. In 1909 the two railroads scheduled daily thirteen southbound and eleven northbound passenger trains between the two cities, with stops at depots in Louviers, Sedalia, Castle Rock, Larkspur, Greenland, Palmer Lake, and Monument. The trip between Denver and Colorado Springs took slightly over two and a half hours: about an hour between Denver and Castle Rock and an hour and a half between Castle Rock and Colorado Springs.[3] Thus, in the early twentieth century, taking the train was more than twice as fast as driving an automobile.

The trains also carried most freight. DC residents shipped their agricultural, dairy, lumber, and rhyolite products north and south and "imported" needed goods. In short, the railroads were the lifeline between DC and the outside world, as well as between the DC towns along the railway.

Transportation through DC changed with the coming of freeways in the 1950s and 1960s. In 1949, the new north-south Valley Highway (US 87) through Denver reached DC. By 1952, it stretched from the Arapahoe County line to Castle Rock as a two-lane cement roadway with extra passing lanes on inclines. Just north of Castle Rock, US 87 merged with US 85 (Santa Fe Road) near the location of today's Douglas County High School at Liggett Road and Front Street. US 85/US 87 then bypassed the town and continued to Larkspur as four lanes.

Hauling Freight Through Douglas County

In 1956, Congress passed the National Interstate and Defense Highways Act; and the new highway became Interstate 25. By 1958, US 85/US 87 had four lanes through DC. The law mandated that interstates also include controlled access, interchanges with overpasses, medians, drainage systems, signage, and, in some places, frontage roads and rest stops.

The Colorado Highway Commission was responsible for finishing I-25. It divided the project into three phases: Arapahoe County to Castle Rock, Larkspur to Monument, and Castle Rock to Larkspur.[4] Phase one included interchanges at Beverly Hills (Castle Pines Parkway/Hess Road), Happy Canyon, and Silver Heights (Meadows/Founders Parkway).[5] Phase two proposed four interchanges at Larkspur, Greenland, County Line Road, and Monument.[6] These plans generated little opposition because those areas were sparsely populated farm and ranch land.

Plans for phase three created controversy because they involved the most populated area between Arapahoe and El Paso Counties. In 1960, one-quarter of DC's entire population lived in Castle Rock (1,152 of 4,816). From the outset, residents complained about the town's northern "interchange" at Cemetery Road (today's Wolfensberger) and Wilcox Street. It consisted of an off-ramp for southbound I-25 motorists and an on-ramp for northbound traffic. Missing were an off-ramp for north-bound autos, an on-ramp for south-bound travelers, and an overpass to connect Cemetery Road and Wilcox Street.[7] To get from one side of the freeway to the other, motorists had to cross the four lanes of I-25, which could be a harrowing experience. Two motorists were killed in March 1962 while trying to do so.[8] Citizens also worried about school buses crossing the freeway, since the nearly completed Douglas County High School was located close to the interchange.[9]

Angry residents petitioned the DC Commissioners to pressure the Highway Commission to change[10] what one citizen called "the most dangerous intersection ever engineered in the state of Colorado."[11] Finally, seven months later, the State Highway Engineer announced that an overpass and sufficient on/off-ramps would be built at Cemetery Road/Wilcox Street and promised similar structures for the rest of the interchanges through the County.[12]

Traffic Stalled Near Castle Rock after the 1965 Flood

The four-lane stretch between Castle Rock and Larkspur required extensive re-engineering. The freeway's existing two southbound lanes became the west-side frontage road, which provided access to the Continental Divide Raceways. The original two northbound lanes became southbound, which required the construction of new northbound lanes and an east-side frontage road between Larkspur and Castle Rock.[13] Unfortunately, the 1965 flood along Plumb Creek destroyed much of the new construction, including the overpass connecting Cemetery Road and Wilcox Street.[14] Consequently, I-25 was not completed until 1968. Once finished, the new freeway reduced the drive time between Denver and Colorado Springs (now 69 miles) to an hour and a half.[15]

How did the new interstate affect the railroads? From the late 1940s, increased auto and airline traffic reduced passenger ridership on the railroads. To reverse this trend, in 1970 Congress established AMTRAK, which identified the most profitable passenger routes, upgraded equipment and service, and increased advertising. The new AMTRAK system made no difference in DC because by then the County's once-busy railroad depots had closed. For example, the AT&SF depot in Castle Rock was decommissioned in 1947 and became a residence in the 1950s.[16] The D&RG depot was closed in 1967. Three years later it was sold, moved to Elbert Street, and remodeled into a residence. In 1997 it became a museum.[17] In Larkspur, the AT&SF depot closed in 1940, then moved to Palmer Lake in 1954; and the D&RG depot permanently closed in 1954.[18] One of the depots in Sedalia relocated and became a residence, and the other was dismantled, and its materials sold.[19] Other depots were demolished. After three-quarters of a century, DC's most efficient means of passenger travel between Arapahoe and El Paso Counties disappeared. Automobile travel became the only alternative.

The interstate also decreased the amount of freight carried by the railroads. Before the interstate system, railroads carried most of the nation's long-haul freight: 90% in 1940 and 80% in 1961.[20] With the coming of the interstates, trucks carried most freight: 70% in 1980 and 87% in 2004.[21] This dramatic turn-around was caused by the deregulation of the trucking industry in the 1970s and the use of semis or 18-wheelers that increased shipping capacity and reduced expenses. Drivers on I-25 must share the road with trucks that play the dominant role in interstate commerce.

During the 1980s, a second freeway was built in DC to accommodate traffic generated by Highlands Ranch, the most populous part of the County. First proposed as Interstate 470, plans changed after unfavorable environmental studies in the early 1970s suggested a divided parkway with cross streets and traffic signals. Finally, it was decided to build a four-lane freeway with interchanges that connected with I-25 in the east and I-70 in the west after passing through Jefferson County. The freeway through DC was built in sections between 1982 and 1990.[22] Thus I-470 became SH 470, which is more popularly known as C-470.[23]

[1] Colorado Historical Society Office of Archaeology and Preservation, *Colorado State Roads and Highways*, National Register of Historic Places, Continuation Sheet, E-22, accessed December 13, 2018, http://legacy.historycolorado.org/sites/default/files/files/OAHP/crforms_edumat/pdfs/645.pdf

[2] *Record-Journal*, January 14, 1927, 4.

[3] "Timecards," *Record Journal*, July 16, 1909, 8.

[4] "Interstate 25 History," *Colorado Department of Transportation*, accessed June 3, 2018, http//www.cdot/gov/about/CDOTHISTORY/50th-anniversary/interstate-25

[5] "More Good News for DC," *Douglas County News*, September 3, 1964, 8; "Douglas County Road Bid In," *Douglas County News*, September 17, 1964, 10.

[6] "Four Interchanges Set for Interstate 25," *Douglas County News*, January 9, 1964, 1.

[7] "Castle Rock Entrance and Exists on Interstate 25," *Douglas County News*, October 11, 1962, 1; *Douglas County News*, October 4, 1962, 1.

[8] *Douglas County News*, March 8, 1962, 1; *Douglas County News*, March 15, 1962, 1.

[9] "Letter from George Kobolt," *Douglas County News*, March 22, 1962, 1, 5.

[10] "Douglas County Commissioners Send Resolution to Ghent," *Douglas County News*, March 22, 1962, 1; "Hiway Department Treated Us Well, Writes Monk, *Douglas County News*, March 29, 1962, 1; Ben Fann, "Is There an Adequate Entrance to Castle Rock?" *Douglas County News*, April 12, 1962, 1, 5.

[11] "Not All True Says Shumate," *Douglas County News*, September 12, 1963, 1.

[12] "Highway Entrances to be Built in 1963," *Douglas County News*, October 4, 1962, 1,3; "Not All True Says Shumate," *Douglas County News*, September 12, 1963, 1; "Douglas County Has Good Tidings," *Douglas County News*, December 19, 1963, 1.

[13] "Highway Entrance to be Built in 1963," *Douglas County News*, October 4, 1962, 1, 3; "Four Interchanges set for Interstate 25," *Douglas County News*, January 9, 1964, 1; "Larkspur Service Road Being Bid," *Douglas County News*, December 10, 1964, 11; "Road Project," *Douglas County News*, December 31, 1964, 11.

[14] *Douglas County News*, August 26, 1965, 13.

[15] "Distance from Colorado Springs to Denver," *Trippy*, accessed on December 13, 2018, https://www.trippy.com/distance/Colorado-Springs-to-Denver

[16] "698 Prairie Hawk Drive, Castle Rock, CO—Town of Castle Rock—Survey of Historic Resources," accessed Feb. 1, 2019, http://douglascountyhistory.org/digital/collection/documents/id/192/rec/1

[17] Susan Consola Appleby, *Fading Past: The Story of Douglas County, Colorado* (Palmer Lake, CO: Filter Press, 2001), 20-21.

[18] Master Timeline—Larkspur Historical Society. Accessed February 4, 2019, https://studylib.net/doc/8645692/master-timeline---larkspur-historical-society.

[19] "Sedalia Scuttle," *Douglas County News*, October 6, 1955, 13.

[20] Richard F. Weingroff, "Moving the Goods: As the Interstate Era Begins," *Highway History*, Federal Highway Administration, accessed February 1, 2019, https://www.fhwa.dot.gov/interstate/freight.cfm

[21] Thomas Gale Moore, "Trucking Deregulation," *The Concise Encyclopedia of Economics*, accessed on February 1, 2019, http://www.econlib.org/library/Enc1/TruckingDeregulation.html; "Trucking Deregulation in the United States: Submission by the United States to the Ibero-America Competition Forum, Sept, 2007, 2, accessed February 1, 2019, http://www.ftc.govsites/default/files/attachments/us-submissions-oecd-and-other-international-competition-fora-ibero-tructing.pdf

[22] "Interstate 470 Colorado," accessed on January 20, 2019, http://www.interstate-guide.com/i_470_co.html.

[23] For an extensive collection of material on the history of transportation in Douglas County, see the *Transportation Books, I, II, and III*, assembled by Douglas Country History Research Center Staff and Volunteers, located in the DCHRC in Castle Rock. See also *100 Years of Colorado State Transportation History* (Denver: CDOT Public Relations, n.d.).

Chapter 46
GROWING PAINS

Larry Schlupp

From 1960 to 1990, Douglas County experienced population growth and demographic change. Its population increased from 4,816 to 60,391. In 1960, the County was overwhelmingly rural; but by 1990 it was only 40% rural. Its pattern of employment changed too. In 1960, 94% of its workers were employed within the County; but by 1980, its in-County workers declined to 24%.[1] During these three decades, DC changed: its population grew, it became less rural, its percentage of commuters increased, and its government struggled to adapt.

During the 1960s, DC grew 75%, thanks especially to the 1955 opening of the U.S. Air Force Academy and the arrival of military retirees from El Paso County. They came because the land was cheaper in DC, and there were new financial opportunities in land development.[2] During the 1970s and 1980s, DC's growth came mostly from the north, due to Denver's booming energy, defense, and technology industries.[3]

Until the mid-1970s, Denver had met its housing needs by annexing land from neighboring counties. But in 1974, activist Freda Poundstone of Greenwood Village in Arapahoe County started a campaign to stop Denver's land-grab policies. She led a ballot initiative to amend the state constitution to require that all future annexations be approved by popular vote. The amendment stopped Denver's annexations and stimulated the growth of Arapahoe, Jefferson, and Douglas Counties.[4]

DC's government was not prepared for sudden growth. The Commissioners had no master plan to guide them or much experience dealing with high-powered developers who wanted to turn farm and ranch land into high-density housing. DC's residents were deeply divided about growth issues. Many landowners were eager to cash in on rising property values. Land that sold for $60 to $100 per acre twenty years before now sold for $2,500.[5] Others wanted to preserve DC's small towns and wide-open spaces. The DC Commissioners were thus caught between people who preferred the status quo and those who demanded unfettered property rights.

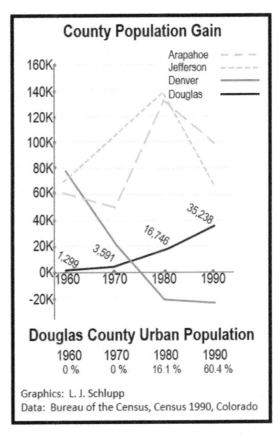

County Population Gain

Arapahoe
Jefferson
Denver
Douglas

Douglas County Urban Population

1960	1970	1980	1990
0 %	0 %	16.1 %	60.4 %

Graphics: L. J. Schlupp
Data: Bureau of the Census, Census 1990, Colorado

After World War II, land developers created "special districts" to provide electricity, water, gas, fire protection, waste management, and other services.[6] Anti-growth counties could stop building projects by refusing to approve these special-purpose districts. In 1965, the Colorado General Assembly sided with the developers by enacting the Special District Control Act. It stipulated that "the burden of proof resides with the commissioners to demonstrate that the district's petition has not met the requirements" mandated by the 1965 law.[7] Under the new rules, DC Commissioners had little choice but to approve nearly all the special district proposals during the 1970s and 1980s.

In 1972 the General Assembly also mandated that all counties produce master plans to guide growth. But in DC, antagonism between pro- and anti-growth proponents made it exceedingly difficult to reach a consensus. Commissioners rejected the first master plan proposal in the early 1970s. In the mid-1970s, they rejected a second proposal after intense opposition.[8] Finally in 1983, eleven years after the state's mandate, the Commissioners approved the DC's first master plan.[9] In the following years, the master plan was reviewed and updated many times.

By then, DC was in chaos. Early on, numerous inexperienced, under-funded, and according to some citizens, underhanded developers were approved for housing projects. After creating special districts, the builders bought land, divided it into city lots, and sold them to eager buyers. But before they put in promised utilities, many developers went bankrupt, leaving their customers responsible for finishing the project themselves. All over the County, there were subdivisions in trouble.

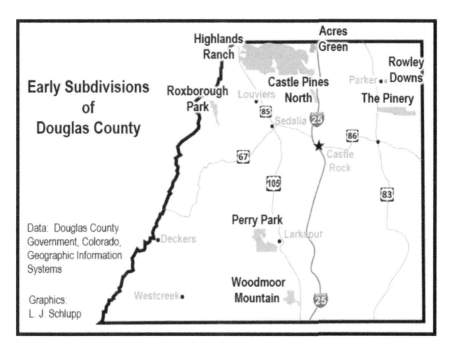

Early Subdivisions of Douglas County

Data: Douglas County Government, Colorado, Geographic Information Systems

Graphics: L. J. Schlupp

Two of the biggest fiascos were Perry Park and The Pinery.[10] In 1967, the Colorado Western Development Company started the 14,000-acre Perry Park Ranch in southwestern DC. But the company soon went bankrupt. After a series of legal battles, in 1977 residents created a new metropolitan district which enabled them to complete the subdivision.[11] In 1971 Terracor, Inc. started The Pinery on 5,500 acres east of Highway 83 and south of Parker with no plan for local governance. By 1976 residents were complaining about a lack of promised services. In 1981 Terracor went bankrupt, and residents turned to the DC government for help. The County refused to solve The Pinery's problems and advised residents to form a metropolitan district. The residents refused, and for the next decade, they rejected all attempts to establish self-rule.

Incorporated Castle Rock had problems too. In 1984, just south of the town and west of I-25, Castle Rock Ranches was approved by the Town Council for 7,900 homes. After four miles of parkway and some utilities were finished, the developer went bankrupt. In 2003 a new buyer changed the name to Dawson Ridge but was never able to resume construction.[12] In the same year, Castle Meadows, a 3,600 acres multi-use development west of US 85, was approved. Financial difficulties required a new buyer who changed the name to Lincoln Meadows but made slow progress. In 1997 Castle Rock Developers bought the Meadows, and two decades later it is approaching its final build-out.[13] Both of these projects sputtered because Castle Rock had not yet started its growth spurt. Supply far exceeded demand.

Douglas County's first northern subdivision was Acres Green, developed by Morris General Contracting in 1971 along the Arapahoe and Douglas County line.[14] At about the same time the Woodmoor Corporation started Roxborough Park in northwest DC but filed bankruptcy in 1974.[15] Also in the 1970s, Parker City Land Corporation built Rowley Downs with plans for other subdivisions totaling a population of 15,000.[16] In the late-1970s, several retired military veterans built the Woodmoor Mountain subdivision in southern DC and later expanded it with the help of a revived Woodmoor Corporation.[17]

Overshadowing all other DC subdivisions was Highlands Ranch. In 1978, the Mission Viejo Company acquired 33.5 square miles in northern DC from Marvin Davis who had obtained it from the estate of Lawrence Phipps II.[18] Shea Properties later purchased Highlands Ranch from Mission Viejo with plans to build a city of over 90,000, at a time when DC's total population was about 25,000. Highlands Ranch became DC's largest community, but its residents have rejected all efforts to incorporate.[19] In 1980 Jack Vickers started Castle Pines North. Bankruptcy followed a series of legal and tax disputes. After a few years, Castle Pines North finally became financially viable. Other subdivisions followed in rapid succession during the 1980s.

Where did DC's new residents come from? The County's major population accelerator in the 1970s and 1980s was the development of the Denver Technological Center, the Meridian Business Park, and Inverness Business

270

Park along I-25 in southern Arapahoe and northern Douglas Counties. Hewlett Packard, Kodak, Honeywell, First Data Corporation, EchoStar, and CH2M employed more than 70,000 people.[20] With the completion of I-25 in the 1960s and C-470 in the 1980s, commuters had easy access to DC, which was quickly becoming a bedroom community for people who worked elsewhere. But DC's most explosive population growth was yet to come.

[1] "Employment-to-Population Ratio, 1980," *1983 Master Plan* (Castle Rock, CO: Douglas County Planning Commission), 12.

[2] Personal interview with Bill Noe, Monument, CO, November 15, 2018. Noe was DC's Planning Director, 1973-1978.

[3] Richard L. Forstall, "Population of Counties by Decennial Census, 1900-1990," *US Bureau of Census*, March, 1995, accessed September 29, 2018, https://www.census.gov/population/cencounts/co190090.txt.

[4] Kevin Weinman, "Invisible Suburbs: Privatized Growth in Suburban Metropolitan Denver, 1950-2000," Ph.D. Dissertation, University of New Hampshire, May, 2017, 131, University of New Hampshire Scholars' Repository, accessed December 16, 2018, https://scholas.unh.edu/cgi/viewcontent.cgi?article=dissertation.

[5] Ibid., 53.

[6] Ibid., 82.

[7] Ibid., 107.

[8] Noe, personal interview.

[9] Weinman, "Invisible Suburbs," 112.

[10] Ibid.,114-130.

[11] Ardis Webb, *The Perry Park Story* (Denver: Ardis & Olin, 1974), 52-54.

[12] Ross Dolan, "Dawson Ridge, Sleeping Giant is Stirring," *Castle Rock Star*, September 28, 2003, 1, 3.

[13] *Douglas County News-Press*, July 20, 1984; *Denver Post*, December 12, 1984; Mary Beth Jannakos, "Meadows Subdivision Sold," *Douglas County News-Press*, October 8, 1997.

[14] "Acres Green, Colorado," *Wikipedia*, accessed November 22, 2018, https://en.wikipedia.org/wiki/Acres_Green.Colorado.

[15] Don Selbie, "Great Moments and People in the History of Roxborough Park," Roxborough Area Historical Society, September 1992, accessed December 12, 2018, http://www.roxhistory.com/uploads/2/4/1/24129156/great_moments_and_peopl e_-_history_rox_park.pdf.

[16] Weinman, "Invisible Suburbs," 146.

[17] Noe, personal interview.

[18] Weinman, "Invisible Suburbs," 155-156.

[19] Ibid., 155-168.

[20] Ibid., 36; Shea Properties, "The Meridian Story," accessed November 19, 2018, http://www.dtcmeridian.com/about/places/the-meridian-story; "Inverness pioneer John O'Meara recalled," *Colorado Real Estate Journal*, accessed February 23, 2019, https://crej.com/news/inverness-pioneer-john-omeara-recalled/.

Chapter 47
HISTORICAL TOWNS

Tim Weber

From 1960 to 1990, parts of Douglas County approached urban sprawl, while other areas hardly changed at all. Among DC's historic towns, Castle Rock and Parker boomed; but Sedalia, Franktown, Louviers, and Larkspur remained small country towns.[1]

Sedalia did not grow between 1960 and 1990. Its location alongside US 85 was certainly advantageous; and the fact that the Denver & Rio Grande and Santa Fe railroads ran through town had once made it a major transportation center for lumber, coal, wheat, cattle, and passengers.[2] But during the 1960s, those "industries" were no longer as robust as they had been; and the flood of 1965 had destroyed part of the town. In the 1980s, even the coming of new businesses like Western Sling (manufacturer of steel cable slings); the Intermountain Rural Electric Association (IREA); [3] and the controversial Cooley Gravel Company did not bring population growth.[4] A housing boom in its distant "suburbs" did not affect the town either. It chose to stay small. According to its Master Plan (1990), "Sedalia residents like the rural character of their community. They want to preserve historical structures, agricultural land uses, and both private and public open lands as an integral part of their rural lifestyle and as a link to their heritage."[5] In short, Sedalia did not want to grow, so its stable population remained in the 200s during this entire period.

Franktown was DC's first county seat (1861). When an election made Castle Rock the county seat in 1874, Franktown became a prosperous farming and dairy area, some of which was severely damaged when the Castlewood Canyon Dam broke in 1933. Thereafter, the town remained small and deeply committed to its rural character. When DC started growing in the 1970s, the Whispering Pines and Whispering Pines North subdivisions were constructed outside of town. Franktown residents considered but rejected incorporation because they feared higher taxes and the annexation of new subdivisions.

Residents also became deeply divided over a modified Master Plan that would have allowed gravel pits to be built along Cherry Creek.[6] During this period, the town's population stayed around 100.[7] One local historian characterized the town's history as "a tale of chances taken, failures met, and vehement resistance to lifestyle changes."[8] The people of Franktown liked things the way they were.

Founded in 1906, Louviers was a self-contained company town, owned and operated by the DuPont Powder Plant.[9] After nearly fifty years of operation, the company scaled back operations in 1962 and allowed residents to purchase their own homes. It also promised that "there will be no subdividing." During the 1970s DuPont stopped making dynamite and reduced its workforce; then in 1988, it closed the plant. Town residents did not want their little town to change, so in 1999 they got the entire town placed on the National Register of Historic Places. To ensure that development would not surround the town, in 2002, DuPont donated 855 acres of open space.[10] Louvers' population remained in the 200s from 1960 to 1990.[11] With no new construction, would-be buyers had to wait for residents to sell, which few of them ever did.

Home in Louivers

Larkspur was one of DC's earliest settlements and became a transportation center for lumber, potash, and dairy products. By the 1960s, numerous businesses served its population of 250. The flood of 1965 washed away its largest employer, Frink's Creamery Company; but there were plans to develop a $31 million "science-business-entertainment complex" with convention facilities, hotels, an amusement park, and a 1,900-foot space tower. The development was never built. In 1979, the town was incorporated mainly to qualify for state and federal funds to replace its defective water system. Soon residents began feuding over the town's governance and direction. Even an approved Comprehensive Plan (1987) did not stop the in-fighting that lasted for decades. There were recalls, attempted recalls, resignations, and continuing ill-will.[12] In DC's population boom, subdivisions were built outside city limits; and in 1976 the coming of the Colorado Renaissance Festival greatly helped its economy. But lingering divisions kept Larkspur's population at about 300.[13]

Parker was already the business center of northeast DC before the County and the town began to grow in the late 1970s. The town decided to incorporate in 1981 after a big project to turn Mainstreet into a "Western-Victorian" tourist attraction and several subdivisions including The Pinery

Mainstreet Parker 1964

went bankrupt. Residents wanted to control their own future, not the County Commissioners. The new town was one square mile and had a population of 285, including those living in the Rowley Downs subdivision. From the beginning, the town board was committed to growth. In 1984 it annexed four subdivisions, which more than doubled the town's size and increased its population to 1,200. Eventually, shopping centers, restaurants, and various businesses proliferated on both sides of Parker Road; and more subdivisions were annexed. Such expansion was guided by a Master Plan (1984) whose goal was to "Create a community with a separate and distinct identity, which encourages and maintains a home town image, provides for quality development, preserves open space, and fosters a sense of belonging."[14] By 1990, Parker's city limits had expanded to thirteen square miles and its population increased to 5,400.[15] Further expansion in the 1990s led many residents to question whether the town was in danger of growing too large.

Castle Rock was both DC's county seat and its largest town until Highlands Ranch was developed in the 1980s. In 1960, almost 25% of DC's population lived in Castle Rock. During that decade, the town grew by only 379 people. During the 1970s, it increased by 2,390; and during the 1980s, it grew by 4,787. Another way to analyze growth is by "housing units." In 1970, there were 547 housing units in Castle Rock; in 1980, 1,515; and in 1990, 8,708.[16] The town grew by annexing new subdivisions, starting in the 1970s.[17] In the early 1980s, the town's size increased from 2,300 to 7,260 acres by annexing several subdivisions. A few years later, the town doubled again when it annexed another six subdivisions containing 7,700 acres. In just four years, the population went from 3,921 to about 6,000. Many citizens did not like such rapid growth or the subdivisions that went bankrupt (See Chapter 46, Growing Pains). Residents divided into pro- and anti-growth groups that regularly put pressure on the town's planning commission and town council. As in Larkspur, there were recalls, firings, and heated public meetings. But almost all efforts to stop or slow down further development failed; and most residents became resigned to growth. With the additional housing came new commercial development and the revitalization of the downtown.[18]

DC's historic towns reacted differently to the County's rapid growth. Some towns wanted to remain rural and chose to stay small. Others embraced growth, often with reservations and some regret, and grew dramatically. It was a matter of choice. Either way, there was a price to pay; and even pro-growth residents grieved over the DC that was lost.

---

[1] Thanks to Hannah Weber, Archivist at the Douglas County Archives and Local History center, for providing valuable research for this article.

[2] Susan Consola Appleby, *Fading Past: The Story of Douglas County, Colorado* (Palmer Lake, CO: Filter Press, 2001), 163.

[3] "IREA Moving to Sedalia next November," *Douglas County News-Press*, December, 13, 1979, 3. Note: DC newspapers may be accessed at Colorado Historic

Newspapers at https://www.coloradohistoricnewspapers.org. Articles may also be found in the Newspaper Clippings Binders Collection, Archives & Local History, Miller Library, Castle Rock.

[4] Appleby, *Fading Past*, 169.

[5] Ibid.

[6] Ibid., 53-54.

[7] "Russellville—History of Franktown," *The Historical Marker Database*, accessed May 20, 2019, https://www.hmdb.org/marker.asp?marker=97969.

[8] Ibid., 47.

[9] Harrison Fletcher, "Blast from the past," *Westworld*, March 11, 1999, accessed May 20, 2019, ps://www.westword.com/news/blast-from-the-past-5059652.

[10] Castle Rock Writers, *Images of America: Douglas County* (Charleston, S.C.: Arcadia Publishing, 2017), 84.

[11] Appleby, *Fading Fast*, 120.

[12] Ibid., 103-110.

[13] "Huntsville—Larkspur Master Timeline," *Larkspur Historical Society,* accessed on April 12, 2019, http://larkspurhistoricalsociety.org/wp-content/uploads/2012/06/larkspurtimeline.pdf.

[14] "Town of Parker Master Plan," November, 1994, 23.

[15] Appleby, *Fading Past*, 127-128.

[16] "1990 Census of Population and Housing: Colorado, Population and Housing Units, 1970 to 1990 (Washington, DC: U.S. Department of Commerce, 1990), Table 9, accessed March 15, 2019, https://www.census.gov/prod/cen1990/cph2/cph-2-7.pdf; "Castle Rock plays a waiting game," *Littleton Independent*, July 2, 1970.

[17] "Sleepy Little 'castle' awoke in past decade," *Douglas County News-Press*, March 20, 1979, C-1; "Looking Back: 1977 in review," *Douglas County News*, January 26,1978, 1, 8.

[18] Appleby, *Fading Past*, 13-16.

Chapter 48

CHANGING WATER RULES

Steve Boand

Surface water supplies in Douglas County are not always plentiful. During the 1960s, its water providers had already begun utilizing the shallow groundwater reservoirs beneath Plum and Cherry Creeks for community water supplies.[1] These alluvial aquifers contain a sizable volume of water during the summer when streamflow dwindles.[2] Parker, Larkspur, Sedalia, Louviers, and Castle Rock were located near such waterways and had a vital interest in their ability to provide additional water supplies.

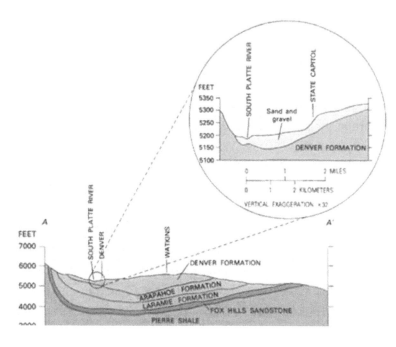

Groundwater is defined in law as "any water not visible on the surface of the ground under natural conditions."[3] Castle Rock transitioned away from using surface water to groundwater in the 1920s. By 1960 the town utilized eight shallow wells to access needed groundwater.[4] The Parker Water &

Sanitation District, formed in 1962, also used groundwater wells for its water supply.[5]

Colorado's surface water allocation system has long operated according to one basic principle: "first in time, first in right."[6] Simply stated, the first person to make reasonable and beneficial use of water has the senior right to that water. The senior water right user is entitled to water before a junior water right is honored.[7] This system became known as the priority system.[8] On that basis, summer water supplies in the South Platte River system were fully allocated between 1860 and 1870.[9] After 1880, water rights were applied to storage supplies because supplies of surface water were severely limited by higher-priority users.[10]

Castle Rock's water rights for its initial water supply system dated from 1880 to the early 1890s.[11] But what the town considered its senior water rights had already been claimed in 1880 by downstream water users.[12] As a result, according to the priority system, the town's water rights did not yield a dependable year-round water supply. In the 1990s, the town realized that their old senior rights were of no use in a dry year when their water rights on East Plum Creek would be zero.[13]

By the mid-1960s, Douglas County had eight water providers.[14] Many of them were in the northern part of the County. The Southwest Metropolitan Water and Sanitation District (WSD) served portions of Littleton in Douglas County.[15] The other water providers were Roxborough, Thunderbird, Southgate, Silver Heights, Dolly-O-Denver and Parker WSDs, and Castle Rock.[16]

During the 1960s, the County's population grew by nearly 3,600 people to 8,407.[17] Castle Rock estimated that its water rights holdings on Plum Creek produced an average of 700 acre-feet per year (AF/Yr).[18] In a dry year, they yielded only 350 AF/Yr, which was sufficient to support a community of approximately 1,400 people.[19] With a population of 1,531 people in 1970, Castle Rock's water supply was already insufficient to supply the town's needs.[20]

The number of wells in DC grew from fewer than 200 in 1960 to 2,649 by 1980,[21] when the County's population increased to just over 25,000.[22] Most of these wells were rather shallow domestic wells, but other wells accessed the deep groundwater from the Denver basin aquifer system.[23] The Denver basin system is a vast groundwater supply underlying central and eastern Douglas County.[24] It is a naturally non-renewable source.[25] Most importantly, it is considered legally separate from the surface and shallow groundwater and is not part of the water rights priority system.[26] This reserve rapidly became essential for DC's growth. Deep groundwater beneath our feet had now become a crucial component of our water supply.

Well Drilling in Castle Rock

Water law changes affected Douglas County and set new directions for growth. The question of how alluvial water wells worked within Colorado's water rights system became a great concern to senior water users downstream of Douglas County.[27] Before 1970, there was no regulation of alluvial wells by the State under the priority system.[28] Technical evidence showed that water from the shallow aquifers was directly connected to streams and rivers.[29] In 1969, the State enacted a new law requiring alluvial well users to replace their groundwater diversions in order to make senior water users whole.[30] These augmentation plans became a requirement, and municipal water providers often headed to water courts to get their plans approved.

The first augmentation plan in the County was developed by the Denver Southeast Suburban WSD for the Pinery in 1972.[31] That plan used deep Denver basin groundwater to replace its junior water use.[32] Nearly all the water district replacement plans in DC used a similar approach using deep groundwater to replace diversions by junior alluvial wells.[33] By 1990, thirty-five augmentation plans were in place across the County.[34]

Castle Rock continued its pursuit of renewable water supplies in October 1987 with the purchase of 1870 and 1881 irrigation water rights on East Plum Creek.[35] A sum of $400,000 was paid for water from the Crook Creek and Hillside ditches south of Larkspur.[36] Approval by the Water Court was needed for the town to use these water rights.[37] Ten parties objected to Castle Rock's plans for the water, including Thornton, Denver, Highlands Ranch developers, and the State Engineer.[38] Water transfers in Colorado typically draw a great amount of interest from water users in the region.

The Court ruled in May 1989 that Castle Rock was entitled to up to 249 AF/Yr of reusable use water from the ditches.[39] That amount was enough to serve between 300 and 600 households, depending on the efficiency of use. One of the challenges of surface water rights in Douglas County, even those dating back to the 1870s, is that they are senior during the summer.[40] Reservoir storage or deep groundwater is needed to meet seasonal- and drought-condition water demands.

The Colorado Water Resources Research Institute reported in 1990 that groundwater reserves from the Denver basin aquifer had not yet been "exploited extensively."[41] The Institute recognized the importance of the Denver basin reserves as a drought supply and recommended that utilization of the Denver basin aquifers should be limited.[42] It is hard to imagine the amount of groundwater the Denver basin aquifer contains. The United State Geological Survey reports that the volume of water in the aquifers is estimated to be 120% of the water held in Lake Erie.[43]

By 1990, State records indicate there were more than 3,850 wells in the County.[44] The County's population had swelled to 60,391 residents.[45] Castle Rock's water supplies in 1990 came from 15 deep wells with more than 80% of the water supply derived from deep groundwater wells.[46] Shallow groundwater supplies were no longer the prime water source across the County.[47]

Water supply issues became contentious as the County entered the 1990s. The Board of County Commissioners empaneled a Water Advisory Board that recommended that the County "require renewable water for existing and future centers of population."[48] The town evaluated its water supply future and determined that the cost of developing and producing deep groundwater for buildout would be "extreme."[49] Thus after 1990, DC began to search for renewable water supplies.

[1] Colorado Department of Natural Resources, *Colorado's Decision Support Systems CWCB/DNR—Well Permits,* accessed March 23, 2019, https://dnrweb.state.co.us/cdss/WellPermits.

[2] S.G. Robson, *Alluvial and Bedrock Aquifers of the Denver Basin—Eastern Colorado's Dual Ground-Water Resource,* Water Supply Paper 2302 (Washington D.C.: United States Geological Survey, 1989), 26.

[3] Joseph Grantham, *Alluvial and Bedrock Aquifers of the Denver Basin* (Denver: Colorado Division of Water Resources, Department of Natural Resources, 2016), 8.

[4] *Findings of Fact: Conclusions of Law, Judgment and Decree Concerning the Application for Water Rights of the Town of Castle Rock, Helen Ema Arfsten, a/j/a Helen E Arsten, James H. Noe, Issac Joen Noe and Ida May Noe.* 87CW240 (District Court, Water Division 1, Colorado, May 11, 1989), 2-5.

[5] Parker Water & Sanitation District, *About Us: The Past & The Future,* accessed April 16, 2019, https://www.pwsd.org/872/About-Us.

[6] Grantham, *Alluvial and Bedrock Aquifers of the Denver Basin,* 3.

[7] Ibid., 2.

[8] Ibid., 2-3.

[9] Colorado Water Resources Research Institute, *South Platte River System in Colorado—Hydrology, Development and Management Issues,* Working Paper (Fort Collins: Colorado State University, 1990), 3.

[10] Ibid.

[11] Town of Castle Rock and the Water Committee, "The Town of Castle Rock Water Resources Management Plan" (Castle Rock, 1992), 31.

[12] *South Platte River System,* 3.

[13] "The Town of Castle Rock Water Resources," 25.

[14] Douglas County Assessor, *Historic Abstracts of Assessment,1966,* accessed February 16, 2019, https://www.douglas.co.us/assessor/taxing-authorities/historic-abstracts-of-assessment/.

[15] Southwest Metropolitan Water & Sanitation District, *About Us,* accessed April 16, 2019, https://swmetrowater.org/about-us/.

[16] *Historic Abstracts of Assessment,* 1966.

[17] Colorado Department of Local Affairs, *Historical Census Data—Counties and Municipalities,* 2019, accessed February 16, 2019, https://demography.dola.colorado.gov/population/data/historical_census/.

[18] "The Town of Castle Rock Water Resources Management Plan," 31.

[19] Douglas County, *Guide to Water Supply Standards* (Castle Rock, February 15, 2019).

[20] *Historical Census Data—Counties and Municipalities.*

[21] Colorado Department of Natural Resources, *Colorado's Decision Support Systems CWCB/DNR—Well Permits,* accessed March 23, 2019, https://dnrweb.state.co.us/cdss/WellPermits.

[22] *Historical Census Data—Counties and Municipalities.*

[23] *Colorado's Decision Support Systems CWCB/DNR—Well Permits.*

[24] Robson, *Alluvial and Bedrock Aquifers of the Denver Basin,* 28.

[25] Ibid.

[26] Grantham, *Alluvial and Bedrock Aquifers of the Denver Basin—Eastern Colorado's Dual Ground-Water Resource,* 13.

[27] David Harrison, Veronica A. Sperling, and Steven O. Sims, "Intro to Ground Water Law in Colorado and Surface-Groundwater Conflicts in the South Platte," *Groundwater in the West,* Summer Conference, June 16-18, 2004 (Boulder: Getches-Wilkinson Center for Natural Resources, Energy, and Environment at the University of Colorado Law School, 2004), 11.

[28] Ibid., 6.

[29] Ibid., 7.

[30] Ibid., 11-12.

[31] *Colorado's Decision Support Systems CWCB/DNR—Well Permits.*

[32] *In the Matter of the Application for Water Rights of the Denver Southwest Suburban Water and Sanitation District and Terracor, Inc. Out of Cherry Creek and its Tributaries, in Douglas County Colorado—Findings of Fact, Conclusions of Law and Decree.* W-6268 (District Court in and for Water Division No. 1, State of Colorado, November 21, 1977).

[33] *Colorado's Decision Support Systems CWCB/DNR—Water Rights Transactions*

[34] Ibid.

[35] Paul DiNucci, "Castle Rock pays $400,000 for Plum Creek water rights," *Douglas County News-Press,* October 17, 1987.

[36] Ibid.

[37] *Findings of Fact, Conclusions of Law, Judgment and Decree Concerning the Application for Water Rights of the Town of Castle Roc, Helen Ema Arfsten, a/j/a Helen E Arsten, James H. Noe, Issac John Noe and Ida May Noe.* 87CW240, 24.

[38] Ibid., 2.

[39] "The Town of Castle Rock Water Resources Management Plan," 31.

[40] *South Platte River System in Colorado,"* 3.

[41] Ibid., 9

[42] Ibid.

[43] Robson, *Alluvial and Bedrock Aquifers of the Denver Basin,* 1.

[44] *Colorado's Decision Support Systems CWCB/DNR—Well Permits*

[45] *Historical Census Data—Counties and Municipalities.*

[46] "The Town of Castle Rock Water Resources Management Plan," 2.

[47] *Colorado's Decision Support Systems CWCB/DNR—Well Permits.*

[48] Douglas County Water Advisory Board, *Water Supply, Demand and Institutional Needs of Douglas County: A Report of the Douglas County Water Advisory Board to the Douglas County Board of Commissioners* (Castle Rock, 1988), 38.

[49] "The Town of Castle Rock Water Resources Management Plan," 7.

Chapter 49

THE ECONOMY TURNS

Larry Schlupp and Tim Weber

In the three decades after 1960, Douglas County went from a mostly agricultural community to a bedroom community for Denver, then, finally, an economically mixed urbanized area. Despite robust growth, the residential tax base did not provide needed public services.[1] *The Douglas County News* proposed a solution: a "more aggressive industrial development program designed to increase jobs in the county, to expand the tax base, and to keep taxes from becoming unsustainable."[2]

Commercial development came slowly at first because not enough land was zoned for commercial use.[3] Gradually, commercial projects were developed: Blair Industrial Park in Parker,[4] Inverness Industrial Park,[5] Titan Industrial Park,[6] Lincoln Park East,[7] and Meridian Business Park. But none could compare to the Denver Technological Center, which provided employment in southern Arapahoe County for thousands of DC residents.

The economy turned upside down during this period. The historically dominant agricultural economy changed the most. During the 1960s and 1970s, the raising of beef cattle replaced the dairy industry as DC's leading agricultural sector.[8] From 1960-1990, land consolidation decreased the number of working ranches/farms from 427 to 200. While agricultural income grew during this period, the assessed valuation of all agricultural activity declined from 20% to only 2%.[9]

By the late 1970s, the construction industry began to gain strength in DC's economy, especially in the northernmost 12 miles of DC.[10] Subdivisions sprang up on former farm and ranch land; but existing towns did not grow significantly until the late 1980s and beyond, often because of the bankruptcies of many subdivisions.[11] The public sector also completed major building projects. Roads were built to connect new subdivisions; and the completion of I-25 and C-470 made commuting into, out of, and through the County easier. The steady population growth required the building of new schools which in the late1980s made the school district the biggest employer in DC (see "Education Explosion," chapter 52). The Sheriff's Department also expanded; and in the 1990s the County completed the Robert A. Christensen Justice Center(see "Evolution of Law Enforcement," chapter 51).

The Building of One of the County's Subdivisions, Perry Park Ranch, Red Rocks Drive Site, and the Echo Hills Townhouses Site, circa 1970

With the changing economy, some businesses closed, and others opened. One that closed was Frink's Creamery. In 1902 Clarence Frink and C.G. Carlson made a small creamery in Larkspur the headquarters for affiliated creameries in Castle Rock, Sedalia, Spring Valley, Franktown, and Monument.[12] The creamery produced milk, butter, cottage cheese, condensed milk, and award-winning Black Canyon Cheese, which it shipped to New Mexico, Texas, and Louisiana. It also supplied sweetened-condensed milk to Denver's major candy and ice cream makers.[13]

Larkspur's Frink Creamery in the Late 1920s and
Dairy Entrepreneur-Owner Clarence Frink

Carlson left the partnership in 1920, so Frink carried on alone.[14] In 1923 he temporarily closed the Larkspur creamery in a dispute with the Colorado Dairymen's Co-operative Association.[15] Frink did not like anyone getting between him and his suppliers.[16] In response, the Co-op attempted to start its own creamery in Castle Rock;[17] but its attempt failed. Its facility became a steam laundry, then a filling station.[18] The Co-op suffered another setback when disgruntled members got an injunction to stop its unfair dues-collection policy.[19] When Frink battled the Co-op, he usually won.[20]

In 1931, Frink moved company headquarters to Denver;[21] but the Larkspur creamery still led DC's dairy industry. Until his death in 1945, hundreds of dairy farmers and creamery workers attended his annual summer picnics in Larkspur.[22] He also made his facilities available for community gatherings. Frink's Creamery hit hard times in the 1960s. In 1961, as usual, it was a sponsor of the Douglas County Fair; but in 1965 it defaulted on a $178,847.35 note owed to the Denver Milk Producers.[23] A few months later, the 1965 Flood destroyed Frink's creamery. It was the end of an era, and the dairy industry in both DC and Denver suffered.

In 1990, the Castle Rock Town Council developed plans for DC's first major retail project. From 1988-1989, the town's budget went seriously into the red, so the newly elected Town Council began looking for new sources of tax revenue.[24] When the Council heard about the new retail concept of factory stores outlets (Colorado's first outlet mall opened in Silverthorne in 1989), it requested and received numerous proposals. One of the new Council members was Steve Boand, who was elected as a write-in candidate, then served as mayor from 1991-1992. He and the rest of the Council lacked expertise in retail business development, so Boand arranged for a friend on the Colorado College faculty to assign his advanced business students to analyze the proposals—at no charge to the County.[25]

In the beginning, the opposition was fierce. Many town merchants feared that the project would put them out of business. Other citizens doubted that shoppers from Denver or Colorado Springs would drive so far to shop. Some people warned that current roads could not handle the anticipated traffic. A few predicted that when the mall failed, it would ruin the town. The Council took all such objections seriously and worked hard to answer questions and overcome problems. After rejecting the first two proposals by developers, it contracted with the Baltimore-based Prime Group, Inc, which had already built seventeen outlets in fourteen states. According to Boand, "We have been very conservative. We wanted to do this right. We want them to show us that they have the financing for the project and the leasing."[26] The Council did its homework and was satisfied that the project would succeed. In those pre-TABOR days, no public vote was required for approval. Once the Council was certain, it moved the project ahead.[27]

Prime broke ground on forty acres in February 1992, and the two-lane I-25 interchange expanded to the multi-lane Meadows Parkway. Throughout the project, Prime Group kept its promises and helped the town work through complicated financing issues. The new mall opened in November to large crowds.[28] Most of the nay-sayers were proved wrong. People came. In fact, in 1994, five million shoppers visited the mall: 72% were from Denver, 20% from Colorado Springs, 5% from Boulder, and 3% from Pueblo. As a result, Castle Rock Factory Stores was the most profitable outlet mall in the country.[29] Prime Group fought off attempts to build a similar mall west of theirs.[30] In 1997, Prime purchased 12.5 acres to the north and added 40 shops to its original 108, which added 300 jobs to its current 1000 employees.[31] Castle Rock's impoverished budget quickly became financially viable thanks to the dramatic increase in new sales tax revenue.

The Factory Outlet Stores marked the end of "business as usual" in Castle Rock and the rest of DC. In the next two decades, other commercial developments in Castle Rock like Safeway, King Soopers,[32] Walmart,[33] Kohl's,[34] and Home Depot did put small stores out of business. The same thing happened elsewhere in DC. In 1996 the Park Meadows Mall opened in Lone Tree. Parker had a retail explosion on both sides of Parker Road, and Highlands Ranch experienced its own retail expansion. But the retail revolution in Douglas County started with the Castle Rock Factory Stores Mall.

[1] Douglas County Planning Commission, *Douglas County Master Plan*, December 6, 1983, 12.

[2] "Industrial development group recommended for County," *Douglas County News*, April 21, 1977, 1.

[3] Gary Wells, "Where to put industry poses problems for Douglas County," *Douglas County News-Press*, December 10, 1980.

[4] Jerry Peterson, "Parker gets county's 1st industrial park," *Douglas County News- Press*, July 2, 1980, 7.

[5] Gail Anderson, "Inverness to add nearly a million square feet," *Douglas County News Press*, February 6, 1980, 1; Gail Anderson, "Inverness development on Douglas County side result of plat OK," *Douglas County News-Press*, June 29, 1982, 1.

[6] "Titan Road Industrial Park clears hurdle," *Douglas County News-Press*, September 25, 1980, 1; Gail Anderson, "Industrial Park off Titan given county's final approval," *Douglas County News-Press*, January 20, 1982, 3.

[7] "Mobil Land Co. finalizes Lincoln Park East purchase," *Douglas County News-Press*, January 9, 1981, 3.

[8] USDA data from Colorado is archived at Cornell University at http://agcensus.mannlib.cornell.edu/AgCensus/getVolumeOnePart.do?year=1992&part_id=842&number=6&title=Colorado.

[9] Douglas County Assessor's Office, *Historic Abstract of Assessment*, 1966, 1970, 1980, 1990, accessed May 26, 2019, https://www.douglas.co.us/assessor/taxing-authorities/historic-abstracts-of-assessment/.

[10] Gary Wells, "Despite Economic doldrums, county development flowering," *Douglas County News-Press*, July 7, 1981, 5.

[11] "Bankruptcies take Douglas County toll, some in holding pattern," *Douglas County News-Press*, March 20, 1979, B-8.

[12] Susan Consola Appleby, *Fading Past. The Story of Douglas County* (Palmer Lake, CO: Filter Press, 2001), 105.

[13] "Texas Inspectors Visit Frink Creamery Plants," *Record-Journal*, August 22, 1924, 1; "Frink Creamery Company Installs New Equipment," *Record-Journal*, January 13, 1928, 1.

[14] Appleby, *Fading Past*, 105.

[15] "Frink Creamery Closes its Doors," *Record-Journal*, June 29, 1923, 1, 8.

[16] "Frink Questioned by Dairy Officers," *Record-Journal*, July 6, 1923, 1.

[17] "Dairymen Plan Local Creamery," *Record-Journal*, July 20, 1923, 1; "Dairymen to Have Creamery Plant," *Record Journal*, July 27, 1923, 1; "Local Creamery Plans Considered," *Record-Journal*, August 3, 1923, 1; "Creamery Plans are Approved," *Record-Journal*, August 31. 1923, 1.

[18] "Dairymen," *Record-Journal*, October 23, 1925, 4; "Steam Laundry to be Established Here," *Record-Journal*, April 26, 1929, 1; "Notice," *Record-Journal*, June 7, 1929, 4.

[19] *Record-Journal*, July 18, 1928, 4; "Dairymen Get Injunction Against State Association," *Record-Journal*, July 19, 1928, 1.

[20] "Dairymen Meet at Larkspur," *Record-Journal*, November 25, 1932, 1.

[21] "Frink Creamery Company Moves Head Offices to Denver This Week," *Record-Journal*, September 11, 1931, 1.

[22] "Frink Creamery Company Notes 50th Anniversary," *Douglas County News*, August 14, 1952, 7.

[23] "Notice of Public Trustee's Sale," *Douglas County News*, January 15, 1965, 4; Interview with Ann Trueblood, accessed April 20, 2019, http://history.douglascountylibraries.org/floods/1965.htm.

[24] Telephone interview with Steve Boand on April 20, 2019.

[25] Ibid.

[26] "Castle Rock awaits OK on Outlet Mall," *Denver Post*, February 11, 1992.

[27] Boand interview.

[28] K.T. Kelly, "New Parcel eyes for outlet mall," *Weekly News Chronicle*, December 6, 1995.

[29] Pete Lewis, "5 million shoppers visit factory mall," *Douglas County News-Press*, January 7, 1995.

[30] K.T. Kelly, "Outlet Mall developer adds to lawsuit," *Weekly News Chronicle*, November 20, 1995; Kelly, "New parcel eyes for outlet mall."

[31] Virginia Grantier, "Factory outlet set to expand," *Denver Post*, January 25, 1997.

[32] "King Soopers," *Douglas County News-Press*, March 19, 1998.

[33] "Walmart opens for business," *Douglas County News-Press*, January 26, 2000.

[34] Ross Dolan, "Kohl's making its way to Castle Rock," *Castle Rock Daily Star*, June 25, 2003.

Chapter 50

THE GROWTH OF DOUGLAS COUNTY GOVERNMENT

Steve Boand

As Douglas County's population increased, so did the size of County government. Its population grew more than tenfold, and the number of local government institutions grew from under twenty to more than one hundred.[1] Growth requires infrastructure; and in Colorado, the goal is to have new growth pay its own way. New communities require a host of services including roadways, water, and sewer service, and fire protection. State and County (or city) approved special districts were created to meet the needs of these new communities. New challenges required new solutions and new responses from local governments. How did County government change during these three decades?

In 1970, County government consisted of two general-purpose governments: Douglas County and the Town of Castle Rock, DC's only incorporated town (1881).[2] Specialized districts included Douglas County RE-1 School District, ten water and sanitation districts, and four fire protection districts.[3] Four additional special purpose districts included the Cedar Hill Cemetery, the Regional Transportation District (RTD), the Urban Drainage and Flood Control District, and Upper South Platte Water Conservancy District.[4] Each of the special districts provided important services to portions of the County, which taxpayers supported by paying specified mill levies. Total property tax revenue for all governmental entities in Douglas County in the early 1970s was less than $2.5 million.[5]

DC added two additional incorporated municipalities during the 1970s. In 1972, DC annexed part of the City of Littleton, most of which was in Arapahoe County.[6] Larkspur became Douglas County's third incorporated community in 1979.[7] The town was one of the first established in DC and became an important rail center for the transportation of lumber, potash, and later dairy products. Frink's Creamery played a crucial role in DC's dairy industry until it was destroyed in the flood of 1965. In the 1970s, Larkspur's population numbered only in the 200s.[8]

Larkspur - Settled 1869, Incorporated 1979

In the 1970s and 1980s, DC had rapid growth. In the 1970s, its population grew 199.1% (from 8,407 to 25,153); and in the 1980s, 140.1% (from 25,153 to 60,391).[9] Most of this growth occurred in northern and northeastern DC, where large communities were built on former farmland. On June 1, 1977, a *Douglas County News-Press* headline announced, "Historic Phipps Ranch to change hands."[10] The 22,000-acre parcel was sold by the estate of Lawrence C. Phipps, Jr. to a group of Denver businessmen headed by oilman Marvin Davis, for a reported price of $14 million. Six months later, the Mission Viejo Company of California, a wholly owned subsidiary of Philip Morris, purchased the land and called it Highlands Ranch.[11]

Construction followed a phased approach, with the first families moving into Highlands Ranch in 1981.[12] The town never sought incorporation, preferring to depend on six special districts, including a water and sanitation district and five metropolitan districts.[13] These special districts were designed to support a well-developed financial plan that remained under the control of Mission Viejo. Consequently, Highlands Ranch remains one of the largest unincorporated communities in Colorado, with a current population approaching that of the City of Pueblo.[14]

Douglas County Courthouse circa the 1970s

The county government suffered a severe blow on March 10, 1978, when DC's historic Courthouse was destroyed by an arsonist. Many County records were lost, including early subdivision plats and masterplans. County citizens helped to locate and restore many records for safekeeping until a new courthouse was erected.[15] Despite the loss, DC kept expanding.

During the 1980s, development approvals in the County and Castle Rock led to the formation of 22 new special districts charged with the construction of public facilities in the Meadows, the Villages at Castle Rock, and the now defunct Dawson Ridge development south of Castle Rock.[16] Parker was incorporated in 1981. The first town budget was $5,600 borrowed from the Bank of the West and $7,500 in donations from the Chamber of Commerce.[17] Parker was founded in the 1860s, but it developed slowly. Parker's first mayor after incorporation, Dean Salisbury, remembered tough times: "We had dirt streets. Highway 83 was looking more like Santa Fe every day. We had no water. The community was just stagnant and going nowhere."[18] The mayor's comments reflected the series of bankruptcies, including the Pinery, that left residents and the town in dire straits (see "Growing Pains," chapter 46).

By the mid-1980s, DC and the rest of Colorado were in the grip of a recession that caught nearly everyone by surprise. Job losses between 1984 and 1986 were "the largest since job data were first compiled."[19] New home construction floundered statewide and fell from more than 50,000 starts in

1983 to slightly over 10,000 by 1989.[20] DC's governments had to grapple with the reality of recession. Housing starts fluctuated in the County: from approximately 500 in 1980, more than 2,000 in 1986, and approximately 1,200 in 1988 and 1989.[21]

Planning in Douglas County in the early 1980s had been based on predictions of steady growth. Special districts in the County had borrowed millions of dollars to construct infrastructure, cover the cost of bond issuance, and make initial debt payments. Bonds had been issued based upon service plans approved by the DC Commissioners, who were also blindsided by the recession. "It does not appear that the Douglas County Commission considered the cumulative effects of these districts competing against each other for housing sales and population."[22]

As the recession continued, numerous new communities experienced bond debt default. It started with the Villages at Castle Rock Metropolitan District #4, Dawson Ridge Metropolitan District, and the Castle Pines North Metropolitan District.[23] In 1989 and 1990, these districts filed for bankruptcy when they could not meet their debt obligations.[24] A year later, the Roxborough Metropolitan District and the Cottonwood Water & Sanitation District near Parker joined the list of defaulters.[25] Many local governments suddenly found themselves in financial trouble.

One outcome of bond debt default was a dramatic increase in residential property taxes.[26] Some districts took preventative actions to resolve actual or probable defaults to protect both the developer and residents.[27] Other communities saw dramatic increases in their property tax bills in the 1980s and 1990s.[28] In response to these issues, the Colorado General Assembly required that mandatory disclosures be incorporated into purchase contracts in special taxing districts.[29] Prospective homeowners were required to evaluate the risk of potential property taxes increases.[30]

By 1990, there were 109 local governments in the County.[31] More than 100 of them were special districts providing fire protection (13), water and sewer (20), and other urban services (69).[32] In addition, the County annexed part of the City of Aurora, which brought the number of incorporated municipalities to five.[33] Total property tax collections in 1991 exceeded $65.7 million.[34] The Douglas County budget approached $30 million from diversified revenue sources.[35] County reserves generated more than $1 million in interest.[36] Between 1981 and 1990 the County staff increased from 187 to 366 employees,[37] a 95% increase. The government had new responsibilities and was becoming big business in Douglas County.

---

[1] Douglas County Assessor, *Historic Abstracts of Assessment.* February 2015, accessed February 16, 2019, https://www.douglas.co.us/assessor/taxing-authorities/historic-abstracts-of-assessment/, 1966 and 1989.

[2] Ibid, 1966.

[3] Ibid.

[4] Ibid.

[5] Ibid, 1970.

[6] Ibid, 1972.

[7] Larkspur Historical Society, *Town of Larkspur, Colorado. Larkspur History,* accessed March 19, 2019, http://townoflarkspur.org/about-us/larkspur-history/.

[8] Ibid.

[9] Department of Local Affairs, *Historical Census Data. Counties and Municipalities,* February 16, 2019, https://demography.dola.colorado.gov/population/data/county-muni-timeseries/.

[10] Sharon Turnes and Tom Munds, "Historic Phipps Ranch to change hands," *Douglas County News-Press,* June 1, 1977.

[11] Ibid.

[12] *Highlands Ranch Reporter,* November 1981.

[13] *Historic Abstracts of Assessment,* 1980.

[14] *Historical Census Data: Counties and Municipalities.*

[15] Shelley Gonzales, "Historic blueprints returned 18 years after they were lost," *Rocky Mountain News,* September 28, 1996.

[16] *Historic Abstracts of Assessment,* 1980.

[17] Penny Perkins, "Salisbury saw stagnant Parker go from dirt streets to new town," *Douglas County News-Press,* January 20, 1988.

[18] Ibid.

[19] Wilson Kendall, *A Brief Economic History of Colorado,* Prepared for the Demography Section, Colorado Department of Local Affairs (Denver: Center for Business and Economic Forecasting, 2002), 11.

[20] Ibid.

[21] "Douglas County Growth and Development Profile" (March 2019), accessed April 16, 2019, https://www.douglas.co.us/documents/douglas-county-growth-and-development-profile.pdf.

[22] Julia Beckett, "The Bankruptcy of Developer District Governments in Colorado: Structural Defects or a Downside of Growth?" Ph.D. Thesis, University of Colorado at Denver, 1995, 92.

[23] Ibid, Appendix A.

[24] Ibid.

[25] Ibid.

[26] Department of Local Affairs, *Special Districts: A Brief Review for Prospective Homeowners.* Special District Assistance (Denver: State of Colorado, 2009), 6.

[27] *In re Villages at Castle Rock Metropolitan District No 4.* 89-B-16240-A (United States Bankruptcy Court, D. Colorado, May 11, 1990), 1-4 .

[28] *Special Districts: A Brief Review for Prospective Homeowners,* 6.

[29] Ibid, 6-7.

[30] Ibid, 7-11

[31] *Historic Abstracts of Assessment,* 1989.

[32] Ibid.

[33] Ibid.

[34] Ibid.

[35] *1990 Douglas County Budget* (Castle Rock:, Douglas County Finance Department 1989), 30.

[36] Ibid.

[37] Ibid, 44.

Chapter 51

EVOLUTION OF LAW ENFORCEMENT

Joan Gandy and Tim Weber

From 1960 to 1990, the Douglas County Sheriff's Office transformed itself. As the County's population increased, the department evolved from a two-person operation to a modern law enforcement agency. Three sheriffs served during this period, and each played a crucial role in the process.[1]

John Hammond was DC's longest-serving Sheriff (1947-1970). During his tenure, the County's population grew from 3,507 to 8,407. When he started, the Sheriff's Office consisted of an elected Sheriff and an appointed Undersheriff, plus a few volunteer deputies who worked as needed. During the 1960s, Hammond hired a few part-time deputies and bought the department's first patrol car. When he left office in 1970, there were four full-time employees.[2] Hammond brought a personal touch to policing. Annually he visited all ranchers and farmers to say hello, drove his own vehicle, wore no uniform, and rarely ever carried a gun. Instead of jailing

John Hammond

juvenile offenders, he gave them a stern talking-to, then returned them to their parents. He even brought non-violent prisoners to the county jail home for Thanksgiving dinner.[3] Hammond utilized common sense: "You can't just go by the book in this county. It takes common sense to be sheriff. Mainly, I just tried to help people."[4]

Sheriff Hammond got national attention in the Adolph Coors III kidnapping case. On February 9, 1960, the CEO of Coors Brewery went missing on his way to work in Jefferson County. His wife Mary received a ransom note demanding $500,000 in small bills. But she never heard from the kidnapper again.[5] The FBI identified Joseph Corbett, Jr. as the prime suspect and placed him on its *Ten Most Wanted List*.[6] On September 11, 1960, a target shooter found human remains and a key chain bearing the initials AC III in a dump off West Jackson Creek Road near Sedalia.[7] Searches uncovered additional bones, clothing, shoes, and a wristwatch, which the Coors family identified.[8] Because the evidence was found in DC, Hammond temporarily wrestled jurisdiction away from Jefferson County and the FBI. When a human skull was found a few days later, DC Coroner Doug Andrews identified it as Coors'.[9] The FBI arrested Corbett on October 29, 1960, in Vancouver, British Columbia. He was tried in Golden, found guilty of murder, and sentenced to life in prison.[10] Corbett was paroled from Canon City on December 12, 1980,[11] and committed suicide on August 24, 2009.[12]

Royal McKinster was the next Sheriff (1971-1982).[13] He pushed hard for more staff and bigger budgets. Within a year, the department grew to nine full-time employees. This number included dispatchers and jailers to provide round-the-clock coverage. The Sheriff and Undersheriff did most administrative and investigative duties, but only three deputies patrolled the County in three eight-hour shifts.[14] A funding shortage in May 1972 nearly led to layoffs and the closure of the jail.[15] McKinster found ways to make do. In the early seventies, he organized the all-

Royal McKinster

volunteer Douglas County Special Deputy Force to provide various services. All funding for training and equipment came from private contributions, not tax money. By the time McKinster left office, there were forty-seven full-time employees.[16]

McKinster's tenure was filled with challenges and controversies. In 1977 a grand jury investigated thirteen allegations against the Sheriff. It concluded that the complaints were over his leadership style, not anything criminal, and declined to indict him.[17] When the DC Court House burned down in 1978, the

Sheriff's Office and jail moved to temporary quarters until a new justice center could be opened at 355 S. Wilcox Street, where the Walgreens now stands.[18] But in November 1979 the Sheriff said he would not take possession because of design flaws and poor construction.[19] Frustrated Commissioners hired a consultant from the National Institute of Corrections to evaluate and make recommendations. He concluded that most problems could be fixed quickly to meet the Sheriff's specifications. Reluctantly, McKinster moved in during January 1980.[20]

Tensions between the Sheriff and the Commissioners continued. In May 1980, McKinster warned that without more money for gasoline and additional jailers, he would cut patrols and take deputies off the streets to run the jail. He declared, "It is an understatement [that] there is not adequate law enforcement in the county. Everyone knows it."[21] At first, the Commissioners resisted by disputing the Sheriff's figures.[22] But in the end, they provided the $58,000 the Sheriff had requested.[23]

In 1982 the district attorney empaneled another grand jury to investigate possible criminal activity in the Sheriff's Office. When three officers cooperated with the grand jury, McKinster fired them. After the officers sued, the Sheriff re-instated them with back-pay and benefits.[24] The DA did indict three other officers, including McKinster's two stepsons, on fifteen felony counts for selling drugs taken from the evidence storeroom and assaulting two under-aged girls. All three officers accepted plea bargains and resigned.[25] This scandal revealed deep divisions and low morale within the department. Few people were surprised when McKinster declined to seek a fourth term.[26]

Stephen Zotos, a former special agent for the Santa Fe Railroad, was elected Sheriff in 1983 when DC's population was about 25,000.[27] When he stepped down twenty years later, DC had grown to over 175,000. During his five terms, he increased full-time employees to 384[28] and revolutionized the DC Sheriff's Office.

Zotos brought a "hard-driven, no-nonsense approach to policing."[29] Between his election and his swearing-in, he wrote the department's first policy manual which emphasized training, professionalism, and performance expectations. He developed a positive and cooperative relationship with the

Commissioners and the public. In the mid-1980s he built a large training facility south of Highlands Ranch which included eight shooting ranges and a repelling tower. Eventually, these facilities served 2,800 law officers from 64 agencies. He also added a track to train emergency vehicle drivers. He organized a SWAT team, bomb squad emergency response team, hostage negotiators, and a large investigation unit. He was one of the first sheriffs in Colorado to develop a victims' assistance program and placed deputies in DC high schools as school resource officers.

Stephen Zotos

One of Zotos' major achievements was the construction of the Robert A. Christensen Justice Center in 1998. When the Sheriff's Office was sued over jail overcrowding (100 prisoners in a space for 30), he got the Commissioners and voters of DC to raise taxes to build the new facility. He also constructed a large substation in Highlands Ranch and raised salaries to attract and keep highly qualified deputies. Morale soared under Zotos. The turnover rate of senior officers remained less than one-per-cent. In 2003, a newly enacted term-limits law forced Zotos to retire. By then, the DC Sheriff's Office was considered one of the premier departments in Colorado.[30]

During this period, only two DC towns started their own police departments: Castle Rock (1960) and Parker (1983). Lone Tree became the third (2004). Highlands Ranch never incorporated and retained the DC Sheriff's department as its police force. During DC's initial population growth, the Sheriff's Office more than met the challenge.

---

[1] For an excellent overview of the history of the DC Sheriff's Office see, Attila Denes, "History of Law Enforcement in Douglas County," *Colorado Sheriff*, vol. XXXIX, no. 3 (Spring, 2019), 22-28.

[2] Alan Isbell, "Heated debate ensues over sheriff's shortfall," *Douglas County News-Press*, June 4, 1980, 2.

[3] Interview with Bonnie Bell, daughter of Sheriff John Hammond, on February 23, 2018, at the Philip S. Miller Library, Castle Rock.

[4] "John Hammond–sheriff for 40 years recounts past," *Douglas County News-Press,* June 18, 1981.

[5] Ray Humphreys, "Bullet Bargainer," *Timely Detective Cases, 1946,* 97-102, 131-132.

[6] "Wanted by the FBI," *Douglas County News,* June 9, 1960, 5.

[7] Philip Jett, *The Death of an Heir: Adolph Coors III and the Murder that Rocked an American Brewing Dynasty* (New York: St. Martin's Press, 2017).

[8] *Adolph Coors Case Files,* Archives and Local History department, Philip S. Miller Library, Castle Rock; Jett, *Death of an Heir,* 173-179.

[9] Jett, *The Death of an Heir,* 177-189.

[10] Dennis Porter, "Coornap: The Investigation into the 1960 Murder of Adolph Coors III," *The Denver Westerners Round Up,* September-October, 2010.

[11] Jett, *Death of an Heir,* 290-291.

[12] Kevin Vaughn, "Adolph Coors Murder: Notorious Killer's Quiet End," *Denver Post,* August 29, 2009.

[13] *Douglas County News,* November 5, 1970, 1.

[14] "D.C. Sheriff's Special Deputy Force," *Douglas County News,* April 13, 1972, 4, 9.

[15] "No Jail in May?" *Douglas County News,* April 27, 1972, 1.

[16] "Steve Zotos," *Douglas County News-Press,* May 26, 1999, 18.

[17] "McKinster's oft-stormy, oft-headlined tenure nears end," *Douglas County News-Press,* May 26, 1982, 1, 6.

[18] "Sheriff's department moves again—421 Perry," *Douglas County News,* Apr. 20, 1978.

[19] "Sheriff to move to Justice Center," *Douglas County News-Press,* Nov. 7, 1979.

[20] Alan Isbel, "Jail failing explained by corrections expert," *Douglas County News-Press,* Jan. 24, 1980.

[21] Alan Isbell, "Patrol may be sacrificed: Budget squeeze leads to sheriff-commissioners show-down? *Douglas County News-Press,* May 13, 1980, 1.

[22] Isbell, "Heated debate ensues over sheriff's shortfall," 1-2.

[23] Alan Isbell, "Sheriff wins county commitment for budget supplement," *Douglas County News-Press,* June 10, 1980.

[24] Karen Naiman, "Sheriff fires 3 DC deputies," *Douglas County News-Press,* May 25, 1982, 1, 16; Karen Naiman, "3 fired deputies allege dismissals unconstitutional," *Douglas County News-Press,* June 8, 1982, 1, 2; Karen Naiman, "Sheriff's officers fired in May are reinstated," *Douglas County News-Press,* July 20, 1982, 1, 3.

[25] "Grand Jury dissolved, DA hints more formal charges are possible," *Douglas County News-Press,* May 26, 1982, 1, 6; "Pressure Mounted, rumors rampant, as

jury worked," *Douglas County News-Press*, 2; "Tension snaps, quietness prevails, waiting over," *Douglas County News-Press*, May 26, 1982, 2.

[26] "McKinster's oft-stormy, oft-headlined tenure nears end," 1, 6.

[27] "Railroad Agent seeks GOP nomination for Sheriff," *Douglas County News-Press*, May 19, 1982, 1, 9.

[28] "Steve Zotos, Former Douglas County Sheriff," Oral Histories Project, Highlands Ranch Historical Society, accessed on March 3, 2019, http://www.highlandsranchhistoricalsociety.org/20180122-Oral_History-Steve_Zotos_Douglas_County_Sheriff.

[29] Attila Denes, quoted in "Steve Zotos."

[30] "Steve Zotos."

Chapter 52

EDUCATION EXPLOSION

Tim Weber

As Douglas County's population grew between 1960 and 1990, so did its school district. In 1958, Douglas County School District RE-1 was organized. It enrolled 1,149 students in two high schools (grades 9-12) and eleven elementary schools (grades 1-8).[1] As DC's population increased from 4,816 in 1960 to 60,391 in 1990, RE-1's student enrollment more than doubled in each decade: from 1,204 in 1960, to 2,705 in 1970, to 6,727 in 1980, and to slightly over 14,000 in 1990.[2]

Two superintendents served DC schools during this period: Dr. Lowell Baumunk (1958-1981) and Dr. Richard O'Connell (1982-2002). In every year of their tenure, the district needed more classrooms (or schools), teachers, support staff, educational supplies, transportation, custodians, and money for utilities.

Douglas County High School under Construction, 1962

During the 1960s, RE-1 was just getting started. In 1958 Parker High School was closed and its 40 students transferred to Douglas County High School. In 1961 a $14 million bond issue was passed to build a new Douglas County High School in Castle Rock and provide additional classrooms in most RE-1 elementary schools. The high school was finished in 1962 and accommodated all 10th, 11th, and 12th graders. Shortly after, the Douglas County Junior High School (RE-1's first) opened in Castle Rock for all 7th, 8th, and 9th graders. In 1964 the district began offering teachers instruction in educational technology;[3] and in 1968, the district's first computer program started in the Junior High School, then spread to other schools.[4] Five of the district's original elementary schools (Gann, Franktown, Indian Park, Larkspur, and Westcreek) closed, and their children transferred elsewhere. Northeast Elementary School in Parker opened.

Financing RE-1 became more complicated in the 1970s. In 1973, the new School Finance Act changed public school financing in Colorado. Both Baumunk and O'Connell complained that the law was unfair to DC and other relatively poor districts. The law was based on a formula determined by dividing each district's assessed tax valuation by the number of pupils. That figure was used to determine how much cash the State Department of Education contributed to the district's general fund and the mill levy that could be charged to the district's taxpayers. When the assessed valuation baselines were established in 1973, DC was still mostly rural and had almost no industry. Thus, according to the superintendents, RE-1 started at a financial disadvantage each year.[5]

The law also limited each district's indebtedness. If the school district's proposed budget exceeded the state's cash contribution and mill levy allotment, which often happened, the district had to borrow money or approve the sale of school bonds. But the funding law restricted district indebtedness to 20% of its assessed valuation. Once the district reached that limit, it had no alternative but to ask voters to raise the mill levy beyond the level approved by the State Board of Education and thereby increase their taxes even more. Furthermore, if voters increased taxes, the state would reduce its contribution accordingly.[6]

Despite these challenges, Baumunk and the school board made progress. During the 1970s, most schools were at or beyond student capacity,[7] so the district built five new elementary schools in Acres Green, Parker, Castle Rock (South Street), Larkspur, and Franktown, along with two new junior high schools in Castle Rock and Parker, which was the first school in DC and maybe Colorado with solar heating.[8] Four schools received additional classrooms including DCHS and Sedalia, South Street, and Northeast Elementary Schools.[9] Because of shortages of space and resources, RE-1 missed the state's deadline (1970) for starting a kindergarten program but did establish one by the mid-1970s.[10]

Tight budgeting and rising inflation raised the issue of teacher salaries, which were in the bottom quarter of metro Denver school districts and lagged behind the state average by almost $1,300.[11] Throughout the 1970s two organizations competed to represent DC's teachers in their negotiations with the district: the Douglas County Educational Association and the Douglas County Federation of Teachers, an affiliate of the AFL/CIO.[12] For most of the decade, the DCEA negotiated rather modest results. In 1971, for example, it secured a $375 increase to the salary scale, which started at $7600.[13] In 1978, teachers selected the DCFT to represent them.[14] It secured a 7-9% salary increase for teachers, a new starting salary of $11,400,[15] and provisions more typical of union bargaining.[16] Baumunk understood that teachers elsewhere had already unionized and became a good partner in the transition. Bob Terwilleger, an English teacher at DCHS and head of the union, called him "the most outstanding educational leader in County history for numerous reasons." [17]

Douglas County RE-1 Schools Administration Building (Castle Rock)

In the 1980s, RE-1 expanded dramatically due to accelerating population growth in northern DC. RE-1 constructed Ponderosa High School (south of Parker),[18] Mountain View Elementary (the Pinery), a junior high connected to

307

Pine Lane Elementary (north of Parker), and Cherokee Trail Elementary (Franktown).[19] The biggest challenge in the decade was the Highlands Ranch area, whose developer Mission Viejo predicted a population of 90,000. As families moved into the development in 1981, Mission Viejo wanted RE-1 to build an elementary school there. O'Connell said that the district required 100 students before construction. When only 50 students could be guaranteed, Mission Viejo and O'Connell worked out an unprecedented deal. The company promised to assume the $3.3 million construction costs for Northridge Elementary School, plus all operating expenses for the first year. RE-1 agreed to lease the school for fifteen years at $1/year, after which it would purchase the school with the school taxes set aside from Highlands Ranch during the leasing period.[20]

Soon other schools were required in Highlands Ranch: Sand Creek Elementary, Eagle Ridge Elementary, and Highlands Ranch Junior/Senior High School. By the end of the 1980s, those schools were over capacity and other schools were being planned.[21]

In 1991-92, the district realigned grades: "middle schools" housed grades 7 and 8 and high schools, grades 9 through 12.[22] In 1990, RE-1 had 1500 employees (including 861 teachers) and was DC's biggest employer. Teachers in the same school often did not know each other.[23] Teacher salaries ranged from $18,338 to $46,430, with an average salary of $26,578. The top salary for elementary school principals was $54,959, and for junior high and senior high principals, $66,603. Superintendent O'Connell received $89,264, which was over nine times larger than Baumunk's $9,400 in 1958.[24]

During this period, the voters of Douglas County had to be willing to raise their own taxes and approve school bond issues repeatedly. Only once did they say no. In late 1980 voters turned down the district's request for a $500,000 tax increase to balance the 1981 budget, which led to significant cuts in educational and other programs.[25] Before his retirement later that year, Baumunk warned that if the people of the County wanted good schools, they would have to pay for them.[26] They never turned down requests for additional school financing. After 1990, RE-1 grew to 8,100 employees (4,400 teachers), 68,000 students, and 91 schools—the third largest school district in Colorado.[27]

[1] James O'Hern and Pat Grippe, *Where Did They Go From Here? A Longitudinal Study of Douglas County High School Students From 1967-1986* (Castle Rock Douglas County School District, 1992), 8.

[2] Ibid, 8- 9.

[3] "Teachers Learn About New Media," *Douglas County News*, November 5, 1964, 3.

[4] O'Hern and Grippe, *Where Did They Go From Here*, 9.

[5] Jerry Peterson, "Next Superintendent In For Tough Time: Baumunk," *Douglas County News-Press*, February 3, 1981, 1.

[6] Ibid.

[7] "$2 Million School Bond Vote Upcoming in Fall," *Douglas County News*, July 30,1970, 1, 8.

[8] "Solar Heat is Still Experimental," *Douglas County News*, April 10, 1975, 10.

[9] "School Officials Get New Office Space," *Douglas County News*, August 27, 1970, 19; "District Notes 13.5 Per Cent Growth in School Enrollment," *Douglas County News*, September 8, 1977, 1.

[10] "Kindergarten Issue Boils," *Douglas County News*, October 2, 1969, 1; "RE-1 Report," *Douglas County News*, December 18, 1969, 9; "Enrollment figures released," *Douglas County News*, October 28, 1975, 2.

[11] "Douglas County Pay Scale for Teachers: A Few Facts," *Douglas County News*, January 31, 1974, 1, 10; Jerry Peterson, "Staff Salaries Take Largest Chunk of Schools' Budget," *Douglas County News-Press*, September 12, 1979, 1, 10.

[12] "Union Asks for Teachers Vote," *Douglas County News*, February 21, 1974, 1; "DCEA to Continue as Teachers' Representative," *Douglas County News*, February 13, 1975, 21; "1", *Douglas County News*, May 16, 1974, 1.

[13] "Teachers Issue Statement," *Douglas County News*, January 3, 1974, 4; "School District Wants To Negotiate," *Douglas County News*, January 31, 1974, 1, 10; "Fact-Finder is Appointed," *Douglas County News*, March 7, 1974, 5; "Teachers and Board Accept Pay Report," *Douglas County News*, May 2, 1974, 16.

[14] "A Pair of Prexies," *Douglas County News*, March 9, 1978, 2.

[15] "All School District Salary Increases 7-9%," *Douglas County News*, January 11, 1979, 2; Peterson, "Staff Salaries Take Largest Chunk of Schools' Budget."

[16] "Teachers Union President Pleased with 2-year Contract," *Douglas County News*, December 28, 1978, 1.

[17] Interview with Robert Terwilleger, May 1, 2019. Terwilleger, a former English teacher and department chair at DCHS, also served as the president of the DCFT.

[18] "There will be a Parker High School," *Douglas County News-Press*, September 16, 1980, 9; "Design Work Restarted on Parker H.S.," *Douglas County News-Press*, June 6, 1980, 1; "Strike Delays Could Postpone Parker High Opening," *Douglas County News-Press*, July 24, 1981, 1, 20.

[19] "Gary Wells, "School District Faces Problems Handling Expected Growth," *Douglas County News-Press*, January 1, 1981, 2.

[20] "Mission Viejo Elementary Needs at least 100 Students to Open," *Douglas County News-Press*, February 18, 1982, 3; Sydney Brown, "Mission Viejo to Pay for School for 50 Highlands Ranch Children," *Douglas County News-Press*, July 21, 1982, 1; "Northridge Elementary Expected to Open in September," *Highlands Ranch Reporter*, August, 1982, 1-2.

[21] "County Needs a New Junior High, 3 Elementary Schools," *Douglas County News-Press*, May 18, 1989, 1, 3.

[22] O'Hern and Grippe, *Where Did They Go From Here*, 11.

[23] Terwilleger interview.

[24] "Schools: Big Money in Administration Salaries," *Douglas County News-Press*, April 14, 1990, 3; "New School District Setup Said Nearing Completion," *Douglas County News*, August 21, 1958, 1.

[25] Jerry Peterson, "Baumunk: Taxes Likely to Go Up," *Douglas County News*, September 10, 1980, 1, 14; Jerry Peterson, "Taxes Going Up, Board Wants Them Higher," *Douglas County News-Press*, November 7, 1980, 3; Jerry Peterson, "School Board Could Slash $485,000 to Balance Budget," *Douglas County News-Press*, December 9, 1980, 6, 9.

[26] Peterson, "Next Superintendent in for Tough Time."

[27] www.dcsdk12.org/about, accessed May 1, 2019.

Chapter 53

FLOODS IN DOUGLAS COUNTY

Joan Gandy

Between 1960 and 1990, the worst natural disaster to hit Douglas County was the flood of June 16, 1965, when fourteen inches of rain fell on Dawson Butte in four hours. "The small natural channels on the steep slopes could not carry the runoff, so water took shortcuts, following the line of least resistance. Creeks overflowed, roads became rivers, and fields became lakes—all in a matter of minutes," reported H.F. Mattai in a 1969 geological survey.[1]

Westside of Dawson Butte Showing Erosions of 1965 Flood, circa 1970

The flood waters swept through Larkspur, Castle Rock, Sedalia, and Louviers, then flowed to the South Platte River below Littleton and roared through Denver and northeastern Colorado, causing major damage along the way.[2] On I-25, two bridges were obliterated near Larkspur; and all six bridges in Castle Rock were washed away, stranding 300-400 cars south of town. Helicopters had to evacuate their passengers.[3] Roads and drainage culverts were destroyed as well as train trestles and roadbeds.[4] In the town of Castle Rock, Sellars Gulch flooded and destroyed a motel, trailer park, and a bridge on Wilcox Street and damaged a few homes.[5] Larkspur's business district was demolished, including Frink's Creamery, DC's largest. The Creamery was never rebuilt, which greatly diminished DC's dairy industry and eliminated hundreds of jobs in the County and in Denver.[6] The flood also damaged farmland and structures in Franktown and Parker and carried away livestock in Newlin Gulch and other parts of the County.

Sedalia was severely impacted by the flood. The bridge over the confluence of the two Plum Creeks was destroyed by a 15-to-20-foot wall of water that also submerged a large part of town. "Residents stood on the banks, watched Plum Creek surge by, and totaled up the damage. They found seven homes, the town's only church, and the grange hall had vanished," reported the *Denver Post*.[7] Tornadoes compounded the already desperate situation, damaging businesses and homes in Palmer Lake, Parker, and Castle Rock. A rancher flagged down a helicopter after a tornado ripped the roof off one of his buildings and hurled a trailer home across his yard. Luckily, the three persons inside the trailer were unharmed.[8]

Out of the flood came stories of heroism and survival. Banding together, DC residents waded through rising water to save their endangered neighbors. Three members of the Hier family risked the surging waters to rescue Sedalia resident Albert Manhart from his flooded home.[9] While his life was saved, the 87-year-old Manhart lost everything but the clothes on his back.[10] Reuben and Priscilla Oman were driving on U.S. 85 when the water pushed their car into a pit. Water and sand flowed into the car while the Omans pressed their faces against the inside roof. After two hours, rescuers spotted the couple, and using a wrecking truck, "they peeled the top off the car. They found the Omans buried up to their faces in sand and mulch—but alive."[11]

Curt Bains braved the already flooded bridge crossing Plum Creek in Sedalia on foot to reach his family. "I saw a horse go by, riding on the roof of a barn. He was still riding, as long as I saw him. Hayricks, barns, trees, and animals went by. I saw my own pick-up go."[12] South of Castle Rock, 16-year-old Jim Lowell hung onto the side of a silo after attempting to rescue his calf. Worried his son's strength was failing, his father John Lowell used a tractor to reach the roof of the barn and pull Jim to safety.[13]

Only a few people in DC died in the flood. Anne Belle Jackson and Harold Young both died in the rising waters. Mrs. Jackson, a mother of five, was driving from Denver to her home in Grand View Estates when she heard of the extreme weather. After her car stalled in the middle of Newlin Gulch, rescuers attempted to throw her a rope. The water came too fast and carried Mrs. Jackson to her death. Mr. Young braved the storm to save his dogs from East Bijou Creek, but the crest of water swept Mr. Young downstream.[14]

Aftermath of 1965 Flood, Looking East from Plum Creek
to Courthouse, Castle Rock

The Douglas County community rallied around the flood victims. A street auction on July 2 in front of the Douglas County Courthouse opened first to flood victims, in hopes they could secure items they lost such as refrigerators at a discounted price.[15] The newspaper offered free use of classified ad space to the people who lost property in the disaster so they could more easily swap, exchange, or request needed items.[16] Neighbors provided fresh water, poured out hot coffee, and dug each other's buried equipment out of the mud.[17] "Yesterday we drove down to Sedalia, and what we saw there makes a column like this seem more than a little unimportant," wrote columnist Mrs. Franklin Doud in the *Douglas County News* a week after the flood.[18] "All the folks along the Platte want the people who suffered through this unbelievable flood to know our thoughts are with them."

A second flood hit Castle Rock on June 24, 1965, causing additional damage to the Spears Motel and two trailer courts.[19] An eight-foot bank of hail was deposited after additional storms in August.[20] In all, the natural disasters in the summer of 1965 caused nearly half of a billion dollars worth of damage.

In the 1970s and 1980s, two additional floods hit DC. In May 1973, heavy rains knocked out electricity and phones and made many roads treacherous west of SH-105. The water cut six- to eight-foot-deep crevasses into the road, isolating the residents of Jackson Creek.[21] "Formerly dry gulches suddenly filled with uncontrollable water, the culverts were unable to carry the load, consequently, the roads in places disappeared rapidly."[22] In the summer of 1983, a July storm brought hail, high winds, and rising waters again to Douglas County.[23] Golf ball-sized hail stripped paint from houses and shattered windows. Ten people were stranded on Castle Rock baseball fields after rising waters blocked the exit roads.[24]

In Douglas County, those who witnessed the 1965 flood will never forget its legacy. "Some stories may be exaggerated in traditional Western style; but when most of 14 inches of rain falls in about 3 hours, it is raining harder than most people have ever seen or will ever see. When one experiences a storm like this and sees the consequences, exaggeration is difficult and pointless. The scars on the landscape, remains of damaged homes, piles of assorted debris, and deposits of sand and gravel along the streams are not fictitious; they are mute evidence that a disaster did occur."[25] After the flood, the Chatfield Dam was constructed (1967-1975) to prevent the South Platte from spreading future flood waters into Denver and beyond. Fortunately, the flood waters that flowed down Cherry Creek were captured by the Cherry Creek Dam, whose water level rose by twelve feet.[26]

---

[1] H.F. Mattai, "Floods of June 1965 in the South Platte River Basin, Colorado," *Geological Survey Paper 1850-B*, 1969, accessed February 14, 2019, https://pubs.usgs.gov/wsp/1850b/report.pdf.

[2] *The Denver Post* published a "Flood Final" insert on June 17, 1965, which provided the most extensive coverage of the flood available.

[3] Ibid.

[4] "Most Area Homeless Not Insured," Flood Final, *Denver Post*, June 17, 1965, 17.

[5] Jessie Robinson, "Castle Rock," *Douglas County News*, June 24, 1965.

[6] "Larkspur," *Douglas County News*, June 24, 1965; Susan Consola Appleby, *Fading Fast: The Story of Douglas County, Colorado* (Palmer Lake, CO: Filter Press, 2001), 105.

[7] C. Carter, "Sedalia's Main Street 'Vanishes' in Torrent," Flood Final, *The Denver Post*, June 17, 1965, 9.

[8] L. Georgia, "Knife of Mud Sickening," Flood Final, *The Denver Post*, June 17, 1965.

[9] Ibid.

[10] "He Lost Everything," *The Denver Post*, June 17, 1965.

[11] A. Curtis and D. Kelly, "Where the flood was born," *Saturday Empire Magazine, The Denver Post*, June 5, 1966.

[12] Ibid.

[13] Ibid.

[14] "Flood Claims Three Lives Locally," *Douglas County News*, June 24. 1965.

[15] "Street Auction July 2nd," *Douglas County News*, June 24, 1965.

[16] *Douglas County News*, June 24, 1965.

[17] C. Walter, "Perry Park Road," *Douglas County News*, June 24, 1965.

[18] F. Doud, "Along the Platte," *Douglas County News*, June 24, 1965.

[19] J. Robinson, "Castle Rock's Second Flood," *Douglas County News*, July 29, 1965.

[20] News clipping, Aug. 23, 1965, *Natural Disasters Floods Book II*, Douglas County Libraries Archives and Local History.

[21] "Jackson Creek Residents Isolated," *Douglas County News*, May 10, 1973.

[22] J. Simeth, "Twin Cedars," *Douglas County News*, May 10, 1973.

[23] J. Adkins, "Hail, high winds strip homes, shatter windows," *Douglas County News*, July 26, 1983.

[24] T. Smith, "Rain washes out fields, stymies tournament play," *Douglas County News*, July 26, 1983.

[25] "Floods of June 1965 in the South Platte River Basin, Colorado."

[26] Flood Final, *The Denver Post*, June 17, 1965, 1, 3.

Chapter 54

HAVING FUN IN DOUGLAS COUNTY

Sarah Stevens

New sources of fun and entertainment in Douglas County emerged in the 1960s and beyond. Residents of the county provided their talents and ideas to foster community. Civic, religious, and social groups, and community-wide celebrations brought people together. In short, the people of Douglas County knew how to make their own fun.

Teens played a significant role in providing programs for everyone to enjoy. Douglas County high schools put on plays, cabarets, and musical performances. Teens and young adults agreed that the county needed to do more for its young people and lobbied accordingly. In 1970, Douglas County High School teens wrote an article published in *Douglas County News* urging the town of Castle Rock to consider creating a teen-centered space.[1] They argued that a recreation center for teens would cut down on drag racing down Wilcox Street and other risky behavior.[2] A few years later, the Douglas County Youth Council welcomed the opening of a teen rec center.[3]

Dancing, particularly square dancing, was a popular activity in DC. Square dancing clubs like the Rock-a-Twirlers of Larkspur and Castle Rock held competitions with other groups throughout the Denver metro area. There was a big rivalry between the Rock-a-Twirlers and the Denver Square Hoppers.[4] Competitions included a dance that required holding lemons in one's mouth and capturing other teams' flags. Members accumulated badges by winning such events.[5] The Rock-a-Twirlers held dances at Kirk Hall at the county fairgrounds, including one for the holidays in December 1964, which anyone could attend for seventy-five cents.[6] The club also gave free lessons.[7] Similarly, the Ponderosa Squares of Parker and Franktown and Elbert County residents held an anniversary ball in Elizabeth, Colorado.[8]

Music and drinking establishments also were popular during this time. John Anderson, a grandson of the original owners of the Rockview Lounge, recounted his time growing up around the establishment. The Lounge had humble beginnings. It began as a birthday party, became a weekly event, then evolved into a popular music venue. Rockview was located south of Castle Rock near what would later become the Continental Divide Raceways. Its band played only country and western music since rock n' roll was not acceptable to its usual clientele of farmers and cattlemen. Known to most locals as The Barn, it could get rowdy, but it was generally known as a great spot for a good time.[9] According to Anderson, people traveled from as far as Fort Collins to drink and dance the night away.[10]

Before the mid-1950s, DC residents watched Hollywood movies in the "School Theater" (the DC High School auditorium) on Wednesday and Sunday nights. In the summer of 1956, the 47 Drive-in Theater opened on Highway 86, just east of Castle Rock.[11] *The Douglas County News* held a contest to name the theater. The winning submission came from Willard Smith of Parker. The number "47" was on the license plate of owner James Peterson.[12] Later, the theater offered free showings to cars with certain "lucky license plate numbers." The theater sometimes kicked off its season with free family-friendly screenings.[13] The drive-in stayed open from late spring to early fall, depending on DC's unpredictable snowfall.[14] Business was not always brisk: between six and thirty cars was typical.[15] In 1969, the drive-in was renamed Castle Rock Cinema.[16]For the first time, DC residents no longer had to cross county lines to see the latest films.

The Continental Divide Raceways opened south of Castle Rock in August 1959 and received national attention in the December 1959 issue of *Sports Car Illustrated*.[17] It offered a 2.8-mile road course, a half-mile oval track, and a 4,200-foot drag strip. The racetrack was a major asset for Colorado since few such venues were operating at the time. Consequently, it attracted large crowds that also frequented Castle Rock businesses. The Raceways also offered its customers spectacular views of the entire facility and the bluffs of southern Douglas County.[18] At the peak of the Raceways' success, it offered sanctioned races and attracted famous racers like A.J. Foyt and Mario Andretti, whose participation was a major draw.[19] Unfortunately, the Raceways closed in 1973 after a major accident, and, owner, Sid Langsam was diagnosed with cancer.[20] It did reopen later but was unable to sustain itself. The venue closed permanently when the property was sold in 1983.[21]

View from the Stands of Continental Divide Raceways

Colorado Renaissance Festival

Another major tourist attraction in Douglas County was the Colorado Renaissance Festival. After losing its original location near Morrison,[22] the

Festival moved to Larkspur in March 1980.[23] The possibility of the festival coming to Larkspur generated both enthusiasm and opposition in the early planning process. While the festival site raised issues of zoning, traffic congestion, and liquor licensing, many people liked the idea. One supporter was Tweet Kimball, owner of the Cherokee Ranch and Castle.[24] She stated that "Something like this could be an asset to the county."[25] She was right — the Colorado Renaissance Festival was an economic boom for DC and offered a unique entertainment opportunity. It also provided local artisans a venue to sell their creations and gave local performers an opportunity for summer employment.[26] The Festival remains to this day a major summer attraction for people along the Front Range.

Douglas County became the home of a major professional golf event. In 1986, Jack Vickers founded The International at the Castle Pines Golf Club as part of the PGA tour. His goal was to create the "best golf tournament on the planet."[27] The tournament was considered unusual because of its modified Stableford scoring system. The system was created by Dr. Stableford for golf competitions at higher altitudes. Many considered it "a better way to score the game than simply adding strokes."[28] According to a sports editor of the *Douglas County News-Press*, the format allowed for a more competitive edge among players and engaged spectators more than in other tournaments.[29] The International attracted major golf professionals and remained a popular event through 2006.

One of the longest-lasting entertainment venues in DC was the Rock Bowl, which opened in 1963 on Wilcox, just south of the Castle Rock city limits.[30] It had a coffee shop and meeting rooms, and its bowling leagues included scores of teams and hundreds of bowlers. When the courthouse burned down in 1978, it made room for the district court. In the late 1980s, Rock Bowl moved 1.5 miles south on Frontage Road in expanded facilities: 20 lanes, a lounge, a Mexican restaurant (Hector's), a big screen TV and video games, a pool table, and banquet facilities, which attracted all kinds of meetings, including wedding receptions.[31] In 1996, Duke's Steakhouse purchased the property and stayed there until it moved to Castle Pines in 2010.

Entertainment and fun in Douglas County emerged from a sense of community. While the county struggled with expansive growth, finding ways to have fun seemed to keep pace. From the small square dances of the 60s and 70s to the Colorado Renaissance Festival, the rich history of DC demonstrated its residents' talents and varied tastes.

[1] What Are You Doing Saturday Nite?" *Douglas County News*, November, 12 1970, 1.

[2] Ibid.

[3] Stan Underwood, "Douglas County Youth Council," *Douglas County News*, June 30 1977, 1.

[4] *Douglas County News*, October 8, 1964, 10.

[5] Ibid.

[6] Advertisement, *Douglas County News*, August, 13, 1964; "Rock-A-Twirlers," *Douglas County News*, May 6, 1965, 4; "Rock-A-Twirlers," *Douglas County News*, September 30, 1965, 13.

[7] "Free Square Dance Lessons," *Douglas County News*, June 18, 1964, 15.

[8] "Square Dance Club News," *Douglas County News*, June 16, 1977, 6.

[9] Advertisement, *Douglas County News*, March 10, 1966, 14.

[10] John Anderson, Oral History, Douglas County Archives and Local History, 2004.2005.015.

[11] Lowell Baumunk, Oral History, Douglas County Archives and Local History, 2004.2005.017.1000. As a high school student, Baumunk was the summer projectionist from 1959 to 1962. "Tentative Opening of Drive-In Theater is Set," *Douglas County News*, July 26, 1956, 1; "Congratulations and Welcome," *Douglas County News*, August 9, 1956, 1.

[12] "Willard Smith, Parker, Winner in Name the Drive-In Competition," *Douglas County News*, May 31, 1956, 1.

[13] "Free Show at 47 Drive-In," *Douglas County News*, May 27, 1963, 1.

[14] "47 Drive-In Closing for Winter Season," *Douglas County News*, October 3, 1957, 12.

[15] Baumunk, Oral History.

[16] "47 Drive-In Now Castle Rock Cinema," *Douglas County News*, May 29, 1969, 1.

[17] "Castle Rock Pictured in National Magazine," *Douglas County News*, December 31 1959,1.

[18] "Another Asset for Douglas County," *Aspen Daily Times*, September, 10, 1959.

[19] "Castle Rock's Continental Divide Raceways," *Denver Post Blog*, October, 17, 2013, accessed March 17, 2019, http://blogs.denverpost.com/library/2013/10/17/colorados-continental-divide-raceways/8889/.

[20] Ibid.

[21] Ibid.

[22] Ray Alvarez, "Arts Festival Request Could Pose Dilemma," *Douglas County News*, December, 14, 1978, 1.

[23] Alan Isbell, "Renaissance Festival Wins Larkspur Board," *Douglas County News*, March 7, 1980, 1.

[24] Ibid.

[25] Ibid.

[26] "Auditions Slated April 15 for Renaissance Festival," *Douglas County News-Press*, April 9, 1980, 3.

[27] "The Spring International Promotional Pamphlet," August 21, 1994. *Golf Tournaments: The International, 1994*; Ephemera Collection; Archives and Local History, Douglas County Libraries.

[28] John Kilin, "Doc Stableford makes impact at International," *Douglas County News-Press*, August 20-23, 1992.

[29] Ibid.

[30] "Rock Bowl Invites Each of You," *Douglas County News*, October 31, 1963," 1.

[31] "Rock Bowl offers best in sports and quality family restaurant," *Douglas County News-Press*, February 28, 1989.

Chapter 55

MORE REPUBLICAN THAN EVER

Tim Weber

For most of its history, Douglas County was sparsely populated, rural, and staunchly Republican. But between 1960 and 1990, DC grew from almost five thousand to just over sixty thousand. At first, most new residents came from El Paso County, but eventually, most newcomers came from Arapahoe County and beyond (see "Growing Pains," chapter 46). Did the arrival of new people alter DC's traditional Republican identity?

The short answer is no. In the eight presidential elections between 1960 and 1988, DC voted Republican seven times. The only exception was in 1964 when Lyndon B. Johnson defeated Barry Goldwater (52% to 48%). In the other presidential elections, Republican candidates won by a wide margin. DC voted for Nixon three times: in 1960 against Kennedy (64% to 36%); in 1968 against Humphrey and Wallace (66% to 28% and 11%); and in 1972 against McGovern (76% to 29%). Other Republican winners included Ford over Carter (66% to 32%) in 1976; Reagan over Carter and Anderson (70% to 18% and 12%) in 1980; Reagan over Mondale in 1984 (79% to 20%); and Bush over Dukakis (70% to 29%) in 1988.[1]

How did these results compare with earlier and later elections? In the fifteen presidential elections between 1900 and 1956, DC voted for Republican presidential candidates ten times and Democrats five times; but in the seven presidential elections since 1992, DC voted Republican *every time,* including the 2016 election in which DC voted for Donald Trump over Hillary Clinton (55% to 37%).[2] Between 1960 and 2016, then, DC voted for Republican presidential candidates fourteen out of fifteen times.

Why did Republican success increase so dramatically after 1960? Most of DC's population growth came from El Paso and Arapahoe Counties, which were both strong Republican enclaves at the time. In fact, all three counties voted the same way in the presidential elections from 1960 to 1988: seven Republicans and one Democrat. Thus, a significant number of new residents were probably already Republicans before they got here.[3] That assertion is confirmed by voter registration figures. During this growth period in DC, registered Republicans always outnumbered Democrats; and frequently, so did Independents. Twice there were more registered Independents than Republicans (1972 and 1974). Of course, not all registered voters cast ballots; and voters did not always support their party's candidates. But overall, Republicans retained a much larger base than Democrats or Independents, which made them difficult to beat.[4]

REGISTERED VOTERS IN DOUGLAS COUNTY			
Year	Republicans	Democrats	Independents
1966	1237	1074	1090
1968	1432	1041	981
1972	2224	1193	2365
1974	2594	1577	2772
1978	4437	2106	4195
1980	6031	2280	5493
1984	7720	2324	5761
1988	16793	5450	13455

How did such Republican numerical superiority affect state and local elections? From 1960 to 1990, DC Republicans won *every* state election for governor except one: Richard Lamb in 1982. In local or county elections, however, Democrats won often, as had been the case in DC's past. During the 1960s, successful Democrats included Charles Prescott, County Clerk and Recorder; C. Douglas Andrews, County Coroner; Donald Williams, County Commissioner; and Robert Metzler, DC School Superintendent. In the 1970s, Democrat officeholders included Royal McKinster Sheriff; Carroll Hier, County Clerk, and Recorder; Joan Skarda, County Assessor; and Gill Whitman, County Commissioner. Some of these Democrats were elected more than once. During the 1980s, however, no Democrats won County elections, which demonstrates the growing power of Republicans throughout the electoral system.[5]

Despite Republican dominance, DC politics became contentious in the 1970s and 1980s. Disagreements about population growth turned neighbor against neighbor and transformed local politics into a war zone. Some residents wanted to sell their acreage to developers at inflated prices, while others wanted to preserve DC's rural heritage. Strong pro- and anti-growth sentiments existed in both political parties, which led to increasing levels of political dysfunction.

Always in the middle of the political fray were the three DC Commissioners who had the final say about DC growth. Like most Colorado counties, in 1970 DC had no master plan for development. Without such guidelines, the Commissioners found it difficult to evaluate the proposals submitted by high-powered developers; and because of changes in state law, they eventually found it difficult to say no to them. As a result, in the 1970s the Commissioners approved many inadequate and under-funded subdivision plans that ended in bankruptcy. Such failures left residents financially liable and looking for someone to blame. True to form, voters elected mostly Republican Commissioners during this period (twelve to three); but party affiliation was a poor predictor of where politicians stood on growth issues.

In 1972 the state legislature mandated that all counties develop their own master plans for growth. DC formed a five-person Planning Commission, but the County Commission rejected many proposed plans because of strong public opposition. The Commissioners often seemed overwhelmed by the consequences of growth, which they generally favored: the lack of paved roads, increasing traffic, inadequate schools, understaffed sheriff's office, too few snowplows, lagging job opportunities within the County, and the recurring questions about long-term water supply. In 1972, the Colorado Land Use Commission expressed concern about the DC Commissioners' ability to deal with such issues, which produced a heated debate over local versus state control. In 1978, without consulting the third Commissioner (a Republican), two pro-growth Commissioners (one from each party) fired the DC director of planning because they concluded he was anti-growth. In the early 1980s, one Republican Commissioner ordered road work in his district without getting approval from his two Republican colleagues.[6] In 1984, two Commissioners met regularly without the third who usually opposed them (all three were Republicans).

Irate voters threatened to recall County officials, and some members of County committees and commissions resigned in protest over heavy-handed tactics. Many citizens criticized the Commission's planning process and overall competence, and public meetings often became volatile and disruptive. In a recent academic study of DC during this period, the author described "a decade-long pattern of amateurism, factionalism, and infighting within the Douglas County Board of Commissioners, Planning Commission, and citizen groups."[7] Pro- and anti-growth rivalry disrupted the decision-making process during the 1980s in DC's three incorporated towns—Castle Rock (1881), Larkspur (1979), and Parker (1981). Disagreements over population growth often seemed that they would tear local governments apart.

After a decade, the Commissioners finally approved DC's first Master Plan in 1983. It was revised many times as changing conditions warranted. But the Master Plan was adopted *after* the Commissioners approved the plan submitted by the Mission Viejo Company for Highlands Ranch. As an experienced developer of huge projects, Mission Viejo's plan was comprehensive, professional, and irresistible. Throughout their decade-long building project, the developers kept control of the special districts created to manage the plan. They also discouraged incorporation, even though Highlands Ranch became DC's largest municipality.[8]

In the sixties through the eighties, DC politics remained under Republican control, but local politics became deeply divided. "A decade-long power struggle occurred within Douglas County governance between property-rights proponents and slow-growth advocates that led to a variety of squabbles, firings, and public debates over control of the county's future."[9]

---

[1] *Dave Leip's Atlas of U.S. Presidential Elections,* accessed May 26, 2017, https://uselectionatlas.org, see also https://en.wikipedia.org/wiki/Douglas_County,_Colorado.

[2] Ibid.

[3] For complete Colorado election results, starting in 1900, see Colorado Secretary of State, *Election Results Archives,* accessed March 7, 2019, https://www.sos.state.co.us/pubs/elections/Results/Archives.html.

[4] Ibid.

[5] Ibid.

[6] Gail Anderson, "Recall drive planned against Commissioner Orcutt," *Douglas County News-Press,* September 3, 1982, 1, 19.

[7] Kevin Weinman, "Invisible Suburbs: Privatized Growth in Suburban Metropolitan Denver, 1950-2000," Ph.D. dissertation, University of New Hampshire, Durham (Spring, 2017), 149-155, accessed March 7, 2019, https://scholars.unh.edu/dissertation/157/.

[8] Ibid, 169-221.

[9] Ibid., 138.

PART SIX

EXPLOSION OF GROWTH, 1990-2020

Chapter 56

THE FASTEST GROWING COUNTY IN THE U.S.

Larry Schlupp

From 1990 to 2020, the nation's economy shifted from goods-producing industries to those sectors impacted by new technologies, services, and tourism. Douglas County became an epicenter of Colorado's economic upheaval, overwhelmed by the influx of huge capital investments and population growth coming from outside its borders. This unrelenting source of dollars and people produced new demands for services that forever changed the demographic and cultural profile of the County. During the 1990s, DC was the nation's fastest-growing county in terms of percentage of population increase (+191%); and it soon became Colorado's highest-ranked county in terms of median household income and educational levels.[1]

In 1992, the U.S. Government redirected $30 billion of its "Cold War peace dividend"[2] to create a new *Information Superhighway* (the Internet), which became the infrastructure for a new communications network. Part of this initial outlay of capital in the mid-1990s was used by *Telecommunications, Inc. (TCI)* and *US West* to lay hundreds of miles of fiber-optic cable in Douglas County. Coincidentally, dozens of private start-up software companies were founded in anticipation of the emerging communications revolution, which started the Dot Com era. But the expanding Dot Com Bubble burst in 2002 because of the lack of firmware products to utilize the software. Of the many new start-up companies, *Netscape* and *AOL* were among the few that survived.[3] Still, the foundation had been laid for the future development of new end-user products in biotechnology, machine tooling, robotics, and digital data storage and usage. Despite the rough start, the Dot Com era led to substantial population growth in Douglas County in the latter 1990s.

From 1990 to 2020, Douglas County's population grew from 60,391[4] to an estimated 358,000.[5] In 1990, Douglas County had 13,249 workers, most of whom commuted to work outside Douglas County. Up to the mid-1990s, Denver Tech Center, the Meridian Business Park, and Inverness Business Park provided most of the outside-of-the-County jobs in companies like *First Data Corporation, EchoStar, CH2M,* and many service-based hotels and restaurants.[6] In 1990, services, retail/wholesale, and leisure/hospitality were the three largest employers of DC residents.[7] Digital communication reached adolescence in 2005 and continued to mature over the next fifteen years. Transmission modes, transmission speeds, content, and technological innovations grew exponentially, rapidly changing traditional industries and creating jobs for highly skilled employees.

Douglas County Population Growth				
Towns	1990	2000	2010	2019
Castle Rock	8,244	20,302	48,231	69,000
Castle Pines	*	2,654	3,614	11,340
Franktown	83	99	395	428
Highlands Ranch	10,181	70,931	96,713	107,216
Larkspur	232	260	183	195
Lone Tree	1,261	6,880	10,218	15,150
Louviers	*	227	237	269
Parker	5,625	23,384	45,297	57,405
Sedalia	205	211	206	214
Roxborough	*	4,446	9,099	10,685
Westcreek	97	105	129	153
Total County	60,391	175,766	285,465	358,000
% Urban	60.4	85.5	86.7	89.8
% Rural	39.6	14.5	13.3	10.2

1990-2010: US Department Decennial Census   * Verified Census
2019: Douglas County and Municipal Estimates   numbers not available.

Douglas County struggled to keep up with population growth and the changing economy. The retail industry exploded with the opening of the Outlets Mall at Castle Rock (1992), Lone Tree's Park Meadows Mall (1996 and 2008 expansion),[8] the Promenade at Castle Rock (2015+), and the many new shopping centers in Parker. Four large hospitals and medical complexes were built in Douglas County: Sky Ridge Hospital in Lone Tree (2003), Centura Health's Parker Adventist Hospital (2004) and Castle Rock Adventist Hospital (2013), and UC Health Highlands Ranch Hospital (2019). New recreation facilities included the PACE Center (Parker), the Miller Activity Complex (Castle Rock), and Highland Ranch's multiple recreation centers. For the first time, multi-theater complexes opened in Highlands Ranch, Lone Tree, Castle Rock, and Parker. The Douglas County Fairgrounds and Event Center underwent numerous updates and expansions and drew thousands of people each year to its various entertainment, educational, and community programs. Big box stores (Costco, Sam's, Home Depot, Lowe's, and Walmart) opened in Lone Tree, Castle Rock, and Parker. By the end of 2019, the major employment industry sectors in Douglas County were professional and business services (18.4%), retail trade (14.8%), and leisure/hospitality (13.0%).[9] This vibrant economy employed 127,529 workers in DC. Of these, 10.6% were government employees and 89.4% worked in privately-owned companies.[10]

Aerial of North Castle Rock Development

As a result, Douglas County became a more transient, commuting, and urban society during the 1990-2020 era. Its net population grew by 297,609 people and reflected the extreme mobility of the U.S. population. Although Douglas County's population growth came from both inside and outside of Colorado, most of the growth came from people moving into the County from other states. Moving survey information[11] indicates that a significant portion of the County's growth came from California and Texas. During the era, all the in-out-and-around migration of the population changed the County's residential environment from rural to urban. In 1990, most of DC's population (60,391) lived in rural areas. Castle Rock was DC's largest town (8,244), and Parker was the second largest (5,625). The County's other historic towns were much smaller: Larkspur (just over 200), Sedalia and Louviers (200s), and Franktown (about 100). Those historic population patterns have changed dramatically since then.

In the last three decades, most of DC's growing population lived in the northern half of the County which stretched along the C470/E470 corridor and then spread southward.[12] Thousands of residents moved into new towns like Castle Pines and Lone Tree. Highlands Ranch was DC's first planned community and became its largest town (over 107,000). Parker increased almost ten-fold (from 5,625 to 57,405) and is listed as a population center within Denver Metropolitan Area (MSA). Roxborough changed from a quiet suburb of Littleton to a separate town and another distinct part of the Denver MSA. Due to its increase in geographical area, population, commerce, and government services, Castle Rock (about 69,000) is now the county seat of one of the most financially progressive counties in Colorado. In contrast, the southern half of Douglas County has remained DC's least populated and most rural area. Instead of new subdivisions, it is characterized by 66,000 acres of County-managed Open Space and Land Conservancies.

DC's demographic profile has changed radically from 1990 to the present.[13] The number of those under 18 grew significantly, as did those over 65. The median age increased from 30 to just under 40. The percentage of the population with college degrees grew from 25% to 65%. The annual median family income in the County grew from $51,620 to just under $130,000. DC also became more racially diverse. Its non-white population grew from 4% to 29%. The median home price increased from $128,500 to $487,500. At the end of the era, 70% of the employees living in Douglas County commuted to work outside the County. The 2008-2009 Great Recession hit DC's construction industry hard, though it was in full recovery by mid-2011. The construction industry took another dip in mid-2014 due to the shortage of construction workers.[14]

334

DC's growth spurt is not over yet. Large housing developments are being planned or are already approved for northern DC: 12,000 homes in Sterling Ranch (south of Chatfield Reservoir);[15] 5,000 homes in The Canyons (between I-25 and Crowfoot Valley Road);[16] 2,400 to 3,378 homes in Hess Ranch (west of Parker);[17] 1,200 homes in Montaine (south of Castle Rock);[18] and 100s of homes in the Trails, Meadowlark, and other developments (on north Crowfoot Road in Parker).[19] The ripple effect of continued growth in DC will be felt for years to come.

---

[1] Personal correspondence with Community Development Supervisor Kati Rider, February 4, 2020. See also "Douglas County Demography, Douglas County Community Development, *US Bureau of Census, 1990, 2000, and 2010.* From 2000 to 2010, Douglas County ranked 16th in the county.

[2] Thomas L. Goodnight and Sandy Green, "Rhetoric, Risk, and Markets: The Dot-Com Bubble," *Quarterly Journal of Speech*, 9, no. 2: 122.

[3] Ibid., 124.

[4] Richard L. Forstall, "Population of Counties by Decennial Census, 1900-1990," *US Bureau of Census*, March 1995, accessed November 29, 2019, https://www.census.gov/population/cencounts/co190090.txt.

[5] *Douglas County Growth and Development Profile*, March 2019, accessed November 18, 2019, https://www.douglas.co.us/documents/douglas-county-growth-and-development-profile.pdf/; Department of Community Development, *DC Demographic Summary,* accessed January 8, 2020, https://www.douglas.co.us/documents/douglas-county-demographics-summary.pdf.

[6] Shea Properties, "The Meridian Story," accessed November 19, 2018, http://www.dtcmeridian.com/about/places/the-meridian-story; John Rebchook, "Inverness pioneer John O'Meara recalled," *Colorado Real Estate Journal*, March 14, 2017, accessed February 23, 2019, https://crej.com/news/inverness-pioneer-john-omeara-recalled/

[7] "Douglas County Jobs," accessed November 19, 2019, https://dcdata-dougco.opendata.arcgis.com/datasets/douglas-jobs-annual-average?selectedAttribute=F51_Information.

[8] Kristi Alrellano and Joey Bunch, "Town gets shopping money," *The Denver Post*, September 10, 2006, accessed January 15, 2020, https://www.denverpost.com/2006/09/10/town-gets-shopping-money.

[9] *DC Demographic Survey.*

[10] U.S. Bureau of Labor Statistics, *Quarterly Census of Employment and Wages, CSVs by Areas: Colorado, Douglas, 2019*, accessed February 10, 2019, https://www.bls.gov/cew/downloadable-data-files.htm. Note: This URL listing

allows the reader to access the *QCEW NAICS-Based Data Files* (midway down the page) for county employment data for individual years, 1990 through 2019, by SIC industries. The employment data for Douglas County was downloaded for each year (1990 to 2019) on an Excel spreadsheet and the percentage relationship between private industries employment and government employment could then be calculated.

[11] *Annual United Van Lines Movers Study*, "Shipment Migration by State" (filtered Excel file), accessed 1.9.2020, https://www.unitedvanlines.com/newsroom/movers-study-2019.

[12] U.S. Department of Commerce, "*Colorado 1990, Census of Population and Housing*," September 24, 1992, 3, accessed November 15, 2019, https://www.census.gov/library/publications/decennial/1990/cp-2/cp-2-7.pdf; U. S. Department of Commerce, "Colorado 2000, Census of Population and Housing," July 3, 2003, 6-7, accessed November 15, 2019, https://www.census.gov/prod/cen2000/phc-3-7.pdf; U. S. Department of Commerce, United States Summary, "Census 2010, Census of Population and Housing Unit Count," September 2012, 53, accessed November 15, 2019, https://www2.census.gov/library/publications/decennial/2010/cph-2/cph-2-1.pdf.

[13] "DC Demographics Summary."

[14] Ibid.

[15] Carlos Illeseas, "Sterling Ranch Clears Hurdle," *Denver Post*, February 21, 2014, 7A.

[16] Jessica Gibbs, "The rise of Castle Pines," *Castle Rock News-Press*, September 26, 2019, 6-7; Jessica Gibbs, "Castle Pines OKs 1,500 more home in the Canyons," *Castle Rock News-Press*, December 19, 2019, 5, 7.

[17] Jill Jamieson, "Hess Ranch development to begin with $41 million sale," *Colorado Real Estate Journal*, April 21, 2018, accessed on January 28, 2020, https://crej.com/news/hess-ranch-development-to-begin-with-41-million-sale/.

[18] Jessica Gibbs, "Planning Commission OKs 1,200 homes proposal," *Castle Rock News-Press*, February 18, 2019.

[19] Town of Parker Active Development Tour—Updated January 7, 2020, accessed January 28, 2020, www.arcgis.com/apps/Shortlist/index.html?appid=7879283391d3453da213a439f2 dca232.

Chapter 57

EXPANDING GOVERNMENTS

Steve Boand

Douglas County swelled with new residents between 1990 and 2020. By far the biggest growth occurred within unincorporated Douglas County where the population grew by 150,306 residents from 45,887 in 1990 to 196,193 people in 2018.[1] The cities and towns also gained 132,150 new residents, with Castle Rock and Parker making up 80% of the increase.[2] As a result, DC governmental structures grew significantly.

The County's tax revenue expanded from $29.9 million in 1990[3] to $312.8 million in 2018.[4] Inflation-adjusted expenditures for services only grew by 18%, from $713 to $842 per resident. Government services expanded to meet citizens' needs, including a new Justice Center in Castle Rock in 1995.[5] Expenditures for public safety and justice services rose from $5.8 in 1990[6] to $79.9 million in 2018,[7] an increase of 620%. The public safety expenditures in 2020 comprised 22% of the county budget, which is 10% above the average for other counties.[8]

Robert A. Christensen Justice Center - circa 1998

Much of the increasing revenues came from escalating sales taxes during the 1990s. Castle Rock's Factory Shops opened in 1992.[9] Park Meadows Mall opened in 1996 and was annexed by Lone Tree in 2007.[10] As a result, these new sales tax revenues were a windfall for Douglas County, rising from zero in 1990[11] to more than $70 million in 2019.[12] The sales taxes were used to support DC's law enforcement, open space, parks and recreations, and road projects. County revenue share backs to the municipalities exceeded $10 million per year.[13] Without sales tax revenue, property taxes would have increased by 33% in 2018 to cover spending.[14]

Government at all levels has been a growth industry over the last thirty years. In 1990, there were 110 local governmental entities providing services.[15] In 2020, that number increased to 268.[16] Of these, 138 were new Metropolitan Districts.[17] These entities helped the County's goal that "new development pays its fair share."[18]

Overall job growth increased in DC by 61% over twenty years. In 2001 there were 82,190 jobs in DC;[19] and by 2019, there were 132,290, with 10.3% of them in government service.[20] The number of Douglas County employees grew from 366 in 1990[21] to 1,218 in 2018.[22] The number of employees per thousand residents served, however, declined from 7.97 in 1990 to 6.21 in 2019, indicating some economy of scale.[23]

There are three different models for local governments in DC. Some towns are *unincorporated*, which requires the creation of metropolitan districts to provide utilities, roads, and other services. In *incorporated* municipalities, local elected officials are responsible for providing such services with taxes collected, then distributed by the state per state laws. A third alternative— *home rule*—enables residents to exercise maximum control over local affairs by drawing up their own charter that allows elected officials to collect and distribute their own taxes and operate apart from many state statutes.[24]

Highlands Ranch is DC's largest unincorporated community (100,000+ population). The Highlands Ranch Metro District provides road construction, the management of parks, sports programs, open space, a variety of other public works, and cultural assets like the Highlands Ranch Mansion.[25] It relies on the Douglas County Sheriff's Office for its law enforcement. Residents have rejected many attempts to incorporate, and more than 95% of residents rate the community as an excellent or good place to live.[26]

Two of DC's newest municipalities have made different choices. Lone Tree was under development in the early 1990s. Soon residents complained about the lack of services and unfulfilled developer promises.[27] The County intervened and stopped all development until promises were kept.[28] By late 1995, 85% of voting residents approved the incorporation of the City of Lone Tree,[29] which then consisted of 960 acres and 13 homeowner associations.[30] To increase local control, residents adopted a home rule charter in 1998.[31] In 2000, the City annexed 3,500 acres straddling I-25 known as RidgeGate.[32] By 2018, the City grew to nearly 10 square miles[33] and a population of 13,860.[34]

Castle Pines North was incorporated by an affirmative vote of 80% in November 2007.[35] Its name was changed to the City of Castle Pines in 2010, and voters approved a home rule charter in 2019.[36] Castle Pines' 2018 population was 10,552, and it is expected to triple over the next twenty years.[37] The City plans to become a "balanced, unified, and sustainable community."[38] Three other DC incorporated municipalities have adopted home rule: Castle Rock, Larkspur, and Parker.[39]

Hidden Mesa Open Space

One benefit of growth is the ability to provide amenities that improve the quality of life. Between 1990 and 2019, state-of-the-art recreation centers, field houses, aquatic parks, multipurpose fields, dog parks, golf courses, ice trails, ice rinks, skate parks, equestrian facilities, and miles of trails were opened across the County in Highlands Ranch[40], Parker[41], Castle Rock,[42] Larkspur,[43] Lone Tree,[44] and unincorporated areas.[45] Castle Rock Parks & Recreation received National Gold Medal Awards for its programs in 2012 and 2018.[46]

Citizens voted for open space protection in 1994 with the approval of a small sales tax.[47] More than 16,980 acres have been protected by County ownership.[48] An additional 44,074 acres of private property are secured by conservation easements.[49] Other communities have also preserved open space, including the 2,500-acre open space preserves managed by the Highlands Ranch Metro District.[50] Castle Rock,[51] Parker,[52] and Lone Tree[53] have collectively set aside nearly 8,000 acres of open space.

The arts gained public support during these three decades. The Colorado Artfest at Castle Rock came of age in the 1990s, bringing artists from around the USA to the County every summer.[54] Parker[55] and Lone Tree[56] opened centers for the performing and visual arts in 2011 to create venues for theater, dance, music, and the visual arts. These arts facilities were made possible by government financial assistance, including participation certifications[57] and revenue bonds.[58]

U.S. News and World Report rated Douglas County as America's Healthiest Community in 2019.[59] DC's open spaces, recreational facilities, community events, educational attainments, community health, and low environmental hazards moved the County to the top of the elite national list.[60] The investments made by local governments have enabled the County to receive such recognition. Such benefits have come from the County's growth.

Douglas County will face a host of growth-related challenges in the future, including traffic congestion and encroachments on open spaces.[61] Communities relying on non-renewable groundwater including Castle Pines[62], Parker,[63] and Castle Rock[64] will face the increasing costs of developing renewable water supplies. Castle Rock forecasts that the implementation of its long-term water supply plan will cost more than $300 million.[65]

Despite these challenges, the future is bright for the people and government services in the County. Every government in DC has a balanced budget.[66] The County's 2019 citizen survey reported that "96% affirm the accuracy of the statement: *Douglas County is a good place to raise a family*".[67] That perception will likely continue for many years to come.[68]

[1] *State Demography Office Data, 2020,* accessed February 9, 2020, https://demography.dola.colorado.gov/data/.

[2] Ibid.

[3] "1990 Douglas County Adopted Budget" (Castle Rock, 1989), 30.

[4] "2020 Douglas County Adopted Budget." *Budget Books (*December 13, 2019), 34, accessed May 21, 2020, https://www.douglas.co.us/documents/2020-adopted-budget.pdf/

[5] Jessica Gibbs, "Growing Castle Pines seeks to build community identity," *Colorado Community Media,* accessed May 20, 2020, https://coloradocommunitymedia.com/stories/growing-castle-pines-seeks-to-build-community-identity,286629.

[6] "1990 Douglas County Adopted Budget."

[7] *Comprehensive Annual Financial Report For The Year Ended December 31, 2018* (Castle Rock: Finance Department, 2019), 34.

[8] *2018 Colorado Local Government Handbook,* Research Publication No. 719 (Denver: Colorado General Assembly, 2018), 13.

[9] "Castle Rock: A look back," *Rocky Mountain News,* November 24, 2006, 43A.

[10] Jane Reuter, "The rise of Lone Tree," *Parker Chrncicle,* December 10, 2011.

[11] "1990 Douglas County Adopted Budget."

[12] "2020 Douglas County Adopted Budget," 9.

[13] Ibid., 7.

[14] *Comprehensive Annual Financial Report For The Year Ended December 31, 2018, 4.*

[15] *Abstract of Assessment and Summary of Tax Rates* (Castle Rock: Office of the Assessor, 1990).

[16] *2019 Abstract of Assessment and Summary of Tax Levies* (Castle Rock: Office of the Assessor, 2019).

[17] Ibid.

[18] "Douglas County 2040 Comprehensive Master Plan" (Castle Rock: Douglas County Planning Commission, August 5, 2019), 6-7.

[19] Colorado Department of Local Affairs, *Jobs by Sector (NAICS),* 2020, accessed May 21, 2020, https://demography.dola.colorado.gov/economy-labor-force/data/jobs-by-sector/

[20] *Douglas County Economic Development Quarterly Report, 4th Qtr, 2019* (Castle Rock: Department of Community Development, 2020), 2.

[21] *Comprehensive Annual Financial Report For The Year Ended December 31, 1990, 44.*

[22] Ibid., 143.

[23] Author's computation.

[24] *2018 Colorado Local Government Handbook,* 15-19.

[25] Highlands Ranch Metro District, *Welcome to Highlands Ranch, Colorado!* 2020, accessed May 18, 2020, https://highlandsranch.org/

[26] "Highlands Ranch Metro District, CO 2019 Citizen Survey" (Boulder: National Research Center, 2019).

[27] Reuter, "The rise of Lone Tree."

[28] Ibid.

[29] "City of Lone Tree Comprehensive Plan," January 19, 2019, 7.

[30] Ibid.

[31] Holly Cook, "Home rule is where Lone Tree's heart is." *Colorado Community Media.* May 29, 2008, accessed June 5, 2020, https://coloradocommunitymedia.com/stories/home-rule-is-where-lone-trees-heart-is,132884

[32] Reuter, "The rise of Lone Tree."

[33] "City of Lone Tree Comprehensive Plan," 7.

[34] *State Demography Office Data.*

[35] *History of Castle Pines*, accessed April 5, 2020, https://www.castlepinesco.gov/city-services/about-castle-pines/history-of-castle-pines/

[36] Ibid.

[37] Gibbs, "Growing Castle Pines seeks to build community identity."

[38] "Castle Pines Comprehensive Plan," April 12, 2016, 6.

[39] *Active Colorado Municipalities*, accessed June 10, 2020, https://apps.douglas.co.us/dcmaps/map.html?mapInstance=subdivision

[40] Highlands Ranch Community Association, *Recreation Centers, 2020*, accessed May 21, 2020, https://hrcaonline.org/about-us/recreation-centers (accessed May 21, 2020).

[41] Colorado Parks and Recreation, *Town of Parker: Facilities, 2020*, accessed May 21, 2020, https://parkerrec.com/225/FACILITIES

[42] *Facilities—Castle Rock Recreation Center, 2020*, accessed May 21, 2020, https://www.crgov.com/Facilities/Facility/Details/Castle-Rock-Recreation-Center-46.

[43] Larkspur, *Parks & Recreation, 2020*, accessed May 21, 2020, https://www.townoflarkspur.org/park-recreation-2020.

[44] Reuter, "The rise of Lone Tree."

[45] *Recreation, 2020*, accessed May 21,2020, https://www.douglas.co.us/about-us/business/recreation/

[46]Castle Rock, "2020 Budget and Financial Planning," *Operating and Capital Improvement Budget, 2019,* 131, accessed June 6, 2020, https://crgov.com/DocumentCenter/View/25427/2020-Adopted-Budget-PDF

[47] Douglas County, *Preservation Efforts, 2020,* accessed May 21, 2020, https://www.douglas.co.us/government/departments/open-space/preservation-efforts/

[48] Ibid.

[49] Ibid.

[50] Highlands Ranch Metro District, *Open Space, 2020,* accessed May 21, 2020, https://highlandsranch.org/services/natural-resources/open-space/

[51] Castle Rock, *Open Space and Trails, 2020,* accessed May 21, 2020, https://crgov.com/1985/Open-Space-and-Trails

[52] Parker, *Lamppostings: Meet Our Department–Parks, Recreation and Open Space, 2020,* accessed May 21, 2020, https://crgov.com/1985/Open-Space-and-Trails

[53] "City of Lone Tree Comprehensive Plan," 35.

[54] Castle Rock Chamber of Commerce, *Artfest Castle Rock Colorado, 2020,* accessed May 19, 2020, https://castlerock.org/castle-rock-artfest/

[55] Parker, *Parker Arts, 2020,* accessed May 16, 2020, http://parkerarts.org/1001/History-of-the-Towns-Cultural-Facilities

[56] Lone Tree, *Lone Tree Arts Center, March 2020,* accessed March 15, 2020, https://cityoflonetree.com/departments/lone-tree-arts-center/

[57] *Parker Arts.*

[58] *City of Lone Tree 2020 Budget,* 34, accessed June 6, 2020, https://cityoflonetree.com/files/Finance/Budget/LoneTreeBudget2020%20-%20web.pdf

[59] Rachel Cemansky, "America's Healthiest Community: Douglas County," *U.S. News & World Report,* March 26, 2020, accessed May 21, 2020, https://www.usnews.com/news/healthiest-communities/articles/2019-03-26/healthiest-community-in-america-douglas-county-colorado

[60] Ibid.

[61] John Agular, "Castle Pines set to double in size as growth in Douglas County continues to surge," *The Denver Post,* December 30, 2019, accessed May 17, 2020, https://www.denverpost.com/2019/12/30/douglas-county-growth-castle-pines/

[62] Hawksley Consulting. "Strategic Renewable Water Implementation Plan Prepared for Castle Pines North Metropolitant District," October 2015, 64.

[63] Providence Infrastructure Consultants, "Parker Water & Sanitation District: 2014 Water & Wastewater Master Plan, Highlands Ranch, 9-5.

[64] Castle Rock, "Water Resources Strategic Master Plan, 2016," xiii.

[65] Ibid.

[66] Colorado Department of Local Affairs. *Active Colorado Local Governments, 2020,* accessed May 21, 2020, https://dola.colorado.gov/lgis/

[67] Douglas County, *Commissioners reveal 2019 Citizen Survey results,* May 17, 2019, accessed May 21, 2020, https://www.douglas.co.us/commissioners-reveal-2019-citizen-survey-results

Chapter 58

DOUGLAS COUNTY SHERRIF'S OFFICE

Sergeant Attila C. Denes

Propelled by a decade of nation-leading population growth, the Douglas County Sheriff's Office in the 1990s entered a period of rapid and sustained development.[1] As Sheriff Stephen C. Zotos ended his second term, the office employed 106 members, including 77 commissioned deputies, and boasted a fleet of 68 vehicles. In 1991, the communications center, which provided emergency dispatching for the sheriff's office and five fire departments, acquired its first computer-aided dispatch system, increasing the efficiency with which the center processed its 53,896 calls for service.[2]

Many operational enhancements followed. In 1992, the county commissioners adopted portions of the Model Traffic Code, allowing the county to retain traffic fines previously deposited in the state's coffers.[3] Regular patrols were augmented by a traffic unit; K-9 officers; a steadily increasing number of school resource officers; reserve deputies; and fully equipped SWAT, bomb, and hazardous materials teams staffed on an on-call basis. In 1993, the Highlands Ranch Law Enforcement Training Foundation, the nation's first privately funded foundation for the training of law enforcement personnel, was established to augment the training provided to over 30 police agencies at the multi-agency training center off U.S. Highway 85.[4]

By 1995, it became clear that the existing justice center, which opened in 1979, was woefully inadequate. In 1995, voters approved sales tax funding—a first in Colorado for a county capital construction project—to build a new facility. The Robert A. Christensen Justice Center opened in June 1998, with its detention center opening two months later. The 284,144 square foot building had an inmate capacity of 284, dwarfing the previous facility, and doubled the number of courtrooms from four to eight. To operate the jail, the detention center staff more than tripled to 112.[5] At the same time, the county's emergency response agencies transitioned from an antiquated VHF radio system to an 800 MHz digital trunked system, which was the first in Colorado.[6] In 1999, the United Fire Dispatch Authority was formed, doubling the number of fire agencies dispatched by the sheriff's communications center.[7] This change, coupled with the unrelenting growth in call volume, resulted in the dispatch staff nearly doubling in 1999.[8] In February 1999, the all-volunteer Douglas County Search and Rescue Team performed its first mission, replacing the agency's long-standing reliance on the all-youth Arapahoe Rescue Patrol.[9]

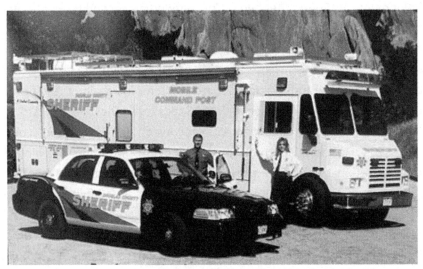

Mobile Command Post and Patrol Car with Deputy Keith Mathena and Dispatch Supervisor Cindi Dieck - 2004

By 2000, the number of deputies more than tripled from the previous decade to 209, while the overall sheriff's office staff increased to 318.[10] The agency reestablished a modern mounted patrol unit in 2000, bringing back the horse as a symbolic and functional support element.[11] In 2001, the High-Tech Crimes Unit, which specialized in white-collar and computer crimes, took up new quarters in the Park Meadows Center substation in Lone Tree.[12] The 1995 enactment of term limits for local officials signaled the eventual end of Sheriff Zotos' 20-year term, but not before the 2002 Hayman Fire charred 137,760 acres to become Colorado's most destructive wildfire, and Douglas County's biggest public safety emergency to date.[13]

Cowboy Sheriffs L to R Sheriffs Tony Spurlock,
Steve Zotos, Dave Weaver, and Mike Acree - 2018

Sheriff Michael L. Acree, a 20-year DCSO veteran and division commander, took office in 2003. He expanded the office's command and supervision structures, bringing in experienced law enforcement leaders from outside the agency, creating a new command rank structure, and doubling the number of sergeants by eliminating the corporal rank and upgrading all existing corporals to sergeants. He also instituted the first patrol car paint scheme change in 20 years, introducing the iconic black-and-white look that caught on with several local police agencies.[14] Sheriff Acree also envisioned the benefits of national accreditation through the Commission on the Accreditation of Law Enforcement Agencies, and set in motion the mechanisms that would ultimately earn the agency the coveted Triple Crown Accreditation a decade later.[15] Sheriff Acree stepped down after two years in office to take a position with the state. His undersheriff, David A. Weaver, a 24-year DCSO veteran and the first person in agency history to become Sheriff after starting as a deputy, was appointed to fill the vacancy in 2005. He was elected in his own right in 2006.[16]

Sheriff Weaver, a fiscal conservative who also understood the need to keep up with the safety needs of a growing community, instituted many changes. Among his first acts were re-establishing the corporal rank and downsizing the command structure to near its 2002 levels. He changed the patrol car paint scheme to an all-black design, increasing the resale value of retired cars. He changed the agency's uniform to a more contemporary and cost-effective design, first replacing the French blue wool pants with a dark blue synthetic material, and later adding a matching dark blue shirt.

Sheriff Weaver greatly expanded the role of volunteers within the sheriff's office. Among the most visible addition was the creation in 2006 of the Community Safety Volunteer (CSV) program. Initially envisioned to provide an added layer of crime prevention and relieve deputies of tasks not requiring peace officer authority, CSVs today serve important roles in every division.[17] Volunteers were also brought into the jail to run inmate programs, and into various support roles throughout the agency.[18]

Several major facility and service expansions occurred under Sheriff Weaver's tenure. A 2006 justice center expansion added two inmate housing units and doubled the number of courtrooms to 16. In 2010, the Elbert County 9-1-1 dispatch center closed, transferring its operations to the renamed Douglas Regional 9-1-1 communications center, and increasing the number of entities served to five law enforcement agencies and 16 fire departments.[19] The $9.5 million, 35,000 square foot Highlands Ranch substation opened in 2011, allowing roughly half of the agency's patrol and investigative staff to deploy directly from the county's most populated area.[20] In 2014, another $29.9 million jail expansion opened, bringing the inmate capacity to 480 and adding a medical housing unit and Special Management Unit for inmates with mental health concerns, as well as a parking structure for fleet and employee vehicles.[21]

Sheriff Anthony G. "Tony" Spurlock was appointed in July 2014 when Sheriff Weaver filled a vacancy on the Board of County Commissioners and was elected sheriff later that year. Among the achievements of his tenure were the 2018 opening of the Unified Metropolitan Forensic Crime Lab, a free-standing facility near Centennial Airport representing a partnership between the sheriff's offices of Douglas and Arapahoe counties, the Aurora Police Department, and the 18th Judicial District Attorney's Office. Sheriff Spurlock also partnered with the Arapahoe County Sheriff's Office to form a joint POST academy that hosts 50-plus cadets annually and created a unique public-private partnership to open a 37-acre driving training track. Having joined the sheriff's office as a deputy in 1980, Sheriff Spurlock has witnessed the agency's staggering growth firsthand. The numbers perhaps tell the story best: by 2020, the agency employed 533 people, of whom 362 were commissioned deputies, the vehicle fleet had grown to 480, and the number of calls handled by the communications center reached 190,842.[22]

[1] Castle Rock Economic Development Council, "Castle Rock is trending up: Demographics and trends," April 16, 2019, accessed April 26, 2020, https://castlerockedc.com/facts-figures/demographics-trends/.

[2] *Douglas County Sheriff's Office 1992-1993 Annual Publication,* 9, 12, 19.

[3] *Douglas County Sheriff's Office 1993-1994 Annual Publication,* 24.

[4] *Douglas County Sheriff's Office 1992-1993 Annual Publication,* 18.

[5] *Douglas County Sheriff's Office 1996 Annual Publication,* 9. *Douglas County Sheriff's Office 2000-2001 Biennial Report,* 14.

[6] *Douglas County Sheriff's Office 1997 Annual Publication,* 19-20.

[7] *Douglas County Sheriff's Office 1998-1999 Biennial Report,* 24.

[8] Ibid., 23

[9] *Douglas County Sheriff's Office Legacy Album, 1861-2013,* 195.

[10] *Douglas County Sheriff's Office 2000-2001 Biennial Report,* 10.

[11] Ibid., 20.

[12] Ibid., 32.

[13] Joey Bunch, "Colorado's Hayman fire set high marks for size, cost, heat and rehabilitation," *The Denver Post,* June 7, 2012.

[14] *Douglas County Sheriff's Office Legacy Album, 1861-2013,* 19.

[15] *Douglas County Sheriff's Office 2013 Annual Report,* 12.

[16] Ibid., 5; *Douglas County Sheriff's Office Legacy Album, 1861-2013,* 19.

[17] *Douglas County Sheriff's Office 2013 Annual report,* 50.

[18] *Douglas County Sheriff's Office Legacy Album, 1861-2013,* 178-195.

[19] Carlos Illescas, "Elbert County to shutter dispatch, route 9-1-1 calls to Douglas County," *The Denver Post,* June 26, 2010.

[20] *Douglas County Sheriff's Office Legacy Album, 1861-2013,* 37.

[21] Ibid., 41.

[22] *Douglas County Sheriff's Office 2019 Semi-Annual Report.*

Chapter 59

SCHOOL CHOICES

Tim Weber

Education exploded in DC in the last thirty years. In 1990 Douglas County School District had about 14,000 students, in 2000 about 34,000, in 2010 around 61,000, and in 2020 approaching 69,000.[1] The District employed about 1,500 persons (861 teachers) in 1990 and in 2020 about 8,300 (4,500 teachers), which made it the County's largest single employer.[2]

Of the eighty-seven DCSD schools in 2020, all but two are in the northern part of the County. Well over 80% of DC schools are in Highlands Ranch, Parker, and Castle Rock. The remainder are in Franktown, Castle Pines, Lone Tree, Littleton (Roxborough), and Sedalia. The only schools in southern DC are Larkspur Elementary School and Cherry Valley Elementary School, south of Franktown on Highway 83. Students from southern DC go to Castle Rock for middle and high school.[3] Students from Westcreek attend school in Woodland Park, El Paso County.[4]

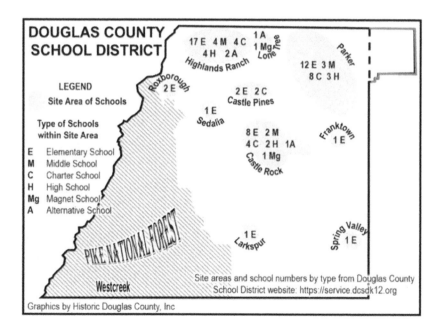

DOUGLAS COUNTY SCHOOL DISTRICT

LEGEND
Site Area of Schools

Type of Schools within Site Area
E   Elementary School
M   Middle School
C   Charter School
H   High School
Mg Magnet School
A   Alternative School

Highlands Ranch   17 E 4 M 4 C   4 H 2 A
Lone Tree   1 A 1 Mg
Parker   12 E 3 M   8 C 3 H
Roxborough   2 E
Castle Pines   2 E 2 C
Sedalia   1 E
Castle Rock   8 E 2 M   4 C 2 H 1 A   1 Mg
Franktown   1 E
Larkspur   1 E
Spring Valley   1 E
Westcreek

PIKE NATIONAL FOREST

Site areas and school numbers by type from Douglas County School District website: https://service.dcsdk12.org

Graphics by Historic Douglas County, Inc

Educational choices are plentiful in DCSD. Two-thirds of its public schools are traditional, neighborhood schools: 45 elementary schools (K-6 grades), 9 middle schools (7-8 grades), and 9 high schools (9-12 grades). The remaining third includes four "alternative" schools: one for students at risk of not finishing high school (Daniel C. Oakes H.S.); another with classes scheduled in the afternoon/evening (Eagle Academy); and two others for students with special educational, behavioral, and life-skill needs (Plum Creek Academy and Transition Bridge Program). There are two magnet schools: one utilizes Outward Bound and Expeditionary Learning models (Renaissance Expeditionary Learning Magnet School, K-6); and the other features the Highly Effective Teaching (HET) model that offers educational experiences to promote reflective thinking (Lone Tree Elementary, K-6). DCSD offers "cyber-schools:" both eDCSD and HOPE Learning Centers give online instruction in multiple locations in DC. The district supports Home Education with teaching guidelines and extracurricular activities. Since 1992, DCSD has offered a tuition-based early childhood education program (pre-K) that now has 42 locations.[5]

Franktown Elementary School - 2015

Charter schools constitute most of DCSD's non-traditional offerings. In 1993, the Colorado legislature passed the Colorado Charter School Act which encouraged innovation and more parental involvement in public schools.[6] DCSD was Colorado's first district to authorize a charter school (Academy Charter School), and today there are eighteen charters in DCSD. Each charter school is an accredited, tuition-free public school of choice that operates under a contract ("charter") between its independent board of directors made up of parents, teachers, and community leaders and the local school board. Each school is thus semi-autonomous: its board defines the school's educational mission, academic standards, curricular design, and governance. According to the law, to achieve their diverse educational goals, charters are given "autonomy in exchange for accountability." While these schools operate free of certain state regulations (for example, they may hire qualified teachers without state certification), their students must take state-mandated standardized tests; and the DCSD school board must make sure that the charters are reaching their stated educational goals. All charters must provide for students with special needs and accommodate English learners. They do not have selective admissions but admit students by lottery.[7]

All charter schools are not the same. Some schools have the STEM curriculum (science, technology, engineering, and mathematics), while others use the STEAM model (science, technology, engineering, arts, and mathematics). Other schools couple Core Knowledge Education and character development. Two schools utilize an intercultural approach and require learning a second language. One school uses a curriculum developed and promoted by Hillsdale College, and another stresses outdoor Adventure Education. In one school, training in the performing arts stands alongside the other subjects.[8]

In addition to DCSD, there are about thirty-five private schools of education in DC, serving around 6,500 students, all of them located in the northern half of the County. About two-thirds offer only preschool-kindergarten programs, while the other third includes elementary, middle, and high schools (Valor Christian High School and Mile High Academy in Highlands Ranch, and Lutheran High School in Parker). One-third of the private schools are faith-based, and two-thirds are not.[9] Between traditional, charter, alternative, cyber, magnet, and religious and non-religious private schools, the people of Douglas County have plenty of educational choices.

The issue of school choice eventually led to some fierce legal battles. On March 15, 2011, the conservative reform-minded majority on the DCSD board established the Choice Scholarship Program. It promised to provide parents with state money (75% of Per Pupil Revenue provided by the state legislature—about $4,575) to use as tuition in approved private schools, some of which were faith-based. Advocates argued that the program allowed parents to find the best education possible for their children; but opponents (including Taxpayers for Public Education and the American Civil Liberties Union) filed suit in the Circuit Court of Denver County, claiming that public funds should not be used to support religious schools. The court agreed. But in 2013, a Colorado appeals court reversed the Denver Court's decision. When this decision was appealed to the Colorado Supreme Court, it decided that providing public funds for religious schools was unconstitutional. Voucher-supporters then appealed to the U.S. Supreme Court, which had recently ruled in a similar case in Missouri (*Trinity Lutheran vs. Comer*) that public funds could be given to religious schools under certain circumstances. The Supreme Court sent the case back to the Colorado Supreme Court for reconsideration in light of that decision.

But the Colorado Supreme Court never reviewed the case. In December 2017, a newly installed anti-voucher DCSD school board, whose election had been financially supported by the American Federation of Teachers Union, voted unanimously to eliminate the voucher program, thus making the court case moot. Accordingly, the Colorado Supreme Court dismissed the case without considering the U.S. Supreme Court's ruling on *Trinity Lutheran vs. Comer*.[10]

A similar dispute followed the tragic shooting at the STEM School of Highlands Ranch on May 7, 2019. In response, the Douglas County Commissioners earmarked $10 million in grants for mental health programs and safety upgrades for both DCSD and private schools.[11] When the old anti-voucher arguments were raised, the Commissioners cited the U.S. Supreme Court's *Trinity Lutheran vs. Comer* decision and found considerable support within Colorado's legal community.[12] Observed Commissioner Lora Thomas,

"We didn't understand how a child who went to a private school was different from any other child."[13] The grant program continued.

In early 2020, the County awarded $6.8 million to DCSD grant applicants for projects and programs, including $56,000 to the STEM School in Highlands Ranch.[14] Then it awarded another $855,000 to two charter schools and a faith-based private school.[15] Meanwhile, the Castle Rock Town Council contracted with DCSD to split the cost of School Resource Officers from the Castle Rock Police Department for one high school and two middle schools. The County Commissioners offered an ongoing $3 million to split the cost with the district for many other SROs coming from the DC Sheriff's Department.[16] Such partnerships contribute to the continuing improvement of education in DC.

---

[1] Douglas County School District, "Student Enrollment Reports," accessed February 11, 2020, https://www.dcsdk12.org/about/our_district/departments/planning_and_construction/student_enrollment_reports.

[2] Douglas County School District, "About: By the Numbers," accessed February 11, 2020, https://www.dcsdk12.org/about.

[3] Douglas County School District, "Schools: School Locator Map," accessed February 11, 2020, https://service.dcsdk12.org/locator/.

[4] See real estate listings for Westcreek, CO.

[5] "About: By the Numbers." The graphic on the website indicates 91 schools, but a check of the list of schools indicates only 87.

[6] Colorado Department of Education, "Part 1—Charter Schools Act," accessed February 12, 2020, http://www.cde.state.co.us/cdechart/csact_part1.

[7] Colorado Department of Education, "Colorado Charter Schools Frequently Asked Questions," accessed February 12, 2020, https://www.cde.state.co.us/cdechart/faq; Douglas County School District, "Charter Schools," accessed February 12, 2020, https://www.dcsdk12.org/cms/one.aspx?portalId=220484&pageId=5758110.

[8] "Charter Schools."

[9] Private School Review, "Top Douglas County Private Schools," accessed February 11, 2020, https://www.privateschoolreview.com/colorado/douglas-county. USA.com, "Douglas County Private Schools," accessed February 11, 2020, https://www.privateschoolreview.com/colorado/douglas-county. Jessica Gibbs, "Douglas County's history with school vouchers," The Castle Rock News-Press, July 4, 2019, 4.

[10] Gibbs, "Douglas County's history with school vouchers," 4. For accounts from different perspectives: Erica Meltzer, "The Douglas County voucher case is finally over," *Chalkbeat*, January 26, 2018, accessed February 20, 2020, https://chalkbeat.org/posts/co/2018/01/26/the-douglas-county-voucher-case-is-finally-over/. Liz Hayes, "Colorado Supreme Court Ends Douglas County School Voucher Lawsuit, A Win for Public Education and Religious Freedom," *Americans United for the Separation of Church and State: Wall of Separation Blog*, January 26, 2018, accessed February 20, 2020, https://www.au.org/blogs/wall-of-separation/colorado-supreme-court-ends-douglas-county-school-voucher-lawsuit-a-win. Leslie Hiner, " A Frank Description of What Really Happened with the Douglas County, Colorado's School Voucher Program," *Engage by Choice*, December 5, 2017, accessed on February 20, 2020, https://www.edchoice.org/engage/frank-description-really-happened-douglas-county-colorados-school-voucher-program/. Nic Garcia, "Douglas County ends controversial private school voucher program," *Denverite*, December 5, 2017, accessed February 20, 2020, https://denverite.com/2017/12/05/douglas-county-ends-controversial-private-school-voucher-program/.

[11] Douglas County, Colorado, "County launches process for schools' access to $10 million in mental health and school safety funds," August 7, 2019, accessed February 20, 2020, https://www.douglas.co.us/county-launches-process-for-schools-access-to-10-million-in-mental-health-and-school-safety-funds/.

[12]Jessica Gibbs, "A debate over public funds for private schools," *Castle Rock News-Press*, July 4, 2019, 4, 6.

[13] Lora Thomas, quoted in Jessica Gibbs, "Douglas County awards more school safety grants," *Castle Rock News-Press*, February 6, 2020, 9.

[14] Jessica Gibbs, "Douglas County awards school district $6.8 million for security," *Castle Rock News-Press*, January 30, 2020, 3-4.

[15] "Douglas County awards more school safety grants."

[16] Jessica Gibbs, "Castle Rock to add a school resource officer in 2019," *Castle Rock News-Press*, July 11, 2019, 3.

Chapter 60
TRANSFORMATION OF DC LIBRARIES

James LaRue

By 1990, the Douglas County Public Library System, under county auspices, ranked near the bottom of Colorado libraries. It was open just 5 days a week and employed about 25 mostly part-time people. There were no children's librarians and just two reference librarians. Its collection, computers, and outreach services ranked lowest in the metro area. Moreover, the County sought to reduce library funding.[1] By 2009, however, Douglas County Libraries had transitioned from the worst in the state to the best in the nation. It employed over 350 people, had one of the highest per capita checkout rates in the world, and 84% of county households had an active library card.[2]

Three factors contributed to the rapid development of the county's library district. The first and most essential factor was a shift in governance and funding structure. The second was the growth of collections, facilities, and services. The third was a profound shift in focus, from library-centric to community-centric.

As a county department, the library was poorly funded and did not get to keep all the money it received. The County deducted charges for computer support, building and grounds maintenance, insurance, and benefits. In

November 1990, under the leadership of the new library director, James LaRue, the library took its case directly to the public. It sought to break away from the county and form an independent library district, funded by a dedicated property tax. The voters approved the change by an almost 2 to 1 margin. The borders of the new Douglas Public Library District followed those of the County, but it was now a subdivision of the state. Funding increased from an ostensible 1.1 million to an actual 2.5 million.[3]

Shortly thereafter, the district signed an Intergovernmental Agreement to separate from the county, transitioning to its own business arrangements. County commissioners retained Trustee appointing authority, although they explicitly handed over the recruitment and recommendation process to the existing board. In 2014, the Commissioners controversially took that authority back.[4] While the County still collected the tax money, it no longer had the authority to control how it was spent.

With reliable funding and an exclusive focus on library services, the library board could make its own plans. At the same time, Douglas County's population took off. In 1990 its population was a little over 61,000, and during the 1990s, the County became the fastest growing County in the country.[5] By 2010 the population had grown to over 285,000. Such growth required the expansion of library facilities. Over the next four years, the new district invested in new branches. The locations and size of the buildings were based on several factors: a 3-to-5-mile service radius, a 1 square foot per capita for the population within that area (.5 sf for building, .5 sf for parking), and a regional focus. The district saw libraries as a key part of civic and economic life, so often sought to place them in the "downtown" of the communities served. All buildings were paid for with cash. There were no bonds or debt.

By 2014, the DC Libraries had seven branch locations. Here is a list that indicates size and type of location: Louviers, 1,000 sq. ft. historic building (1967); Parker, 20,000 sq. ft. remodeled bowling alley (1995); Lone Tree, 10,000 sq. ft. new construction (1998); Highlands Ranch, 45,000 sq. ft. new construction (2000); Castle Rock, 45,000 sq. ft. renovated Safeway (2003); and Castle Pines, 11,500 sq. ft. rented storefront (2009).[6]

During these growth decades, a quiet revolution took place in library collections. First came increases in the library's purchases of print materials. Most current titles were on library shelves the same day they showed up in bookstores. Next came a growth in non-print items, increasingly in new formats: for example, audiobooks and CDs were replaced by playaways and downloadables; VHS formats were replaced with DVDs, then streaming movies; and periodical indexes went from paper to CD to online. In 1996, Douglas County Libraries linked to the Internet and offered both access to the collections of other libraries and links to a variety of electronic databases. The library expanded its Local History collection from a single box of archival materials to a small but surprisingly rich department at the Philip S. Miller Library in Castle Rock. From 2010-2015, Douglas County Libraries developed an innovative collection of eBooks, which it purchased and hosted locally. This effort, the DCL Model, was featured in many national and international magazines and newspapers.[7]

During this period, services expanded. Most libraries were open 7 days a week and offered more story times, the library's best strategy for the promotion of literacy. In the late 2000s, the library added "sensory story-times"[8] for children on the autism spectrum. Reference services were offered in person and online. The library launched a series of signature annual programs.[9] Among them were Shakespeare in the Park, consisting of live performances in tents (2001); Fantasy Fest which celebrated the worlds of science fiction and fantasy (2001); and Page to Stage, a live theater that brought literature to life for Douglas County School District students (2002). The latter program won the 2007 John Cotton Dana Award, the American Library Association's "most prestigious award" that honors outstanding library public relations. Such innovative programs increased library usage across the board. By 2010, the library had a per capita checkout of 27 items, more than 3 times the national average.[10]

Throughout its history, the library has gone to the voters four times.[11] In 1990, when its performance as a library was at its lowest, voters strongly supported the establishment of the district. In 1996, as the library began to win awards for its work, voters narrowly approved the increase of the mill levy from 2.5 to 4. In 2006, when the library was among the highest performing in the nation, a funding increase lost narrowly. In 2007, along with the school district, the library overwhelmingly lost another election, on the verge of a recession. The library learned that growing use does not always mean growing support.

But library leaders also came to a new realization: it is not the job of a community to make a great library. It is the job of the library to make a great community. To that end, the district began to deepen its relationships with the business community. Small businesses increased their support; library staff began serving on the boards of area Chambers of Commerce and other political entities, including municipal governments, and joined in county-wide programs such as the Douglas County Youth Initiative, the Volunteer Database, and more.

In 2014, James LaRue retired from his position as library director.[12] He was replaced by Robert Pasicznyuk, who oversaw, over the next 6 years, the construction of new buildings, on donated land, in Parker, Lone Tree, and Castle Pines, as well as renovations of the Highlands Ranch Library.

---

[1] James LaRue, "September 19,1990," The HBW Report," accessed May 5, 2020, https://laruesviews.blogspot.com/1990/09/september-19-1990-hbw-report.html.

[2] James LaRue, "July 16, 2009-DCL number one!" accessed May 5, 2020, https://laruesviews.blogspo.come/2009/07/july-16-2009-dci-number-one.html

[3] Douglas County Libraries, "Timeline," 1990. Available from DCL Archives and Local History.

[4] James LaRue, "Douglas County Libraries and the Board of Commissioners," March 17, 2013, accessed May 5, 2020, http://jaslarue.blogspot.com/2013/03/douglas-county-libraries-and-boar-of.html

[5] Census 2000 PHC-T-4, "Ranking Tables for Counties: 1990 and 2000," 6, accessed May 5, 2020, https://www.census.gov/population/www/cen2000/briefs/hpc-4/tables/tab02.pdf.

[6] Douglas County Libraries, "Timeline," 1967, 1995, 1997, 1998, 2000, 2003, 2009.

[7]National Public Radio, "Ebooks Strain Relationships between Libraries, Publishing Houses," August 5, 2013, accessed May 5, 2020, https://www.npr.org/2013/o8/05/209114978/e-books-srain-relations-beween-libraries-publishing-houses.

[8]Laura Baldassari-Hackstaff, Sheila Kerber, Ruth Ann Krovontka, and Laura Root Olson,"Sensory-Enhanced Storytime at Douglas County Libraries: An Inclusive Program," Public Library Online, January/February, 2014, accessed May 5, 2020, http://publiclibrariesonline.org/2014/05/sensory-enhanced-storytime-at-douglas-county-libraries-an-inclusive-program/.

[9] Douglas County Libraries, "Timeline," 2001, 2007.

[10] Andrea Hamilton, "Colorado Public Libraries Outpace National Trend on Circulation per Capita, 1988-2000," accessed May 5, 2020, https://www.lrs.org/documents/fastfacts/183circcous.pdf?lrspdfmetric=no

[11] Douglas County Libraries, "Timeline," 1990, 1996, 2006, 2007.

[12] Lisa Crocket, "Director Jamie LaRue Retires from Douglas County Libraries," *The Castle Pines Connection*, accessed May 5, 2020, https://www.castlepinesconnection.com/director-jamie-larue-retires-from-douglas-county-libraries/.

Chapter 61

PROGRESS ON SUSTAINABLE WATER

Steve Boand

The last six decades of water history were times of perpetual change. Growth in the county outstripped the capacity of local streams to provide water. Castle Rock moved from open ditches and reservoirs to groundwater wells.[1] Shallow water wells were the next source and supplied communities and agriculture along Cherry[2] and Plum Creeks for decades.[3] In the late 1960s, water laws evolved to reflect the reality that the shallow groundwater near streams is a part of the surface water system.[4] That meant that shallow water wells were now subject to administration and potential curtailments by State water officials.[5] Alluvial wells and the junior water rights common in Douglas County could no longer be counted upon to provide water during droughts.[6] Colorado's climate is fickle and unpredictable,[7] but the need for water is constant. New solutions were needed.

During the 1960s it was discovered that Douglas County sits atop billions of gallons of deep groundwater in layered aquifers to depths of 3,000 feet.[8] This deep groundwater is only slightly connected to Colorado's surface water system.[9] Water from the deeper layers of the Denver basin can be utilized outside of Colorado's priority system where "first in time is first in right."[10] The upper aquifers of the Denver basin typically provide very high-quality drinking water.[11] In addition, once obtained, deep groundwater can be used and reused.[12] Pumping deep groundwater from the Denver basin aquifers quadrupled by 2000 and constituted "about 70% of the water supply for the south Denver metropolitan area."[13]

There is one big catch: deep groundwater is not naturally renewable and once used, it cannot be replenished.[14] The time is coming when deep groundwater will no longer be the primary local municipal water supply.[15]

Economics is the key issue for water providers using deep groundwater. The United States Geological Survey determined that while the deep groundwater supplies are vast, the costs of producing water from deep wells will increase fifty-fold as the water is withdrawn.[16] The long-term use of deep groundwater will cost more as pumping depletes the aquifers.[17] Increasing costs for pumping will make "further investment in wells increasingly questionable."[18]

In 2010, Castle Rock had 52 deep groundwater wells in production which provided 100% of its water supply.[19] Between 2007 and 2011, the Town spent $3 million per year on new well construction and old well rehabilitation.[20] Still, deep well production declined an average of about 4% per year.[21] Castle Rock determined that "after investing $250 million in nonrenewable groundwater, the Town would not be able to meet its water demands and would have to invest in a renewable water supply."[22]

Castle Rock explored several water ventures for its renewable water future, beginning in 2011.[23] By 2014, the Town was successful at securing a new water supply from Weld County. In 2014 and 2016, the Town obtained an additional 2,500 acre-feet-per-year supply from the north.[24]

In Colorado's competitive and ever-tightening water markets, the cost of replacing existing local water sources is both substantial and unavoidable. Castle Rock estimates the cost of replacing deep groundwater at $300 million.[25] The Castle Pines North Metropolitan District's plan for developing new water sources costs approximately $106 million.[26]

Rueter-Hess Reservoir, Total capacity of 75,000 acre-feet

Water storage has become a key element in nearly every water supply program in Colorado.[27] The Reservoir Era began in the late 1870s as summer river flows became scarce.[28] Since then, all water providers have recognized that water storage was an essential element in bolstering existing water supply systems. This realization led to the construction of new reservoirs for runoff and aquifer water storage.[29] The Chatfield Reservoir was constructed to store reallocated water held in earlier water storage venues and is expanding to hold even more.[30]

Rueter-Hess Reservoir served the same purpose. Planning began in the early 1990s and construction was completed in 2012 by the Parker Water & Sanitation District. The district's foresight and commitment to garnering approval and completing construction is a lynchpin in the County's water future. The reservoir can store 75,000 acre-feet of water.[31] While Cherry Creek and the small creek tributary to the Reservoir contribute some water to Rueter-Hess, most of its water will need to be imported from elsewhere, including Castle Rock, Castle Pines, and Stonegate.[32]

Chatfield Reservoir - Chatfield State Park and Front Range Backdrop

Centennial Water & Sanitation District is the County's largest water provider servicing Highlands Ranch. The district has long recognized the need for a diversified water supply. While Centennial has 50 deep groundwater wells,[33] it has also developed 10,685 acre-feet of water reserves in three nearby reservoirs, plus Chatfield Reservoir[34] Renewable water (snow melt and rain run-off) comprised 85% of Centennial's water supply over the past thirty years.[35]

Water providers came together in 2006 to form the South Metro Water Supply Authority (SMWSA) to develop renewable water supplies for its members.[36] Their efforts have led to the development of a regional water-sharing partnership called WISE (Water, infrastructure, and Supply Efficiency). As it develops, WISE will provide an average of 7,225 acre-feet per year to its members including ten Douglas County water providers.[37]

WISE water is not a consistent water supply. The amount of water will vary from year to year as the supply of water changes for two major partners: Denver Water and the City of Aurora.[38] In years when Denver and Aurora do not need all their water, the SMWSA Authority can buy their unused water to help reduce its reliance on nonrenewable groundwater.[39] Additional dependable water supplies will need to be developed to make sure water is available every year.[40]

Water for new development will continue to be a challenge in the future. For example, the Sterling Ranch project has pieced together its water supply from Aurora, the WISE program, and Castle Rock.[41] The State conducts a limited review of county subdivision plans for general supply and impact on other water rights. Developers are required to present an incremental plan for supplying water. In the case of Sterling Ranch, the State noted that while current water supplies are adequate for the early stages of development, the Dominion Water & Sanitation District (Sterling's supplier) has not yet secured all the water needed for the completed project.[42] The cost and complexity of assembling a municipal water supply is a tremendous challenge for new communities that takes years of effort and intense financial planning.

The water supply strategy for nearly all water providers for 2050 includes developing renewable water supply and limiting deep groundwater use. Castle Rock plans to use 75% renewable water and only 25% non-renewable sources.[43] By 2018, only 18% of the Town's water supply was renewable.[44] Similar plans are in place for ten of the County's water providers including Castle Pines, Parker, and Highlands Ranch. Partnerships and cooperative water development are key to sustainable water supplies. Progress is being made. Success will require discipline by elected officials, water managers, and an involved citizenry.

[1] "Amended Findings of Fact, Conclusions of Law, Judgement and Decree Concerning the Application for Water Rights of the Town of Castle Rock, 1987," *Consolidated Cases* 86CW378 and 86CW379 (District Court, Water Division 1, Colorado, October 15, 1987), 46.

[2] *Findings, Judgement, and Decree Concerning the Application for Approval of Plan for Augmentation Including Exchange for Parker Water and Sanitation District, 1992*, Case No. 83CW348(A) (District Court, Water Division No. 1, State of Colorado, July 30, 1992), 4-7.

[3] Castle Rock Utilities Department Water-Resources Division, 2017, *Water Resources Strategic Master Plan 2016*, Castle Rock, CO: 4-6.

[4] Susan M. Ryan, "Colorado's Answer to the Tributary Well Question: Maximum Utilization of Surface and Ground Water through Conjunctive Use," *American Bar Association 31st Annual Water Law Conference*, 2013, 1.

[5] Ibid., 5

[6] Ibid., 4

[7] Thomas B McKee, Nolan J. Doeskin, John Kleist, Catherine J. Shrier, and William P. Stanton, *A History of Drought in Colorado: Lessons Learned and What Lies Ahead* (Ft. Collins, CO.: Colorado Climate Center, Colorado State University, 2000), 14.

[8] S.G. Robson, "Bedrock Aquifers in the Denver Basin, Colorado—A Quantitative Water-Resources Appraisal," *U.S. Geological Professional Paper 1257* (Washington, DC: United States Government Printing Office, 1987), 18.

[9] Susanne S. Paschke, ed., "Groundwater Availability of the Denver Basin Aquifer System, Colorado," *U.S. Geological Survey Professional Paper 1770* (Washington, DC: U.S. Geological Survey, U.S. Department of the Interior, 2011).

[10] Greggory J. Hobbs, *Citizen's Guide to Colorado Water Law* (Denver: Colorado Foundation for Water Education, 2004), 10-11.

[11] Nancy J. Bauch, MaryLynn Musgrove, Barbara J. Mahler, and Suzanne S. Paschke, "The Quality of Our Nation's Waters: Water Quality in the Denver Basin Aquifer System, Colorado 2003-2005," *Circular 1357* (Washington, DC: U.S. Geological Survey, 2014), 4.

[12] Hobbs, *Citizens Guide*, 9.

[13] Bausch, et al, *The Quality of our Nation's Waters*, 1.

[14] *Water Resources Strategic Master Plan* (Castle Rock, CO: Castle Rock Utilities Department, Water-Resources Division), 4-10.

[15] Ibid.

[16] S. G. Robson, "Alluvial and Bedrock Aquifers of the Denver Basin: Eastern Colorado's Dual Ground-Water Resource," *U.S. Geological Survey Water Supply Paper 2303* (Washington DC: United States Government Printing Office, 1989), 25.

[17] Robson, *Bedrock Aquifers,* 42

[18] Hawksley Consulting, "Strategic Renewable Water Implementation Plan Prepared for Castle Pines North Metropolitan District" (2015), 7.

[19] Castle Rock Water Engineering, *Water Master Plan Update* (Castle Rock: Town of Castle Rock, 2011), 5.

[20] Ibid., 3.

[21] Ibid., 5.

[22] Castle Rock Water Department, *Comparative Analysis Report: Legacy Water Projects Alternative Sources of Secure Water Supply* (Castle Rock: Town of Castle Rock, 2012), 2.

[23] *Water Resources Strategic Master Plan, 2016* (Castle Rock: Castle Rock Utilities Department Water-Resources Division, 2016), 4-20.

[24] Ibid.

[25] Ibid, vii.

[26] Hawksley Consulting, *Strategic Renewable Water Implementation Plan*, 64.

[27] Neil Grigg, *Citizen's Guide to Where Your Water Comes From* (Denver: Colorado Foundation of Water Education, 2005), 26.

[28] Colorado Division of Water Resources, *Water Development History* (April 22, 2014), accessed February 8, 2020, http://dwrweblink.state.co.us/dwrweblink/0/doc/2810691/Electronic.aspx?searchid=f808fa0f-cb38-4b04-9b54-2c7f324bd6ec.

[29] Centennial Water and Sanitation District, *Water Supply Fact Sheet*, accessed February 8, 2020, https://centennialwater.org/wp-content/uploads/2012/04/WaterSupplyFactSheet2012.pdf.

[30] Castle Rock Water, *Super Master Plan*, xiii.

[31] Parker Water & Sanitation District, *Rueter-Hess Reservoir*, accessed February 8, 2020, https://www.pwsd.org/DocumentCenter/View/1434/2018-Rueter-Hess-Reservoir-Information-Flier-PDF.

[32] Ibid.

[33] Centennial Water & Sanitation District, *2016 Water Efficiency Plan*, 2

[34] Ibid.

[35] Ibid.

[36] South Metro Wise Authority, "South Metro Wise Authority Formation and Organizational Intergovernmental Agreement," accessed March 30, 2020, https://www.sec.gov/Archives/edgar/data/276720/000110262415000024/exh10_2a.htmsec.govAgreement, 4.

[37] Ibid.,1.

[38] Denver Water, *Your Water: WISE*, accessed March 30,2020, https://www.denverwater.org/your-water/water-supply-and-planning/wise.

[39] Ibid.

[40] South Metro Water Supply Authority, *2016 Regional Master Plan Update*, 14.

[41] Colorado Division of Water Resources, "Sterling Ranch Preliminary Filing 5, SB2019-004, SE/4 of Sections 10 and portions of Section 31, all in T6S, R68W, Water

Division 1, Water District 8," *Water Supply Review*, April 1, 2019 (Denver: Department of Natural Resources, 2019).

[42] Ibid.

[43] Castle Rock, *Water Resources Strategic Master Plan 2016*, xi.

[44] Town of Castle Rock, "Municipal Drought Management Plan", 1.

Chapter 62

BIG COUNTY POLITICS

Tim Weber

When Douglas County's population increased dramatically after 1990, so did the number of new voters. In the seven presidential elections between 1992 and 2016, the number of voters grew from 40,060 to 192,617.[1] How did these new voters identify themselves politically? Did population growth change the County's historic voting patterns in national, state, and county elections?

From its founding in 1861, Douglas County has been known as a Republican stronghold, though it has occasionally voted Democratic in national, state, and especially county elections. In recent decades, however, Republicans have gained overwhelming political dominance. In the last sixty years, DC voted Republican in fourteen of fifteen presidential elections. LBJ was the exception in 1964. During the 1980s, no Democratic candidate for a national, state, or county office won in Douglas County.[2] In the 1990s, the only victorious Democrat was Governor Roy Romer, who won twice (1990 and 1994). Since then, DC Republicans have won every national, state, and county election where party affiliation is declared.[3] How did Republicans sustain such consistent electoral power after the arrival of 150,000 new residents?

DC's voter registration rolls provide some answers. Most new residents registered as Republicans or, increasingly, Unaffiliateds, the new term for "Independents." In the 1980s, registered Republicans outnumbered Democrats by two and sometimes three to one. From 1996 to 2006, Republicans outnumbered both Democrats and Unaffiliateds *combined*. As a result, with only two exceptions in the last four decades, registered Republicans ranked first, Unaffiliateds second, and Democrats a distant third on the rolls. The unavoidable conclusion is that most of the people who moved into DC during and after the 1990s either were already Republicans when they got here or became Republican (or Unaffiliated) after they arrived.[4]

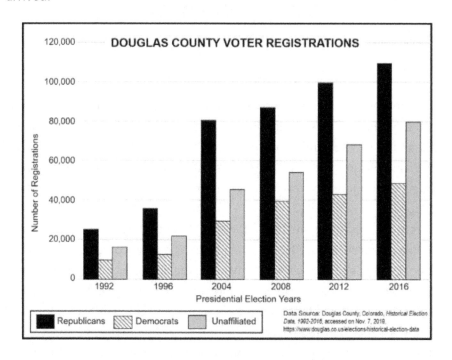

Registered Unaffiliateds were not far behind Republicans. From the 1960s through the 1980s, registered Unaffiliateds numbered between 69% and 95% of the Republican totals. Twice (1972 and 1974) they outnumbered Republicans. In the last three decades, the number of these Unaffiliateds ranged between 57% and 69% of Republicans; but during the Trump-Clinton election of 2016, they increased to 73%, then to 88% in the mid-term election of 2018. Why did the ranks of Independents grow so much in the last two elections? As American politics have become more contentious and divided, many voters preferred not to identify with either major party. Also, changes in Colorado election law allowed Independents to vote in either Republican or Democrat primaries. Practically speaking, many voters registered as Unaffiliated because it meant fewer mailings and robocalls. In the last two election cycles, Republican registrations declined slightly (1.3%); Democrats increased slightly (3.8%), and Unaffiliateds surged (19%).[5] Such statistics make it clear that Unaffiliated voters can determine election outcomes, though to overcome the Republican advantage in registered voters,

Unaffiliateds must break overwhelmingly for Democratic candidates. Up to now, that has not happened.

DOUGLAS COUNTY REGISTERED VOTERS AND GENERAL ELECTION TURNOUTS						
Year	Republicans	Democrats	Unaffil-iated	Other	Totals	Turnout
1992	25,019	9,623	16,555	50	51,247	59.6%
1996	36,640	12,801	22,472	74	71,987	71.2%
2000	NA	NA	NA	NA	103,853	83.36%
2004	81,382	30,402	46,172	309	158,265	86.41%
2008	87,737	39,857	57,944	654	183,045	83.22%
2012	100,301	43,300	68,927	1,660	214,188	79.22%
2016	109,469	48,676	79,774	3,627	241,547	79.74%

Another factor in changing voter registration rolls is the increase in "Others' which refers to third-party affiliations (Libertarian, Green, Socialist Workers, Prohibition, American Constitution, etc.). During the 1990s, the number of registered Others grew from 50 to 74. In 2008, the number increased to 654. By 2016, registered Others grew to almost 4,000. But such an increase still amounts to less than 2% of registered voters.[6]

RESULTS OF DOUGLAS COUNTY GENERAL ELECTIONS 1992 - 2016			
Year	Republican	Democrat	Other
1992	G.H.W. Bush: 18,592	B. Clinton: 9,991	Perot: 11,477
1996	Dole: 32,120	B. Clinton: 16,323	Perot: 3,623
2000	G.W. Bush: 56,007	Gore: 27,076	3,142
2004	G.W. Bush: 80,651	Kerry: 39,661	889
2008	McCain: 88,108	Obama: 61,962	1,751
2012	Romney: 104,397	Obama: 61,094	2,593
2016	Trump: 102,573	H. Clinton: 68,657	16,270

Of course, in the end, voter registrations do not count, only actual votes do. When it comes to casting ballots, registered voters often cross party lines or do not vote at all. In the last thirty years, voter turnouts in general elections have ranged from 59.6% (1992) to 86.41% (2004). The results in three presidential elections show the relationship between voter registrations and actual votes.

- 1992: George H.W. Bush received 18,592 votes, 6,427 *fewer* than registered Republicans. Bill Clinton received 9,991 votes, 368 *more* than registered Democrats. But Ross Perot, a third-party candidate, tallied 11,477 votes in comparison to only 50 registered Others. No-shows numbered slightly over 20,000 (40.4%).

- 2008: there were 88,108 votes for John McCain, 367 *more* than registered Republicans; 61,960 votes for Barak Obama, about 22,000 *more* than registered Democrats than registered Others. Almost 31,000 registered voters stayed home (16.78%).

- 2016: Donald Trump received 102,573 votes, 6,896 *fewer* than registered Republicans; and Hillary Clinton, 68,657 votes, about 20,000 *more* than registered Democrats. Twenty-five third-party candidates received close to 16,300 votes, which was about four and a half times *more* than registered Others.[7] Of the third-party candidates, the top two vote-getters were Libertarian Gary Johnson (10,212) and Green Party candidate Jill Stein (1,477). No-shows increased to nearly 49,000 (20.26%).[8]

In all three elections, Republicans won handily, though they struggled to secure their large, registered base. Twice, Democrats attracted thousands of voters more than registered Democrats but still fell short of victory. Most of them had to be Unaffiliateds. In 1992 many crossover Republicans voted for either Clinton or Perot; and in 2008, Obama attracted both Republican and Unaffiliated voters. In 2016, Trump lost Republican voters to Clinton or third-party candidates, though he still won easily. The percentage of no-show registered voters was over 40% in 1992, almost 17% in 2008, and about 20% in 2016. There is no way of determining who stayed home and why. Despite the steady increase of Unaffiliated registrations, they have not ended the Republican winning streak; and the effects of registered non-voters on election results are impossible to determine. It seems certain that election results could be different if more registered voters went to the polls.

Are there discernible trends to predict DC's political future? In the last three decades, the growth in voter registrations has been uneven: Republicans grew by 438%, Unaffiliateds by 566%, Democrats by 664%, and

374

the Others by 9593%! Such percentage increases can be misleading. Republicans still hold a slight lead over Unaffiliateds in registered voters; Democrats are still about half those of Republicans or Unaffiliateds, and Others are still too few to qualify realistically as "spoilers" in most elections. Up to now Unaffiliated have divided their votes in ways that allowed Republicans to maintain their unbroken winning streak. But only time will tell when or if the Unaffiliateds begin to tilt elections in other political directions.

How do political insiders evaluate present DC politics? Randy Reed served on the Castle Rock Town Council from 2002 to 2010 and as Mayor from 2006 to 2010. He has stayed attentive to County politics. He has seen changes in the body politic, especially the increasing number of Unaffiliateds. He notes the deep divisions among Republicans over the Trump candidacy in 2016, which led many to stay home in that election. Many Unaffiliateds (and Republicans?) supported Hilary Clinton, but Trump was still able to win a sizable victory. Reed predicts the continued growth of Unaffiliateds whom he expects to vote less Republican than in the past.[9] Political change does not come easily in DC.

---

[1] Douglas County, Colorado, *Historical Election Data, 1992-2016*, accessed on Nov. 7, 2019, https://www.douglas.co.us/elections/historical-election-data/.

[2] Ibid.

[3] Ibid.

[4] To check the following analysis, see the summary chart of voter registration data.

[5] Ibid.

[6] For the changing data on Other registrations, see the attached chart.

[7] "Cumulative Report—Official," Douglas County, Colorado—2016 General Election, November 8, 2016, accessed November 11, 2019, https://www.douglas.co.us/documents/2016-ge-election-results.pdf/.

[8] Department of State, State of Colorado, *2016 General Abstract Results*, accessed November 11, 2019, https://www.sos.state.co.us/pubs/elections/Results/2016/General/2016GeneralAbstractResultsCertAndReport.pdf.

[9] Randy Reed, telephone interview, December 7, 2019.

Chapter 63
HIGHLANDS RANCH

Tim Weber

In the recent history of Douglas County, nothing comes close to the development of Highlands Ranch. In 1979, four years *before* DC had a Master Plan, the Planning Commission and Board of Commissioners approved what would become the County's largest development ever.[1] Forty years later, what still surprises about HR is not its size but that it remains *unincorporated.*

Highlands Ranch Entrance Sign with Logo

In 1978, the Mission Viejo Company, a wholly owned subsidiary of Philip Morris Company (Marlborough cigarettes) acquired a purchase option of $26 million on the 33.5 square miles Highlands Ranch (HR), then owned by oilman Marvin Davis. It wanted to develop a community of 90,000 people (DC's population was then 25,000) in five phases over the next 20 or 30 years. Mission Viejo seemed up to the job. It had recently finished a large, planned community in Orange County, California and could demonstrate impressive financial stability, which was important to DC officials since so many previous subdivisions had gone bankrupt before completion.

Its plan for HR was all-inclusive and detailed. It promised a variety of housing levels and options, abundant open space and recreational facilities, plus commercial and industrial areas to provide adequate jobs for residents. After much consideration, DC leaders concluded that it was better for one experienced contractor to develop the entire community than for multiple contractors to develop it in smaller pieces.

Looking back, the deciders in DC seemed overwhelmed by the scope of the project and not having a Master Plan for guidance. The approval process was long and had many obstacles. Opponents in DC thought that Mission Viejo's project would destroy the County's rural character, but they had no alternative plan and were unable to show any fatal flaws in the company's proposal. The largest obstacle to final approval was the company's water plan. The state rejected the plan because it relied on unrenewable water sources. Eventually, after several legal challenges and adjustments, an acceptable plan was finalized. After the plan was approved, Mission Viejo and Marvin Davis closed the deal; and the contractor hit the ground running.[2]

To attract buyers, Mission Viejo knew it needed schools and infrastructure. To secure HR's first elementary school in 1982, the company covered $3.3 million in building costs, paid operational expenses for the first year, and agreed to a fifteen-year lease by Douglas County Schools at $1 per year, following which the district would repay the company with HR taxes set aside during the lease period.[3] After the first school, new school construction never stopped. By 2020, HR had 38 public and private schools, about 30% of all schools in DC.[4] New residents also needed public services—roads, utilities, recreation, fire and police protection, which Mission Viejo provided by creating five Metropolitan Districts (1980), one for each phase of development, the Centennial Water and Sanitation District and the South Metro Fire Rescue District. The HR Community Association offered recreational and community events.[5] As an unincorporated community, HR relied on the Douglas County Sheriff's Office for law enforcement.[6] To guarantee that its plans were always followed, the company made sure that most board of director positions for the Metro Districts were filled with its own employees. As a result, HR residents had little role in governing their own community.[7]

Eventually, many residents wanted to explore incorporation. In 1992, 1997, and 1998, resident groups studied the feasibility of a public referendum on the issue; but the company-controlled Metro Districts effectively blocked their efforts. Finally, in 2006, the company consolidated four Metro Districts into a single HR Metropolitan District after approval by 70% of voters in a special election with only a 15% turnout.[8] Consolidation improved the governing process, but voter participation in Metro District board elections has remained low. In fact, by 2020, turnout was down to 4%.[9]

Almost from the beginning, traffic problems plagued HR. The phased construction of C-470 (1985 to 1990)[10] included four interchanges paid for by HR: US 85, Lucent Boulevard, Broadway, and University. The state highway department underestimated HR population growth. It had predicted 27,000 in 2000 but got 70,000,[11] resulting in higher traffic volume than expected. In 2020 a more recent project added 12.5 miles of express (toll) lanes to C-470.[12]

Mission Viejo opened 400 acres to other builders in 1984 and sold out to Shea Homes in 1997. Despite good intentions, under Mission Viejo, HR remained essentially a rather high-priced bedroom community. Shea Homes was better at developing promised commercial and industrial areas. In 1999 Shea Homes opened HR Business Park with the Shea Center, which soon attracted Lucent Technologies, Qwest Communications, a subsidiary of Visa, and other firms.[13] The Chamber of Commerce of Highlands Ranch was organized in 2000 and has grown to 275 members since changing its name to the Chamber of Northwest Douglas County and including businesses from Roxborough to Lone Tree.[14]

By 2020, HR was a "full-service" community with an abundance of retail, recreational, and health care opportunities. For example, the HR Town Center opened in 2004, with 37 stores;[15] other retail centers were built throughout the community, and patrons flocked to 530 restaurants.[16] There are four recreational centers;[17] two golf courses;[18] twenty-six parks; acres of open space; miles of trails,[19] and a 24-screen AMC Theater. Children's Hospital Colorado, South Campus, and UCHealth Highlands Ranch Hospital are acute care facilities,[20] plus there are several neighborhood health clinics for outpatient care.

Highlands Ranch Veteran's Monument

HR residents rate their community extremely high.[21] Mission Viejo and Shea Homes mostly kept their original promises, though the price of real estate remains high, with a shortage of affordable housing; and most workers commute outside HR. The community is close to build-out, and HR's growth in population has been steady. The first residents arrived in 1981. By the end of the first decade, the population was 17,000. By the end of the second decade, it had grown to 70,000. After thirty years (2011), it was 93,000. By its fortieth anniversary, HR expects to have a population of over 100,000.

When HR began, DC's population was only 25,000; and even though many County residents wanted DC to remain rural, they knew that some growth was inevitable. HR was the turning point in deciding that important issue. After the project was approved, DC no longer asked *if* there will be growth, but *how much*.[22]

---

[1] Kevin C. Weinman, "Invisible Suburbs: Privatized Growth in Suburban Metropolitan Denver, 1950-2000," Ph.D. dissertation, University of New Hampshire, 2017, 154.

[2] Ibid., 154-168.

[3] "Mission Viejo Elementary Needs at least 100 Students to Open," *Douglas County News-Press*, February 18, 1982, 3; Sydney Brown, "Mission Viejo to Pay for School for 50 Highlands Ranch Children," *Douglas County News-Press*, July 21, 1982,

1; "Northridge Elementary Expected to Open in September," *Highlands Ranch Reporter*, August 1982, 1-2.

[4] See Chapter 26: Educational Choices.

[5] "Highlands Ranch Community Association," accessed June 26, 2020, https://www.foxnews.com/.

[6] Douglas County Sheriff, "Highlands Ranch Substation," accessed June 26, 2020, https://www.google.com/maps/dir//Douglas+County+Sheriff+-+Highlands+Ranch+Substation,+9250+Zotos+Dr,+Highlands+Ranch,+CO+80129/@39.5451431,-104.9916676,14.13z/data=!4m8!4m7!1m0!1m5!1m1!1s0x876c824f64d58931:0x9fcaea784e5a6f57!2m2!1d-104.9967718!2d39.5482894. Douglas County Sheriff, "Where is 'unincorporated' Douglas County?" accessed June 26, 2020, https://www.dcsheriff.net/sheriffs-office/where-is-unincorporated-douglas-county/.

[7] Weinman, "Invisible Suburbs," 181-197.

[8] Ibid., 199-216.

[9] Elliott Wenzler, "Metro district candidates see weaknesses in election process," *Highlands Ranch Herald*, May 12, 2020.

[10] David Wetzel, ed., *100 Years of Colorado State Transportation History* (Denver: CDOT, 2010), 78-79, 113.

[11] Weinman, "Invisible Suburbs," 260-262; Emily C. Dooley, "Commuter traffic outgrowing C-470," *Highlands Ranch Herald*, May 11, 2000.

[12] David Gilbert, "C-470 project moving toward completion, CDOT says," *Colorado Community Media*, February 24, 2020; Mark Harden, "C-470 express lanes now open across south metro," *Colorado Community Media*, June 14, 2020.

[13] Citadel National Construction Group, "Lucent Technologies Highlands Ranch Campus," accessed June 26, 2020, https://citadelgroup.org/projects/lucent/; Tamara Monahnan, "Visa to move into Highlands Ranch Business Park," *Colorado Community Media*, July 26, 2000.

[14] Alex DeWind, "Chamber changes name to reflect larger community," *Highlands Ranch Herald*, October 16, 2018, accessed June 26, 2020, https://highlandsranchherald.net/stories/chamber-changes-name-to-reflect-larger-community,271693.

[15] "Highlands Ranch Town Center: list of stores," accessed June 26, 2020, https://www.mallsinamerica.com/colorado/highlands-ranch-town-center

[16] Open Table, "Best restaurants near me in Highlands Ranch, CO," accessed June 26, 2020, https://www.opentable.com/nearby/restaurants-near-me-highlands-ranch.

[17] Highlands Ranch Community Association, "Recreation Centers," accessed June 26, 2020, https://hrcaonline.org/about-us/recreation-centers.

[18] Golf Advisor, "Highland Ranch Golf Courses," accessed June 26, 2020, http://www.golfcolorado.com/courses/highlands-ranch/.

[19] Highlands Ranch Metro District, "Parks . . . a Gathering Place in Highlands Ranch," accessed June 26, 2020, https://highlandsranch.org/services/parks-open-space/parks/

[20] "Children's Hospital Colorado, South Campus, Highlands Ranch," accessed June 26, 2020, https://www.childrenscolorado.org/locations/south-campus-highlands-ranch/?utm_source=google&utm_medium=local&utm_campaign=localmaps&utm_content=109; "UCHealth Highlands Ranch Hospital," accessed June 26, 2020, https://www.uchealth.org/locations/uchealth-highlands-ranch-hospital/

[21] Alex DeWind, "Residents provide views about community in survey," *Colorado Community Media*, accessed June 26, 2020.

[22] Statistics provided by Sherry Eppers of the HR Metro District

Chapter 64

NORTHEASTERN DOUGLAS COUNTY

Catherine Traffis

Long-time residents of northeastern Douglas County are the first to say that the last three decades of population growth have exceeded their wildest expectations. What was once a rural area with a tiny population is now a sprawling suburb with planned communities and wide, fast roads. The rate of growth is troubling to some, but newcomers searching for a great place to raise a family are delighted to be part of it.

North Parker Road - 1980s

Parker has made many "best places to live" lists in recent years and is growing quickly. Between 1935, when a devasting flood ended Parker's Colorado & Southern railroad service, and the time of the town's incorporation in 1981, the population grew from about 100 to just 285.[1] By 1990, however, new houses began to spring up and the town's boundaries grew, bringing the population to 6,000. By 2014, the population had skyrocketed to nearly 50,000[2]—and that does not include the large populations living in the unincorporated communities of The Pinery, Stonegate, and Dove Valley. By 2020, the population reached 58,578;[3] and at full build-out, Parker is expected to be around 102,000.[4]

A constant barometer of Parker's growth has been the expansion of its main artery, Parker Road (CO-83). It is easy to find old-timers who still remember it as a dirt road that kids could dart across whenever they wanted, but woe to the child who attempts such a feat today! Parker Road has become a six-lane Goliath running through the center of town, with cars traveling at near-highway speeds. Along Parker Road and its cross streets are numerous shopping centers and many big box stores such as Walmart Supercenter, Super Target, Costco, Sports Authority, Office Depot, Best Buy, and Murdoch's.[5] One of the major traffic shifts came in 1998 when E-470 was built out to Parker Road, attracting new homeowners and shoppers looking for an easy commute.

As new homes came to Parker, many great institutions followed. It now has 22 schools and the award-winning Parker Adventist Hospital. One of the Town of Parker's brightest achievements in the past decade has been the establishment of Parker Arts and the building of its main space, the PACE Center (2011).[6] With the help of a lottery grant, Parker Arts also restored a secondary space, the 1914 Schoolhouse at Mainstreet.

The Colorado Horse Park was another notable addition to Parker in recent decades. Founded in 1992 by Helen Krieble, the 148-acre park is the largest horse park west of the Mississippi and brings hundreds of visitors to The Pinery area every year, hosting more than 40 events annually.[7] Historically, equestrian skill has always been a point of pride in Douglas County; and horse lovers were thrilled that the park was acquired by another owner when Helen retired in 2014.[8]

If one still needs evidence that Douglas County was the fastest growing U.S. county in the mid-nineties, one only needs to look next door to Lone Tree. The development of the area—so tantalizingly poised for commuting at the junction of I-25 and C-470—had been decades in the making when the city incorporated in 1996: it comprised just 1.5 square miles and was home to about 3,000 people. Today it encompasses 10 square miles, has an enviable daytime economy, and has a population of almost 15,000.[9] Park Meadows Mall opened in 1996, on a spot where cows were grazing in the fields just two years before. The retail behemoth billed itself as "Colorado's only shopping resort" and was an instant hit.[10] Today, it is still the beating heart of Lone Tree's hustle and bustle and even boasts its own light rail station. The mall is surrounded by other retail establishments, including many restaurants and big box stores like Costco and Best Buy.

In the early 2000s, ranch land turned into upscale homes in communities such as RidgeGate, Heritage Hills, Centennial Ridge, and Carriage Club. The city is tastefully planned, with one-third of its land dedicated to open space. Another wise decision the locals made was to preserve the area's most historically significant ranch. With state funding, the Schweiger Ranch was made into a living history museum.[11] Other significant achievements in the City of Lone Tree are the Lone Tree Cultural Arts Center, which opened in 2011, and big employers such as SkyRidge Medical Center, Kaiser Permanente, and Charles Schwab.[12]

Restored Schweiger Ranch House

Incidentally, the name "Lone Tree" was not derived from a particular lone tree. Although there is an old one-room schoolhouse by that name near Larkspur, the choice of the name appears to have been a developer's decision. It has a cowboy feel and nicely ties the community to the golf club of the same name. Residents did often ask for the location of the legendary tree, however. On Arbor Day 1998, the mayor and citizens remedied the situation by planting a Colorado blue spruce at Lincoln and Yosemite and dubbing it "The Lone Tree."[13]

One consequence of northeastern Douglas County's growth has been the need to develop a sustainable water supply. In 1991, the Parker Water and Sanitation District embarked on what would become a 20-plus-year mission to build a dam and reservoir for its service area, which includes most of Parker and parts of Lone Tree, Castle Pines, and unincorporated Douglas County.

PWSD's first site choice was Castlewood Canyon, but after a protracted legal battle with the Colorado Division of Parks, it was decided that the open space needed to be preserved. PWSD then turned its attention to the land of Mrs. Rosie Reuter-Hess, whose family had been ranching in the area near what is now I-25 and Castle Pines Parkway for more than 70 years. Reluctant at first to sell her land, she eventually agreed; and the result is the Rueter-Hess Reservoir, which will keep the locals from overusing precious deep-water aquifers for generations to come.[14] Parts of Rosie's original homestead still sit at the foot of the dam.

At full build-out, recreation will play an exciting role at Rueter-Hess Reservoir. Although it will be several years before enough funding is in place to open the reservoir to the public, the master plan includes pedestrian, equestrian, and mountain biking trails; non-motorized boating; a water exploration play area; picnic and camping areas; scenic overlooks; ADA-accessible interpretive walks; fishing; an incline challenge; a sledding hill; and winter sports.[15]

Before the reservoir was excavated, archaeologists examined the site, which is part of Newlin Gulch. Just as expected, they found an abandoned gold mine that was once part of the less-than-successful Newlin Gulch Mining District. The mine, in which a local man perished in 1922, now lies at the bottom of the reservoir.[16] The archaeologists did make another discovery, however, that was much more intriguing: They found evidence of human habitation dating back 9,000 years.[17] So when current residents put down roots here, it is really nothing new.

---

[1] Chris Michelwicz, "Echoes of Parker's Past—The Changes: 1995-2014," *Parker Chronicle,* December 11, 2014.

[2] Ibid.

[3] World Population Review, "Parker, Colorado Population 2020," accessed May 6, 2020, https://worldpopulationreview.com/us-cities/parker-co-population/.

[4] Michelwicz, "Echoes of Parker's Past—The Changes: 1995-2014."

[5] Parker Community Business Directory, "Retail Big Box Store Shopping Directory, Parker CO," accessed May 7, 2020, https://www.parkercolorado.net/big-box-retail-store-directory-in-parker-co/.

[6] Parker Arts, "The History of the Town of Parker's Cultural Facilities," accessed May 4, 2020, https://parkerarts.org/1001/History-of-the-Towns-Cultural-Facilities.

[7] Colorado Horse Park, "Partnership Led by Mark Bellissimo Signs Contract to Acquire Colorado Horse Park," *The Chronicle of the Horse*, accessed December 19, 2014, https://www.chronofhorse.com/article/bellissimo-contract-acquire-colorado-horse-park.

[8] Elizabeth Hernandez, "Colorado Horse Park in Douglas County to Continue as Equestrian Center," *Denver Post*, December 20, 2014.

[9] United States Census Bureau, "Quick Facts: Lone Tree City, Colorado," accessed May 3, 2020, https://www.census.gov/quickfacts/lonetreecitycolorado.

[10] Janet Forgrieve, "Park Meadows Still Packs 'Em In," *Rocky Mountain News*, August 18, 2006.

[11] "The Schweiger Ranch," *History*, accessed May 3, 2020, https://schweigerranch.org/history-of-schweiger-ranch/.

[12] Meghan Lopez, "The City of Lone Tree is bracing for more growth, planning for the future," *The Denver Channel*, October 11, 2019, https://www.thedenverchannel.com/news/our-colorado/the-city-of-lone-tree-is-bracing-for-more-growth-planning-for-the-future.

[13] Kathleen McCoy, "Lone Tree: From One Small Tree," in *Douglas County, Colorado: A Photographic Journey*, ed. Castle Rock Writers (Castle Rock, CO: Douglas County Libraries Foundation, 2005), 95.

[14] Parker Water and Sanitation District, "Naming Rueter-Hess Reservoir," accessed May 5, 2020, http://www.pwsd.org/2331/Naming-Rueter-Hess-Reservoir.

[15] Parker Water and Sanitation District, "Rueter-Hess Reservoir 2016 Master Plan," accessed May 8, 2020, http://co-reuterhessrecreationauthority.civicplus.com/DocumentCenter/View/69/2016-Recreation-Master-Plan-PDF?bidId=.

[16] Parker Area Historical Society, "Newlin Gulch Mining District," accessed May 8, 2020, https://www.parkerhistory.org/newlin-gulch-gold-mining-district.

[17] Parker Water and Sanitation District, "An Introduction to Rueter-Hess Reservoir," accessed May 5, 2020, https://www.pwsd.org/2193/Rueter-Hess-Reservoir.

Chapter 65
NORTHWESTERN DOUGLAS COUNTY

Char Nauman and Rebecca Holm

In the last thirty years, the Northwestern part of Douglas County has had substantial suburban growth, while its historic towns of Sedalia and Louviers have resisted all expansion opportunities.

Gabriel's Restaurant and Tuscan Bar - Sedalia 2020

While the northern half of DC experienced a population explosion, the town of Sedalia did not grow at all. In the years between 2000 and 2019, its population increased by *three*, from 211 to 214. Unlike other DC towns, Sedalia rejected the strategy of annexing new subdivisions being built nearby. Instead, the people adopted a Master Plan in 1990 that refused such rapid growth. Instead, it affirmed the town's small, rural character.[1] Townspeople had many of its old structures designated as historic landmarks: the Sedalia Fire Department (1933), the Sedalia School House (1891), and the Sedalia Water Tank (1890). The Manhart House (1878), which had been home to Sedalia's most prominent pioneer family of merchants,[2] was transformed into

Gabriel's Italian Restaurant (1985), an upscale eatery that now rivals Bud's Bar (1948) as the town's most popular stopping place. In 2009, local history buffs moved and restored a Victorian cottage that became the Sedalia Museum and Gardens.[3] Consequently, by 2019, the town remained only 1.36 square miles and contained only 91 housing units,[4] despite its strategic location along US 85 (Santa Fe Road), which provided easy access to the jobs and amenities of Arapahoe and Denver Counties. Once the citizens of Sedalia adopted a no-growth policy, they stuck to it.

Louviers is Northwestern DC's only other remaining historic town, located a few miles north of Sedalia on US 85. Founded in 1906 by the DuPont Powder Plant, Louviers was a "company town" where workers lived in houses owned and maintained by DuPont and manufactured dynamite for the western U.S. In the early 1960s, DuPont scaled back operations and allowed workers to purchase their own homes. When Dupont closed the plant in 1988, residents decided to keep things the way they were. In 1999, they succeeded in getting the whole town placed on the National Register of Historic Places so that it became nearly impossible to alter the status quo.[5] In 2002, DuPont donated the 855 acres surrounding the town as open space to provide a buffer zone against future development.[6] Consequently, the town covers only 1.55 square miles. While the population stayed in the 200s from 1960-1990, it now numbers 347 (2019).[7] There are no commercial properties in Louviers; and because additional residential developments have been ruled out, would-be buyers must wait for current residents to sell their homes.

Sterling Ranch Entrance - Roxborough 2020

The residential development of Northwestern DC has been primarily in the Roxborough area, which is close to the South Platte River, the Dakota Hogback, and Pike National Forest. The impetus for the development of this area was the completion in 1975 of the Chatfield Reservoir by the Army Corps of Engineers for flood control of the South Platte River and Plum Creek. The development occurred between Chatfield State Park in the north and Roxborough State Park in the south.

Starting in the 1980s, construction began on several subdivisions in the Roxborough area and has continued to the present: Roxborough Village East and West (built between the1980s and 2015); Chatfield Farms (2005-2020); the upscale Estates at Chatfield (2014+); and the private golf club and resort community of Ravenna in Waterton Canyon (2007). The largest subdivision in the area is Roxborough Park, which extends from Waterton Road in the north to Roxborough State Park in the south and includes the Arrowhead Golf Course.[8] It qualifies as a Census Designated Place consisting of 9.3 square miles and has experienced significant growth in the last two decades. Its population was 4,446 in 2000 with 1,637 housing units. It grew to 9,099 with 3,312 housing units in 2010. It is estimated that its population in 2019 was 10,090.[9]

In 2015, Sterling Ranch became DC's latest master-planned community. It is located south of Titan Road, between Roxborough Park Road in the west and US 85 in the east. After build-out in twenty to twenty-five years, it will consist of 12,000 homes in nine "villages" on 3,400 acres and have a population of 33,000 residents. It will be Colorado's first high-speed fiberoptic community, with lines going to each "smart" home.[10] None of these developments are incorporated or have home rule. They are governed by multiple metropolitan districts that use their taxing power to provide needed services.

Northwestern Douglas County has a unique historical site. In 1960 rancher Charles Lamb discovered bones while digging a stock pond. They turned out to be from a Columbian mammoth. In several digs, archeologists uncovered bones from other extinct Ice Age animals (camels, bison, horses, llamas, and over two dozen other mammoths) and various human implements used to hunt them. As residential development closed in on Lamb's 240-acre ranch, he sold off parcels. In 1995, the Archeological Conservancy helped purchase

35 acres surrounding the diggings, then in 2006, the Lamb Spring Archaeological Preserve was established. Digs continue and free guided tours are available.[11]

The area offers two exceptional recreational areas, Roxborough State Park and Chatfield State Park, which opened in 1975. The former offers exceptional scenery, hiking, biking, birding, cross-country skiing, and snowshoeing in the winter.[12] Chatfield State Park's list of activities is longer: boating, fishing, camping, biking, hiking, horseback riding, and birding. To meet future agricultural and municipal water needs, the Chatfield Storage Reallocation Project was begun in 2017. The project will increase Chatfield Dam's water storage capacity by 20,600 acre-feet, which will raise its water level by 12 feet and require a reconfiguration of its shoreline recreational facilities.[13]

To meet the region's future water needs, the Roxborough Water Treatment Plant was built in 2017.[14] It is the first facility in Colorado to utilize ultraviolet light as the primary disinfectant, which reduces chlorine dosage and disinfection byproducts. By increasing reusable water, the use of non-replaceable deep groundwater can be slowed.

Other additions to Northwestern DC in recent times are a new cemetery and extensive road work. In 2015, Seven Stones Chatfield Botanical Gardens Cemetery became the first new cemetery in the County since Castle Rock's Cedar Hill Cemetery in 1875. Located on North Rampart Range Road, Seven Stones incorporates artistic memorials, modern technology, peaceful courtyards, and creative landscapes.[15] Nearby Titan Road has been widened with added turn lanes, roundabouts, and traffic lights to accommodate Lockheed Martin's Titan rocket project and increasing traffic into Sterling Ranch. Waterton Road is being extended from Rampart Range Road, past Sterling Ranch, to Moore Road.[16] Plans are underway to finish the widening of US 85 from C-470 to Happy Canyon and Daniels Park Roads, which will alleviate the increasing traffic of commuters and workers in the growing number of industrial facilities along the highway.[17]

Northwestern DC has grown since 1990, thanks to new subdivisions, and will continue to do so, the water supply permitting.

[1] Susan Consola Appleby, *Fading Past: The Story of Douglas County, Colorado* (Palmer Lake, CO: Filter Press, 2001), 169.

[2] "Historic Properties," *Douglas County, Colorado*, accessed June 8, 2020, https://www.douglas.co.us/about-us/historic-preservation/historic-properties/.

[3] *Sedalia Museum and Gardens*, accessed on June 8, 2020, https://sedaliamuseumandgardens.org/.

[4] "Sedalia, CO: Facts and Data," *CO HomeTownLocator*, accessed June 8, 2020, https://colorado.hometownlocator.com/co/douglas/sedalia.cfm.

[5] Harrison Fletcher, "Blast from the past," *Westworld*, March 11, 1999, accessed May 20, 2019, ps://www.westworld.com/news/blast-from-the-past-5059652.

[6] "Louviers," *Colorado Encyclopedia*, accessed June 8, 2020, https://coloradoencyclopedia.org/article/louviers.

[7] "Louviers, CO: Facts and Data," *CO HomeTownLocator*, accessed June 8, 2020, https://colorado.hometownlocator.com/co/douglas/louviers.cfm.

[8] "Community," *Roxborough Living*, accessed June 8, 2020, http://www.roxboroughliving.com/.

[9] "Roxborough Park, CO: Basic Facts," *CO HomeTownLocator*, accessed on June 8, 2020, https://colorado.hometownlocator.com/co/douglas/roxborough-park.cfm.

[10] "Fast Facts About Sterling Ranch," accessed June 8, 2020, https://www.sterlingranchroundup.com/sterling-ranch-cheat-sheet.

[11] "Lamb Spring Archeological Site," *Colorado Encyclopedia*, accessed June 9, 2020, https://coloradoencyclopedia.org/article/lamb-spring-archaeological-site; *Lamb Spring Archeological Preserve*, accessed June 9, 2020, http://www.lambspring.org/.

[12] "Roxborough," *Colorado Parks and Wildlife*, accessed June 8, 2020, https://cpw.state.co.us/placestogo/parks/Roxborough/Pages/default.aspx.

[13] *Chatfield Storage Reallocation Project*, accessed June 9, 2020, https://chatfieldreallocation.org/.

[14] "Water Treatment Plant," *Roxborough Water and Sanitation District*, accessed June 8, 2020, https://www.roxwater.org/projects/water-treatment-plant/.

[15] Christy Steadman, "Cemetery breaks ground in Douglas County," *Castle Rock News-Press*, April 27, 2015, accessed on June 9, 2020, https://castlerocknewspress.net/stories/cemetery-breaks-ground-in-douglas-county,187043? *Seven Stones*, accessed June 8, 2020, http://www.discoversevenstones.com/tag/seven-stones-cemetery/.

[16] "Waterton Road Extension Phase I," *Douglas County, Colorado*, accessed June 8, 2020, https://www.douglas.co.us/road-work/state-highway-and-county-road-widening-projects/waterton-road-extension-phase-i/.

[17] "US 85 Corridor Improvements," *Douglas County, Colorado*, accessed June 8, 2020, https://www.douglas.co.us/road-work/state-highway-and-county-road-widening-projects/us-85-corridor-improvements-in-douglas-county/.

Chapter 66

DOUGLAS COUNTY'S CROSSROADS

Tim Weber

The Crossroads area covers much of the center of Douglas County. It stretches along both sides of CO 86 from Castle Rock to Elbert County and straddles I-25 from south of Castle Rock to Castle Pines' border with Lone Tree. This area includes DC's two historic county seats—Franktown and Castle Rock. In response to DC's post-1990 growth, the former decided to remain small and rural; and the latter chose to grow. Castle Pines, the area's newest city, has adopted an aggressive plan for rapid growth.

Franktown Intersection Highways 86 and 83

Franktown was DC's first county seat (1861). It is located at the intersection of CO 83 and CO 86. Through the nineteenth and twentieth centuries, its population remained small but stable, ranging from the 100s to the 200s. As high-density subdivisions encroached from the north after 1970, residents refused to incorporate, fearing higher taxes, the annexation of new subdivisions, and the loss of their rural character. They opposed a controversial master plan, a proposal to increase gravel mining along Cherry Creek, and an effort to change the town's name.[1] Without incorporation, Franktown depended on DC's Planning Commission and County Commissioners to protect its rural identity, which they did. The County has approved only developments with large lots: Whispering Pines, Whispering Pines North, Castlewood North, Bannockburn, Burning Tree Ranch, the Meadows at Russellville, Legacy Pines, and others.[2]

Because residents opposed high-density developments, after 2010, the Franktown Citizens Coalition II mobilized against "Franktown Village" which proposed 286 single-family homes, duplexes, and townhomes and 180,000 square feet of retail and commercial space at the south-east corner of CO 86 and 83. For over five years, the Coalition showed up at DC Planning Commission meetings and lobbied against the project.[3] Finally, in 2017, the developer withdrew his proposal. When asked why they kept up the pressure for so long, the leader of the Coalition explained: "We wanted to protect our little place."[4]

The people of Franktown are not against *all* development. In 2018, they applauded the County's approval of Fox Hill, a "shared farming community" of 365 acres near Flintwood Road for 92 $1 million homes on one- to four-acre lots.[5] This subdivision did not threaten Franktown's rural way of life. The Town has rejected almost all commercial development. Nearly all Franktown businesses are clustered around its historic intersection. The Town has grown, but only slightly. In 2019, there were 428 people within its 2.94 square miles.[6]

Castle Rock was DC's second county seat (1874), its first incorporated town (1881), and its third home-rule municipality (1987). Its population kept pace during DC's recent growth spurt. In 1990, the Town had about 14.5% of the County's total population (8,708 of 60,391); and in 2020, it grew to nearly 20% (69,661 of 351,154). Castle Rock is unique in that it hosts both its own town government and Douglas County's.

The 1990s were a turning point for Castle Rock. The Town built new Fire and Police Stations on Perry Street and a Town Hall on Wilcox Street. The County erected the Philip S. Miller Building and a new façade for the DC Administration Building on Third Street, along with the Robert A. Christensen Justice Center at I-25 and US 85, for the DC Sheriff's Office, detention center, and County and District Courts. Other County buildings included a branch of DC libraries, the DC School District headquarters, and the DC Fairgrounds and Events Center. The multi-level parking structure at Third and Jerry Streets was a joint town/county project.

From 1990 to 2020, there was retail growth and downtown renewal.[7] The Factory Stores Outlets opened in 1992 and expanded in 1997. Stores and restaurants were renovated on Perry and Wilcox Streets, including the Courtyard on Perry. The Great Recession of 2008 brought town budget cuts, staff layoffs, and a halt to downtown construction.[8] But by 2011, thanks especially to the Downtown Alliance,[9] new projects like the White Pavilion (Rink at the Rock)[10] and Festival Park[11] were completed. In 2014, the Promenade at Castle Rock, a 166-acre, 900,000 square feet retail project opened next to the Outlets.[12] More recently, two new "high-rise" mixed-usage projects (Riverwalk and Encore) on Wilcox are expected to bring more residents, office space, retail, and parking spaces downtown.[13] The Castle Rock Adventist Hospital opened in 2011,[14] and the Arapahoe Community College Sturm Collaboration Campus began classes in 2019.[15]

In 2014, Philip S. Miller Park started welcoming visitors. It grew to a 320-acre facility and offered many attractions, including a 200-step Climbing Hill, zip lines, an amphitheater, picnic facilities, a playground, and Miller Activity Complex (MAC), a fieldhouse with indoor playing fields, a large play structure, and a pool.[16] Castle Rock has 18 other parks, 3 trails, and 6 open spaces.[17]

Philip S. Miller Activity Complex with Hiking Incline,
Zip Line Tower, and Complex Entrance Sign Photo

Expansion brought both benefits and challenges.[18] Some people opposed growth, as raucous Planning Commission and Town Council meetings attest. A group of residents tried unsuccessfully to recall two Council members in 2016.[19] But nothing could stop new subdivisions from being built in all directions.[20] Castle Rock has a plan for meeting future water needs, but progress toward achieving its goals is slow.[21] Traffic congestion continues, despite non-stop road improvement projects.[22] In Castle Rock, it seems, there are only two seasons: winter and road construction. The Town currently occupies 33.86 square miles[23] but is likely to get bigger.[24]

Castle Pines is Crossroad's newest community. The first homes were built around two Jack Nicklaus-designed golf courses: Castle Pines Golf Club (1981) and the Country Club at Castle Pines (1986). This community became the unincorporated Village at Castle Pines. By 2009, multi-million-dollar homes were built on lots costing over $500,000.[25] In 2019, the Village covered 4.4 square miles and had a population of 4,138.[26]

Castle Pines North developed on the Village's northside. It was incorporated in 2008 and changed its name to the City of Castle Pines in 2009. A lean and efficient city government organized quickly, and new businesses moved to Castle Pines Parkway.[27] Growth became the city's biggest challenge. West of I-25 were two parcels off Lagae Road which contained 1,000 new housing units. East of I-25, The Canyons consisted of 3,300 acres, which extended from the Reuter-Hess Reservoir to the Sapphire Pointe subdivision in Castle Rock. When this property was annexed, it doubled the City's size. In 2009, Shea Homes proposed building 2,500 houses in The Canyons; then in 2018, it wanted approval for another 1,000 multi-family units. In 2019, it asked for 1,500 more—for a total of 5,000 housing units.[28] In addition to including many housing types, Shea Homes intends to include open space, miles of trails, parks, and recreational facilities.

Such plans worried many residents of Castle Rock who predicted perpetual traffic gridlock on Crowfoot Valley Road; but Shea Homes promised to ease congestion by building Canyonside Boulevard, to connect The Canyons to I-25.[29] The City of Castle Pines presently occupies 9.57 square miles and has a population of 11,219.[30] Some predict that by 2040, it will grow to 30,000.[31]

[1] Susan Consola Appleby, *Fading Past: The Story of Douglas County, Colorado* (Palmer Lake, Colorado: Filter Press, 2001), 47-59.

[2] Douglas County, "Subdivision Fillings," accessed June 13, 2020, https://apps.douglas.co.us/dcmaps/map.html?mapInstance=subdivision.

[3] Tom Skelley, "They've drawn a line in the sand," *Douglas County News-Press,* January 23, 2017; Tom Skelley, "Planners say no to Franktown Village," *Douglas County News-Press,* June 20, 2017.

[4] Tom Skelley, "Franktown citizens celebrate as developers withdraw application," *Douglas County News-Press,* July 28, 2017.

[5] Nick Puckett, "New farming community developing in Franktown," *Douglas County News-Press,* August 7, 2018.

[6] "Franktown, CO Profile: Facts and Data," *CO HomeTownLocator,* accessed May 9, 2020, https://colorado.hometownlocator.com/co/douglas/franktown.cfm.

[7] Mike DiFerdinando, "Downtown vision developing," *Castle Rock News-Press,* January 12, 2015; Mike DiFerdinando, "Town grapples with identity amid business, population change," *Castle Rock News-Press,* March 24, 2015.

[8] Rhonda Moore, "Castle Rock lays off workers," *Castle Rock News-Press,* May 18, 2009.

[9] "Downtown Castle Rock: Downtown Development Authority," accessed June 19, 2020, https://www.downtowncastlerock.com/dda; "Downtown Castle Rock: Creating and Maintaining a Vibrant Downtown," accessed June 19, 2020, https://www.downtowncastlerock.com/.

[10] Rhonda Moore, "Rink on the Rock gets green light," *Castle Rock News-Press,* September 1, 2012; Rhonda Moore, "Grand Opening at White Pavilion in downtown Castle Rock includes ice cream social for hundreds," *Douglas County News-Press,* May 15, 2013.

[11] "Festival Park Reimagined," *Town of Castle Rock, Colorado,* accessed June 19, 2020, https://crgov.com/2388/Festival-Park-Reimagined.

[12] Virginia Grantier, "New outlet mall nears approval," *Castle Rock News-Press,* November 26, 2013; Staff report, "Promenade at Castle Rock continues to grow," *Castle Rock News-Press,* March 28, 2016; Jessica Gibbs, "Castle Rock's first Whole Foods to open in April," *Castle Rock News-Press,* March 13, 2020.

[13] Jessica Gibbs, "Riverwalk approaches partial opening in Castle Rock," *Castle Rock News-Press,* December 3, 2018; Jessica Gibbs, "Downtown Development gets early approval in Castle Rock," *Castle Rock News-Press,* August 28, 2019; Jessica Gibbs, "Castle Rock Town Council approves Encore development agreement," *Castle Rock News-Press,* September 12, 2019.

[14] Centura Health, "Castle Rock Adventist Hospital," accessed June 19, 2020, https://www.centura.org/locations/castle-rock-adventist-hospital; Jessica Gibbs, "Castle Rock Adventist rings in fifth anniversary," *Castle Rock News-Press,* August 6,

2018, accessed June 19, 2020, https://castlerocknewspress.net/stories/castle-rock-adventist-rings-in-fifth-anniversary,267542?

[15] Jessica Gibbs, "Sturm Collaboration Campus opens in Castle Rock," *Highlands Ranch Herald*, August 19, 2019.

[16] Town of Castle Rock, Colorado, "Philip S. Miller Park," accessed June 19, 2020, https://crgov.com/2051/Philip-S-Miller-Park; "Residents celebrate additions," *Castle Rock News-Press*, May 17, 2016.

[17] Town of Castle Rock, Colorado, "Facilities," accessed June 19, 2020, www://www.crgov.com/Facilities.

[18] Shanna Fortier, "Castle Rock growth praised, condemned in discussion," *Castle Rock News-Press*, April 11, 2016.

[19] Shannah Fortier, "Councilmember Ford speaks out on recall," *Castle Rock News-Press*, May 23, 2016; Shanna Fortier, "Valentine protests her recall from town council," *Castle Rock News-Press*, May 26, 2016; Jessica Gibbs, "Castle Rock petitioners cancel recall against Councilmember Valentine," *Castle Rock News-Press*, September 10, 2016.

[20] Rhonda Moore, "Castle Rock a top town for development," *Castle Rock News-Press*, April 10, 2009; Shanna Fortier, "Another 155 homes coming to Castle Rock," *Castle Rock News-Press*, December 6, 2015; Jessica Gibbs, "Town council approves 1,200-home development plan," *Castle Rock News-Press*, March 11, 2019.

[21] Rhonda Moore, "Castle Rock mulls long-term water proposals," *Castle Rock News-Press*, September 16, 2011; Rhonda Moore, "Castle Rock approves WISE agreement with Denver and Aurora water," *Castle Rock News-Press*, May 15, 2013; Rhonda Moore, "Castle Rock switches to chloramine to treat drinking water," *Castle Rock News-Press*, May 20, 2013; Staff report, "Castle Rock Water recognized as industry leader," *Castle Rock News-Press*, June 6, 2016; Jessica Gibbs, "Castle Rock preparing to turn wastewater into drinking water," *Castle Rock News-Press*, April 22, 2019.

[22] Chris Michlewicz, "Roadwork in final phases," *Castle Rock News-Press*, July 28, 2009; Staff report, "Construction to being soon on Founders Parkway," *Castle Rock News-Press*, February 4, 2011; Virginia Grantier, "Castle Rock's largest road construction project begins," *Castle Rock News-Press*, November 5, 2013; Jessica Gibbs, "The 'Gap' project on I-25 south of Castle Rock won't significantly affect environment, report says," *Castle Rock News-Press*, July 2, 2018; Jessica Gibbs, "Castle Rock adopts plan for downtown mobility," *Castle Rock News-Press*, July 22, 2019; Elliott Wenzler, "Transportation plan predicts growth patterns in Douglas County," *Douglas County News-Press*, October 7, 2019; Jessica Gibbs, "CDOT lays out vision for I-25 through Douglas County," *Castle Rock News-Press*, October 21, 2019.

[23] "Castle Rock, CO Profile: Facts and Data," *CO HomeTownLocator*, accessed May 9, 2020, https://colorado.hometownlocator.com/co/douglas/castle-rock.cfm.

[24] Jessica Gibbs, "Douglas County, state growth scrutinized," *Castle Rock News-Press*, August 5, 2019.

[25] Michele Sample, "Lots available at golf community," *Castle Rock News-Press*, February 13, 2009.

[26] "Castle Pines Village, CO Profile: Facts and Data," *CO HomeTownLocator*, accessed May 9, 2020, 2020, https://colorado.hometownlocator.com/co/douglas/castle-pines-village.cfm

[27] Michele Sample, "Happy anniversary, Castle Pines North," *Castle Rock News-Press*, February 12, 2009; Michele Sample, "Castle Pines Chamber turns a year old," *Castle Rock News-Press*, June 19, 2009.

[28] Jessica Gibbs, "New development could bring thousands of homes, people to Castle Pines," *Castle Pines News-Press*, April 21, 2017; Jessica Gibbs, "Castle Pines OKs 1500 more homes in The Canyons," *Castle Pines News-Press*, December 16, 2019.

[29] Gibbs, "New development could bring thousands of homes, people to Castle Pines."

[30] "The City of Castle Pines, CO Profile: Facts and Data," *CO HomeTownLocator*, accessed May 9, 2020, https://Colorado.hometownlocator.com/co/douglas/castle-pines.cfm.

[31] Jessica Gibbs, "Growing Castle Pines seeks to build community identity," *Castle Pines News-Press*, September 23, 2019, accessed June 22, 2020.

Chapter 67

DIVIDE COUNTRY AND THE PIKE

Bill Noe

One early pioneer settler of Douglas County's Divide Country said, "Take care of the land and the land will take care of you."[1] This pioneer motto and approach prevailed from the 1860s into the 1990s until the area began losing its historic agricultural life-based population. In the northern part of DC especially, growing population patterns have replaced farms and ranches with their crops and livestock with asphalt, high-density housing, and urban sprawl.[2] The Divide County and the Pike National Forest of southern DC, named after the watershed of the Palmer Divide, have largely been spared such drastic changes. Many of the Divide's large working ranches were subdivided into small acreage ranchettes whose owners work in the metropolitan areas of Douglas, Arapahoe, and El Paso Counties. Larkspur (pop. 205) is the only incorporated town in the Divide Country whose population is estimated to be 6,200 or two percent of Douglas County's 358,000 residents.[3]

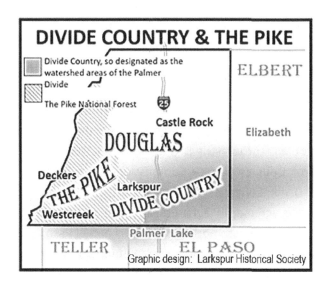

403

Living in Divide Country is expensive. Residential property taxes in Divide Country increased greatly over the last three decades. Property taxes on a smaller three-bedroom house on ten acres increased 30% between 2017 and 2019.[4] As a result of elected officials' past decisions, Douglas County became a "Bedroom Community" that lacked a significant commercial-industrial tax base.[5] Many younger families were priced out of Divide Country due to high ownership costs and few moderately priced homes.[6] Multiple generations of families living in Douglas County have become almost nonexistent.[7]

The Divide's historic large agricultural production of livestock, crops, lumber, and other farm products is now little more than a memory. Few Divide residents make their sole income from producing traditional agricultural products. Legal and illegal Marijuana growing facilities are infiltrating Divide Country, potentially becoming the most significant agricultural crop of the future. Many Divide Country residents dislike this new industry in their backyards and prefer more traditional agricultural uses for their properties.[8]

Employment in Divide Country now includes service workers, the self-employed, and government employees. Most residents commute outside of the Divide area to work in major employment centers that need professional and skilled workers. Many retirees also make the Divide their home. Unfortunately, poor planning in earlier decades did not require area developers to build the necessary regional infrastructure to support the Divide in the twenty-first century, creating traffic problems not only for the residents but the entire Front Range. Commuters pass through Divide Country on I-25 and Highway 83 to employment centers in Denver and Colorado Springs at least twice a day. Thousands of trucks move freight through Divide Country on the same highways, and over one hundred freight trains move products through the Divide on historic 1800s rail-beds.[9]

The Board of Douglas County Commissioners has supported the rural atmosphere of Divide Country.[10] The Board's actions have attempted to keep low-density, large acreage in agricultural usage as a buffer between the metropolitan spreads of both northern Douglas and El Paso Counties. Divide Country's residents enjoy and value their connection to the rural land of scenic open vistas, green pastures, and forested areas. Douglas County Division of Open Space and Natural Resources[11] assists in the acquisition and management of Open Space and Conservation Easements. Douglas Land Conservancy (DLC) works with landowners to acquire private conservation easements which are not open to the public. Open space and conservation easements account for approximately 63,037 acres of protected land.[12] The vegetation of the rural land in Divide Country helps offset the negative effects of greenhouse gases coming from the more densely populated areas. Recently completed, the Colorado Front Range Trail, which provides a continuous trail from the Wyoming border to New Mexico border, passes through Divide Country.[13] Many other trails and scenic areas are located on Divide Country's many open spaces parcels. The Pike National Forest offers ample recreational opportunities.

Southern Douglas County's Divide Country

The residents of Divide County are greatly concerned about the extraction of groundwater, much of which is transported outside of the Divide area. The extraction of groundwater has substantially lowered the water table in the last three decades, forcing many well-using residents to re-drill their wells. "While some Douglas County water providers have water rights to the South Platte, Cherry, and Plum Creeks, their allocations do not provide enough water to satisfy the renewable supplies necessary to fulfill the existing water demands of the County."[14]

The health of forests has created a "Fear of Fire" for many in eastern Colorado during the last three decades. Many fires in the Pike National Forest, in both public and private ownership tracts, have greatly contributed to this fear. The largest fire recorded in Colorado's history happened in 2002.

The Hayman Fire[15] devastated 138,000 acres, 133 homes, and lasted 20 days. A large portion of this fire occurred in DC's portion of the Pike National Forest. It began near the south county line near Westcreek, moved north, and exited DC near Deckers. In the past thirty years, there have been hundreds of fires in the forests of Douglas County, from small blazes started by lightning strikes to large fires involving thousands of acres. Unfortunately, the majority of all wildfires are caused by humans. Non-resident environmental activists have eliminated almost all productive usages of the Pike Forest: sawmills, mining operations, stone quarries, and agricultural grazing. Such restricted use of the forests has undercut its health by increasing the fuel supply for wildfires. Also, the lack of coordination between urban and forested areas for fire mitigation increases the threat of wildfires spreading from the forests into more urban areas. As a result, for the foreseeable future, fire now presents a much greater risk to human life than it did in the past.[16]

Colorado's huge population increase in the last three decades mostly lives in the Front Range corridor and the northeastern part of the County and has massively contributed to much heavier human use of the Pike National Forest. In addition to Mother Nature's re-occurring droughts and harmful insects, motorized sport and off-trail recreation vehicles, widespread trash accumulation, vandalism in camping and parking areas, and human overuse of pristine forest areas have significantly degraded the quality of the forest. Regrettably, outside financially backed political and special interest organizations often override County decisions and impact forest quality negatively. On the positive side, many people continue to enjoy the forest and treat it with care and respect. The Pike National Forest continues to provide important watershed areas and water storage and provides habitat for wildlife and rare vegetation. Volunteers are actively working with the United States Forest Service to create a balance between recreational use and forest management that increases the healthy condition of the native forest environment, enabling Pike National Forest to continue to be a valuable resource to Douglas County and other Front Range residents.[17]

---

[1] Charles Fred Noe, personal interview with Bill Noe. Eagle Mountain Ranch, Greenland, Colorado, 1952.

[2] "Urban sprawl," *Merriam-Webster Dictionary*, accessed January 29, 2020, https://www.merriam-webster.com/dictionary/urban%20sprawl.

[3] *Divide Country Population-Demographics / Neighborhood Info Larkspur, CO, 80118*, accessed April 1, 2020, https://www.movoto.com/demographics/co/80118/.

[4] *DC Assessor State Parcel, 2771-170-00-006*, 2017 to 2019 property tax, no improvements added, accessed April 3, 2020, https://apps.douglas.co.us/assessor/web/#/details/2020/R0179493.

[5] Douglas County Assessor, *2019 Abstract of Assessment and Tax Summary of Levies*, accessed March 29, 2020, https://www.douglas.co.us/documents/2019-abstract-2.pdf/.

[6] The median home value in 80118 is $684,525. Zillow, *Larkspur*, accessed April 2, 2020, https://www.zillow.com/larkspur-co-80118/home-values/.

[7] Demographics, *Neighborhood Info Larkspur, CO, 80118*, accessed April 1, 2020, https://www.movoto.com/demographics/co/80118/.

[8] 86% of farmers earn less than $10k Income per year, US Agricultural Census, *2017 Douglas County*, accessed April 1, 2020, https://www.nass.usda.gov/Publications/AgCensus/2017/Full_Report/Volume_1,_Chapter_2_County_Level/Colorado/st08_2_0001_0001.pdf.

[9] *Douglas County Transportation Master Plan-Existing Conditions, September 2019*, accessed April 3, 2020, https://www.douglas.co.us/documents/2040-transportation-master-plan.pdf/.

[10] Rural Atmosphere, *Douglas County Comprehensive Land Use Plan* (DCCLUP), Copy in Archives and Local History, Philip S. Miller Library, Castle Rock.

[11] *Douglas County Open Space and Natural Resources*, accessed March 31, 2020, https://www.douglas.co.us/dcoutdoors/trails/open-space-trails.

[12] *Douglas Land Conservancy* (DLC), accessed March 31, 2020, https://douglaslandconservancy.org.

[13] *Colorado Front Range Trail in Divide Country,* accessed April 3, 2020, https://www.douglas.co.us/dcoutdoors/trails/open-space-trails/colorado-front-range-trail.

[14] Douglas County, CO, *Water Supply: Ground Water Resources*, accessed April 3, 2020, https://www.douglas.co.us/water/water-supply/.

[15] *Tragic and Destructive North American Wildfires—1950 to Present*, accessed March 20, 2020, https://www.thoughtco.com/tragic-destructive-north-american-wildfires-1342904.

[16] *Grim Lessons Learned and Warnings from California Fire Stories,"* accessed March 20, 2020, https://www.govtech.com/em/preparedness/Grim-Lessons-Learned-and-Warnings-from-California-Fire-Stories-.html.

[17] Pike National Forest Report Summary, "Influence of Forest Structure on Wildfire Behavior and the Severity of Its Effects," accessed March 20, 2020, https://www.fs.fed.us/projects/hfi/docs/forest_structure_wildfire.pdf.

CREDITS FOR PHOTOGRAPHS AND GRAPHICS

Chapter	Image	Credit
1	Projectile Points, Drill, and Scraper	Douglas County History Repository
2	Kit Carson and John Fremont	Public Domain
3	Approximate Tribal Boundaries	Historic Douglas County, Inc.
4	Jim Baker	Public Doman
5	Early Trails Map	Author: Lee Whiteley
	Trader's Cart	Author: Lee Whiteley
6	1859 Migration & Settling Map	Historic Douglas County, Inc.
	Sarah Coberly	History Colorado
	Daniel C. Oakes	History Colorado
7	1860 Territorial Map	Public Doman
	James Frank Gardner	Douglas County Libraries Archives & Local History
8	Hubert and Miriam Fonder	Douglas County Libraries Archives & Local History
9	Camp Weld Peace Conference	History Colorado. 10025492a
10	Twenty Mile House and Barn	Douglas County Libraries Archives & Local History
	Weaver House, Corral and Stable, Sedalia	Douglas County Libraries Archives & Local History
11	Benjamin Quick House	Larkspur Historical Society
12	Colorado Southern Stop at Parker	Parker Area Historical Society
	Castle Rocks Quarries	Fair Use from Robert M. Ormes, "Tracking Ghost Railroads in Colorado," Century One Press, Colorado Springs, 1976
13	Denver and Rio Grande Railroad Depot	Douglas County Libraries Archives & Local History
	Douglas County Courthouse	Douglas County Libraries Archives & Local History
	Population Chart	Historic Douglas County, Inc.
14	Methodist Episcopal Church, Castle Rock	Douglas County Libraries Archives & Local History
	Sedalia School	Douglas County Libraries Archives & Local History
15	Izett Steward Farm and Dairy	Beverly Higginson Noe
	Milk Cans at Larkspur AT&SF Depot	Larkspur Historical Society

16	Curtis Oakland Ranch	Douglas County Libraries Archives & Local History
	Rancher's Wife, Katherine Shuebert with Cattle Herd	Douglas County Libraries Archives & Local History
17	Coal, Rhyolite, and Gold in Douglas County	Historic Douglas County, Inc.,
18	Newspaper Ads Collage	Historic Douglas County, Inc.
	Weaver Boarding House, Plum Avenue Sedalia	Douglas County Libraries Archives & Local History
19	Social at the Case Grange	Douglas County Libraries Archives & Local History
	Three Regions of Douglas County 1900	Historic Douglas County, Inc.
20	Davis Harmon Waite	The Denver Public Library, Western History Collection, Z-1966
	Elias M. Ammons	The Denver Public Library, Western History Collection, Z-4906
21	David Rice Williams	Douglas County Libraries Archives & Local History
	William Dillon	Loyola University Chicago School of Law
22	Mechanized Corn Picker on Bihlmeyer Ranch	Douglas County Libraries Archives & Local History
	Threshing on the Lorraine Ranch, Spring Valley	Larkspur Historical Society
23	Castle Rock Water Works Pumping Station	Douglas County Libraries Archives & Local History
	Hauling Telephone Poles	Telephone Pioneers of America
24	Line Up and Sign Up	Record Journal of DC June 12, 1918
	Robert Rowley and Soldiers	Douglas County Libraries Archives & Local History
25	Frederick and Anna Deopke Family	Douglas County Libraries Archives & Local History
	Population Chart	Historic Douglas County, Inc.
26	Dr. George E. Alexander	Castle Rock Museum
	Mary Briscoe	Douglas County Libraries Archives & Local History (NOTE: Photo has been altered to remove photo scanning error From original to digitized copy.)

27	Douglas County Major Ground Water Sources	Historic Douglas County, Inc.
	Spring Valley Silo Filing	Douglas County Libraries Archives & Local History
28	Diamond Jack	Public Domain
	Nanichant Inn, Perry Park	Larkspur Historical Society
29	Herbert Hoover	Public Domain
	Woodrow Wilson	Public Domain
30	Lookout Station on Devil's Head	Douglas County Libraries Archives & Local History
	William R. Kreutzer	Larkspur Fire Protection District Fire Marshal: Randy Johnson
31	Chart on Distribution of the Labor Force	Historic Douglas County, Inc.
	Silica Brickyard and Bricks	Douglas County Libraries Archives & Local History
32	Castle Rock Public School (Cantril School Circa 1905	Douglas County Libraries Archives & Local History
	East Elevation of Charlford during Construction	Douglas County Libraries Archives & Local History
	Louviers Village Clubhouse 1917	Douglas County Libraries Archives & Local History
33	Daniels and Fisher Tower	The Denver Public Library, Western History Collection, Z-22931
	Elias Ammons	Public Domain
	Helen (Josie) Doepke	Douglas County Libraries Archives & Local History
34	Christmas Star over Castle Rock 1940	Douglas County Libraries Archives & Local History
	Civilian Conservation Corp SCS-7-C 1938	Douglas County Libraries Archives & Local History
35	Douglas County Votes in Presidential Elections 1932-1956	Historic Douglas County, Inc.
	Dwight David Eisenhower	Public Domain
	Franklin Delano Roosevelt	Public Domain
36	Castlewood Dam before the Flood. Note the water leaking frome the dam in the center and to the right.	History Colorado. 10047528
	Wall of water from the Castlewood Dam collapse as it	History Colorado. 10030620

	moved down Cherry Creek through Denver	
37	Gasoline Ration Card	Public Domain
	USS Colorado BB45 off Tinian, July 24, 1944	Public Domain
38	John Hammond	Douglas County Libraries Archives & Local History
	L to R - Perry Ridenour, Martin Nelson, and Dale Ridenour (Murder at the B & B)	Douglas County Libraries Archives & Local History
39	US 85 North of Castle Rock circa 1930	Douglas County Libraries Archives & Local History
	US 85 South of Castle Rock, 1950	Douglas County Libraries Archives & Local History
40	Paul Synder	Leny Yoder
	Shady Drive – Highway 85 through Castle Rock	Douglas County Libraries Archives & Local History
41	Douglas County 1930-1960	Historic Douglas County, Inc.
	Greenland Ranch Reserve Champion Feeder Cattle circa 1950s	Bill Noe
42	Cherokee Castle	Cherokee Ranch and Castle Foundation
	Highlands Ranch Mansion West Extension	Highlands Ranch Metropolitan District
43	Douglas County High School 1943	Douglas County Libraries Archives & Local History
	Dr. Lowell Baumunk 1973 DCHS Huskies	Douglas County Libraries Archives & Local History
44	Philip S. Miller 1915	Douglas County Libraries Archives & Local History
	Philip S. Miller	Douglas County Libraries Archives & Local History
45	Hauling Freight through Douglas County	Douglas County Libraries Archives & Local History
	Traffic Stalled Near Castle Rock after the 1965 Flood	Douglas County Libraries Archives & Local History
46	County Population Gain	Historic Douglas County, Inc.
	Early Subdivisions of Douglas County	Historic Douglas County, Inc.
47	Home in Louivers	Douglas County Libraries Archives & Local History

	Mainstreet in Parker 1964	Douglas County Libraries Archives & Local History
48	Alluvial and Bedrock Aquifers of the Denver Basin – Eastern Colorado's Dual Groundwater Resource	Public Domain (U. S. Geology Survey, 1989)
	Well Drilling in Castle Rock	Public Domain (U. S. Geology Survey, 1989)
49	Larkspur's Frink Creamery in the Late 1920s and Dairy Entrepreneur-Owner Clarence Frink	Larkspur Historical Society
50	Douglas County Courthouse circa 1970s	Douglas County Libraries Archives & Local History
	Larkspur – Settled 1869, Incorporated 1979	Larkspur Historical Society
51	Royal McKinster	Douglas County Libraries Archives & Local History
	John Hammond	Douglas County Sheriff's Office
	Stephen Zotos	Douglas County Sheriff's Office
52	Douglas County High School under Construction	Douglas County Libraries Archives & Local History
	Douglas County RE-1 Schools Administration Building (Castle Rock)	Douglas County Libraries Archives & Local History
53	Aftermath of 1965 Flood, Looking East from Plum Creek to Courthouse, Castle Rock	Douglas County Libraries Archives & Local History
	Westside of Dawson Butte Showing Erosions of 1965 Flood, circa 1970	Douglas County Libraries Archives & Local History
54	Colorado Renaissance Festival	Douglas County Libraries Archives & Local History
	View from the Stands of Continental Divide Raceway	Castle Rock Museum, Gavin Richey
55	Registered Voters in Douglas County	Historic Douglas County, Inc.
56	Aerial of North Castle Rock Development	The Castle Pines Connection, Castle Pines, Colorado
	Douglas County Population Growth	Historic Douglas County, Inc.
57	Hidden Mesa Open Space	Douglas County Open Space & Natural Resources

	Robert A. Christensen Justice Center - circa 1998	Douglas County Sheriff's Office
58	Cowboy Sheriffs (L to R) Sheriffs Tony Spurlock, Steve Zotos, Dave Weaver, and Mike Acree — 2018	Douglas County Sheriff's Office
	Mobile Command Post and Patrol Car with Deputy Mike Mathena and Dispatch Supervisor Cindi Dieck – 2018	Douglas County Sheriff's Office
59	Douglas County School District	Historic Douglas County, Inc.
	Franktown Elementary – 2015	Historic Douglas County, Inc.
60	Douglas County Libraries	Douglas County Libraries
61	Chatfield Reservoir	Wikipedia Commons Media
62	Douglas County Registered Voters	Historic Douglas County, Inc.
	Douglas County Voter Registrations	Historic Douglas County, Inc.
	Results of Douglas County General Elections	Historic Douglas County, Inc.
63	Highlands Ranch Entrance Sign with Logo	Highlands Ranch Metropolitan District
	Highlands Ranch Veterans' Monument	Highlands Ranch Metropolitan District
64	North Parker Road – 1980s	Parker Area Historical Society
	Restored Schweiger Ranch House	Historic Douglas County, Inc.
65	Gabriel's Restaurant and Tuscan Bar Sedalia 2020	Historic Douglas County, Inc.
	Sterling Ranch Entrance – Roxborough 2020	Historic Douglas County, Inc.
66	Franktown Intersection Highways 86 and 83	Wikipedia Commons Media
	Philip S. Miller Activity Complex (MAC) with Entrance Sign Inset in Lower Left Corner	Historic Douglas County, Inc.
67	Southern Douglas County's Divide Country	Bill Noe
	Divide Country & the Pike	Larkspur Historical Society

INDEX

415

419

F

G

M

O

N

P

425

Made in the USA
Middletown, DE
22 October 2022

13301095R00249